PAUL DE GRAUWE
LUCAS PAPADEMOS

The European Monetary System in the 1990s

Longman
London and New York

Longman Group UK Limited 1990
Longman House, Burnt Mill, Harlow
Essex CM20 2JE, England
and Associated companies throughout the world.

Published in the United States of America
by Longman Inc., New York

First published 1990

British Library Cataloguing in Publication Data
The European monetary system in the 1990's.
1. European Community. Monetary systems. European Monetary system
I. Grauwe, Paul de II. Papademos, Lucas
332.4566094
ISBN 0-582-06455-4
ISBN 0-582-06456-2 pbk

Library of Congress Cataloguing in Publication Data
Grauwe, Paul de.
The European monetary system in the 1990s / Paul de Grauwe and Lucas Papademos
p. cm.
Includes bibliographical references.
ISBN 0-582-06455-4 ISBN 0-582-06456-2 (pbk.)
1. European Monetary System (Organization) 2. Europe 1992.
I. Papademos, Lucas. II. Title.
HG930.5.G675 1990 90-35555
332.4'5'094–dc20 CIP

Set in Linotronic 200 10/12pt Times

Printed in Great Britain
by Bath Press Avon

Contents

Introduction

Paul De Grauwe and Lucas Papademos

1. Introduction

The prospects for significant progress towards monetary union in Europe have improved considerably since 1989 when the Delors Committee published its report. A few years ago scepticism about the chances that Europe would ever achieve a true monetary union was rampant. Today in 1990 the probability that this will occur during our lifetime cannot be dismissed.

However, problems abound on the road towards European monetary unification. In August 1989 economists from all over Europe and America convened in Athens (at the invitation of the Bank of Greece) to discuss these problems. They included both academic economists and 'practical men' from central banks and international institutions.

It was found useful to organize the proceedings of this conference along major themes. Some of the themes had to do with the past operation of the European Monetary System (EMS), others were prospective and related to the question of how the system is likely to function in the future, and how it can be transformed so as to advance on the road towards monetary union.

2. A new EMS?

It is clear that the EMS is now (in 1990) a quite different institution from what it was initially. During the first five years of its existence the frequency of realignments was very high, occurring on average more than once a year. As a result, the credibility of the fixity of exchange rates within the EMS was very low, so that frequent speculative crises arose. This in turn forced those members with weak currencies to maintain relatively deflationary policies to avoid these crises.

Things have changed significantly during the second half of the 1980s. These changes were made possible by a combination of institutional reform (most of which came about as a result of the Basle-Nyborg Agreement) and a greater convergence of the inflation rates within the system. As a result the credibility of the fixity of exchange rates has been enhanced considerably. Thus it can be said that at the end of the 1980s we had a 'new' EMS compared to what it was at the start of the decade.

Several chapters analyse some of the consequences of the existence of this 'new EMS'. In chapter 4 Giavazzi and Spaventa draw attention to the potential for instability of the present situation, which can be described as follows. The (traditionally) high-inflation countries (France, Italy, Spain) have high nominal interest rates relative to the low-inflation countries. At the same time, however, the credibility of the fixity of exchange rates of these currencies (FF, lira, peseta) has reduced the probability of a devaluation in the short run. This induces capital movements from the low-inflation to the high-inflation countries which, in the new environment of free capital mobility, are likely to be large. The availability of foreign capital then creates a boom in the high-inflation countries, which tends to undermine the anti-inflationary stance of these countries. In addition, it leads to an increase of current account deficits in these countries, to an accumulation of foreign debt and ultimately to the question whether the situation is sustainable. It will be remembered that this is the same argument that Alan Walters used in his influential book, *Britain's Economic Renaissance* (1986), against the participation of the UK in the exchange rate mechanism of the EMS.

Bini Smaghi and Micossi expand on this theme in Chapter 6. They point out that these 'perverse' capital movements have an inflationary potential for the system as a whole. This inflationary potential arises from the fact that the centre country (Federal Republic of Germany, FRG) sticks to its policy of monetary control (thus sterilizing the capital outflows) while the other countries who receive capital inflows are unable fully to offset the domestic monetary effects of these inflows. This asymmetry in the system leads to a net creation of liquidity in the EMS.

This situation is reminiscent of what happened at the world level during successive cycles in the movements of the dollar. When the dollar was weak, capital was moving into European countries and Japan. The authorities of these countries (who intervened in their foreign exchange markets) found it difficult to contain the expansionary monetary effects of their dollar purchases. Since the Federal Reserve kept its monetary policy independent from what happened in the dollar exchange markets, a net growth of money stocks in the world ensued, adding to inflationary pressures. This was the situation during the 1970s, and has been described by McKinnon in several publications. Exactly the opposite happened during the first part of the 1980s, when capital was moving into the USA, and when central banks sold dollars. As a result, a net deflationary effect on the world money stock ensued.

Something similar may be going on in the EMS. During the first half of its existence, the endemic weakness of the high-inflation currencies led to a deflationary monetary potential in the whole system, as these countries were forced to follow relatively restrictive policies. The turnaround that occurred since 1987 may have put the EMS into an expansionary cycle.

3. How asymmetric is the system?

The nature of the interactions within the EMS has been quite different from that envisaged by the founding fathers of the system. The existence of the European Currency Unit (ECU) was generally seen as an instrument that would allow relatively symmetric relations between the major partners of the system. The EMS has operated in a very different way, and the ECU has not been important in the actual operations of the EMS.

There is now a widespread consensus that the EMS operates as a DM zone, where the German authorities set their monetary policies independently from what happens in the rest of the system. In this view the other countries peg to the DM and are therefore forced to adjust their monetary policies (in particular their interest rates) to conform with the monetary conditions prevailing in the FRG.

This view was challenged by Fratianni and von Hagen in Chapter 5. They note that although the German authorities have usually determined their monetary policies independently, a relatively large degree of monetary independence was also maintained in other major countries (France and Italy). This relative independence was made possible by the existence of capital controls and by regular realignments. Whether this will remain possible in an environment of free capital mobility is doubtful. In this new environment of financial integration, the system will either have to move towards a strengthening of the *institutional* integration or it will face severe disturbances.

Needless to say, the views of how the system has worked in the past, as defended by Fratianni and von Hagen, were challenged by several conference participants, in particular by Jacques Melitz. He noted that the implication of the Fratianni – von Hagen analysis is that the much vaunted source of inflation discipline of the EMS for such countries as France and Italy never really existed. Few participants were willing to accept that conclusion. And yet the fact remains that EMS countries have in general not been able to disinflate their economies during the 1980s at a quicker pace than industrial countries outside the EMS.

There are other such surprises about how the EMS has worked during the 1980s. One such surprise comes from its effect on trade. In Chapter 8 Sapir and Sekkat analyse the issue of whether the greater stability of the intra-EMS exchange rates has affected the pricing mechanism of exports within the EMS as compared to extra-EMS exports. They were unable to find any significant difference in the pricing strategies of exporters inside and outside the EMS which could be related to the volatility of the exchange rates. It is not the first time that econometric studies have been unable to find a significant effect of exchange rate volatility on international trade. These studies also lead to scepticism about the potential welfare gains of fixed exchange rate systems compared to flexible exchange rate systems.

4. How will the transition towards EMU be organized?

How will the future look for the EMS? In trying to tackle this issue the conference participants concentrated their attention on the question of how the transition towards full monetary integration could be organized. The question of whether full monetary union (one European central bank, one European currency) would be good or bad for Europe was discussed very little, despite a warning of Paul Krugman in Chapter 3 that the economic cost-benefit calculus of a full monetary union in Europe may not necessarily be positive. Everybody, however, took for granted his conclusion that even if the economic benefits may not be overwhelming, it would still be worth while moving towards full monetary union because of the political benefits, for example one currency as a first (and necessary) step towards a European nationhood. However, agreement on how to reach this political Nirvana proved to be much more difficult.

A first major contribution was provided by Niels Thygesen (Chapter 1) who discussed alternative blueprints for the transition towards full monetary integration. His analysis and his proposals on how to organize the transition have been influential in shaping the ideas of the members of the Delors Committee. As there are many roads leading to Rome, there are many paths towards monetary union. The great benefit of Thygesen's blueprint is that it is just one such possible path that could be used to start the journey immediately. Economists have the habit, however, of asking the question whether it is the best possible road, and refusing to take the first step before they are sure that no other road exists that would lead to the objective quicker.

A major bone of contention in this whole discussion was the question of how fiscal policies of the nation-states should be coordinated. One of the more controversial proposals of the Delors Committee was to introduce binding rules on the size of the national budget deficits. This would have to be applied not only in full monetary union but also during the transition phase. This idea has been defended by Rieke in Chapter 2, and also by most of the participants to the panel discussion (Ch. 13), in particular by Gunter Baer and Antonio Costa. Other participants, however, argued that such rules are not necessary to manage the transition (some would even go as far as to argue that it is not necessary even in the final stage of full monetary union). In addition, according to these critics of the *Delors Report*, these rules are not desirable, and may increase the potential for conflict during the transitional stages.

5. How large should the future monetary union be?

In Chapter 3 Paul Krugman has argued that economic analysis applied to this question would almost certainly lead to the conclusion that a unified monetary area from Denmark to Portugal and from Ireland to Greece is not optimal. In other words that the optimal currency area is smaller than the whole of the European Community. The question of how large the optimal size would then be was not tackled. Probably rightly so. Instead the participants asked the more relevant question of how and under what conditions the non-participants could join the EMS.

Two schools of thought emerged. One represented by José Viñals (Ch. 9) who discussed the Spanish entrée into the system, and Francisco Torres (Ch. 10) who discussed the Portuguese case, argues that by joining the system the present outsiders will gain from the anti-inflationary reputation of the EMS, thereby making disinflation in these countries less costly. The second school of thought as represented by Lucas Papademos (Ch. 11), who analysed the Greek case, turns this around and argues that the outsider (in this case Greece) must first converge more to the average EMS inflation before considering joining the system.

The controversy can probably be most easily resolved by noting that it will always be relatively simple to force somebody to step into line with the others if he or she is willing to do so. However, force and discipline will usually not work if the willingness to step into line is absent. This may make all the difference today between Spain on the one hand, and the UK and Greece on the other. In addition, when as was noted by Papademos, the divergence between the outsider and the EMS is too large, no fixed exchange rate commitment will be credible.

This leads us to the question of UK participation in the exchange rate mechanism of the EMS. In Chapter 12 Michael Artis analyses the reasons why the UK has refused, up to now, to join the system. He makes it very clear that many of the economic reasons advanced by the UK government were useful in covering up a more basic one which was political and ideological. It remains true, however, that at least during the first five years, the UK had a good economic case for staying outside the system. During the first half of the 1980s the UK government was involved in an anti-inflationary policy which turned out to be a shock therapy (it is unclear whether this was intentional). During that period the UK was certainly more successful in its anti-inflationary policy than most of the EMS members. And although unemployment increased drastically in the UK during that period, the same happened a little later in the EMS countries. It is very doubtful if the UK government could have implemented this drastic anti-inflationary policy if it had chosen to participate in the EMS.

Here again things have changed in recent years. Many economists would argue today that if the UK had joined around 1987 it could have avoided the resurgence of inflation which has since been plaguing the UK.

The issue of seigniorage which has been discussed in many conferences dealing with the entrance of Mediterranean countries into the EMS was declared dead by Daniel Gros in Chapter 7. The issue is well known – southern European countries have a weak fiscal system, i.e. the marginal cost of increasing taxes is high in these countries. The optimal tax literature then tells us that it will be optimal for these countries to rely more on the inflation tax (seigniorage). By joining the low-inflation EMS, these countries lose this source of revenue and are forced to rely on the more costly increase in taxation. Thus, these countries would do well not to tie their currencies rigidly to low-inflation currencies.

Daniel Gros rejected this reasoning on the ground that it loses sight of another source of inefficiency which makes the EMS discipline more desirable. Southern European countries have relatively large fiscal deficits and public debts. The authorities of these countries therefore have a strong incentive to use surprise inflation in order to reduce the real burden of the debt. The public perceives this incentive and comes to anticipate a higher inflation rate. This problem can be solved by a commitment to a fixed exchange rate. The evidence provided by Daniel Gros suggests that the efficiency gain from such a committment would be larger than the efficiency loss of a lower revenue from seigniorage.

On the whole the consensus of the participants at the conference was that southern European countries and the UK would gain from their participation in the exchange rate mechanism of the EMS.

This conference was made possible by the generous hospitality of the Bank of Greece. It was unique not only because it was organized in Greece but also because of its format. It had the right mix of economists from central banks, international institutions and universities. The interaction of viewpoints from these different organizations led to exciting discussions, and to new insights for the participants. We hope that the readers of this book will experience the same thrill from the clash of ideas that occurs when theory and practice are confronted.

Opening address

Mr Demetrios Chalikias,
Governor of the Bank of Greece

Let me start by welcoming you to this Conference which has been organized jointly by the Bank of Greece and the Centre for European Policy Studies. I would also like to thank each and every one of you for responding to our invitation. It is after all your participation which makes this Conference possible and guarantees its success.

The timing of this Conference is very appropriate, for this is an important year regarding the process of European monetary integration. First, it marks the 10th Anniversary of the EMS. Second, the process of Economic and Monetary Union in the Community gained fresh momentum in 1989 with the completion of the Delors Report and with the decisions of the European Council in Madrid. The road leading to the final objective of economic and Monetary Union, however, may turn out to be a long one. There are a number of important issues, both political and economic, which must be addressed carefully before we can proceed to launch the critical second stage proposed in the Delors Report. That is why I feel that Conferences like this one, which bring together distinguished members of central banks, the academic community and international institutions, can contribute to a better understanding of the issues and problems we have to tackle.

In opening this Conference, I would like to share with you my views on certain issues which I feel are important to the monetary integration of Europe. First, I will refer to some of the implications of two principles considered essential for governing the process of economic and monetary union, namely the principles of parallelism and subsidiarity.

Another important issue concerns the timing of the proposed stages towards EMU. Although I do not disagree with the view that the time when these stages should be implemented is a matter calling for a political decision, I would like to stress that it also depends on economic factors, partly reflecting the new conditions that will emerge after the complete liberalization of capital movements and the full integration of financial markets.

Progress towards economic union is important in the advancement of monetary integration: they must therefore go together in order to avoid imbalances. Progress towards economic integration requires action in three areas: competition policy aimed at strengthening market mechanisms; macroeconomic coordination, especially in the budgetary field; and structural and regional policies. I will concentrate on the last two policy areas. This does not mean that I consider competition policy less important. On the contrary.

In the area of economic policy, the Delors Report focuses mainly on the implementation of a coherent fiscal policy. In the absence of a sizeable Community budget, the only feasible alternative seems to be that the Community governments should agree on an overall budgetary stance, with specific objectives that would take the form of binding rules for each country. These rules would refer to overall deficits and to the methods of financing them. The proposed rules may go too far, however, and may be unnecessarily restrictive. Some of the suggested constraints leave the national governments with very little fiscal discretion, less than that enjoyed in existing federal systems, where individual states retain greater fiscal autonomy. A first question is whether this is feasible. With widely divergent 'propensities to run deficits' in the various EC countries, it might prove difficult over the coming years to bring about a convergence in the fiscal field similar to that seen in existing federal systems.

A relevant question is whether, and to what extent, it might be feasible to rely on market forces to impose fiscal discipline and bring about fiscal convergence. National budget deficits will have to be financed in any case. Monetary union might facilitate their financing, since investors would not incur currency risk in their lending. This implies that interest rates might increase less than otherwise. Thus, it might be argued that monetary union would provide room for more, not less, flexibility in fiscal policy. On the other hand, debt servicing costs might increase as a result of the integration of capital markets and of the inability of governments to monetize part of their debt or impose financial regulations ensuring public sector borrowing on privileged terms. Such regulations are certainly inefficient economically, but are used in some countries. Finally, it might be argued that monetary integration will force member countries to make significant fiscal adjustments in order to avoid undesirable consequences on output and employment, which may result if national fiscal policies are fundamentally inconsistent with the monetary policy pursued at the European level.

Therefore, I think, it would be worth considering whether fiscal discipline can be obtained either through binding rules or through the market mechanism. Of course, a possible solution for the implementation of an effective macroeconomic fiscal policy at the Community level might be a Community budget of sufficient size. But this is against the 'principle of subsidiarity', according to which 'the functions of higher levels of government should be as limited as possible and should be subsidiary to those of lower levels'.

Thus, the question remains whether an effective fiscal policy can be implemented at the Community level, in the absence of a large Community budget and/or effective fiscal coordination. If the answer is negative, the only macroeconomic instrument available for the regulation of domestic demand within the EMU might be the common monetary policy implemented by the European System of Central Banks. This, however, should not be an acceptable solution, both in conditions of overheating and, equally, when the economy is in recession. In the first case, interest rates might have to be pushed to an excessively high level, thereby laying the burden of adjustment on investment rather than on consumption. In the second case, the stimulation of domestic demand might create money at a rate incompatible with the objective of price stability.

Let me turn now to structural and regional policies. Since economic and social cohesion is a basic objective, economic union presupposes the strengthening of structural and regional policies. Historical experience has shown that economic integration tends to aggravate rather than reduce economic divergences between developed and less developed areas in the union, particularly if most of the benefits stem from increased economies of scale or reduced transport costs. Consequently, structural and regional policies should be further strengthened. This would allow the structurally weaker countries and regions to grow and converge faster towards the Community average and it would also help minimise the adverse impact of integration by reducing the economic and social tensions that might develop in the transitional period. It is worth noting that the Delors Report rightly stresses that the objective of regional policies should not be the subsidization of income but the enhancement of productivity and opportunities. It might prove necessary, however, to specify more concretely the required policies that would minimise potential divergences which can result from the liberalization of capital movements and the adoption of a common monetary policy.

Finally, I would like to comment on the issue of timing of the steps leading towards the final objective. Although the Delors Report specifies the stages necessary for achieving EMU, it allows for a degree of flexibility which is necessary considering that different countries are characterised by different macroeconomic conditions and stages of economic development. The Report avoids suggesting any explicit timetable, except for the beginning of the first stage, which was adopted by the European Council. The timing of the subsequent two stages is to be determined on the basis of the experience to be gained during the process of integration. The advantage of this flexibility is particularly relevant for the beginning of the second stage, since member states must have the time in the first stage to adjust policies and economic conditions without exacerbating existing economic problems and creating social tensions. This will facilitate full participation in the EMS of certain non-ERM countries, by giving them time to adjust policies and create the conditions that will allow them to accept the EMS exchange rate discipline. More generally, it will facilitate the adjustment of the economies and policies in many member states in the new environment of increased economic and financial integration. In particular, the full liberalization of capital movements and the integration of financial markets will reduce the independence of national monetary policies. Increased economic interdependence will entail changes in market structures and will necessitate a more effective coordination of national policies.

Let me conclude by wishing you all a stimulating and productive conference.

PART ONE

A NEW EMS IN THE 1990s

CHAPTER ONE

Institutional developments in the evolution from EMS towards EMU

Niels Thygesen*

1. Introduction

An initial question which has to be addressed by someone writing a paper under the present title is to define what constitutes 'an institutional development'.

When they negotiated the European Single Act in 1985, European Community (EC) governments stated that the institutional changes required to implement an economic and monetary union (EMU) – an objective to which they reiterated their commitment – would have to be dealt with according to the procedures of Article 236 of the Rome Treaty, i.e. by unanimous agreement by the governments of the member states and by subsequent ratification by all national parliaments (Art. 102A of the treaty as revised by the Single Act). An extension of the European Monetary System (EMS) into a second stage through an agreement among the central banks, subsequently confirmed unanimously by governments under the simpler procedures of Article 235 would not be adequate. This had long been the view of some national monetary authorities with respect to the setting up proposed in the 1978 EMS agreement of a European monetary fund to pool some of the international reserves of member states and centralize part of presently national decision-making on monetary policy. That position, namely that even modest elements of innovation require confirmation by treaty revision, is confirmed in the *Delors Report* in its discussion of the establishment of a European reserve fund which would initially pool 10 per cent of the international reserves of participants (Delors Committee 1989: paras 53–4).

An interpretation which classifies any step that modifies the present informal and essentially voluntary cooperation in the EMS in any significant way as 'institutional' may seem excessively wide. Nevertheless, I shall follow it in the present chapter. The *Delors Report* did not shrink from the responsibility of defining the institutional prerequisites for managing an EMU; the main element would be a high degree of centralization of monetary authority in a European system of central banks (ESCB), underpinned by a capacity vested in the Council of Economics and Finance Ministers to set 'binding rules' for national budgetary policies.

*The author acknowledges helpful discussions with Daniel Gros, and critical comments from André Szasz and Michele Fratianni, but he assumes sole responsibility for remaining weaknesses and biases in the chapter. No effort has been made to update the chapter beyond December 1989.

A second word in the title of this chapter suggests, however, that focusing on the institutional differences between the present EMS and the final stage of EMU would be too confining, though easier than analysing the transitory arrangements. Writing about 'institutional developments' obliges one to concentrate on the process of change which the approach in stages in the *Delors Report* has described in more summary form than the final destination. The following sections will accordingly deal primarily with stages one and two and particularly the latter. The main interest is in stage two, which has been labelled by some as 'soft union', since intra-EC exchange rates could still be modified and centralized budgetary power remains limited to recommendations to national governments, while some joint decision-making is to be established in the monetary area.

This focus can in my view be justified by the following simple consideration: if one cannot argue fairly convincingly that such a stage is both desirable in itself as an improvement over the present EMS and as a necessary preparation for and experimentation with the fully joint management procedures envisaged for the final stage, the process of moving from the EMS to EMU may not get under way at all. Why should member states embark on the time-consuming and politically risky road towards a treaty revision without being confident that the intermediate stage marks progress relative to the already rather well-functioning system which exists today? President Jacques Delors said, in presenting the *Delors Report* to the European Council, that its recommendations should not be regarded as sacrosanct. While this is certainly true as regards the more detailed proposals, it is hard to believe that a fundamentally different approach will be adopted which does not admit the need for some collective management through an ESCB-like institution prior to the fixing of exchange rates, the main step at the start of the final stage.

The following sections draw rather freely on several contributions to the Collection of Papers prepared by members of the Delors Committee, writing in a personal capacity, including in particular my own paper. I do so not to try to invoke any greater authority, because members who, like myself, tried to introduce more detailed proposals for turning a joint monetary policy cannot claim any major success in having these ideas discussed fully in the Delors Committee itself. The latter was, probably rightly, primarily concerned with putting together a short, rather non-technical report on the nature of the main political choice of moving towards EMU, addressed to the European Council. The committee as a whole found it premature to go into much detail about the design and implementation of policy in stages one and two, a task that is now on the agenda of the so-called competent bodies, the EC Monetary Committee and the Committee of Central Bank Governors, as they prepare for stage one and for the intergovernmental conference to be started before the end of 1990. That, however, makes these proposals particularly topical; and the area is one in which academic research, both theoretical and empirical, could be potentially very helpful.

The rest of the chapter is in three substantive sections: section 2, the first and shortest, looks at the limited scope for further developments of the EMS in the first, pre-institutional, stage; in section 3 a number of analytical and operational considerations relevant primarily to stage two are reviewed. Section 4 looks at some critical comments on the institutional approach.

2. Stage one

It is possible to be brief with respect to the first stage – and not only because 'institutional developments' in a formal sense depend on the adoption of a revised treaty, marking only the end of stage one and the transition to stage two. There are substantive reasons as well.

Stage one caused few objections when the *Delors Report* was discussed by the Council of Finance Ministers (ECOFIN) and by the European Council, and practical preparations for starting it in July 1990 are moving ahead by an updating of the framework within which the Committee of Central Bank Governors operates and of the procedures for economic and fiscal policy coordination through the ECOFIN Council. In the monetary area the main innovation is that a higher profile is sought for the Committee of Central Bank Governors. The committee would from time to time express opinions on monetary and exchange rate policy in individual member states; but that would be possible also under the present rules dating from 1964. Such opinions may be addressed publicly to individual governments. The committee is to report annually to the European Parliament and the European Council. Recommendations would be made by majority vote, but they would not be binding for participants. The committee would normally be consulted in advance of important national decisions on the course of monetary policy. The committee will work on the basis of a more structured subcommittee system and it would draw upon a more permanent research staff.

These proposals seem perfectly reasonable; they reflect a natural preference to let an extension of the voluntary cooperation, marking the present EMS, carry the load as far as at all possible. The EMS has proved capable of developing pragmatically, most recently with the so-called Basle-Nyborg Agreement of September 1987 which facilitated intramarginal interventions and coordinated interest-rate responses in periods of tension. What is the scope for moving, within a basically unchanged institutional structure, towards a qualitatively better EMS than we know today?

There are two reasons for thinking that this scope is limited and hence that the first stage should be short. One reason was underlined as a by-product of the work undertaken as a background to the *Delors Report*, the other is more in the nature of conjecture.

The Delors Committee conducted a small questionnaire study among the EC central banks to clarify the scope for moving ahead in coordination without treaty changes. Crudely summarized, the smaller participants did not see major problems in going further in the direction of submitting their monetary policy decisions to *ex ante* coordination within the Committee of Central Bank Governors. But most of the larger countries did not think it possible to move in this direction without significant changes in national legislation and in the treaty. The reason for this was either that monetary authority is at present divided between the central bank and the political authorities, or that the central bank itself has a decision-making structure which makes it impossible for it to delegate, through its president or others, competence, even of a non-binding nature, to a European body. The former of these two situations corresponds roughly to the situation in France and in the United Kingdon (UK) and the latter to that in the Federal Republic of Germany (FRG).

In these circumstances it would be reckless to assume that improvisation in coordination, despite the goodwill of participating members of the Committee of Central Bank Governors, could avoid the tensions that have marked the EMS experience from time to time in the past and which would become more likely with a wider membership, including the UK. Some upgrading of monetary competence from the present national level to the Community level would seem to be required to achieve any qualitative improvement, and this in turn can only come about through a treaty revision which attributes such competence in a relatively precise way. Hence the linkage of the first stage and the convening of an inter governmental conference. The endorsement by the European Council of procedure and momentum, though not of a precise outcome, confirms that the first stage should be seen essentially as a period for deciding upon change rather than as a major qualitative change in itself.

The second reason is that the enlargement of membership in the EMS which is the other main ambition for the first stage is bound to be somewhat upsetting relative to the past working of the system. As shown in Chapter 4 by Giavazzi and Spaventa in this volume the EMS is already being modified by the experience of a long period without realignments. The credibility effects of this process are such as to make the system more symmetric and less dominated by the Deutschmark (DM). This process would be furthered by new participants, once they have established a sufficient degree of credibility for their policy commitment; the Spanish entry in June 1989 (though with a wide band) has provided an example. The UK has been more specific than in the past as to her readiness to see sterling become part of the exchange rate mechanism, though still without any commitment to a firm timetable. Full participation of Portugal and Greece has never been viewed by the authorities of these countries with the ideological hostility close to that shown by the UK government, but given the excess inflation in these two countries their participation is some way off, and possibly beyond the horizon of 1992 which could in other respects be seen as the natural end year for stage one. (As noted in the *Delors Report*, a delayed timetable for some member states is not a decisive argument for the others not to advance to a subsequent stage as long as the former are prepared to commit themselves to the objectives of the final stage.) The extension of full EMS participation to the Spanish and UK currencies and the transition to narrow margins of fluctuations for the lira and the peseta cannot avoid putting additional strain on the habits of cooperation that have developed, even with the best will of the authorities concerned. This second factor makes it unlikely that stage one could in itself lead to a qualitative improvement in cooperation. Indeed, it reinforces the argument for embarking on the process of treaty revision in order to be confident of retaining even the results that have been achieved through the EMS.

Similar remarks apply, almost *a fortiori*, to what is suggested for closer economic and fiscal policy coordination in stage one. The 1974 decision of the ECOFIN Council on convergence has now been replaced by a new procedure, establishing a process of mutual surveillance and policies based on agreed indicators, and, in particular, precise quantitative guidelines and medium-term orientations for budgetary policy coordination and concerted budgetary action by the member countries. It is difficult, however, to see readily why the existing framework with its already elaborate and demanding procedures is inadequate. In the budgetary policy area stage one may be seen as a period during which the ECOFIN Council and the committees that advise it begin to experiment with the formulation of what would in the final stage become binding budgetary rules. Could voluntary efforts bring about the desirable minimum correction of budgetary divergence? That is possible, yet by not means certain, but the prospect of ultimately binding rules would provide an incentive for early action.

3. Stage two

The *Delors Report* proposes no detailed blueprint for the transitory second stage of 'soft union' when the ESCB begins operations. Paragraphs 55–57, and particularly para. 57, mention some broad ideas which are further developed in the Collection of Papers as possible avenues to be explored.

Once exchange rates are irrevocably frozen at the transition to stage three, a common monetary policy is required and will have to be formulated collectively by the governing bodies of the ESCB. In contrast, during stage two when realignments may still occur, national authorities will retain the final say concerning their exchange rates and hence their monetary policies. But the same considerations that lead to the conclusion that the final fixing of parities requires a common monetary policy also imply that to the extent that exchange rates become *de facto* stabilized, and recognized to be unlikely to change, national monetary policies will, in practice, become ever more severely constrained. Increasing exchange rate stability therefore requires a framework for cooperation and coordination of national monetary policies. The more explicit the degree of exchange rate fixity, and the higher the degree of capital mobility, the closer must be the coordination and the extent to which the overall policy stance of the participants has to be decided in common.

In his contribution to the Collection of Papers Lamfalussy (1989) refers to three possible approaches in stage two. The first is for the participating central banks to set up a jointly owned subsidiary, whose facilities they would share in performing certain of their functions, notably a significant share of their transactions in the domestic money and in foreign exchange markets, without requiring any formal transfer of authority. The second is to assign a small number of monetary instruments to the ESCB while leaving others for national decisions or non-binding coordination. The third is to implement a gradual but formal transfer of decision-making power from the national to the ESCB level. The three approaches may perhaps be labelled pooling of (1) operations, (2) instruments and (3) authority.

The three approaches should be seen as complementary rather than mutually exclusive. Indeed, (2) and (3) are difficult to distinguish, since both, in order to be effective, would require the introduction of some hierarchical order in the relations of the ESCB governing bodies and the constituent national monetary authorities. They will be treated as a combined approach in the following. However, (1) is qualitatively different in requiring no formal transfer of authority; in that sense it might even be pursued in stage one, particularly if the more detailed designs of the other two approaches prove time-consuming to negotiate.

POOLING OF OPERATIONS

The pooling of operations would consist in the establishment of a common operations facility incorporating foreign exchange and domestic money market activities in a jointly owned subsidiary. Each central bank would staff its own operations, but at some point the initially seconded national staffs could be merged into a single unit. The use of common facilities would ensure that each individual participant would be fully aware of the operations of other participants, a state of affairs not existing at the present day in the management of foreign exchange reserves, apart from interventions proper, or to domestic money market operations while at the same time presenting a common appearance in the markets. Private market participants would be unable to determine the source of instructions for operations by the jointly owned trading floor. There could no longer be occasionally conflicting signals to the markets.

To these two general advantages one may add that centralization of operations would provide a more efficient training ground for national foreign exchange and money market operators than the daily consultations by telephone in the present system. The approach would facilitate efforts to develop a more convergent framework for the design and implementation of monetary policy, including the domestic aspects of the latter, and hence prepare for fully joint management in stage three. Centralization may also offer some potential for cost savings.

Despite all these virtues and the prospect of postponing the need for treaty revision which it offers the pooling of operations in itself seems too limited an objective. Operations would be merely an aggregate of the instructions received with no one visibly in charge of the consistency of policy over time or of preventing actions at cross purposes within any period of time. The approach would therefore need to be complemented by the two other approaches in the course of stage two. To implement either would, however, require some consensus about the objectives ultimate and intermediate and the design of monetary policy and use of instruments which cannot be said to exist today, at least not in any explicit form. The following pages tentatively address these three issues, mindful that they require substantial efforts of macroeconomic analysis, study of empirical regularities and assessment of practical feasibility to be meaningfully discussed. Reference is made to Table 1.1 for a summary of the points made in the following.

	Collective	National/relative
Ultimate objectives	Maintain approximate medium-term stability of producer prices in the internal market Maintain sustainable current account position for area *vis-à-vis* rest of the world	Keep growth in nominal private final demand close to targeted path in each country
Intermediate objectives	Keep growth of monetary aggregate for area as a whole within targeted interval	Keep growth in domestic credit DCE within targeted interval in each country Keep stable exchange rates *vis-à-vis* other currencies within the area
Instruments available	General (and differentiated) reserve requirements against national domestic credit expansions (DCEs) Intervention policy *vis-à-vis* third currencies	Intervention rates and policy in intra-area currency band. Interest-rate differentials within area (Small) parity realignments

TABLE 1.1 Ultimate and Intermediate Objectives of Monetary and other Macroeconomic Policies and the Instruments of Monetary Policy

POOLING OF INSTRUMENTS AND AUTHORITY

As regards *the ultimate objectives* of monetary policy there is some guidance in the *Delors Report* (para. 32):

> The system (i.e. the ESCB) would be committed to the objective of price stability;
> Subject to the foregoing, the System should support the general economic policy set at the Community level by the competent bodies;. . .

How could this general mandate be made effective in collective terms for the Community as well as nationally so that both the aggregate thrust of monetary policy and the compatibility of its national components become subject to monitoring? There appear to be two main contenders for the role of the collective price objective.

The first is to use medium-term stability of *average producer prices in the internal market* for goods as an indicator. The increasing competition and specialization resulting from the completion of the internal market will tend to make prices for internationally traded goods more homogeneous, gradually removing the scope for price discrimination between national markets. A weighted average of national producer price indices for the participating countries, expressed in a common unit, e.g. the ECU, would provide an increasingly reliable indicator of a common price trend. There is evidence from earlier periods of stable exchange rates, notably the gold standard, that close convergence in producer prices is observable in an exchange rate regime of the firmness envisaged, see e.g. McKinnon and Ohno (1988).

While such an index would give meaningful expression to a common price performance in the Community, it might be desirable to focus particularly on the domestic (i.e. internal to the EC) sources of inflation in producer prices for which ESCB monetary policy would be most directly accountable. A deflator of value added in manufacturing industry calculated as a weighted average for the internal market would leave out of account the inflationary (or disinflationary) shocks such as terms-of-trade changes resulting from swings in the prices of energy or of other intermediate imports or of raw materials. Such external shocks generate fluctuations in the inflation rate which may in practice have to be in part accommodated by variations in the collective money supply. An ultimate objective expressed in terms of stability in the average of national value-added deflators would not be radically different from the course followed in the Community in the 1980s; the second oil price shock led to a temporary acceleration of producer prices in Europe, even in the FRG, while the 1985–86 decline in import prices for raw materials, energy and other intermediate inputs (as well as in the dollar) temporarily pushed the rate of change of producer prices below zero in the low-inflation EMS countries.

In short, by aiming to keep the rate of inflation measured by an average of national value-added deflators within a narrow band close to zero, say between 0 and 2 per cent, or to keep the average increase in producer prices within a slightly wider band, similarly centered around a minimal rate of inflation, the ESCB could give specific content to the notion of a stability-oriented monetary policy and simplify the monitoring of its policies.

The other main contender is a broadly based index such as *a Community-wide consumer price index*, widely perceived as reflecting the cost of inflation to the economy. In an area as large and diverse as the Community, national price trends measured by consumer prices may, however, diverge substantially between countries even over the medium term, because the weight of non-traded goods and services in this index is substantial and price trends for these goods are less directly constrained by the process of market integration. It might be confusing to public opinion to announce a collective price objective around which substantial variation in national performances persisted.

A collective price objective formulated in terms of an essentially common indicator, such as average producer prices, may be sufficient for guiding the aggregate thrust of monetary policy. However, for the purpose of linking up with monetary instruments or with national macroeconomic objectives which will continue to have great importance throughout stage two and into stage three, the collective objective could be supplemented by criteria of national performance, consistent with the common inflation objective. One possible way of doing so, broadly in line with trends in national policy-making in a number of industrial countries in the 1980s would be to set targets for the rate of increase of some measure of nominal income for each participating country.

To be more specific, objectives for the rate of increase in private final demand (private consumption, business fixed investment and residential construction) might be thought of as the national income measure most relevant in the context of monetary policy. For each participating country the national and Community authorities would make a judgement on the unavoidable rate of inflation in private final demand prices expressed in the national currency, and on a rate of increase of real demand judged feasible in the light of trend capacity growth and the initial situation. The national inflation rates thus calculated would typically average a little above the collective objective for producer prices in the Community, because the broader price indices for final demand would comprise non-traded goods and services for which productivity increases are typically slower than for the sectors producing internationally traded goods in the EC market. National inflation rates in terms of final demand prices might also diverge slightly year by year, as the differentials in productivity between sectors are unlikely to be uniform across countries. Gradually goods market integration would tend to impose approximate parallelism on national price levels in this broader sense, as the range of traded goods expands and factor mobility increases. Various forms of nominal income targeting have appeared in national policy-making in the 1980s when the confidence in monetary aggregates as intermediate targets was weakening, while a return to objectives for the growth of real output was perceived as potentially inflationary. Maintaining a suitable measure of nominal income close to a steady growth path provides a framework for monitoring national economic policies and for coordinating them internationally, as is recognized in some of the main proposals for improving a global policy coordination and reforming the international monetary system, see e.g. Williamson and Miller (1987) and Frankel (1989).

In the present context nominal income targeting would provide a linkage to potential intermediate objectives at the national level and through them to decisions relating to a money-supply process which will remain, at least through stage two, largely national in execution if not in design. Such a framework would be suitable for the coordination of monetary and fiscal policies in the Community in so far as it would facilitate the identification of policy conflicts. The latter would arise if the execution by the ESCB of its mandate for ensuring price stability were to be eroded by the sum total of national fiscal policies, implying a growth rate in nominal final demand in one or more countries inconsistent with the objective for average inflation. In this way the framework would pinpoint requirements for fiscal coordination in an analytically more satisfactory way than by simply looking at the size of budget imbalances relative to gross national product (GNP), or to national savings, as a basis for imposing 'binding rules' on such imbalances. By monitoring both the national component of ESCB monetary policy and fiscal policy in terms of the same nominal income targets, the risk of open conflicts is reduced.

Fiscal and other non-monetary policies are clearly seen in the *Delors Report* as providing the main instruments for achieving external equilibrium. It does not say explicitly that internal price stability always has to take precedence over the external stability of the participating currencies, though it envisages no significant degree of commitment to stabilize the latter. Interventions in third currencies would be carried out 'in accordance with guidelines established by the ESCB Council' (*Delors Report*, para. 57 on stage two) and subsequently 'on the sole responsibility of the ESCB Council in accordance with Community exchange rate policy' (*Delors Report*, para. 60 on stage three) and such interventions could be designed either as an additional instrument for influencing trends in the aggregate EC price level or with a view primarily towards external equilibrium in the broader sense of helping to maintain a sustainable current account position for the area as a whole *vis-à-vis* the rest of the world. The concern with finding a proper policy mix expressed elsewhere in the *Delors Report* suggests that the latter interpretation is the more appropriate, but also that no major conflict with the prime objective of price stability was envisaged.

In principle, it would be possible to gear monetary instruments directly to ultimate objectives. If the Community-wide index of producer prices were to accelerate and information on prices could be available with a time-lag of one to two months such an observed development would provide an indication that average interest rates in the Community should be raised to contain money creation. If the growth rate of nominal demand in a particular country were to run well ahead of the agreed national target that would after a somewhat longer information lag trigger a country-specific response by the tightening of one or more policy instruments in the country concerned. With high capital mobility and credibility for the stability of exchange rates inside the area, the scope for differentiated national monetary actions would be limited, so such actions would have to be in part non-monetary. Symmetric responses could be envisaged if a deceleration of average inflation or a shortfall of nominal demand became observable. Simple feed-back rules of this type could provide a stabilizing framework within which both average and nationally differentiated departures from targets were dampened.

But further attention to the way changes in monetary instruments influence the ultimate objectives of average inflation and the rate of growth of nominal demand in the participating countries through monetary and/or credit aggregates is advisable for at least two reasons. First, formulating policy with respect to one or more appropriately chosen aggregate(s) will improve the understanding of monetary policy and enhance its credibility; it will become easier to monitor the actions of the ESCB than in the situation where policy performance is assessed only on the basis of the ultimate objectives over which monetary policy has, within any given shorter time horizon, only a limited influence. Second, if reserve requirements are to be applied as one of the main instruments of the ESCB, they have to be seen to work in a broadly similar way in the participating countries by relating to a monetary or credit aggregate which is related in a stable way over longer periods to the ultimate objectives.

A possible procedure would consist in setting a collective target for aggregate annual money creation in the participating countries, consistent with the objective for average inflation. Abstracting temporarily from net interventions in third currencies by the participants, total additions to the broad money stock (M2 or M3) would be matched by the sum of domestic counterparts to money creation in each country, since purchases of other currencies by one participating central bank are offset by sales elsewhere within the system. In principle, there would be no sterilization of interventions in partner currencies. The task of controlling total money creation would then consist of applying instruments which influence, through incentives or obligations, the readiness of each central bank to keep domestic credit expansion (DCE) close to a targeted and collectively agreed rate for the country in question. Setting the latter through a collective decision-making process in the ESCB would constitute the core of the *ex ante* coordination effort. The process would assist in making mutually consistent the national objectives for the growth of nominal demand from which the national DCEs are derived. Deviations between actual and targeted DCE would in turn give some early information on deviations between actual and targeted growth in nominal demand. A procedure of this nature has been outlined in some detail by Russo and Tullio (1988).

It cannot be claimed with confidence that (1) national DCEs can be closely controlled or (2) that they are tightly linked to nominal demand over shorter periods of time, two desirable characteristics of intermediate monetary objectives, as analysed meticulously by Bryant (1980). A recent Organization for Economic Cooperation and Development (OECD) study shows a fairly weak quarter-to-quarter relationship between DCE (and different monetary aggregates) and changes in nominal demand for the four largest EC economies. On the other hand, a clear tendency for both to decelerate has been observable in the FRG, France and Italy (but not in the UK) since the early 1980s. (see Fig 1.1).

Despite the evidently high degree of slack in the relationship of DCE and nominal demand, using the former as an intermediate objective may be justified by two considerations: (1) it provides the most direct linkage to total money creation in the area; and (2) it is an extension, in the direction of symmetry, of the present informal practice in the EMS in which most countries, with the significant exception of the FRG, look to rates of DCE relative to others in the EMS as the consistent underpinning for the main intermediate objective of maintaining stable exchange rates in the EMS. For the FRG the shift from the present intermediate objective (target for broad money, M3) to a DCE target, with in principle no provision for sterilization, should be acceptable, provided overall money creation in the area were seen to be more directly subjected to stability-oriented, collectively agreed decisions and efficient instruments for implementing them, as is proposed in the *Delors Report* through the establishment of the ESCB with a mandate to pursue price stability.

Total money creation would depart from the sum of national DCEs to the extent that non-sterilized interventions *vis-à-vis* third currencies were undertaken by the ESCB directly or by one of the participating central banks. There is no presumption that such interventions would be sterilized; efforts to stem what was considered excessive depreciation of the area's currencies *vis-à-vis* the dollar through sales of dollars might well require some overall tightening of monetary conditions and higher average interest rates for the Community as a whole, and vice versa in the case of purchases of dollars to stem overly rapid appreciation of the participating currencies. The degree of sterilization would be a matter for discretionary decisions arrived at collectively through the ESCB Council. The latter would also, in consultation with the participating central banks, take a view on which currency or currencies to use in dollar interventions. One important criterion in reaching such decisions would be to maximize the cohesiveness of the currencies within the system as that finds expression in the exchange markets. Guidance would also be found in the degree of correspondence in each country between a central bank's DCE objective and the observed

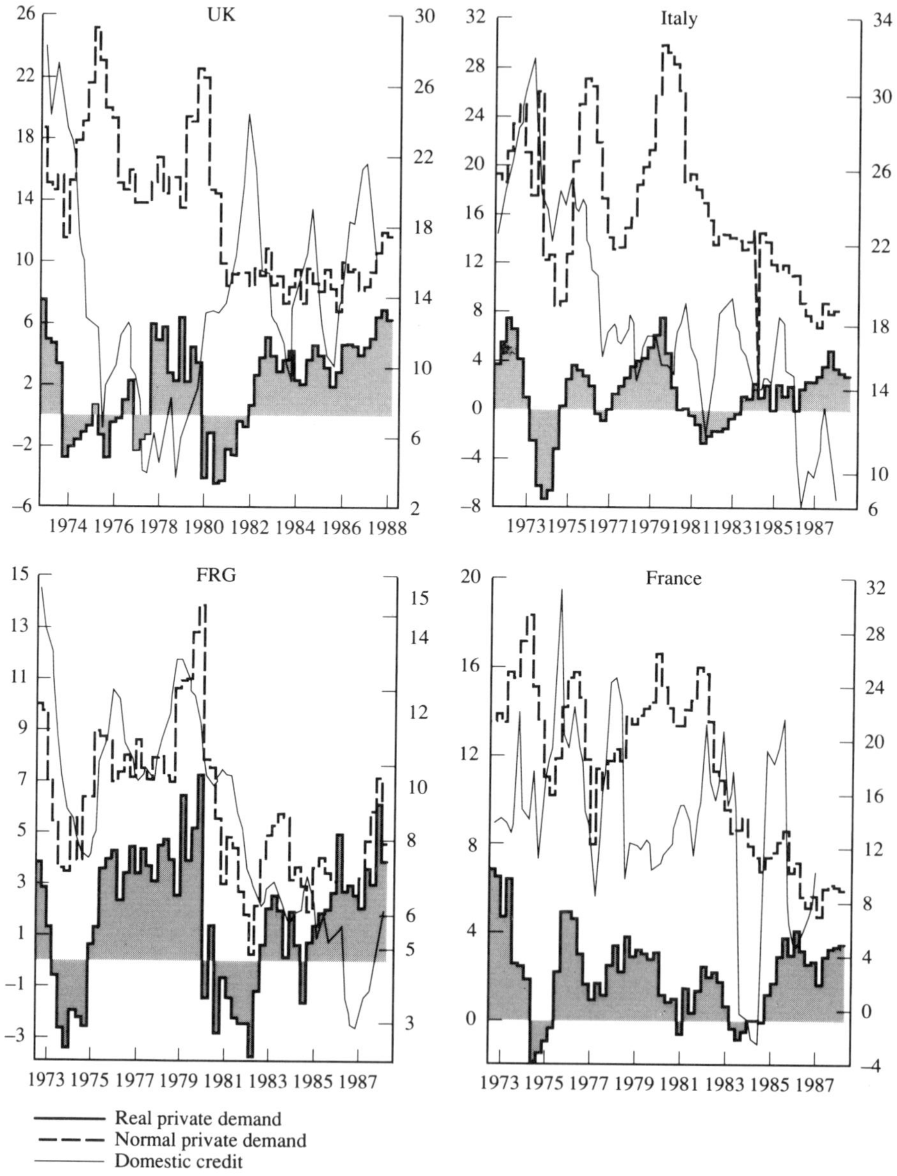

FIG. 1.1 Domestic credit expansion and growth rates in nominal and real private demand (Source: Delors Report (1989), Collection of Papers, p. 164)

growth in credit, including potential effects of sterilization operations linked to interventions in third currencies which the ESCB may assign to that particular central bank.

For the individual central bank the main short-term intermediate objective would continue to be the maintenance of stable exchange rates *vis-à-vis* other participating currencies. Some *ex ante* coordination of DCE objectives should make that task easier on average; but in practice, the DCE objective may, in particular situations, have to be overridden to maintain exchange rate stability.

Instruments Available

Even prior to the attribution of any particular instrument to the ESCB the collective formulation of ultimate and intermediate monetary objectives would in itself constitute a major step towards *ex ante* coordination. The participating central banks could widen their exchange of information on their respective formulations of domestic monetary policy, notably by giving the reports prepared by a special group of experts for the Committee of Central Bank Governors (the 'Raymond group') a more deliberately common analytical framework along the lines above. Similarly, the reports prepared by another expert group on exchange market interventions (the 'Dalgaard group') could begin to be used in a more forward-looking way to formulate intervention strategies rather than to review the past record. Closer coordination could begin to replicate the effects of a more advanced stage, even while the policy analysis and recommendations emerging from it remain advisory, as is the case for stage one.

Yet it is unlikely that anything resembling closely a common monetary policy could be conducted merely through discussions, but without vesting in the ESCB genuine decision-making power with respect to at least some significant instruments of monetary policy. Indeed, that is the rationale of suggesting the set-up of the ESCB for stage two before the irrevocable fixing of parities which makes a common monetary policy a simple necessity. But there are difficulties in determining how monetary authority might be shared between a centre (the ESCB Council and Board) and the participating national central banks. The efficiency of operations requires that there should never be any doubt in the financial markets, among national policy-makers or elsewhere as to which body has the responsibility for taking particular decisions. Monetary authority is less easily divisible than budgetary authority where elements of decentralization and even of competitive behaviour between different levels of government, or within the same level, may be observed in national states.

Four types of policy decisions could be considered as being at the core of any design of a workable pooling of instruments or responsibilities within an ESCB in stage two:

1. Adjustment of short-term interest differentials;
2. Intervention policy *vis-à-vis* third currencies;
3. Changes in reserve requirements;
4. Changes in intra-area parities (realignments).

Reference may again be made to Table 1.

The *adjustment of relative short-term interest rates* is the central instrument in managing the present EMS and the main candidate for gradual pooling of authority. A high degree of coordination and occasionally *de facto* joint, or at least bilateral, decisions have been observed. Participants have developed, particularly since the so-called Basle-Nyborg Agreement of September 1987, a flexible set of instruments for containing incipient exchange market tensions: intramarginal intervention, wider use of the fluctuation band and changes in short-term interest rate differentials. This combination has proved fairly robust in most periods of tension since September 1987. But a risk remains that the experience of earlier periods of tension will be repeated; then public criticism and mutual recrimination between ministers of finance occasionally intensified tensions and made monetary management very difficult. The main examples of such episodes are December 1986, January 1987, November 1987 and to a minor extent April 1989. The participation of additional currencies in the EMS in the course of stage one, notably sterling, which has traditionally been managed with considerable involvement on the part of the UK Treasury and even of the Prime Minister, will make it urgent to strengthen procedures for genuine coordination further and to make an early transition to the more joint form of management of stage two.

Decision-making in this sensitive area would still remain in national hands in stage two, but the launching of the ESCB at the beginning of stage two would in itself imply that national governments find it more difficult than in the past to involve themselves directly in the management of exchange crises. In the course of stage one the Committee of Central Bank governors may already have begun to perform more efficiently the role of a multilateral arbitrator that has been missing occasionally in the past. A common analytical framework for the intermediate targets as outlined above would give more explicit guidance as to who should adjust to whom. If the proposal to develop a joint operational facility for exchange and money market operations is pursued that would in itself bring participating central banks into more continuous contact with respect to their transactions in their domestic financial markets and facilitate coordinated action on interest rates.

Gradual upgrading of decision-making on relative interest rate adjustment from the purely national level to a Community body, in the first stage the Committee of Central Bank Governors, from the second stage the ESCB Council, will not in itself ensure that the average level of interest rates in the participating countries is appropriate, though it should tend to make such an outcome more likely than the present system and minimize the latter's occasional inefficiencies of interest rate escalations and tensions. To get a firmer grip on the average level of rates, the attribution to the ESCB of an instrument which permits a collective influence on domestic sources of money creation would be necessary. Such an instrument is described briefly below in the form of the ability of the ESCB to impose compulsory reserve requirements on domestic money creation and gradually to develop a market for a European reserve money base with its own lending rate.

A second instrument for which some degree of joint management could be envisaged is *foreign exchange interventions in third currencies*. There are two potential arguments for developing a joint policy: (1) the medium-term need to contribute to the containment of major misalignments, and (2) the smoothing of short-term volatility *vis-à-vis* third currencies.

The former argument can hardly be assessed without making a judgement on the feasibility of a more managed global exchange rate system and the degree of commitment by other major monetary authorities, notably in the USA, to support, through interventions and domestic monetary adjustments, any understanding reached on the appropriate level of the main bilateral exchange rates. Given the experience of the period since 1977 and the major present current account imbalances, projected to persist well into the 1990s, it would be hazardous to assume that an emerging joint dollar policy of the EMS countries would be anything more than *ad hoc* guidelines for managing some further collective appreciation of the EMS currencies as smoothly as possible. This will put the cohesion of the EMS currencies to a severe test, but it will also provide a unique opportunity, as was the case in 1985–87, for reconciling low inflation in Europe with a relatively expansionary monetary policy in the Community, hence contributing to an improved and satisfactory price performance in the transition period from the present more decentralized operation towards EMU.

As regards the task of smoothing short-term volatility, it must be noted that tensions among EMS currencies have often in the past decade been triggered by financial disturbances from third currencies, notably movements in the dollar. The currencies participating in the EMS were seen by the markets as being sensitive in different degrees to such disturbances. These perceived differences had their origins in varying degrees of controls on capital movements and in expectations of the likelihood of divergent policy reactions to the external financial disturbances. For example, a depreciation of the dollar was normally expected to strengthen the DM relative to most other EMS currencies, because (1) the DM had the largest domestic financial base and the most liberal regime for capital flows, and (2) the non-German authorities in the EMS were seen as more prone than the Bundesbank to try to avoid the contractionary effects of the appreciation of their currencies. The tensions caused by these real or perceived differences in structure and/or behaviour were occasionally mitigated by an EMS realignment. Conversely, in periods of an appreciating dollar, outflows from Europe were observed to be particularly strong from the DM area, reflecting closer substitutability between the US dollar and the DM than that prevailing for other EMS currencies, but presumably also a perception of decreasing probability of a realignment within the system. In recent years the liberalization of capital movements in France and Italy and some smaller EMS countries, the widening of continental European financial markets and the improved cohesion of the EMS economies have weakened the earlier negative correlation between movements in the US dollar (in effective exchange rate terms) and movements in non-DM currencies in the EMS bilaterally *vis-à-vis* the DM, see Giavazzi and Giovannini (1989). But the tendency for dollar movements to affect the EMS currencies differentially may persist in a moderate form into stage two. The task remains in that case to ensure that such tensions, if they are unwarranted by more fundamental economic divergence, do not persist and force realignments.

While this could in principle be achieved through joint guidelines for decentralized interventions by the participating national central banks, a visible capacity to intervene jointly in third currencies, and to do so in ways that further the cohesion of the EMS, is potentially important. Without a presence in the major exchange markets the ESCB would lack the capacity to check the impact of external financial disturbances on EMS stability at source. Hence 'a certain amount of reserve pooling' (*Delors Report*, para. 57) as well as mutual holdings of ample working balances in EMS currencies would be desirable in stage two.

It is impossible to determine *a priori* what percentage of external official reserves would have to be pooled in order to create a credibility effect in the financial markets for an emerging joint intervention policy. Leaving the percentage low, say 10–20 per cent, as proposed by some members of the Delors Committee as a possible step in stage one (*Delors Report*, para. 53), might run the risk of complicating existing cooperative procedures without making a qualitative difference, though even with limited pooling some beneficial effects could be expected from the learning experience of coordinating interventions through the same trading floor, see also de Larosière (1989). And pooling of reserves would have the clear advantage over pooling of operations that it would force the participants to formulate guidelines for interventions. Presumably the share of total interventions undertaken by the ESCB would exceed its share of total reserves.

Joint interventions in third currencies by means of pooling of part of exchange reserves did not win general favour in the *Delors Report* (para. 54) as a proposal for the first stage; 'too much emphasis might be put on external considerations relative to the correction of imbalances within the Community'. This argument would not apply to an ESCB capacity to intervene in stage two along with the attribution of other monetary instruments with more direct domestic implications for the participants as proposed here.

A third instrument, perhaps specifically assigned to the ESCB, would be the ability to impose *variable reserve requirements* on domestic money creation.

Whereas the two first instruments (and the fourth to be discussed below) are directed primarily at relative adjustments within the EMS, changes in required reserve ratios affect the overall thrust of monetary policy. International monetary agreements, including the Bretton Woods system and the EMS, have typically been more explicit on relative than on aggregate adjustment in the participating countries. The EMS procedures for relative adjustment may leave something to be desired, as explained above and they may leave too much discretion to national monetary authorities to remove ambiguities and tensions. Yet more attention has been given to these procedures than to discussion of whether monetary policy has an appropriate aggregate thrust.

The Bretton Woods system and the early EMS did not have to face up to this issue directly, because both systems were protected by a mixture of capital controls for the short term and some scope for changing the exchange rate in the longer term. The post-1983 EMS has had more difficulty in avoiding the issue. In the absence of some aggregate monetary target for the whole system, an implicit monetary rule emerged: monetary policy in all participating countries tended to be determined, via the ambition to hold more rigidly fixed nominal exchange rates, mainly by that of its largest and least inflationary participant. The practice in the EMS that reserves used for intervention in defending a weak currency have to be reconstituted within the span of a few months is that convergence, provided that exchange rates do remain fixed, will be towards the low inflation in the FRG and not towards some average as would be the case if intervention credits provided a more permanent safety net. In that case efforts at sterilization would have become more widespread in the weaker currency countries, and aggregate money creation could have drifted upwards.

By using the degree of freedom of aggregate monetary policy for implicitly attaching policies to the domestic monetary target in the FRG the EMS succeeded for a number of years since 1983 in becoming 'a zone of monetary stability' in the double sense of promoting both exchange rate and price stability, as argued, among others, in Gros and Thygesen (1988). The challenge in the recent more symmetric EMS has been to protect the system against the effects of erosion of this quality. That is particularly difficult in a system which remains voluntary and decentralized. In stage two (and stage three) the challenge remains to design intermediate objectives and monetary instruments so as to make an extension of monetary stability likely. The pooling of authority with respect to an instrument enabling the ESCB to influence domestic sources of money creation in each participating country would be the prime example of the third approach referred to above.

The EMS would in any case have to be revised as the leadership role of the largest country is already weakened and will be eroded further during stage one, as additional currencies join the EMS and short-term capital transactions are fully liberalized. This process affects the size of potential flows in the new member countries, in those countries that undertake additional liberalization, notably France and Italy, and in the FRG itself. The ability of the Bundesbank to keep a preferred domestic monetary target as close to a desired path as has typically been the case for the past 15 years may weaken further. Financial integration increases the risk of policy errors and hence the incentive for all participants, including the Bundesbank, to modify the present paradigm. Another factor working in the same direction is the increasing ease, as the credibility of fixed exchange rates becomes more well founded, with which all non-German participants can attract inflows of capital by maintaining short-term rates only moderately above those in the FRG. The improved substitutability between participating currencies inexorably pushes the thinking of all monetary authorities in the direction of aggregate money creation in the area and to the formulation of intermediate objectives for domestic money creation consistent with an aggregate target and, finally, to designing procedures whereby the latter can be kept roughly on their agreed course; Ciampi (1989) provides an analysis of the options available. (The following two paragraphs merely restate the main principles of the scheme, while the rest of the present subsection enlarges on it.)

The essential feature is that the ESCB should be empowered to impose uniform or differentiated reserve requirements on either the increase in the monetary liabilities of each national central bank or on the credit extended by them to their respective domestic sectors. This requirement would be met only by holding reserves with the ESCB; the supply of reserves would be entirely controlled by the latter through allocations of a reserve asset (official ECUs) to each central bank corresponding to the demand for reserves which would arise if agreed targets for money creation or DCE were observed. Both cost and availability considerations would provide central banks with an incentive to stay close to declared objectives. The ESCB would have to be given some discretion in extending or withdrawing reserves to provide marginal accommodation. The new system could largely replace the present method of creating official ECUs through temporary swaps of one-fifth of gold and dollar reserves as well as the credits extended through the very short term facility of the European Fund for Monetary Cooperation.

The system would create a monetary-control mechanism analogous to that through which national central banks, who use reserve requirements, influence money and credit creation through their banking systems. It would introduce a certain hierarchy in the relationship between the ESCB and its constituent national central banks, while leaving some freedom for each national central bank in designing its domestic instruments.

The reserve requirements might alternatively be applied directly to DCE in the total national banking system, i.e. the domestic sources of broad money creation. The advantage of this method would be to assign the collective monetary instrument more directly to a natural intermediate objective (DCE) underpinning fixed exchange rates, but it might introduce more slack in the control mechanism, as it would no longer apply to items that appear on the balance sheet of the central banks for which the latter could be regarded as more directly responsible.

In the proposals by Ciampi (1989), the ESCB would not have any direct contact with commercial banks or with financial markets in general. Its sphere of operation would be confined to transactions with the second tier of the three-tier system, the national central banks. This would be unduly confining from the time during stage three when a common currency is introduced. To manage a common currency the ESCB would need to have direct transactions with commercial banks, as does any national central bank at present. To prepare for this during the earlier part of stage three, possibly even in stage two, it may be useful to explore in what ways the ESCB could be put into a position to have some direct influence on liquidity conditions without always relying on its ability through guidelines and incentives to exert its influence indirectly via the national central banks. In any case, since legislation enabling the ESCB to deal directly with financial markets in the final stage of EMU would also be part of a comprehensive treaty revision, attention to the nature of such contacts is not premature.

One way to give the ESCB such influence would be to allow it to make open-market operations in national markets. The ESCB might, for example, use the securities it has acquired from the national central banks for such open market transactions. Initially, one could impose limits on the total amount of purchases and sales which can be made within any given period. This would be especially important at the start, when the ESCB would mainly be purchasing securities, since its initial stock would be small. These limits could be raised over time, allowing in stage three the operations of the ESCB to become more important than those of the national central banks in their respective markets.

A different and complementary approach, more directly in extension of the reserve requirements system applied to national central banks, would be to introduce a uniform European reserve requirement on commercial bank deposits, or on increases thereof. A small fraction of such deposits would be held with the ESCB and denominated in ECUs. A federal funds market, in which the ESCB as the only issuer would have strict control of the total supply, could then develop in which commercial banks would trade among themselves the reserve balances they need to satisfy the European reserve requirement. The approach would imply that the ESCB be given direct influence on a market which reflects system-wide liquidity conditions.

The approach could be implemented by giving the ESCB the authority to set, within limits set in its statutes, a compulsory reserve requirement on all deposits of Community residents with Community commercial banks. To give banks initial access to deposits with the ESCB, the latter could initially buy the appropriate amount of securities in the market; hence the system could be regarded as complementary to the idea outlined above to permit the ESCB to undertake limited open-market transactions in initial periods. The securities purchased could be denominated either in ECUs or in national currencies, provided, if introduced in stage two, the proportions of the latter correspond to the weights in the ECU basket. Once the initial amount of reserves has been created and absorbed into required reserves, the ESCB could engage in additional marginal accommodations by supplying federal funds through modest discretionary open-market operations. A tightening of the federal funds market would come about if required reserves were to run ahead of the process of supplying them; and a rise in the federal funds rate would induce banks to slow down the underlying deposit creation. The approach is compatible with the usual range of operating procedures for a central bank from interest-rate to reserves targeting.

Different operating procedures would presumably be appropriate as the ESCB extends its authority from stage two to stage three and to the ultimate management of a single currency, but the basic mechanism would not have to be modified. In effect, the ESCB could, from its beginning, act in some respects as a true central bank, reinforcing its more indirect and orchestrating functions inherent in the way that the earlier proposals constrain it to being a bank for the central banks only.

Suggesting some form of reserve requirements as the major instrument for an emerging joint policy to influence the domestic sources of money creation as a complement to the control over the external sources which a joint exchange rate and intervention policy *vis-à-vis* third currencies would provide is bound to raise critical questions on the approach. Although reserve requirements have historically been the prime method by which central banks have achieved monetary control in most countries, reliance on that instrument is limited in the Community today, see e.g. the survey by Kneeshaw and van den Bergh (1989). In most industrial countries the banking system has become indebted to the central bank to an extent that makes it dependent on the terms on which marginal accommodation of reserve needs is provided. The mechanisms suggested illustrate ways in which an analogous influence may be brought to bear through a reserve requirement system on the relationship between the ESCB and the participating central banks (the three-tier system) and gradually extended to financial markets in general. A direct contact between the central institution and financial markets would provide a smooth passage to the final stage when the ESCB is to manage a common currency.

The three instruments proposed so far, collective guidance of relative interest-rate adjustments, joint interventions in third currencies with a definitively pooled part of foreign exchange reserves and imposition of variable reserve requirements on domestic money creation, are prime examples of shifts towards the European level of decision-making authority in well-specified areas of the kind that could be considered for stage two and extended into stage three.

It remains to consider how the one decision in the EMS which is today subject to *de facto* joint decision-making, namely realignment of central rates, could be handled in stage two. Would there be a case for vesting authority over this instrument with the ESCB as part of monetary management rather than leaving it as in the present EMS with the ECOFIN Council? There are arguments both for and against such a transfer.

A major purpose of setting up elements of a collective monetary authority in the ESCB *before* the irrevocable fixing of parities which marks the transition to the third and final stage of EMU is to constrain realignments and eliminate the need for them. A more specific objective would be to ensure that the occasional and rare recourse to them will be made in sufficiently small steps to preserve continuity of market exchange rates around realignments. This has been an important feature in the containment of speculative pressures in the recent EMS experience. If financial market participants would interpret a transfer of authority for making the residual small realignments to the participating central banks as part of the ESCB's task as a signal of an intended tightening of the EMS in the transition to full EMU, such a transfer could prove stabilizing and hence desirable.

Putting the question in this way, however, suggests the counter-argument, namely that governments might not succeed in conveying such a signal. They might instead feel relief at not having, as in the present EMS, to bear the political burden of visibly initiating a realignment and without a new, more hidden, discipline inherent in membership of a union with irrevocably fixed exchange rates. The Council of the ESCB might be faced with *fait accompli* situations in which only a realignment would ease tensions and with national policy-makers blaming either private speculators or the central bankers themselves for the outcome. This would imply a deterioration relative to the recent performance of the EMS.

On balance, these arguments suggest that the decisive considerations in assigning the authority to undertake realignments are how close participants have come to meeting the prerequisites for full union. It would be dangerous, if feasible, to shift the responsibility for deciding on realignments to the ESCB in stage two, if any major divergence of economic performance has persisted into that stage. But it would be desirable to shift that responsibility if the need for realignments were generally accepted as residual only, and if adequate monetary instruments for underpinning fixed rates had been assigned to the ESCB along the lines proposed above. A tentative conclusion is that the authority to decide on realignments could become part of the mandate of the ESCB in stage two, but that this is less of a priority than the attribution of the other, day-to-day, instruments of an increasingly collective monetary policy.

4. The institutional approach: an alternative in competition?

Section 3, on institutional developments in stage two as an evolution from the present EMS towards the final stage of EMU, puts at the centre the gradual pooling of operations, instruments and monetary authority in an emerging ESCB. An outline of this kind is too cautious for those relatively few who believe the conditions will soon be ripe for full-scale monetary unification, if not with the issue of a single currency, then at least with the fixing of parities. This chapter has, as does the *Delors Report*, assumed that this longer-run vision could be unrealistic without further experimentation in the more mandatory cooperative framework of stage two to gain experience in making common judgements and decisions.

But the institutional approach is also criticized by those who find it too cumbersome and bureaucratic and inferior to the simpler disciplining mechanisms which operate in the present-day EMS through a mixture of market mechanisms and competitive relationships between the participating central banks and their respective monetary policies. The latter type of criticism is found most frequently among German officials and economists, see e.g. Kloten (1989) and Vaubel (1989). It has also found strong expression in the contribution to the Collection of Papers by Jaans (1989). This line of reasoning has also been taken up in the memorandum submitted to the ECOFIN Council by the UK authorities, UK Treasury (1989). It is important to evaluate briefly the strategy that these critics have in mind and whether it represents a visible alternative.

In the present-day EMS market perceptions of the relative merits of participating currencies and the underlying monetary policies and performances of the economies have forced the central banks to adopt an increasingly external orientation of monetary policies. The present mechanism is marked by informality and, usually, by speed of reaction as market tensions, movements of the currency in the band, and reserve flows combined with peer pressure cannot long be neglected. Occasionally, there are inefficiences in the competitive process among the central banks if interest rates escalate throughout the EMS without alleviating existing intra-system tensions, or if the price leadership exercised by the Bundesbank through its *de facto* responsibility for relations with third currencies is delayed due to uncertainties surrounding the likely reactions of other EMS central banks.

With the pooling of international reserves and authority over specific other instruments of policy, market pressures would become more remote as the initiative for adjustment shifts from the national towards the collective level. As the most visible indicators of policy inconsistencies disappear, national policy-makers may feel less constrained than in the present system. At the same time collective decisions with respect to the instruments assigned to the governing bodies of the ESCB may become delayed, as more time is allowed for evaluating macroeconomic performance within the area than in the present more decentralized and vulnerable system. This would be aggravated if the decision-making process in the emerging ESCB were complicated, requiring careful building of a near-consensus or elaborate coalitions.

The substitution of political or bureaucratic bargaining for more decentralized decisions entails dangers of this type, just as the merger of several oligopolistic suppliers into a monopoly may lead to welfare loss for the consumer. Could it be safer, as suggested by this line of reasoning, to preserve some degree of competition also among the suppliers of national moneys, allowing the consumers of monetary services to exercise more choice and judgement? Why should competition be confined to goods and financial services and not extended to the supply of monetary services? What checks will exist to restrain the behaviour of the ESCB as an increasingly monopolistic supplier?

A general discussion of the relative merits of the competitive approach versus the institutionalist approach advocated in the *Delors Report* and in the present chapter would be too demanding. My own view is that the advocates of the competitive approach who wish to retain the elements of such an approach in the present EMS, or possibly to replace it by a less institutionalized arrangement than the ESCB of a gold-standard type, see e.g. Goodhart (1989), exaggerate the benefits of competition in this area and underestimate the instabilities of both a nominal and a real kind which it could encourage within the EC. Safeguards could be built into the integration process in stage two, and beyond, to contain the weaknesses of the institutional approach, particularly if all of the three approaches outlined as features of the institutional evolution are pursued as complementary.

The autonomy of the governing bodies of the ESCB, in particular their freedom from political influence from either national governments or Community political authorities, will strengthen the capacity of those central banks that have limited autonomy nationally to take effective part in collective decision-making and help to preserve the speed of reaction which has typically been observed in the present EMS. Pooling of operational facilities and the assignment of some monetary instruments to collective management could both improve efficiency and limit the risks of delay through diffusion of responsibility and maximize the transparency of policies. It could prove more important to centralize elements of decision-making than to pool implementation in a new institution. Conceivably, joint facilities could be built in a national central bank, as was proposed for foreign exchange interventions in the Bundesbank in Thygesen (1988), provided assignment of the instrument in question to the ESCB had been decided. This would have the virtue of preserving continuity with features that are seen by most as assets in the present arrangements. But they might not be realistic in the longer-run perspective of the final stage of EMU and the issue of a common currency.

Finally, by emphasizing that monetary policy in the emerging ESCB would be guided by a general mandate to pursue price stability and intermediate monetary targets to underpin that mandate, an appropriate balance between rules and discretion could be achieved as in the present EMS. Monitoring performance on the basis of these criteria would make the fears of those who see a risk of a new institution developing into a self-serving bureaucracy, well protected against public scrutiny and criticism, appear unfounded.

5. Concluding comments

In a perceptive critical comment at a conference two years ago, well before the recent debate on the evolution towards EMU had started, Jean-Jacques Rey (1988) remarked that institutional arrangements on the EMS might have to envisage shifts of responsibilities of three different kinds: (1) within each country from the government to the central bank; (2) from the national to the Community level; and (3) at the Community level towards an operational centre. The evolution outlined in the *Delors Report* during stage two would imply all three, if all the proposed changes in decision-making and implementation are considered. This chapter has deliberately focused on that stage and on its institutional aspects, confident that a more systematic assessment both of the performance of the EMS which is the point of departure and of the final stage of EMU will be taken up in other papers at the conference.

References

Bryant, R.C. (1980) *Money and Monetary Policy in Interdependent Nations*, The Brookings Institution, Washington, D.C.

Ciampi, C.A. (1989) An operational framework for an integrated monetary policy in Europe, in Collection of Papers of *Delors Report*, pp. 225–32.

Committee on the Study of Economic and Monetary Union (the Delors Committee) (1989) *Report on Economic and Monetary Union in the European Community (Delors Report)* (with Collection of Papers), Office for Official Publications of the European Communities, Luxemburg.

de Larosière, J. (1989) First stages towards the creation of a European Reserve Bank – the creation of a European Reserve Fund, in Collection of Papers of *Delors Report*, pp. 177–84.

Frankel, J. (1989) A modest proposal for international nominal targeting, *NBER Working Paper*, No. 2849, National Bureau of Economic Research, Cambridge, Mass.

Giavazzi, F. and **Giovannini, A.** (1989) *Limiting Exchange Rate Flexibility: The European Monetary System*, MIT Press, Cambridge, Mass.

Goodhart, C. (1989) The *Delors Report*: was Lawson's reaction justifiable?, Financial Markets Group, London School of Economics, Special Papers No. 15, London, (unpublished).

Gros, D. and **Thygesen, N.** (1988) The EMS: achievements, current issues and directions for the future, *CEPS Paper*, No. 35, Centre for European Policy Studies, Brussels.

Jaans, P. (1989) The basic difference between the frameworks for policy-decision making provided by the EMS and EMU, in Collection of Papers of *Delors Report*, pp. 221–3.

Kloten, N. (1989) Der 'Delors–Bericht', *Europa Archiv* **44** (9), 251–60.

Kneeshaw, J.T. and **Van den Bergh, P.** (1989), Changes in central bank money market operating procedures in the 1980s, *BIS Economic Papers* No. 23, Bank for International Settlements, Basle.

Lamfalussy, A. (1989) A proposal for stage two under which monetary policy operations would be centralized in a jointly-owned subsidiary, in Collection of Papers of *Delors Report*, pp. 213–19.

McKinnon, R. and **Ohno, K.** (1988) Purchasing power parity as a monetary standard, Memorandum No. 276, Center for Research in Economic Growth, Stanford University, Stanford, Calif. (unpublished).

Rey, J.J. (1988) 'Comment' in De Grauwe, P. and Peeters, T. (eds) *The ECU and European Monetary Integration*, Macmillan, London.

Russo, M. and **Tullio, G.** (1988) Monetary policy coordination within the European Monetary System: is there a rule? in Giavazzi, F., Micossi, S. and Miller, M. (eds) *The European Monetary System*, Cambridge University Press, Cambridge.

Thygesen, N. (1988) Decentralization and accountability within the Central Bank: any lessons from the US experience for the potential organization of a European central banking institution? (with comment by Jean-Jacques Rey), in De Grauwe, P. and Peeters, T. (eds) *The ECU and European Monetary Integration*, Macmillan, Basingstoke and London.

Thygesen, N. (1989) A European central banking system – some analytical and operational considerations, in Collection of Papers of *Delors Report*, pp. 157–75.

United Kingdon Treasury (1989) *An Evolutionary Approach to Economic and Monetary Union*, London.

Vaubel, R. (1989) Überholte Glaubenssätze, *Wirtschaftsdienst* **VI** 276–9.

Williamson, J. and **Miller, M.H.** (1987) Targets and indicators: a blueprint for the international coordination of economic policy, *Policy Analyses in International Economics 22*, Institute for International Economics, Washington, D.C.

Comment: André Szasz

It is impossible in my brief remarks to do justice to Professor Thygesen's most interesting chapter. Two main elements can be distinguished.

First, his view on the relative roles of stage one and stage two and his argument that the preparation of EMU should take place mainly in stage two.

In Professor Thygesen's view there is little scope for further development towards EMU in the present situation, i.e. without institutional changes. Therefore stage one should be short. In this, he agrees with those member countries in whose view stage one should only be as long as it takes to have an intergovernmental conference agree on a change in the treaty and have it ratified.

Second, based on his view of stage two, the content he gives to it: replacing the present non-symmetric system with the DM as the anchor of stability by a symmetric system. This envisages a system in which monetary policy is assumed to be largely depoliticized, based on targets for DCE and where decisions on external monetary policy are taken centrally, meaning in effect surrender by the FRG of its money market policy.

The central assumption for stage two in Professor Thygesen's chapter is the freedom of the ESCB from political influence. It is on that assumption that he bases his proposals to replace the DM as the anchor of stability by a system of common decision-making, based on symmetry. It is on this assumption of independence in stage two that I have my main doubts, as follows:

1. The implication is that none of the national central banks are directed by their governments how to vote in the ESCB: for some countries this means a drastic change in both national law and attitude.
2. Independence of a central bank should be based both on clear legal provisions and on general political acceptance which can only follow from tradition. In most European countries such a tradition is lacking. If within a short period we replace the present institutional framework by a Community system where the Bundesbank – perhaps supported by one or two others – can be overruled, then pressure will be strong indeed on many governors within their own countries to insist on different priorities.

All this the more so, since in the field of budgetary policies nothing will be changed (we will have recommendations, just as at present) so that an excessive burden will remain on monetary policies.

No doubt some would see this symmetrical situation as an improvement over the present one. But that would not necessarily bring us nearer to EMU; it would rather be an incentive to keep things as they are, and not to tackle the really controversial issue: sovereignty in budgetary policies.

The alternative approach is to let the preparation for EMU take place mainly in stage one. That would imply a continuing role for the DM as the anchor of stability.

There is an increasing tendency within the EMS to pursue the hard currency option and to accept its implications for interest rate policies. If this tendency continues it means that governments accept that their central banks have to give the same priority to price stability as does the Bundesbank, without political interference. In time member countries would get used to the situation in which in practice, central banks are no longer subject to political directives as is now the case in several participating countries.

This development would mean a *de facto* movement in the direction of a common currency even in the absence of institutional changes. It would only be sustainable if in fact, even if not in theory, DCE would play an increasing role in policy-making.

1. The hard currency option by the other participants would mean for the FRG that it would be largely deprived of the exchange rate as a tool for

adjustment. This would only be acceptable if the FRG could continue to pursue price stability with its remaining policy tools and tighten monetary policies if necessary. But tightening would only help if an excess money supply was caused by domestic factors, not by inflows.

2. For the other participants it would mean that in case of outflows they have to take early measures to stem them. If they refuse to do so the hard currency option could not be maintained for long.

Thus, a growing *de facto* autonomy of central banks in all participating countries could go together with the emergence of a common analytical framework in the course of the first stage. As a result it would become possible for central banks to develop their consultations in the direction of *de facto* common decision-making which is – as Professor Thygesen also remarks – more important than pooling implementation. Of course, as a model for monetary integration it is less appealing than Professor Thygesens's, but it might turn out to be more realistic.

In this view stage two should be brief. It should only be introduced when:

(a) convergence warrants it, implying control over public finance and increased autonomy of central banks in all participating countries; and therefore
(b) EMU is actually within reach.

This approach would prevent the risk of introducing a stage two lacking the benefit of a stability anchor and lasting indefinitely. It may also avoid an unnecessary showdown with the UK, which at present in substance – if not in words – rejects EMU but which might take a different view once the success of stage one and of the internal market makes itself felt.

CHAPTER TWO

Alternative views on the EMS in the 1990s

Wolfgang Rieke

1. The EMS: past performance

A decade after its birth in 1979 the European Monetary System (EMS) is widely regarded as a success on which further progress can be built. During the earlier part of that whole period, the scepticism voiced initially in some quarters was largely validated. Serious tensions could only be resolved by recourse to realignments whose frequency became itself a source of doubt as to how long the system would last. In these circumstances the mere fact that the system has survived may already have been taken as a sign of success. But only the relative absence of tensions and the infrequency of realignments, the greater progress in reducing domestic inflation to levels that offered the prospect of lasting exchange rate stability, and other indications of greater convergence of economic performance in the later half of the decade give real credibility to a positive assessment of the EMS experience.

It can still be argued that the EMS remains at best a qualified success. Important members are either not participating in the exchange rate mechanism (ERM) which is at the core of the system, or are adhering to a special regime. Moreover, even though exchange rates between ERM currencies have behaved in a less volatile manner than those *vis-à-vis* – or between – major third currencies such as the dollar, yen and sterling, and large overshooting of purchasing power parity (PPP) or equilibrium rates has been avoided, these are not achievements to which the EMS has exclusive claim. A number of non-EMS members in Europe have been as successful in their parallel efforts to secure internal and external monetary stability. But perhaps it can be claimed that the performance of some EMS participants might have been less good outside the EMS.

Some of the achievements of the EMS, including the greater domestic price and exchange rate stability than under a free-floating regime, are not as soundly based on appropriate policies and performance of individual member countries as might be necessary for its lasting success. Fiscal discipline in several member countries is clearly recognized as inadequate even by those responsible for it, and remains a potential source of trouble. Equally, the large external payments imbalances within the Community must be a cause for concern even at times when they do not seem to be a source of market tension and realignment speculation. The ease with which they are being financed by spontaneous or other capital flows should not give rise to false optimism.

Among the many reasons for the relative success of the EMS, the determination of participating countries to restore domestic price stability as a necessary condition of lasting exchange rate stability probably ranks first. Flexible application of monetary policy instruments cum intervention has increasingly come to play its role in reducing exchange market tensions, depending on the circumstances and the status of individual EMS currencies. The Deutschmark (DM) has been widely accepted as an 'anchor' of the system, based on the Bundesbank's stability-oriented monetary policy.

By contrast, many of the rules written into the central bank agreement on the EMS have played only a secondary role. This may actually have helped the smooth functioning of the system more than it has impeded it. Interventions at the margin and very-short-term financing through mutual central bank credit booked at the European Monetary Cooperation Fund (EMCF) has played a decreasing role, as intra-marginal intervention gained favour with most partner central banks. Such intervention is mostly made in DM, with permission given by the Bundesbank depending on the circumstances; it has encouraged a large build-up of DM reserves. Settlement in ECUs, US dollars or other reserve assets has accordingly been limited and the large short- and medium-term credit facilities have hardly been used at all, to the great relief of major creditor central banks whose monetary policy might have been more seriously impaired. The divergence indicator, a watered-down version of the ECU-based intervention and settlement system initially preferred by some partners, has hardly played the role expected of it.

Use of the DM as a preferred intervention currency and its role as 'anchor' of exchange rate stability was not an explicit component of the original design of the EMS, though it was perhaps unavoidable to begin with. The adoption of the 'parity grid' rather than an ECU-based intervention system, must have strengthened the DM's claim to that role. It was certainly not a role sought or imposed on the system by its largest partner.

It has been claimed that the 'sceptics underestimated the ability of the EMS to meet the different circumstances of members' (IMF, 1989). It is probably even more true that they underestimated the participating countries' ability and determination to deal effectively with the causes of uncontrolled inflation and to accept the rules of a fixed rate system with its most powerful member setting the standard to be followed by others. This experience may lend support to the view that almost any reasonable set of rules can be made to work if countries are prepared to respect them and keep their house in order to begin with. But it also confirms the view that a system of fixed but adjustable exchange rates needs a firm 'anchor', which in present circumstances can only be provided by a major partner currency and the monetary policy that stands behind it. In any case, these seem to mark the key points to which attention must be paid as the EMS enters the 1990s.

2. The EMS in the 1990s

At the conclusion of their Madrid Summit the heads of state and government confirmed their intention to move forward to EMU and they accepted the *Delors Report* as *the* basis for the first stage which is to begin on 1 July, 1990, but only as *a* basis for the later stages, leaving room for alternative approaches to be considered in due course. It is not clear as yet what the components of alternative approaches would be. But after the critical reactions to the *Delors Report*, certain key areas which they will try to address differently can be cited:

1. The appropriate balance between community competence and national sovereignty, especially in the area of budgetary policy.
2. The weight and resources to be attributed to Community structural and regional policies.
3. The arrangements for monetary union and the status of a future European central banking system, including its 'democratic accountability'.

Some of the criticism appears to have been inspired by interpretations of the *Delors Report*'s findings which seem to give less than full justice to the discussions within the expert group.

For one thing, EMU as conceived by the Delors Committee would not give the Community full or even partial control over individual members' budgetary policies. The appropriate balance of powers would be guided by the 'principle of subsidiarity' referred to in the *Delors Report*, confining 'the attribution of competences to the Community . . . specifically to those areas in which collective decision-making was necessary' and leaving 'all policy functions which could be carried out at national (and regional and local) levels without adverse repercussions on the cohesion and functioning of economic and monetary union . . . within the competence of the member countries' (Delors Committee 1989: para 20). While a wide range of decisions would remain the preserve of national and regional authorities, 'given their potential impact on the overall domestic and external economic situation of the Community and their implications for the conduct of a common monetary policy, such decisions would have to be placed within an agreed macroeconomic framework and be subject to binding procedures and rules' (Delors Committee 1989: para. 19).

These conclusions take account of the fact that the Community budget will in all likelihood cover only a small portion of total public revenue and expenditure for some time to come. Close coordination and where necessary directly enforceable decision-making by the European Council in cooperation with the European Parliament in the macroeconomic and budgetary field, to the extent to which this is necessary to prevent imbalances that might threaten monetary stability, should thus be seen as a substitute for wholesale transfer of budgetary powers from the national to the Community level rather than as a means to enforce such a transfer.

The scope for such coordination and common decision-making will be hotly debated in the run-up to the intergovernmental conference which will be convened in due course to negotiate a new EMU treaty. But it is already relevant to the first stage of EMU and constitutes an important part of the agenda of the EMS in the 1990s. Accepting the arguments set out by Professor Lamfalussy and others on the issue, 'fiscal policy coordination would appear to be a vital element of a European EMU and of the process towards it.' (Lamfalussy 1989). In negating the need for certain rules and procedures the arguments on the other side fail to take the experience of many countries within and outside the Community adequately into account. Membership of the EC and of the EMS has provided certain countries with the necessary backing, though not with any guarantees, for much larger public borrowing abroad than would otherwise have been feasible at comparable cost. In some cases reliance on market discipline clearly has not resulted in timely correction of economic and financial policies that are dictated by domestic political pressures. Refusal of direct access to central bank credit in a future EMU will not necessarily prevent indirect recourse to monetary financing, and declarations of 'no bail-out' may not be taken as seriously as intended, given the potential repercussions for financial institutions and other systemic risks. Even if they are taken seriously, this by itself would not lead to a set of fiscal policies within the Community that would satisfy the requirements of an appropriate policy mix. It risks leaving monetary policy 'out on a limb'.

Reference to the less developed countries (LDCs) debt problems, to insolvency problems of savings and loan institutions in the USA, etc. all justify serious doubts about the wisdom of wholesale reliance on financial market discipline. Borrower governments are far more resistant to interest rates or other financial market disciplines than private borrowers, and it is not surprising that the existence of market disciplines is more often than not supported by statutory limitations on public deficits and the mode of its financing.

The critical comments on the *Delors Report*'s repeated reference to the need for enlarged structural and regional funds may be interpreted as a healthy reaction to sometimes exaggerated and unrealistic demands coming from the poorer countries. The calls for greater convergence of incomes, living standards and employment opportunities as a condition of full participation in a project leading to EMU raise important issues. They underline the need for an adequate measure of solidarity among the partners, involving the special responsibility of its richer partners. But it must also be recognized, as the *Delors Report* does explicitly, that 'excessive reliance on financial assistance through regional and structural policies could cause tensions' (Delors Committee 1989: para. 29). After all, even within individual countries disparities exist which will be far from fully offset by financial transfers or other measures having similar effects. And such transfers can under no circumstances be substitutes for action taken in the poorer countries to deal with the multiple causes of misallocation of available resources.

It can thus be assumed that reference in the *Delors Report* to the need for substantially enlarged structural and regional funds was in large part intended to draw the attention of the heads of state and government to the potentially large costs involved rather than as a wholesale endorsement by the central bank governors of the need for large financial transfers or other measures.

The views expressed by a group of central bank governors in their personal capacity as members of the Delors Committee may well be given different weight depending on the subject. On the appropriate monetary arrangements and the status of a European central banking system in a future EMU, their unanimous verdict in favour of a firm commitment to price stability and political autonomy deserves to be taken most seriously. Though many partners may find this difficult to accept in the context of their national political circumstances and legal arrangements, they might see advantages in a pre-defined commitment to price stability and full political autonomy of a future European central banking system, given the special political circumstances in which monetary policy would have to be conducted in the Community. Absence of political union, or the very loose type envisaged by some observers for the Community, suggests that monetary arrangements based on a clear commitment to the task which monetary policy can most effectively pursue, namely price stability, and on a status of autonomy from political interference directed at it from either national governments or Community authorities would best meet a variety of concerns that may exist.

As stated, discussion of these key issues and its outcome will also have a critical bearing on the content and speed of progress towards EMU in the first stage. The agenda for that first stage is clearly set out in the *Delors Report*. It is in its essentials identical with that of the EMS in the 1990s, in so far as 'it would aim at a greater convergence of economic performance through the strengthening of economic and monetary policy and coordination within the existing institutional framework' (Delors Committee 1989: para. 50).

In the monetary field, action in the first stage is to be taken along several lines, including:

(a) the completion of a single financial area;
(b) full participation of all Community currencies in the ERM;
(c) removal of all impediments to the private use of the ECU;
(d) redefining the mandate of the Committee of Central Bank Governors.

It can be assumed that the necessary Community Directives for the establishment of 'a single financial area in which all monetary and financial instruments circulate freely and banking, securities and insurance services are offered uniformly throughout the area' (Delors Committee 1989: para. 52) will be in place shortly so as to be promptly enforced in all member countries. The creation of a single financial area must be seen as essential to the further evolution of the EMS in the context of EMU. It is also highly relevant in so far as monetary integration and policy coordination should be able to rely more on market forces playing their proper role rather than on mechanistic rules seeking to achieve 'symmetric' adjustment to yield the expected results.

Removal of all impediments to the private use of the ECU may face greater obstacles if it is meant to place the ECU on an equal footing with domestic currencies, after having been treated like any other foreign currency so far. In any case, the ECU in its present form as a basket is unlikely to be of more than symbolic significance even if its role as a financial instrument continues to expand.

Full participation of all members in the ERM under the same set of rules would do away with an imbalance of rights and obligations which remains a potential threat to the system, and it may give support to the notion of a two-speed process towards EMU, with incalculable implications. As mentioned, non-participation and a wider band were considered appropriate as a temporary device to give countries time to adjust to the full constraints of the EMS and to find the right exchange rate level for their participation on a durable basis.

The time for entering the fixed rate mechanism after an extended period of free floating may never look ideal, especially for a currency like sterling. For various reasons, sterling may at times still be exposed to forces that are different from those affecting other currencies, including particularly the DM as the key currency of the EMS. The present time may seem specially ill-suited for entry, given the obstinately high British inflation rate and some of its underlying causes. The proponents of entry would expect participation to strengthen the authorities' ability to deal effectively with inflation, if only because it would give added credibility to its anti-inflation strategy. But the opposite result could not be wholly excluded if the use of monetary policy cum intervention to defend the agreed exchange rate margins were to conflict with the need to secure greater price stability.

However, taking an optimistic view, after a decade of experience with the EMS, the system might on the whole be able to cope with any tensions arising from the participation of sterling, provided the British authorities are willing to apply their own monetary policy fully to the task. The example of other EMS currencies that were beset by high inflation and exchange rate instability in the past would seem to justify such guarded optimism, even though sterling may be considered 'a special case'.

The single most prominent action in the monetary field involves the strengthening of cooperation and coordination of monetary policy by way of redefining the tasks and procedures of the Committee of Central Bank Governors. It can be argued that the changes proposed by the *Delors Report* could be put into effect without changing the relevant Council decision of 1964, which was sufficiently broad to cover a wide range of tasks. This might, however, deprive the proposed action of its political content.

The case for cooperation and economic policy coordination at various levels has been amply demonstrated with reference to the G-7 process, which seeks to reduce global payments imbalances and secure reasonably stable exchange rates in an environment of non-inflationary growth (Frenkel *et al.* 1988a, b). Its proponents point to the linkages between national economies and the spillover effects of policy action taken by countries individually as well as to the feed-backs of excessive exchange rate volatility, especially misalignments, which can only be adequately dealt with in the context of policy coordination seeking to optimize some sort of global economic policy function.

The arguments against undue reliance on policy coordination are also well documented (Feldstein 1988). They stress the risks involved if individual countries systematically seek to escape their responsibilities for keeping their house in order, while relying on others to assume their share of the adjustment burden as defined in a cooperative framework. Targeting the exchange rate is seen as inopportune because it eliminates one important adjustment instrument and imposes policies on individual countries that will prove unsustainable over the long term.

In the Community, closer policy coordination at all levels, including monetary policy, is increasingly seen as an essential complement of the commitment to fixed though adjustable exchange rates in the EMS, the progressive integration of financial markets based on unrestricted capital flows, the completion of the internal market and the whole process leading to EMU. The preference for stable over fully flexible exchange rates in itself amounts to an option in favour of cooperation and policy coordination over *laissez-faire* for all. Progressive liberalization of capital movements and financial market integration is seen to add a wholly new dimension, as monetary policy autonomy will be progressively reduced under fixed exchange rates and free capital flows.

There is much evidence that monetary policy decisions are now taken in a spirit of greater mutual recognition of their spillover effects, though the weight given to exchange rate considerations will differ according to countries' priorities and circumstances, as well as the status of the respective currency. For the Bundesbank domestic price stability takes precedence over exchange rate stability if a choice needs to be made, while some other partners insist on a stable or fixed exchange rate as the most effective means of securing domestic price stability.

As long as inflation rates diverged substantially a simple 'follow-the leader' formula seemed perfectly acceptable as it added credibility to the efforts made to bring down inflation. As inflation rates move closer to the lowest possible norm, this state of affairs is increasingly called into question. It is alleged that it has resulted in an asymmetry of adjustment and financing burdens which favours the strongest partner, thus giving rise to growing inequities. Some critics even claim that it imposes a deflationary bias upon the system, in so far as it prevents certain countries from pursuing their optimal growth/inflation trade-off. By contrast, the *Delors Report* found that 'the System has benefited from the role played by the Deutsch mark as an "anchor" for participants' monetary and intervention policies' and thus failed to give support to such criticism (Delors Committee 1989: para.5).

In any case, the arguments for closer cooperation or common decision-making in the monetary policy area leave important questions unanswered. The central questions relate to the objectives to be pursued by monetary policy and the methods to be applied. The assertions of an asymmetry resulting in a deflationary bias of the EMS suggest that the consensus on the primacy of price stability as an objective of monetary policy may be less firm than is often alleged. It appears to leave substantial room for disagreement about the degree to which other objectives should be actively pursued with the help of monetary policy within the constraints of reasonable price stability. The recent spurt of economic growth and the resurgence of inflationary pressures may again have put a damper on the willingness of individual governments to accept undue inflation risks while actively pursuing other objectives. But very high unemployment will remain a constant invitation to call on monetary policy to be less concerned about the dangers of inflation and to exploit its potential to stimulate overall demand, even though this may at best be of very short-term benefit.

The debate about the appropriate autonomy status for central banks and the degree to which the Committee of Central Bank Governors should be expected to support Community objectives also suggest an inclination in some quarters to adhere to concepts that carry with them considerable potential for discord. Central bank autonomy appears sometimes to be equated with excessive concern with inflation risks and undue neglect of other objectives of public policy.

But even assuming for a moment a general willingness to give price stability precedence over other objectives, important questions remain to be dealt with. In his treatment of some of the relevant analytical and operational issues involved, Thygesen (1989: 160) states that 'the judgment on the performance of monetary policy . . . would hinge on an interpretation of the objective of price stability', and he offers 'two main contenders for the role of collective objective', namely the medium-term stability of average producer prices in the internal market for goods or a Community-wide consumer price index. And he claims that ways could be found to link up the common inflation objective with national macroeconomic objectives, which will continue to exist so long as the final stage of EMU has not been achieved.

Thygesen recognizes that for a number of reasons, among them the different weight of non-traded goods and services which are less subject to the effects of market integration, national consumer price trends would continue to diverge substantially even over the medium term. He concludes that 'it might be confusing to public opinion to announce a collective price objective around which substantial variation in national performances persisted.' (Thygesen 1989: 161). What he does not say is that such a collective price objective would then have to be measurably higher than zero, depending on the likely range of divergent performances and their variation over time, unless he assumes that below-zero price performance in individual countries is as likely to occur as above-zero price performance.

The concept of price stability may indeed be subject to some qualification *ex post*, if only to take account of statistical properties of the price index against which the success of monetary policy is to be measured. For certain purposes such as monetary targeting, it may also have to be qualified at the technical level, albeit within narrow limits. But to be credible as a policy objective *ex ante* price stability must be equated with zero inflation, however measured. The existence of different rates of hard-core inflation in various Community countries would not seem to be consistent with the adoption of zero inflation as a common objective. An average of such core inflation rates would by definition not satisfy the high core inflation countries, and it would tend to drive up the average over time if low-inflation countries allowed their inflation rate to move closer to the average. It is not entirely clear whether an average producer price index would deal with this problem, even though in a fixed exchange rate system producer prices might on past experience converge more than consumer prices.

As a practical way out, Thygesen suggests nominal income targeting as a means to link national economic policy formulation in a situation involving still diverging inflation rates with the collective price objective and inflation rates, and the aggregate thrust of monetary policy based on it. He counts on goods market integration to impose approximate parallelism on national price levels as the range of traded goods expands and factor mobility increases.

National income targeting as a guide for monetary policy is open to well-known objections which seem largely to have been confirmed by practical experience. It is essentially a medium-term concept given that monetary policy affects both price and output developments with substantial lags. It also invites attempts to achieve an optimal trade-off between inflation and output growth which is likely to result in higher-than-intended inflation as the limits of monetary stimulation are tested. The very notion of a trade-off is likely to give an inflationary bias to the actual working of a system based on a national income framework.

While technical expertise will be required to give operational content to close coordination of monetary policies between central banks, no particular method chosen will provide a substitute for a clear commitment to price stability as a guiding principle. Lack of such a commitment will itself be a cause of added difficulty confronting many countries in their efforts to achieve non-inflationary economic growth, if only because economic agents will seek to protect themselves against the adverse consequences of inflation which their government and central bank may be inclined to tolerate. Interest rates are then likely to rise spontaneously as inflationary expectations increase, thus frustrating the intentions of the authorities to exploit a perceived trade-off through an easier monetary policy.

The difficulties confronting an approach to coordinated monetary policy in the Community based on a narrow definition of price stability as a guiding principle suggest that it would be unrealistic to assume that the system could do without an 'anchor' of stability provided by the most widely used and most stable currency. Even if a mechanism were put in place that relies on coordination procedures giving all partners equal weight, monetary policy management for the Community as a whole would probably need such an 'anchor' to function properly. Since the ECU is unlikely to qualify for that role in its present form and for some considerable time to come, the DM remains the prime candidate.

Apart from its own statutory commitment to monetary stability, the ability of the Bundesbank to pursue a monetary policy geared to domestic price stability remains crucial to this task, whereas other partners may continue to regard the defence of their central rate within the EMS as best suited to the achievement of their objectives. Some members have already materially come close to being co-partners in the 'anchor' function, even though the primary focus of the markets will be on exchange rate relationships with the DM as a matter of convenience. Among the major partners, France is moving clearly in that direction, based on a price performance approaching that of the Federal Republic of Germany (FRG) and a policy mix which increasingly gives support to a claim of co-responsibility for the stability 'anchor' of the system. Indeed, other members should consider participation in the EMS as an open invitation to compete for the role as 'anchor' or – perhaps more realistically – a share in that role.

In this sense, currency competition would thus be a major component of a strategy aimed at progressive convergence towards the lowest price denominator and offering the prospect of lasting exchange rate stability at the same time. Cooperation and policy coordination efforts, while avoiding automatic or strictly rule-based obligations of central banks to take particular action or avoid it, could thus be expected to further the progressive formation of a core group of countries pursuing parallel (though not in all respects identical) policies producing convergent results. Objection to one important currency and its central bank acting as 'anchor' would thus be defused. In its place a stable core group would increasingly share the role of 'anchor', based on the successful pursuit of monetary stability and growing substitutability of their currencies in private use. As mentioned, a single integrated financial market based on free capital movements would be essential to this strategy, allowing market participants to choose freely between currencies and forcing all partner central banks to take heed of market signals.

As part of the ongoing process exchange rates would presumably still have to be adjustable, to deal with continuing price disparities and underlying imbalances. To the extent that high-inflation countries have adhered to somewhat overvalued exchange rates, correction may sooner or later be necessary unless they can improve their inflation performance beyond that of other partners. The existing external payments imbalances within the Community give support to this view, even though they may currently be financed without undue difficulties. Only at a fairly late stage in the integration process leading to EMU will it be possible with the necessary degree of conviction to declare exchange rates fixed. The possibility of exchange rate adjustment as dictated by the need to restore competitiveness and deal with underlying imbalances is not to be seen as a substitute for an approach that stresses cooperation and policy coordination, but as a safety-valve without which that process could well break down before it has achieved its final goal, EMU.

Undue rigidity of exchange rate arrangements was one of the causes of the breakdown of the Bretton Woods system of fixed but adjustable exchange rates at the global level. The EMS has avoided this rigidity, even though exchange rate adjustments have often only been made under severe market pressure and are increasingly considered as undesirable under almost any circumstances. Equally, the absence of a stable global 'anchor' has been a cause of breakdown, once the USA failed to live up to its responsibility for overall economic balance as a necessary condition of a stable dollar. An inadequate commitment to cooperation and policy coordination at all levels no doubt contributed to the eventual breakdown of the Bretton Woods system, but it was not the central cause. It can even be argued that economic policy cooperation was at its zenith at the time, before withering away in the early phase of floating rates. But at no time was it a substitute for the efforts of countries 'to keep their house in order' and avoid protracted internal and external economic imbalances, or for the existence of a stable currency 'anchor'.

References

Committee on the Study of Economic and Monetary Union (the Delors Committee) (1989) *Report on Economic and Monetary Union in the European Community* (the *Delors Report*) (with Collection of Papers), Office for Official Publications of the European Communities, Luxemburg.

Frenkel, J.A., Goldstein, M. and **Masson, P.** (1988a) International coordination of economic policies: scope, methods, and effects, in Guth, W. (ed) *Economic Policy Coordination*, International Monetary Fund, Washington, pp. 149–92

Frenkel, J. A., Goldstein, M. and **Masson, P.** (1988b) *International Macro-economic Policy Coordination*, Group of Thirty, New York.

IMF (1989) The European Monetary System in the context of the integration of the European financial markets, IMF Occasional Papers, Washington.

Lamfalussy A. (1989) Macro-coordination of fiscal policies in an economic and monetary union in Europe, in Collection of Papers of *Delors Report*, pp. 91–125

Thygesen, N. (1989) A European central banking system – some analytical and operational considerations, in Collection of Papers of *Delors Report*, pp. 160–1

Comment: Paul De Grauwe

The chapter by Dr Wolfgang Rieke is a thoughtful analysis of how the future of the EMS may look like. As a person closely associated with the institutions that have formed the backbone of the EMS, Dr Rieke is ideally placed to evaluate the future developments in the system.

In my comments I focus on two issues that play an important role in Dr Rieke's chapter, and that will continue to loom large in the future developments of the system, i.e the future role of the FRG in the EMS, and the role of fiscal policies in the system during the 1990s.

THE FUTURE ROLE OF THE FRG IN THE EMS

As will be clear from a number of papers presented at this conference, there is no consensus among economists about the past and present role of the FRG in the system.

There are two views. One can be called the conventional view. According to this view, the FRG sets its monetary policy independently from what happens in the rest of the system. The other members peg their currency to the DM, and in so doing, are forced to follow German monetary policy leadership. In fact, the FRG determines monetary conditions in the system; the EMS is, in reality a DM zone.

In some recent empirical papers this view has been challenged. It has been noted that more symmetry seems to exist in the system than is commonly assumed. True, the FRG may be the most important member of the system. However, monetary developments in some other countries also affect the system as a whole.

I do not want to discuss the merits of these views here. These are discussed in Fratianni and von Hagen (Ch. 5), and Bini Smaghi and Micossi (Ch. 6).

What I want to do is to look into the future. Given the lack of consensus about the role of the FRG in the system in the past, one may argue that it is very hazardous to make pronouncements about its future role. Yet in this case it may be easier to predict the future than to interpret the past. In any case these forecasts can be considered as what the French call 'une fuite en avant'.

Let me concentrate on stage one as envisioned by the *Delors Report*. (The other stages are clouded in even greater uncertainty as to make predictions even more unreliable.) Although I have reservations based on the empirical evidence, let me also take the view that the FRG has dominated the system up to now. How is this hegemonic position going to evolve once capital movements are completely liberalized ?

I will argue that this process will make the EMS less asymmetric, less dominated by the FRG. I see two reasons for this.

First, the existence of capital controls in France and Italy in the past not only gave these countries some limited scope for independent interest rate developments, it also made life easier for the German monetary authorities to control their domestic money market. Capital controls insulated the French and Italian financial markets from short-term disturbances outside France and Italy. It also (partly) insulated the German market from French and Italian disturbances. This two-way insulation is disappearing and will soon be completely eliminated. This will also tend to make the German financial markets more dependent on what happens in France and Italy than in the past. This will make it less likely that the FRG can set its monetary policies independently.

A second and more fundamental reason why liberalization of capital movements is more likely to lead to more symmetry within the system has to do with the political economy aspects of the problem. Freedom of capital movements will make a significantly higher degree of convergence of monetary policies necessary among the major EMS partners than has been the case up to now.

It is doubtful, however, that such a convergence could be of the hegemonic type where the FRG determines the good and adverse climates in the system, and the others follow passively. This is the kind of very asymmetric relation that exists between the Netherlands and the FRG today, which works rather well because the Netherlands is willing to take this subordinate role without feeling that its pride is hurt. It is unlikely to be a good guide for the relations between France and the FRG. The economic power of France relative to the FRG is such that an asymmetric functioning of the EMS (with the FRG setting the system-wide monetary policy) is not a long-run option for the EMS. Sooner or later such a system will lead to open conflict between the two major EMS countries. This conflict could jeopardize the whole system.

Today fears of such a conflict seem remote. In the last few years a remarkable consensus has emerged among the major EMS countries about the role of monetary policy. Contrary to the view prevailing less than 10 years ago, there is now a surprising agreement among EMS central bankers that the objective of monetary policy is price stability and nothing else. Not so long ago, most European central bankers admitted that another goal of monetary policy consisted in stabilizing the business cycle. This is still an objective of American monetary policy-making; it has completely receded to the background in the EMS.

This remarkable shift in opinion of what constitutes the goal of monetary policy explains to a large degree why countries like France have been willing to subordinate their monetary policies to a low inflation target and to follow the German lead. However, the consensus that has now been achieved, is not necessarily a permanent one. A turnaround in the business cycle, which in 1989–90 looks bright, may shake it, and may lead individual central bankers to shift their priorities away from price stability. This would certainly lead to conflict among EMS members, and would disturb the consensus that was achieved in 1989–90.

The preceding argument also makes clear that in order to avoid future conflict, steps towards institutionalizing the monetary cooperation within the EMS are of great importance. It is to the merit of the Delors Committee members to have seen this need very clearly, and to have proposed concrete steps towards achieving it.

THE ROLE OF FISCAL POLICIES

Dr Rieke defends the view, which is also prominent in the *Delors Report*, that rules on fiscal deficits should be imposed, as a prerequisite for monetary integration. This is certainly one of the more controversial aspects of the *Delors Report*. And it has met with a lot of criticism of economists.

Let me first enumerate some arguments that one can develop to propose such fiscal policy rules. There are basically two. First, in a monetary union the fiscal authorities of different regions profit from the reputation the others have accumulated in following sound fiscal policies. At the same time, those with sound reputations suffer from the bad reputations of the fiscally laxer regions. There are thus externalities involved. These externalities lead to inefficient outcomes, and require some control on each others' behaviour.

Second, a lack of control on fiscal policies may make the conduct of the system-wide monetary policies more difficult. Too much of a burden may be put on the monetary policy branch if there is insufficient coordination of fiscal policies. European monetary policies may then be forced to correct mistakes made by national fiscal authorities. It is now widely recognized that this has been a problem of the American economic policies during the 1980s when the Federal Reserve had to pick up the pieces of fiscal policy that for too long was excessively expansionary.

These are powerful arguments which have certainly been in the minds of the Delors Committee members when they proposed strict rules on government budget deficits.

There are, however, equally powerful arguments against imposing these rules on national fiscal policies in a future monetary union in Europe.

The traditional theory of optimal currency areas suggests that when a country joins a union it loses an important instrument of policy. Thus, if exogenous shocks occur which reduce the country's competitiveness (e.g. an increase in its unit labour costs), it will face a problem of adjustment. Since the exchange rate is fixed it will need to go through a deflationary process to restore external equilibrium. This will be costly in terms of employment.

As is well known, the cost of this adjustment process is reduced if there is mobility of factors of production between regions. In that case the unemployed in a weak region will move out, seeking better employment prospects in other regions.

A second factor tending to reduce the adjustment costs in monetary unions occurs when the budget process is centralized. In such a union the problem for the region which has lost competitiveness is mitigated by fiscal transfers.

Europe now seems to be moving towards monetary union. Labour mobility between countries, however, is relatively limited. Automatic fiscal transfers to countries experiencing a loss of competitiveness does not seem possible in the near future. Thus, countries which are hit by shocks leading to a loss of competitiveness will be forced into a more painful adjustment than would be necessary if they could use the exchange rate. Therefore, it seems logical to conclude that fiscal policies should be left as much as possible to the discretion of the national authorities. This is in fact going to be the only policy instrument available to the national authorities. It is therefore very surprising to find in the *Delors Report* a call for constraints on national fiscal policies. It seems to me that as long as there is no European-wide automatic transfer scheme (which will take a long time to achieve), it would be inappropriate to take away a national instrument which can be used to soften the effects of competitiveness shocks.

The case of the Netherlands and the FRG during the 1980s illustrates the argument made here against imposing rules on national fiscal policies. The Netherlands and the FRG formed something close to a monetary union. The guilder/DM rate was practically unchanged during the last 10 years. And yet fiscal policies were widely divergent. For example, the government debt in the FRG increased during the 1980s from 30 to 46 per cent of gross domestic product (GDP). In the Netherlands it increased from 40 to 85 per cent of GDP. In fact the growth of the government debt in the Netherlands was faster than in Belgium and in Italy over the same period.

This rapid increase in the Dutch government debt was the result of the fiscal accommodation of the recession of the early 1980s which was particularly severe in the Netherlands. One wonders what would have happened if Delors-type rules on fiscal deficits had been imposed on the Netherlands during that period. The historical evidence suggests that they were unnecessary.

It is interesting to note that the northern FRG was hit by a similarly severe shock as the Netherlands (and Belgium) during the early 1980s. Table 2.1 shows the growth rates in the Benelux countries and in northern and southern FRG. Table 2.2 presents the increases in unemployment during the period 1979–83 when these regions were hit by a series of unfavourable disturbances. The northern FRG, of course, could rely on the automatic budgetary solidarity provided by the federal budget. No such mechanism existed in the Benelux countries. It was therefore imperative that some fiscal independence was maintained by these countries.

The Dutch case also makes clear that central controls on the budgetary process are not really necessary. Despite large Dutch budget deficits, the guilder/DM rate was extremely stable. At no point did the budgetary deficits spill over into the foreign exchange market, the Dutch authorities having convinced the market that the budgetary deficits would in no way affect their monetary policies which remained fully committed to the exchange rate target.

TABLE 2.1 Average yearly growth of output during 1980–87.

	%
Northern FRG	1.23
Belgium	1.5
Netherlands	1.25
Southern FRG	2.5

Source: For the FRG *Statistisches Jahresbuch*, 1988; for Belgium and the Netherlands, OECD, *Economic Outlook*, December, 1989

Note: Northern FRG comprises Nordrhein-Westfalen, Nieder-Sachsen, Hamburg, Bremen, Schleswig-Holstein; South Germany consists of Hessen, Rheinland-Pfalz, Saarland, Baden-Württemberg, Bayern

TABLE 2.2 Unemployment 1980–1987

	1980	1983	1987
Northern FRG	4.7	11.0	11.5
Belgium	7.8	13.0	11.1
Netherlands	6.4	14.9	12.5
Southern FRG	3.5	7.5	6.4

Source: For the FRG, *Statistisches Jahresbuch*, 1988; for Belgium and the Netherlands, OECD, *Economic Outlook*, December, 1989

Note: Northern FRG comprises Nordrhein-Westfalen, Nieder-Sachsen, Hamburg, Bremen, Schleswig-Holstein; South-Germany consists of Hessen, Rheinland-Pfalz, Saarland, Baden-Würrtemburg, Bayern

The previous argument was based on the automatic stabilizing role of the budget. There is a second argument against the Delors view that some central control on national fiscal policies is necessary to make a monetary union workable. It is based on the political economy aspects of this view. Implicit in the idea that the central authorities should control and check the fiscal policies of the lower levels is the assumption that the central authorities are more fiscally orthodox, and in general wiser, than the lower levels (national and regional) of decision-making. However, why this is the case is unclear.

What are these European institutions that will have to formulate rules on national fiscal policies? Surely, they will have to include the European Parliament. Decisions to set rules on fiscal deficits involve spending and taxation. Taxation without representation, however, will not be accepted. As a result, the European Parliament will be at the core of the decision process.

But then the question arises why the Members of the European Parliament (MEPs) will be less sensitive to the same political pressure that leads to undisciplined behaviour at the national level. After all, the MEPs come from the same countries and will obey the same political pressures. In other words, there is no reason to believe that the controller will behave more responsibly than the controlled.

I want to stress that I am not against a centralization of national fiscal policies in Europe, not even one that goes much further than that proposed in the *Delors Report*, if that is what the European electorate wishes. We should, however, have no illusions that such centralization will make a European monetary policy easier to conduct. It could easily be the other way around. Twelve national fiscal authorities may often behave irresponsibly. They do not, however, behave in the same way all the time. Often their actions compensate each other, thereby putting only limited pressure on a future centralized monetary policy. A future central European fiscal authority, however, that behaves irresponsibly, may put much more strain on the European monetary authorities than 12 irresponsible national authorities. The problems encountered by the US monetary authorities during the 1980s vividly illustrate that this may also be a serious problem of a monetary union in Europe that attempts to force more centralization of the budgetary process.

Comment: Loukas Tsoukalis

This is a very interesting contribution which examines the development of the EMS in the context of the transition to an EMU. In the limited space available, I propose to concentrate on some specific issues raised by Dr Rieke, namely, the alleged deflationary bias of the system and the related issue of the coordination of macroeconomic policies, the flexibility of the ERM and the transfer of resources.

There is broad agreement among economists regarding the contribution of the EMS to the reduction of exchange rate instability among participating currencies. The experience of the EMS has been extremely valuable for participating central banks as part of the gradual learning process leading to the establishment of a collective system of management of intra-European exchange rates. There is also widespread acceptance of its role as an effective instrument in the fight against inflation; a link which is not, however, easily proven through the available econometric evidence.

The evaluation of the EMS experience needs to be situated within a wider macroeconomic context, especially in view of the unfavourable performance in terms of economic growth of the participating economies in the early years of the operation of the system. Dr Rieke refers to the anchor function of the DM and the role of the

Deutsche Bundesbank in setting the monetary standard for the other
is already a substantial body of literature referring to the credibility
linking of other currencies to the DM, translated into a lower deflationary
economies concerned. But there is no agreement on this issue. The advantage for some (Giavazzi and Pagano 1988) of tying one's hands to the DM anchor is the cost of the deflationary bias of the system for others (Tsoukalis 1989), which is in turn associated with German macroeconomic policy priorities.

This raises the question of policy coordination. Though there is general agreement regarding the need for close coordination, if not centralization, of monetary policies in the context of EMU, no such consensus exists with respect to fiscal policies. This promises to be one of the most controversial issues in forthcoming negotiations. Two comments will be made on this point.

It is interesting that, while there has been a whole debate about the alleged deflationary bias of the EMS, the *Delors Report* concentrates on the need to control the size and financing of national budget deficits, thus implying a fear about excessive inflationary tendencies inside a monetary union. The rather restrictive approach adopted by the Delors Committee, as regards the national margin of manœuvre in the area of fiscal policy, is also very different from the attitude expressed in the Padoa-Schioppa Report (1987: 85), where the authors refer to the experience of other federal systems which usually impose no strict controls on state budgets and where 'the effective restraint . . . is the sanction of the capital market'.

The emphasis of the Delors Committee on binding rules as regards national budget deficits should be, at least partly, a reflection of its own composition: central bankers keen on imposing controls on irresponsible(?) politicians. On the other hand, a distinction can be drawn between the final and the intermediate stages of EMU. During the latter, there may, indeed, exist an inherent deflationary bias, because of the fear of speculative pressure against the exchange rate arising from independent reflationary action, which in turn leads to a trade deficit due to import leakages. At the final stage of EMU, with irrevocably fixed exchange rates, the situation can be qualitatively different. The elimination of the balance of payments constraint could lead to irresponsible national fiscal policies, financed through borrowing, while the reaction of capital markets could be 'too slow and weak or too sudden and disruptive' (Delors Committee 1989 p. 24).

In favour of the close coordination of national fiscal policies, there exist a number of arguments which are not only limited to the perceived need to impose effective constraints on inflationary deficit financing. First of all, the size of the EC budget is likely to remain very small in the foreseeable future, which means that it will not be able to play any important stabilization role for the EC economy as a whole. Hence the need to define the macroeconomic policy stance (and more specifically, its fiscal component) through the coordination of national policies. Even more so, since some national budgets will continue for a long time to dominate by their sheer size. On the other hand, the long experience of fiscal laxity in some countries and the evident inability of financial markets (see, e.g., the international debt crisis of the early 1980s) to act as effective and efficient constraints on sovereign actors militate in favour of a close coordination of national policies.

Coordination does not necessarily imply convergence; on the contrary and, as with many other areas of economic policy, coordination at the EC level could mean increased differentiation which takes into account the different economic conditions prevailing in the member countries. It could also be argued that, in the transition towards EMU, fiscal instruments should become more flexible in the pursuit of macroeconomic goals, as monetary policy is directed more and more towards the exchange rate target.

Clearly, the experience so far with the intergovernmental coordination of fiscal policies is not at all encouraging. This is true of the EMS experience and also of the various attempts made at the international level through the G-3, G-5 and G-7. Short of a major redistribution of political power and effective legitimacy between national and Community institutions, it is indeed difficult to envisage how sovereign national parliaments will be prepared to accept serious constraints from outside on their powers of spending and taxation.

What is at stake is about who will determine the macroeconomic priorities for the EC as a whole, and how, in fact, will the priorities themselves be determined. And this task cannot be entrusted to one member by default. Assuming that there are real trade-offs between different policy objectives, as for example between inflation, growth and unemployment (which may still be not such an unorthodox view among economists), then there is also room for different interests and priorities among countries. The reconciliation of the priorities of a rich and risk-averse country, with a declining population, and those of a developing country, with strong demographic trends and high unemployment, which is the complex reality of the Community of Twelve, requires a political system which is much closer to a federation than a system of intergovernmental cooperation. Whether the EC is ready to give birth to such a system in the near future remains to be seen. But the argument that the combination of high trade interdependence, capital market integration and exchange rate union does not require close and effective coordination of national macroeconomic policies appears totally unconvincing.

Another important question refers to the degree and kind of exchange rate flexibility during the intermediate stages of EMU. The experience of recent years points to an excessive rigidity of exchange rates in the ERM due to the heavy reliance of some countries on the exchange rate as an anti-inflation instrument. This has, in turn, led to a certain misalignment of currencies and to growing bilateral trade imbalances. Since the forthcoming liberalization of capital movements is likely to add another factor of instability in exchange markets, it might be imprudent to call for further restrictions on the use of the exchange rate as a policy instrument. This would also apply to proposals to do away quickly with the wider margins of fluctuation currently used by the lira and the peseta and, why not, other EC currencies which could be expected to join the ERM during the first stage of EMU. Here again, flexibility and some differentiation of rules, instead of uniformity, may be the right approach towards economic integration in a heterogeneous Community.

Progress towards EMU has usually been closely associated with a significant transfer of resources through the EC budget, largely seen as a means of compensating for the loss of policy instruments at the national level. It is undoubtedly true that large inter-country transfers, on the scale of those taking place between rich and poor regions within the borders of EC member countries, are not feasible in the near future. They would require a degree of social and political cohesion and a sense of *Gemeinschaft* which do not as yet exist inside the Community. I would agree absolutely with Dr Rieke that such transfers should not be 'a substitute for action taken in the poorer countries to deal with the multiple causes of misallocation of resources'. Yet, the experience of other federations, the FRG included, suggests that large redistribution through the central budget constitutes an integral part of an economic union. The equalizing effects of the market mechanism can hardly be relied upon.

References

Committe on the Study of Economic and Monetary Union (the Delors Committee) (1989) *Report on Economic and Monetary Union in the European Community* (the *Delors Report*) (with Collection of Papers), Office for Official Publications of the European Communities, Luxemburg.

Giavazzi, F. and **Pagano, M.** (1988) The advantage of tying one's hands: EMS discipline and central bank credibility, *European Economic Review*, vol. 32 June, pp. 1055–82.

Padoa-Schioppa Report (1987) *Efficiency, Stability and Equity*, Oxford University Press, Oxford.

Tsoukalis, L. (1989) The political economy of the European Monetary System, in Guerrieri, P. and Padoan, P.C. (eds), *The Political Economy of European Integration*, Harvester Wheatsheaf, London.

CHAPTER THREE

Policy problems of a monetary union

Paul Krugman

Over the past decade the major nations of Western Europe have decisively turned their back on flexible exchange rates, and embarked on what seems to be a path towards ever growing monetary integration. The adjustable-peg European Monetary System (EMS) has become increasingly credible over time, with realignments becoming smaller and rarer. And in the last few years the idea of a common European currency has moved with remarkable speed from intellectual plaything to realistic possibility.

The politics of this change in outlook are fairly apparent. First of all, disillusionment with the volatility of floating rates came sooner and stronger within Europe than elsewhere, partly because of the sheer size of trade flows within the region, partly because fluctuating exchange rates turn the management of European Community institutions, notably the Common Agricultural Policy, into an administrative nightmare. At a deeper level, monetary union is a natural political counterpart (though the economic logic is less clear) to other moves that attempt to use closer European economic integration to end the long stagnation of the European economy from the mid-1970s to the mid-1980s – that attempt, as the Brussels jargon has it, to 'use the Community dimension to reinforce growth'.

The first wave of the new drive to seek a solution to Eurosclerosis in greater European integration was, of course, the complex set of measures referred to as '1992'. Whatever the ultimate success of 1992, it is a fairly uncontroversial initiative from the point of view of economic theory. Greater integration of markets brings gains that are well understood in principle, though poorly measured in practice. One may believe that the claims for 1992 are exaggerated – my own guess is that the Cecchini Report is over-optimistic by a factor of two or three – but the qualitative character of the gains is clear.

The push for closer monetary union represents the natural political continuation of 1992: having achieved a stunning political success in their drive to eliminate barriers to trade in goods and services, the advocates of European economic union are looking for new frontiers to tear down. Yet from an economist's point of view trade integration and monetary union are very different kinds of action. The economics of international trade are relatively well understood (in principle, if not quantitatively), and the nature of the gains from trade, whether from comparative advantage, exploitation of scale economies or increased competition are not controversial. The economics of international money, by contrast, are not at all well understood: they hinge crucially not only on sophisticated and ambiguous issues like credibility and coordination, but on even deeper issues like transaction costs and bounded rationality. So the sudden enthusiasm for monetary union has carried us into largely uncharted territory.

The purpose of this chapter is to present a brief overview of some issues raised by European monetary union. The chapter takes the form of a somewhat rambling essay: I sketch out a few models, while trying to present as coherent a discussion as I can of the issues that at present defy formal modelling, and make no attempt to integrate the analysis into a coherent framework. The best defence I can offer is that monetary union is inherently a messy subject – and that becoming aware of that inherent messiness is the first part of wisdom in this field.

Although the title of the chapter refers to problems of policy under a monetary union, a substantial part is actually concerned with a somewhat different subject: the advantages and disadvantages of substituting a common currency for an adjustable-peg system of the kind that most of Western Europe already lives under. There are several reasons for spending a good deal of time on this question. First is that the issues of more or less fixed versus flexible exchange rates have already been the subject of a huge if not exactly conclusive literature, while the effects of going on from stable rates to an actual common currency have been less fully worked over. A second justification for focusing on the question of a common currency is that it is an idea whose time has apparently come, yet creation of such a currency is far from being a done deal. It seems particularly useful to review the issue now given that politicians are busy taking sides with very little basis in the scribbling of academics of this or any other year – the enthusiasm with which some have adopted the idea, and the dismay with which others regard it, are based more on gut reactions than on careful analysis. Finally, thinking about the costs and benefits of a common currency as compared with more modest schemes like EMS-style fixed rates helps us to think about what policies are needed to make either kind of system work.

The chapter is in six sections. Section 1 addresses some general 'philosophical' issues regarding monetary economics in general and monetary union in particular. Section 2 reviews the traditional optimal currency argument, which applies both to the question of whether to form a monetary union and the question of whether to take the final step to a common currency. Sections 3 and 4 examine some more newfangled arguments involving coordination and credibility. Section 5 briefly examines whether monetary union also demands coordination of fiscal policies. Section 6 presents a different argument regarding monetary union, which links it to the imperatives of political integration.

1. Money and monetary union: some general considerations

I want to begin the discussion in this chapter with two 'philosophical' points. The first is that monetary economics in general, and the economics of international monetary arrangements in particular, cannot be addressed using presumptions from our usual economic rules of thumb. The second is to stress the importance of defining the alternatives to be discussed: I want to argue that the most interesting alternatives are floating rates, an adjustable-peg system and a common currency.

Let me start with the question of how to think about monetary economics. Most of what economists think they know comes from microeconomic theory, and in particular from the model of frictionless, competitive general equilibrium. From this model comes the general presumption that markets work, that government interference reduces welfare unless there is a clear-cut market failure. For many policy issues the presumptions of simple microeconomics give clear guidance. Unfortunately, in monetary economics, almost by definition, standard microeconomic presumptions are of little help. Simple microeconomics assumes an absence of frictions; monetary economics is precisely about frictions, and the institutions that are devised to cope with them.

Consider the main roles of money. Although the traditional Jevons classification gives four roles of money – medium of exchange, unit of account, store of value, standard of deferred repayment – it is the first two that are essential. Yet neither role makes sense in the kinds of models that underlie most of our policy judgements. A medium of exchange is needed to reduce transaction costs, yet standard economic models do not allow for transaction costs, and indeed even the most sophisticated models have trouble incorporating such costs in a coherent way. The role of money as a unit of account presumes that people need a short cut for making economic calculations – that they cannot keep the whole vector of relative prices in their heads. This is reasonable enough. Yet once we allow for the possibility that people cannot use all the information they have, we are into the world of bounded rationality, a difficult area where we know that many of the standard presumptions of economics need to be questioned.

Now admittedly there have been a number of efforts on the part of economists to incorporate money in a systematic way into their models – typically through approximate ways of representing the medium of exchange function, such as the so-called Clower constraint that requires that individuals have cash in advance of any purchase. These models provide little useful guidance for evaluating international monetary arrangements, however, for two main reasons. First, as nearly all of their creators would admit, they are incomplete: at best they give a stylized account of the role of money as medium of exchange, but they have nothing to say about its unit of account role. Since both the costs and benefits of monetary unions depend crucially on the role of national versus multinational standards as units of account, this is a vital omission. Second, formal analyses of money nearly always assume that use of a single currency is imposed by fiat of a single government. This assumption looks like a reasonable approach for many purposes, but unfortunately it immediately takes many of the issues concerning monetary union off the table. So there is not much guidance to be had in standard economic theory for the key monetary issues facing Europe.

My point in proclaiming our ignorance is to emphasize that economic theory does not give us any simple presumptions about monetary unions. In particular, one cannot appeal to any presumption in favour of free markets. For one thing, in the inherently second-best world of monetary arrangements there is no reason to assume that markets get it right; for another, alternative international monetary arrangements may be equally well characterized as free-market (or unfree-market). Which is more nearly a free-market system: flexible exchange rates, fixed exchange rates or a common currency? The answer is not obvious, and even if we could decide on some ranking of freeness, no policy conclusion would follow.

Let me turn next to the question of what alternatives we should discuss. This chapter could make a number of comparisons: fully flexible rates versus target zones, or absolutely fixed rates versus adjustable pegs, etc. I would argue, however, that for Europe right now the interesting issues are the comparison between flexible rates, an adjustable-peg system and a common currency.

The first reason that these are the interesting choices is that within Europe these are the choices currently on the table. The UK is still debating whether to join the exchange rate mechanism of the EMS; for the rest of Europe the longer-term question is whether that mechanism evolves into something more.

One might, of course, want to discuss intermediate choices: why not discuss the desirability of British 'shadowing' of the European Currency Unit (ECU), or of a transition of the EMS from adjustable pegs to more rigidly fixed rates? The answer on the one hand is that I do not believe that a target zone and an adjustable peg are very different in their economic impact; as recent research has shown, target zones tend to stabilize exchange rates toward the middle of the band while they are credible, and to be subject to speculative attacks just like fixed rates when they are not. On the other hand, I would argue that the case of an adjustable-peg system is more fundamental than that of a totally fixed system, at least as long as we have a comparison with a common currency on the table. Any system of national currencies is, potentially, one in which exchange rates *could* change. This possibility may not be exercised very often, but the possibility of realignment is one of the crucial differences.

This concludes the philosophical set-up of the chapter. Now we can proceed on to the analysis.

2. The optimal currency area approach

The traditional starting-point for discussion of issues concerning monetary union has been via the so-called optimal currency area approach. In more recent discussion, new ideas concerning policy coordination and credibility have become more fashionable. However, the optimal currency area approach is still very useful as a first step, and probably more fundamental. Thus as a way of organizing our thoughts, it is important to review it.

The basic optimal currency area argument may be illustrated by imagining that Europe consists of only two countries, France and the Federal Republic of Germany (FRG). Let us imagine that these countries have some difference in their export mix – say France exports cheese, the FRG wurst. And let us also suppose that the world market is subject to occasional shocks that shift the relative demand for cheese and wurst.

Should France and the FRG maintain separate currencies? If so, should the exchange rate between these currencies be fixed, or should it be allowed to float? Let us consider these questions in reverse order.

The basic argument for allowing the exchange rate to float is that it eases the process of adjustment to shocks. Suppose that the world relative demand for cheese falls, necessitating a fall in the relative price of French goods and labour. Then it will ordinarily be easier for this change in relative prices to be accomplished via a decline in the French franc (FF) against the Deutsch mark (DM) than via some combination of inflation in the FRG and deflation in France. In particular, if prices and wages are sticky, changing the exchange rate avoids the necessity for a French recession. So allowing the exchange rate to float has obvious macroeconomic advantages.

It might seem that these same advantages could be achieved in a discretionary fashion even within a currency union (but not with a common currency), by having a rate that is fixed by the central banks but adjusted when necessary. The problem with such a system is that it is subject to speculative attacks when the market thinks an exchange rate change may be in prospect; in order to limit such attacks, the central banks must try to make credible their commitment not to change parities too often, and the attempt to retain credibility will inhibit their ability to make exchange rate adjustments. This problem should not be overstressed – an adjustable-peg system can work, and need not forsake all the advantages of exchange rate flexibility – but an adjustable-peg system, because of the need for credibility, tends to become less effective at smoothing macroeconomic adjustment than a pure float.

Returning to our example, what are the disadvantages of floating? The answer is that they are microeconomic. Fluctuating exchange rates will impose costs due to uncertainty;[1] these costs will be larger if the exchange market is speculatively inefficient, producing excess volatility (and all available evidence suggests that this is in fact the case). Essentially, a floating exchange rate will tend to degrade the unit of account function of both national moneys.

A transition from floating to fixed rates, then, would impose a cost – increased difficulty in adjusting relative prices – and a benefit – decreased uncertainty and confusion about the values of national moneys. Notice that both the cost and the benefit depend on the unit of account function of money: the tendency of firms to set prices that are sticky in nominal terms, on one side, and the importance of a stable standard in calculations, on the other. But the unit of account function of money is essentially a bounded rationality issue, so that even in this most simple exercise in international monetary economics we are in deep theoretical waters.

This means that the next step, which is the elaboration of the conditions under which a fixed rate is desirable, is highly speculative. None the less, the optimal currency approach makes the plausible assertion that a fixed rate is more desirable, the more closely linked are the two economies.

FIG. 3.1

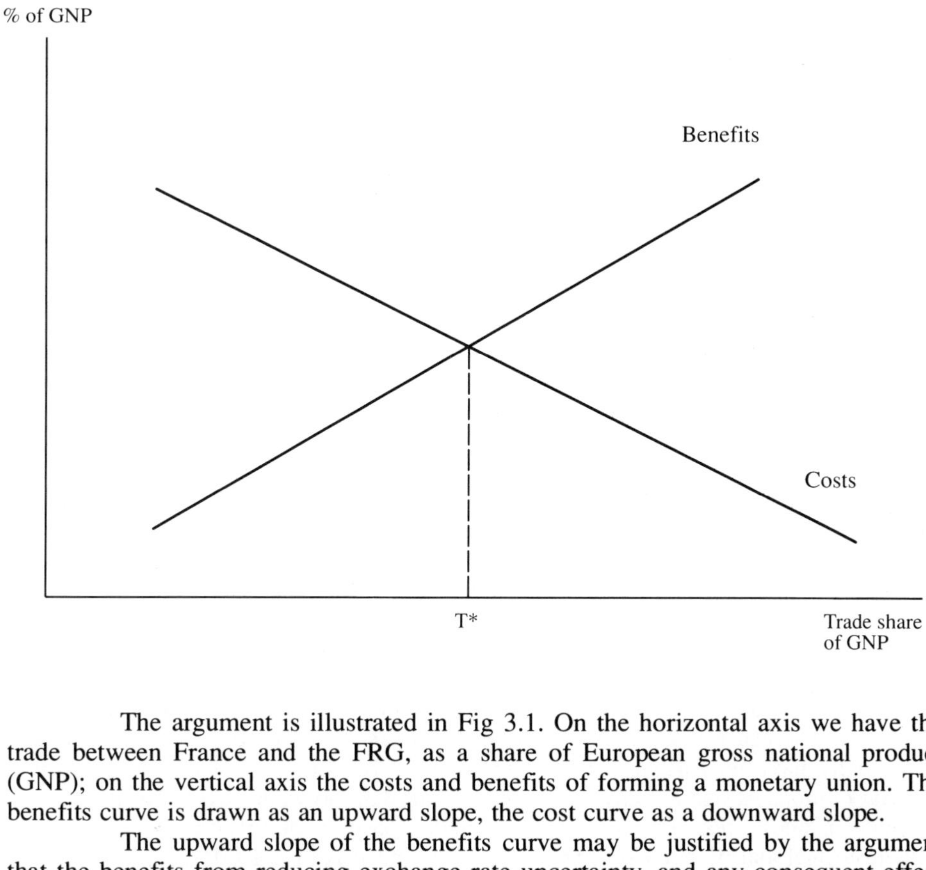

The argument is illustrated in Fig 3.1. On the horizontal axis we have the trade between France and the FRG, as a share of European gross national product (GNP); on the vertical axis the costs and benefits of forming a monetary union. The benefits curve is drawn as an upward slope, the cost curve as a downward slope.

The upward slope of the benefits curve may be justified by the argument that the benefits from reducing exchange rate uncertainty, and any consequent effect of a monetary union in enhancing the unit of account function of each country's money, will be larger as a percentage of GNP, the larger the share of international trade in GNP. This seems fairly obvious, even though we do not have any idea how large these benefits may actually be.

The downward slope of the cost curve may be justified by two arguments. One is fairly concrete: the size of required price adjustments to accommodate any given external shock is likely to be smaller, the larger the initial trade within the monetary union. Consider the effect of simultaneous rise in demand for wurst and decline in demand for cheese that worsens France's trade balance with the outside world by 1 per cent of its GNP, with a corresponding improvement in the FRG's balance. To offset this shock, France would have to improve its balance with the FRG by an amount equal to 1 per cent of its GNP; this would have to be accomplished through a decline in French relative wages and prices that makes French goods more competitive *vis-à-vis* German. Clearly, the size of the required fall in wages will be less if French exports to the FRG are initially 20 per cent of GNP than if they are initially only 1 per cent. For any given Phillips curve, then, the cost of accommodating the shock without changing the FF–DM exchange rate will be less the more trade there is between France and the FRG.

The other, somewhat vaguer reason for downward-sloping costs lies in the effect of large-scale trade on the adjustment of prices and wages themselves. If France has extensive trade with the FRG, it becomes possible that French wages will be explicitly or implicitly indexed to the DM, so that exchange rate adjustment will become ineffective in any case. That is, depreciation of the FF will not succeed in lowering relative French wages and prices, it will simply cause French inflation.

The crossing-point of the curves then defines the critical level of integration: if trade exceeds the level T^*, a fixed rate system is preferable to floating.

Many discussions of optimal currency areas add a further observation, that the degree of factor mobility makes a difference. Suppose that labour moves easily and freely between the FRG and France. Then when the demand for cheese falls, French workers can move to the FRG and start making sausage. This will reduce both the need for wage adjustment and the costs of incomplete adjustment, lowering the costs of a fixed rate system and thereby making it more desirable.

The thought experiment conducted here considers whether two given countries should form a monetary union. If one could measure the costs and benefits involved, however, the exercise could be turned around to ask how the world should optimally be carved up into currency areas. Assuming that the optimal size of such an area is less than the whole world but bigger than the typical country, such areas would consist of regional blocs of countries that do much of their trade with each other – such as Western Europe, North America and perhaps the western Pacific.

Unfortunately, the assumption that the optimal currency area is intermediate in size between a large country and the world is not based on any real evidence. We actually have no particular reason to suppose that Europe is the right size for a monetary union. At one extreme, one could claim that the whole world constitutes the optimal currency area. This is a fairly popular position at the moment, under the influence of global monetarists like McKinnon, and it is also a safe position, since it is not going to happen.

The contrary positon is, in the current political climate, near-heresy, but it is perfectly possible to make a case that Europe is too large for monetary union to be desirable. We might note the following points. First, the large countries of Europe do not do all that much trade with each other; the average intra-Community trade of the four major economies is only 15 per cent of GNP, less than Canada's trade with the USA, yet Canada has not made a monetary agreement a priority. Second, exchange rate changes are hardly ineffective at changing relative wage rates within Europe – one need only look at the UK's roller-coaster competitiveness from the mid-1970s to the mid-1980s as a demonstration. Third, labour mobility among the European nations is in fact hardly enough to provide much of an alternative to exchange rate adjustment.

But if Europe is not an optimal currency area, why should we think that the USA constitutes one? Well, actually maybe it is not. Would not it have been helpful at some times in the recent past to have been able to devalue the Midwestern dollar? The idea of floating rates within the USA seems absurd, and not simply because the USA has much higher internal factor mobility than Europe. However, the reasons why it seems absurd probably stem more from issues of political symbolism than from any solid evidence that the costs would exceed the benefits.

The optimal currency area concept is very far from giving an operational guide to policy. None the less, it is useful as a way of organizing our thoughts, and at least of revealing what we do not know. It can also be modified quite easily to consider the next question, that of comparing a fixed rate system with a common currency.

A transition from an adjustable-peg system like the EMS to a common currency would generate a concrete if rather mundane benefit: the elimination of foreign exchange transaction costs. It would also generate some further unit-of-account-type gains by removing residual uncertainty. On the other hand, adoption of a common currency would remove any remaining flexibility, imposing another cost.

The saving on transaction costs ought not be dismissed, even though it sounds rather boring. Admittedly, transaction costs in the interbank market for foreign exchange, on which financial institutions swap funds, are negligible. Firms engaging in international trade, however, to say nothing of tourists and business travellers, must buy foreign exchange retail, paying a spread of 2–3 per cent.

Is this a significant number? If one has in mind some spectacular pay-off to the creation of a common currency, then the answer is no. However, the costs of transacting foreign exchange in Europe are of a roughly similar scale to typical estimates of those costs of crossing borders (delays, administrative costs, etc.) that 1992 is supposed to eliminate. It is widely hoped that eliminating border costs will bring indirect benefits through industry rationalization and increased competition that exceed the direct savings on transport itself. So a common currency would in this mundane way be comparable to the border-eliminating measures of 1992 as a force for European growth.

These gains from reduced transaction costs obviously depend on the scale of trade; in a less clear-cut way, the unit-of-account gains probably do the same. On the other hand, the costs of eliminating the option of exchange rate realignments will once again be less, the larger is trade. So the cost–benefit diagram for the transition from monetary union to common currency will look the same as that for transition from flexible rate to monetary union. Presumably the size of the optimal area for common currency will be smaller than that for more modest monetary union, so that (if the sizes are the right order of magnitude) the optimal world will have a hierarchy of common currency areas organized into currency blocs that in turn float against one another.

This, then, is the traditional optimal currency area approach. It still, in my view, captures the most fundamental considerations. In recent discussions, however, other issues – notably those of coordination and credibility – have come to play an increasingly important role. This partly reflects intellectual fashion (this is the age of game theory), partly the particular context of the EMS in the 1980s. My guess is that when the dust has settled the old optimal currency area approach will still occupy centre stage while these new approaches will look oversold and dated. However, it is worth spending at least a little time on these newer issues.

3. Coordination and the central bank role

Twenty years ago, advocates of floating rates argued that they would allow nations to pursue independent monetary policies. It has become apparent since then that the independence of nations under floating rates is much less than imagined, and that indeed there are important issues of coordination. Somewhat ironically, monetary union is now being advocated by some as a way of resolving coordination problems that arise under floating rates. In the simplest version of this story, countries under floating rates have an incentive to engage in beggar-thy-neighbour disinflation: any individual country, by pursuing a tight monetary policy, can appreciate its currency and thereby achieve a rapid reduction in inflation. Unfortunately, if everyone tries to do this they find that they have chosen a deeper recession than they would have chosen faced with the true collective inflation–output trade-off.

Fixed rates eliminate this problem by imposing the necessity of coordinated monetary policies. However, coordination does not become magically generated by the decision to fix rates. Some additional rules of the game are needed, and what we have learned is that in essence what is needed is the designation of someone as central banker.

This may seem like too flat a statement. At the level of pure economic analysis, all that we can say for sure is that a system of fixed exchange rates requires coordination of monetary policies. The famous *N*-1 problem, which points out that there is one less exchange rate than there are currencies, makes the need for some agreement on who does what into a kind of theorem. This need could in principle be met by some kind of symmetrical coordination of policies. Indeed, the EMS is a symmetric system on paper. In practice, however, symmetry is not what results. It is now widely accepted that fixed rate systems, when they work, almost always do so in part because one national central bank takes on the implicit role of central banker to the system as a whole.

It is arguable that even the classical gold standard in its last decades was really a Bank of England standard; it is much more apparent that Bretton Woods gave central monetary authority to the Federal Reserve, despite an apparent external discipline imposed by the role of gold. The EMS, however, provides the most instructive case: a system that is fully symmetric at a formal level is generally regarded as a German monetary area at a practical level.

The reasons for German pre-eminence are now familiar: since the FRG is the most credibly anti-inflationary of the major European economies, it is useful for other nations to follow the FRG's lead as a way of borrowing credibility – a bit of policy slipstreaming that is helped by the lucky coincidence that the economy with the sternest managers is also the largest. What is particularly interesting is the way that this strongly asymmetric system is entirely implicit, a matter of latent rather than manifest function. This difference between formal structure and practical outcome has turned out to be useful to all concerned; one of the main difficulties with a move to a common currency might be that the ability to cloak reality would be reduced, as we will see in section 4. For now, however, let us simply note that the difference between implicit roles that flourishes under the EMS could not continue with a common currency, for when fixed rates are replaced by a common currency, no ambiguity about who the central bankers really are can be tolerated.

The point that a common currency requires explicit designation of a single central bank is pretty obvious, but it may be worth spending a little time emphasizing why. In much recent work on monetary economics, issues of seigniorage are greatly overplayed, largely because it is something we know how to model. The need for a central bank, however, is one of those issues in which the problem of seigniorage really does play a key role.

Imagine that a group of countries were to try to form a currency union without establishing a common central bank, so that each national bank would have the right to issue community money. Evidently there would be an externality. Each bank's credit creation would generate seigniorage for itself, while generating inflation that falls on all countries; the result would be a bias towards excessive inflation.

Of course externalities of this kind are common in many international contexts, including pure floating, and countries often manage to live with them or make rough accommodations that manage them well enough. However, the conflict over seigniorage among members of a monetary union would be much worse than the usual coordination problem, for one key reason. This is that inequalities of size, which usually reduce coordination problems, would in this context greatly worsen them. When we consider problems of international policy coordination, we usually conclude that the existence of a dominant player – an FRG versus Greece situation – tends to resolve the issue, because the small player ends up following the large player's lead. This general point is sometimes grandly dubbed the theory of hegemonic stability. In a currency union without a central bank, however, the situation would be reversed. Small players would be aggressive in creating money, swamping the big players. The reason is that the small players would find that the benefits of an additional real ECU of seigniorage are just as large for them as for the big players, while the costs of an additional point of inflation are much less.

A simple algebraic example may help make the point. Consider a currency union consisting of two countries that retain independent central banks. One country has a population n_1; the other a smaller population n_2. Assume for simplicity that the countries are very similar except for the difference in their populations, with each having a per capita real demand for money m (assumed inelastic with respect to the rate of inflation), and with each bank having the objective function

$$W = r - \beta\pi^2, \qquad [1]$$

where r is per capita seigniorage, and π the rate of inflation.

It is straightforward to show that the rate of inflation in this imaginary union will be

$$\pi = (n_1 r_1 + n_2 r_2)/m(n_1 + n_2). \qquad [2]$$

Now suppose that each country were to try to choose a level of seigniorage, taking the other country's level as given. Then the first-order conditions would be

$$\pi = (n_1 + n_2)/\beta n_1 \qquad [3]$$

for the first country, and

$$\pi = (n_1 + n_2)/\beta n_2 \qquad [4]$$

for the second.

Clearly we have a problem. The second country, with its smaller population, will try to collect seigniorage up to the point where inflation reaches a higher level than the larger country will tolerate. A literal interpretation of this model is that the large country would try furiously to pull money out of the system while the small country pushes it in as fast as its printing presses allow; a realistic interpretation is that if the central banks of Greece and the FRG were both to have the right to print ECUs, Greece would abuse the privilege and quickly drive the FRG out of the system in disgust.

The essential difference from a system of fixed exchange rates is that under that system Greece cannot hope to extract seigniorage from the population of the FRG. With a common currency, however, the weakness of a bank's home turf would not impair the value of its notes, and so the usual leader–follower relations would break down.

So a common currency requires explicit designation of a central bank. This is a major difference from a fixed exchange rate system where national currencies are retained, because under such systems the central banking role may remain implicit. Under Bretton Woods the Federal Reserve effectively acted as central banker to the world, in a way that was only half acknowledged by the formal system; under the EMS the Bundesbank has come to play the central role in a wholly unlegislated way. With a common currency, however, the designation of a central bank would have to be a formal process. As I will argue below, this will normally change the outcome, quite possibly in an undesirable way.

4. Credibility

The EMS is now widely regarded as having done as well as it has because it is a device that allows less self-controlled countries to take a ride on German credibility. This is by way of a caricature, but it is sufficiently valid to serve as a useful way of approaching the problem. Let us review the argument briefly, then ask two questions: is the success likely to persist in a future era when other nations do not need to assume Teutonic coloration as badly, and would this credibility-enhancing function be enhanced or worsened by a move to a common currency?

The credibility argument can be stated in brief using a version of a now standard model. Suppose that each European nation is able to choose its rate of inflation π, given an expected rate of inflation π^E already built into wage contracts. Suppose also that each country has a loss function that penalizes it for deviations from target levels of employment and inflation. Employment, however, depends on the deviation of actual inflation from that expected; and we assume that each country has a target employment that is higher than the 'natural rate' that results when actual and expected inflation are equal. Then a quadratic version of such a loss function would be

$$L = (\pi - \pi^E - \alpha)^2 + \beta\pi^2,$$

where the constant term α captures the desire of the government to achieve higher employment than the natural rate, and β is a measure of distaste for inflation.

A country trying to minimize this loss function *ex post*, that is, given π^E, will choose π so that

$$\pi = \alpha/(1+\beta) + \pi^E/(1+\beta).$$

If wage-setters know this, however, they will set wage contracts based on an expected π that is then validated by the government. The end result is that the government fails to achieve its goal of raising employment above its natural rate, and pays a price in inflation for its known desire to do so.

The equilibrium is shown in Fig. 3.2. For each of the several governments shown there, we show a reaction function of π as determined by π^E. Equilibrium in each case is where the reaction function crosses the 45-degree line. For Italy the equilibrium is at point I; for Germany, which we suppose has either more modest goals for employment, greater distaste for inflation or both, at point G. Disregard the schedule labelled Europe for the moment. In this kind of model, then, the willingness to sacrifice to obtain low inflation achieves its end without the need actually to pay the costs. A government can therefore gain from anything that enhances its anti-inflationary credibility.

The now standard argument for the EMS is apparent. Suppose that the Italians, by making some kind of moral commitment to the EMS, are able credibly to promise to match German inflation performance. Then they obtain the German expected rate of inflation, and are able to achieve the superior German result, at point G.

Fig. 3.2

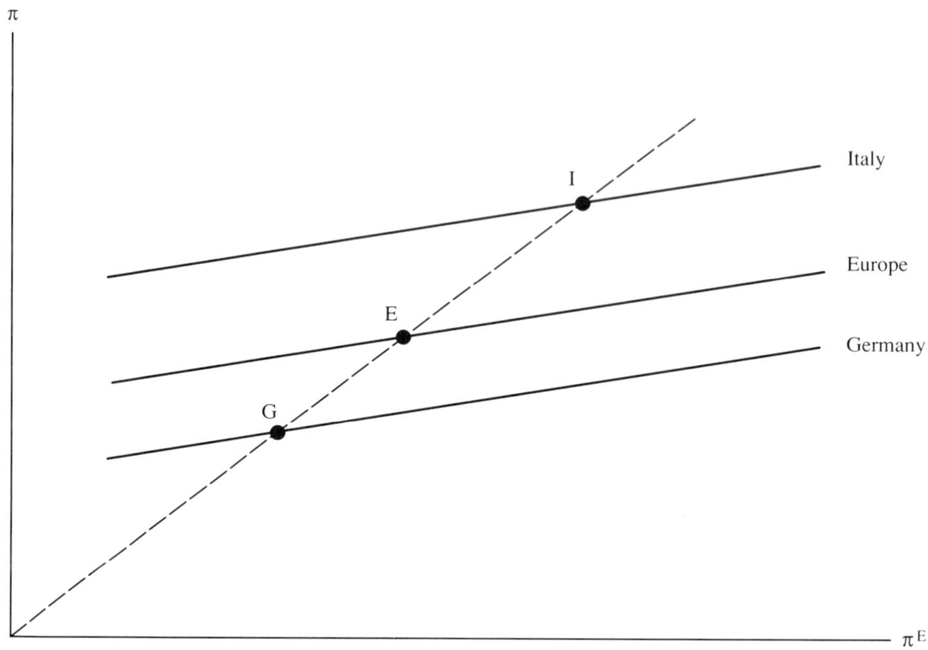

This is clearly an overstated argument. It places much more weight on rationality in price determination than the evidence warrants, and ignores the costs of loss of flexibility. None the less, it allows us to approach the remaining issues: will this argument remain valid as the FRG's special role fades, and will it be reinforced or weakened under a common currency?

There is no simple answer to the first question. One cannot expect the FRG always to be a monetary paragon, so that if the system depends ultimately on the implicit German role it will eventually be in trouble. Among the reasons that Bretton Woods fell apart was that the USA went from being a pillar of responsibility on which other countries could lean to a source of imported inflation; the FRG will not always be as German as it is now. However, Europe is somewhat different from the Bretton Woods group of nations in that it is more symmetric. If there comes a day when the FRG has an inflation problem and France does not, they could conceivably reverse roles, because Germany is not overwhelmingly the largest European economy.

Indeed, one could argue that the EMS, which may eventually contain four roughly equal-sized economic powers, could in time develop into a system in which there is *de facto* competition for the hegemonic role. In this case the national central bank perceived as having the most conservative monetary policy would tend to emerge as the *de facto* European central bank, but with that status always provisional.

Now for the next question: would credibility be better or worse under a common currency?

At first sight, one might think that it would necessarily be worse, since commitment to fixed rates is always provisional as long as national currencies remain; a fixed rate system is always in some sense still an adjustable-peg. Establishment of a common currency is a more credible commitment than a mere promise to stabilize exchange rates. It is not easy to opt out of a common currency, as Panama has found; nor is it easy to impose capital controls or otherwise seek monetary independence.

Yet there is an alternative argument that suggests to me that a common currency might actually provide less credibility as an anti-inflationary device than an EMS-type system. The reasons are as follows: under the apparent symmetry of the EMS, it is possible for the inflation-prone countries to sacrifice their monetary independence implicitly, without any formal political humiliation. With a formal designation of a central bank, this would no longer be possible, and the views of the inflationary nations would have to be reflected – whether they like it or not. Thus the credibility of the system would actually be less.

Consider Fig. 3.2 again. Suppose that the FRG and Italy form a monetary union, and that the central bank reflects the views of both. Then the European central bank's reaction function would lie intermediate between the German and Italian schedules, leading to an outcome at E: better than Italy under floating rates, but worse than the common outcome at G under fixed rates!

This is clearly too extreme a result. It comes from a model in which there is never any reason to want a more expansionary monetary policy *ex ante*, in which a central bank that is indifferent to employment does just as well in terms of employment as one that makes employment a priority, and achieves this result with lower inflation. A more realistic model would allow some role for active stabilization policy, and in this model Italy might prefer to have a seat on the central bank's board, even though that bank's credibility might suffer slightly as a result. I have also neglected the point that Italy might have problems being fully credible in its commitment to stabilize its exchange rate.

None the less, the basic result that everyone's credibility might actually be worse with a common currency than with mere fixed rates may serve as a useful corrective to excessive enthusiasm about a European currency.

5. Fiscal policy

An issue that has arisen both from 1992 and from movements towards monetary unification is whether a highly integrated economy requires fiscal as well as monetary and trade policy coordination. This is a heated issue; it may be useful to throw some cold water on the subject.

The basic case for coordination of fiscal policy is similar to the general case for policy coordination: it is based on externalities between the major nations. Consider the following example: a group of countries has established a credible monetary union; never mind, for the moment, who acts as central banker. Suppose also that despite the existence of some kind of union central banker, it is true both that countries have individual current account targets, and that fiscal policy is an essential tool of stabilization policy. Then there will be a potential deflationary bias in the system. Each country will be tempted to follow a tight fiscal policy in pursuit of a current account surplus, but the collective result of these policies will be low output for everyone without much current account improvement.[2] Thus it becomes necessary to have coordination of fiscal as well as monetary problems.

How reasonable is this concern? I am sceptical on one theoretical and two practical grounds. The theoretical question is, what happened to monetary policy? The argument here depends on the Keynesian view that a sufficiently expansionary fiscal policy is needed to achieve a desired level of demand. As long as someone is playing the central bank role, however, there is no particular reason why monetary policy cannot do the job instead. Since it is aggregate demand for the whole of Europe, not local demand, that is the issue, it is hard to see why the level of fiscal stimulus matters very much.

As a practical matter, what stands out first is that the active use of fiscal policy for stabilization purposes has become fairly rare in any case in the last decade. So it is hard to see why it should suddenly become a major issue for European monetary union. Furthermore, there is the always useful comparison with the USA, with its federal system: if fiscal coordination is so important, why has the USA found it unnecessary to police state and local budgets?

On the whole, the case for fiscal coordination seems much weaker than that for monetary coordination, and it is hard to work up much enthusiasm for it.

6. Monetary and political union

The discussion presented so far does not convey an overwhelming case for European monetary union, still less for creation of a European common currency. The theory of optimal currency areas suggests that a monetary union should take place when the relevant countries are very closely integrated, to the point where the costs of foregoing exchange rate flexibility are small and the costs of uncertainty about rates large; Europe is still arguably too large and poorly integrated to fit the criteria. That same theory suggests that optimal areas for common currencies are smaller than optimal areas for fixed rates, so *a fortiori* the case for a common European currency is questionable.

None the less, creation of a common European currency is strongly advocated by many of Europe's political élite, for reasons that have little to do with economics. And they are probably right in their advocacy. For monetary union may well be a necessary counterpart of closer European political unity, whether or not it is actually the best thing from a strict economic point of view. I have previously noted that while a reasonable economic case can be made for having regional currencies inside the USA that can be realigned against one another, this idea seems absurd. The time has now come to sketch out why it seems impossible, and correspondingly why Europe may need a common currency.

Suppose that we make the following argument: a unified polity requires full freedom of movement of goods, services and people. Historically, governments have acted in ways that suggest that easy movement across the polity is a crucial aspect of political identity: examples include the practice of charging a flat postal fee for domestic mail, regardless of distance, and the often costly construction of transportation routes that follow political rather than national geography (e.g. the Canadian railway system).

If freedom of economic movement is a crucial symbol of political unity, then part of this freedom is the ability to use as legal tender in all parts of a polity the same currency that one uses elsewhere. It is a powerful symbol of Canadian existence that a resident of Vancouver can use dollars in Montreal but not in Seattle; there would not be much of a Canadian identity left if this was otherwise.

Now one might imagine that European currencies could circulate side by side, with DM legal tender in France and FF the same in the FRG. This would, however, raise two problems. If the currencies really were accepted equally, we would have the competitive seigniorage problem discussed in section 3. More likely, however, the most widely used currency would tend to crowd out the others through a cumulative process. So Europe would end up with a single currency anyway; clearly it would be politically necessary in this case that the currency be issued by a community rather than a national bank.

Now the argument that in free currency competition Europe would tend to converge on a single currency, may seem to demonstrate to many readers that Europe is an optimal currency area – after all, that is the free-market outcome. Here, however, the philosophical points of section 1 apply. Given the inherent second-best nature of monetary economics, free-market outcomes have no special appeal: the market is not always right. It is perfectly possible that market forces may lead to the existence of too few currencies in the world. I find it quite reasonable to guess that Europe is too large, diverse and poorly integrated to benefit economically from a single currency.

I also think that a single currency for Europe is an excellent idea. Economic efficiency is not everything. A unified currency is almost surely a necessary adjunct of European political unification, and that is a more important goal than the loss of some flexibility in adjustment.

Notes

1. It is sometimes thought that the costs of exchange rate uncertainty are summarized by the effect of exchange risk in discouraging international trade and investment. It is then argued that the absence of any clear negative effect of exchange rate volatility on trade volumes shows that the costs have been negligible. However, the effects of uncertainty may take other forms than simply adding risk. Uncertainty may make investment decisions sluggish in response to cost changes, because of the option value of waiting and seeing; or it may lead firms to construct excess capacity, to take advantage of exchange rate swings; or it may simply degrade the quality of decisions. So the fact that trade has continued to grow in spite of volatile exchange rates tells us little about the actual costs of that volatility.
2. Daniel Cohen and Charles Wyplosz have suggested a reverse scenario. In their version members of a monetary union are indifferent to the effect of their policies on current balances inside the union, and therefore follow fiscal policies that lead to a larger-than-optimal current deficit of the union against the rest of the world. While the logic of the model given the assumptions is impeccable, I am not persuaded that this is a realistic characterization of the problem.

CHAPTER FOUR

The 'new' EMS

Francesco Giavazzi and Luigi Spaventa

1. Introduction

In the past three years, the countries that belong to the exchange rate mechanism of the European Monetary System (EMS) have experienced a very rapid process of financial integration. Most exchange controls – in the form of constraints on portfolio investment and foreign trade financing, or dual exchange markets, where capital account transactions are kept isolated from current account transactions – have been lifted, and the few remaining regulations are scheduled to be removed in the next few months.

While the process of financial integration was taking place, important changes have occurred in the mode of working of the EMS. The abolition of exchange controls has been accompanied by the transition to more fixed exchange rates. For three years now there have been no changes of the central parities – a sharp difference from the previous eight years of operation of the EMS, when central parities used to be realigned once every year, at least. Early in the most recent period, strong speculative pressures against some 'weaker' currencies, like the French franc (FF) and the lira, were resisted obstinately, unlike in the past, and with success. On more than one occasion the offer by the Federal Republic of Germany (FRG) of an across-the-board appreciation of its currency, often vainly solicited in the past, was turned down: aversion to parity changes, once confined to the smaller (northern) members of the system, has now become common to all – including the newcomer, Spain.

While these developments were occurring, the process of convergence of infra-EMS inflation rates seems to have come to an end: an inflation differential between the FRG and 'weaker' countries persists, though in different degrees. At the same time domestic demand has grown more rapidly in 'higher-inflation' countries. Higher inflation and faster growth of domestic demand are reflected to some extent by changes in the current account position, and more fully by changes in the infra-EMS trade balances.[1] These imbalances are projected to grow further in the near future.

This side of the European experience raises the question of what will be the effects of financial integration and the commitment to fixed exchange rates on the speed and the output cost of disinflation. Are the microeconomic benefits associated with free trade in financial assets going to come at the macroeconomic cost of growing intra-European imbalances?

The decision to fix exchange rates and liberalize capital movements before the convergence of inflation rates has been accomplished would normally be applauded by some and objected to by others. Both sides would, however, agree that it must cause hardships, in the shape of a contraction of output induced by real appreciation, and of capital outflows and loss of reserves resulting from repeated speculative attacks on the currency. The difference of views would only arise out of a different relative assessment of costs and benefits: the supporters believing that the disciplinary effects on inflation of the policy shift are sizeable, and valuing them more than the costs; the opponents being doubtful about those effects, and attributing a greater weight to the costs. Recent developments, however, seem to have faulted both the supporters and the opponents. There have been no hardships; but neither has there been a disciplinary effect.

In this chapter we attempt to provide an explanation for these developments, based on the effects on expectations of the change in EMS regime. Section 2 discusses the facts: why are we talking of a 'new' EMS? In section 3 we analyse the effect of the regime shift on inflation, and on the output cost of disinflation. We start describing the 'old' EMS, which, at least in the more recent years, very much resembled a crawling-peg regime. We then analyse the adjustment process initiated by the authorities' decision to fix the nominal exchange rate. We consider first the case where the policy shift has no effect on expectations. Next we ask how credibility affects the adjustment. We show that the answer critically depends on the degree of financial integration – and in particular on the ability of domestic residents to borrow in foreign currency.

Our conclusions on the consequences of the new EMS regime are mixed. The impact effect of financial integration and of a credible commitment to fixed exchange rates seem at first to jeopardize the attempts to disinflate. In the longer run, however, they may become important assets, which speed up the disinflation and dampen its output cost.

2. Some facts on the 'new' EMS

THE EFFECTS OF FINANCIAL INTEGRATION: CAPITAL FLOWS

Figure 4.1 shows diffences in the growth rate of domestic demand. The faster-growing group is led by Italy and Spain, the two EMS countries with a higher inflation; France is in the middle, while the FRG and the northern countries lag behind. Higher growth in the former countries has gone together with higher investment rates, especially in equipment.

Differences in growth rates are reflected in current account imbalances; the latter, however, have not affected exchange rate stability. Current account deficits have been over-financed by capital inflows. Exchange rate stability and financial inte-

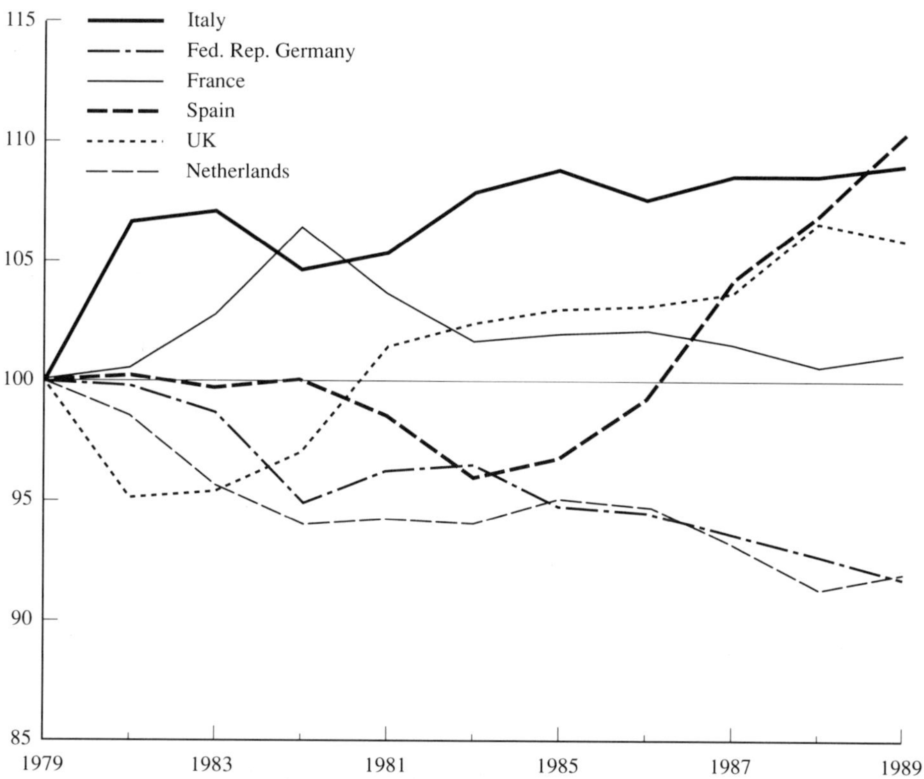

FIG 4.1 Relative and domestic demand in the EMS (1979 =100)
Source: OECD

gration have stimulated capital flows from lower inflation and lower growth areas into countries with higher inflation and faster growth of domestic demand. Monetary authorities in the latter countries have sterilized the increase in reserves, to prevent an undesirable monetary expansion and a reduction in domestic interest rates. When full sterilization has proved difficult, they have attempted to discourage the inflows through administrative controls and/or have accepted some appreciation of the exchange rate. In short, the monetary targets set by the weaker countries in order to control domestic demand have over-fulfilled the requirements set by the exchange rate objective.

Italy and Spain provide good examples of these developments. In Italy, following the last realignment in January 1987, the lira started to depreciate relative to the Deutschmark (DM), as had happened after previous parity changes. To keep within the band the central bank raised the nominal interest rate differential *vis-à-vis* the FRG by 200 basis points. A large speculative attack was resisted in the summer, and a number of occasions in which a decision to realign would have been natural were not seized. Early in 1988, expectations shifted. Capital started to flow in, notwithstanding a reduction in the interest rate differential *vis-à-vis* the FRG (Fig. 4.2).

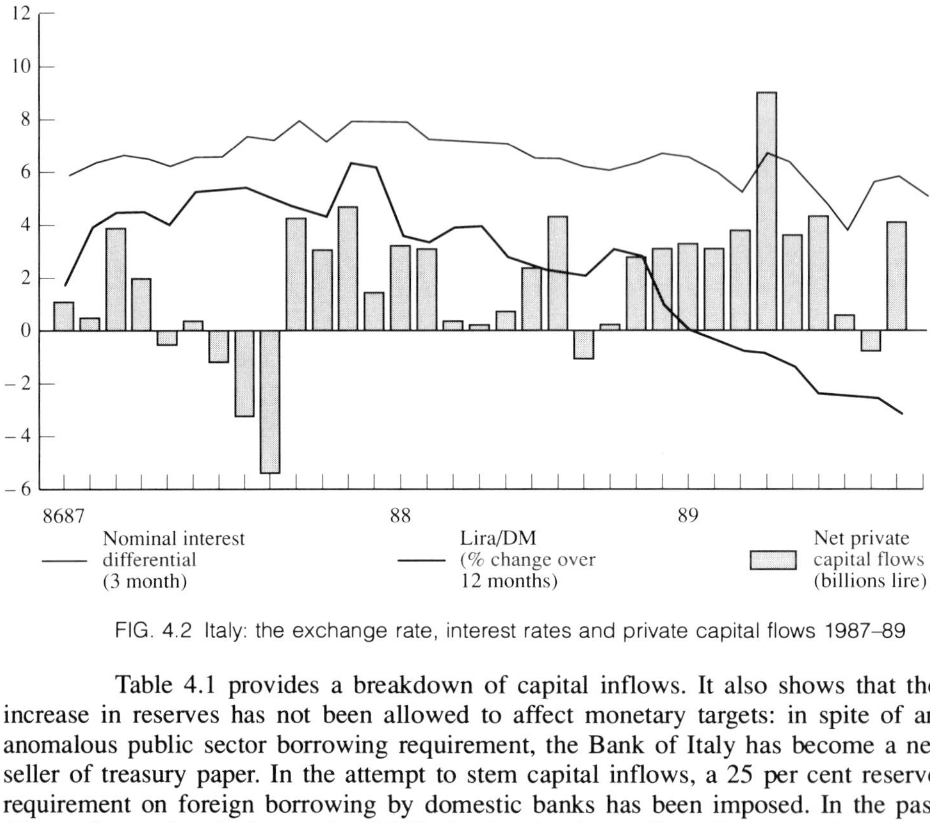

FIG. 4.2 Italy: the exchange rate, interest rates and private capital flows 1987–89

Table 4.1 provides a breakdown of capital inflows. It also shows that the increase in reserves has not been allowed to affect monetary targets: in spite of an anomalous public sector borrowing requirement, the Bank of Italy has become a net seller of treasury paper. In the attempt to stem capital inflows, a 25 per cent reserve requirement on foreign borrowing by domestic banks has been imposed. In the past 12 months (ending in September 1989) the lira has been allowed to appreciate up to 3 per cent with respect to the DM, while the Italian inflation rate remains 4 percentage points above the German rate. The monetary targets set by the Bank have been fully respected. Credit targets, instead, have been substantially exceeded: but this is part of the story we shall tell later.

Table 4.2 provides similar data for Spain. Even before joining the EMS, the Spanish authorities had made it clear that they were shunning a weak currency option. Again, the size of capital inflows is impressive.

There are two differences with respect to Italy: the limited dimension of commercial banks' borrowing suggests that long-term capital has been more important; sterilization has been less effective. Credit targets have been largely overshot, as in Italy.

We note another remarkable similarity between the two countries. In 1989 the Bundesbank has twice increased German interest rates. This move was promptly followed by other EMS members, but not by Italy and Spain, the two countries with the higher inflation differential with respect to the FRG.

TABLE 4.1 Italy: the current account, private capital flows and central bank sterilization (billion lira)

	1988	1989 (Jan.–October)
Current account	–12,285	–17,958
Private capital flows	+23,186	+24,895
Of which:		
Change in net foreign liabilities of comm. banks	+10,219	+10,739
Change in Central Bank reserves	+10,906	+17,676

	1987	1988	1988 (Jan.–September)	1989 (Jan.–September)
Change in monetary base (bn. lire)	13,946	12,957	6,462	8,921
Of which:				
Increase in reserves	6,756	10,947	5,225	19,062
Treasury financing	8,820	2,295	3,442	–8,266
Other	–1,631	–667	–2,205	–1,875
M2 (% change)				
Target	6–9	6–9		
Outcome	8.3	7.7		
Credit to non-state sector				
Target	7.0	6–10		
Outcome	10.3	15.5		

Source: Bank of Italy.

The recent experience in Italy and Spain has a precedent. In Denmark, controls on capital inflows were abolished in the fall of 1983, when the authorities made a firm commitment to a stable parity. Figure 4.3 shows that a steep fall in Danish interest rates was insufficient to prevent the large capital flows – mainly (as in Italy) through foreign borrowing by commercial banks – induced by the credibility of the government's commitment.

THE EFFECTS OF FINANCIAL INTEGRATION: EXCHANGE RATE EXPECTATIONS

There were two common arguments in favour of capital controls in the EMS: (1) capital controls help to stabilize domestic interest rates; (2) capital controls eliminate

TABLE 4.2 Spain: the current account, private capital flows and central bank sterilization (billion pesetas)

	1988	1989 (Jan.–July)
Current account	–348.9	–723.1
Private capital flows	1,693.0	1,193.3
Of which:		
Change in net foreign liabilities of comm. banks	302.6	108.2
Change in Central Bank reserves	961.8	793.9

	1987	1988	1988 (Jan.–July)	1989 (Jan.–July)
Change in Monetary base (bn. lire)	747	224	733	1,826
Of which:				
Increase in reserves	1,653	922	793	839
Treasury financing	291	–40	–384	–62
Other	–1,197	–658	324	1,049
ALP (% change)				
Target	6.5-9.5	8–11		
Outcome	14.2	11.0		
Credit to non-state sector				
Target		12.5		
Outcome	14.5	16.4		

Source: Bank of Spain.

the possibility of speculative attacks against the reserves of the central bank

With perfect capital mobility, whenever a discrete change in the exchange rate is expected, interest rate differentials widen sharply. In proximity of a devaluation, equilibrium interest rates on overnight assets can easily exceed 100 per cent! In general, expectations of exchange rate devaluations increase the volatility of short-term nominal interest rates to levels that are considered unacceptable by most central banks, though there is no widely agreed-upon welfare justification for the desirability of targeting nominal interest rates.[2]

Further, when a devaluation is expected, even a jump in domestic interest rates adequate to prevent the reallocation of international financial portfolios may not be sufficient to avoid a speculative attack on the reserves of the central bank. To escape the loss of purchasing power of the domestic money stock caused by a devaluation, holders of high-powered money may be induced to sell the domestic currency to the central bank in exchange for foreign currency just before the

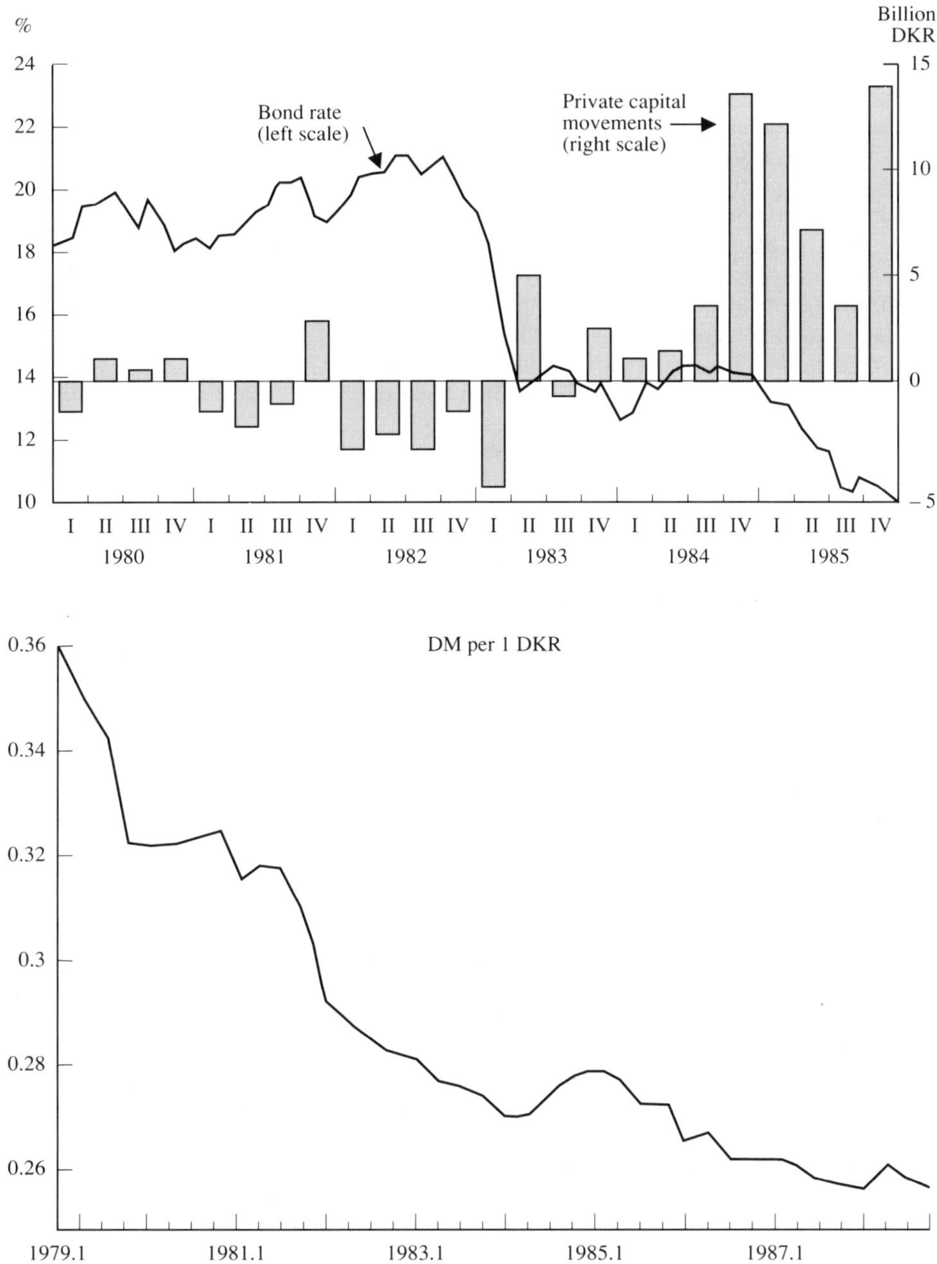

Fig. 4.3 Exchange rate stabilization, interest rates and private capital flows, Denmark: 1982–83

devaluation, then buy it back after the devaluation. Speculative attacks on central banks' reserves can thus occur even when domestic interest rates are allowed to jump to equilibrate financial portfolios. This problem could be especially bothersome to central banks, since the magnitude of the expected devaluation does not affect the size of the speculative attack. The reluctance of central banks to suffer large swings in their foreign exchange reserves is another argument for prohibiting the purchase of foreign exchange by domestic residents, for reasons that are not related to the financing of international trade.

The likelihood of sharp increases in domestic rates and of speculative attacks is enhanced by the possibility that the expectation of a devaluation will be self-fulfilling. A 'confidence crisis' may force the central bank to devalue even if 'fundamentals' are consistent with the exchange rate target. In such cases capital controls eliminate the possibility of multiple equilibria.

These arguments have been often used to suggest that the EMS would not survive the abolition of exchange controls.

The process of financial integration that has taken place in the Community since 1985–86 has practically removed all controls on portfolio investment. The only remaining restrictions, in countries such as France and Italy (at the end of 1989), are on bank deposits – residents being prevented from holding deposits denominated in foreign currency. These restrictions are still effective in dampening the fluctuations in demand for high-powered money that accompany expectations of exchange rate changes. Interest rates, on the contrary, already bear the full burden of adjusting to the portfolio shifts that may be induced by expectations of exchange rate changes.

The top section of Table 4.3 compares the variability of onshore and offshore interest rates in France, Italy and the FRG before and after liberalization. The offshore rate is the interest offered on Eurodeposits issued in London, and denominated in the three EMS currencies; onshore rates are offer rates in the domestic money markets in Paris, Milan and Frankfurt. Table 4.3 gives figures for three periods. During the first two periods exchange controls in France and Italy isolated the domestic money market from the international financial market; the third period starts at the time of the abolition of exchange controls. In the FRG international financial transactions are unrestricted throughout the sample. We have split the sample referring to exchange controls into two, to account for the greater 'turbulence' observed in the EMS up to the realignment of March 1983. Data are daily, and variability is defined as the standard error of the detrended time series of interest rates divided by the mean.

As expected, financial liberalization in France and Italy has eliminated the gap between onshore and offshore rates: the variability of the two series is now practically identical. This is in contrast to the early 1980s when exchange controls were effective at reducing the volatility of domestic interest rates relative to that of Eurorates.

However, contrary to what could have been expected, the gap has been closed, more than by an increase in the volatility of onshore rates, by a significant reduction in the volatility of offshore rates. This observation is consistent with three different hypotheses. First, interest rates worldwide may have become more stable. An alternative hypothesis points to the effects of exchange controls on the volume of Eurodeposits denominated in lire and FFs: exchange controls increase transaction

TABLE 4.3 Variability of onshore and offshore interest rates (1-month deposits)

	DM		FF		Lire	
	Offshore	Onshore	Offshore	Onshore	Offshore	Onshore
12.11.80–31.3.83	0.141	0.146	0.482	0.146	0.262	0.060
1.4.83–31.7.87	0.093	0.087	0.132	0.059	0.126	0.079
1.4.88–21.10.89	0.061	0.056	0.051	0.046	0.050	0.032

Average bid–ask spreads in the Euromarket (1-month deposits)

	DM	FF	Lire
12.11.80–31.3.83	0.014	0.033	0.067
1.4.83–31.7.87	0.026	0.023	0.047
1.4.88–21.10.89	0.021	0.015	0.048

Source: Data Resources Inc., FACS Databank.

Note: Data are daily, and interest rates are per annum. The measure of variability refers to bid rates. Variability is defined as the standard error of the detrended time series of interest rates divided by the mean. The average bid–ask spread is computed as [*i* (ASK – *i* (BID)]/[*i* (ASK) + *i* (BID)](0.5).

costs in the currencies that are subject to such controls, and thus limit the number of agents who actively trade for portfolio purposes in those currencies. The outcome is that offshore markets will be relatively thin, and in some cases 'market thinness' may raise the volatility of asset prices. Finally, the reduction in the volatility of offshore rates may be an indication that exchange rate expectations have stabilised.

The data in Table 4.3 tend to reject the first two interpretations. If we take the DM as the standard, we see that the change in the volatility of interest rates on DM deposits cannot fully explain the stabilization of Eurorates in lire and FFs: between 1983–87 and 1988–89 the variability of DM Eurorates falls by 50 per cent, while that of Eurofrancs and Eurolire falls by 250 per cent. The lower section of Table 4.3 reports the average spread between bid and ask rates in each subsample. These spreads tend to widen in thin markets. If financial liberalization had rapidly deepened the Euromarket we should observe a fall in the average bid-ask spread. Although there is some evidence that bid-ask spreads have fallen in the Eurofranc market, spreads on deposits denominated in Italian lire have remained almost unchanged. The evidence thus suggests that the transition to greater freedom of capital movements and to growing integration of financial markets has stabilized exchange rate expectations; these in turn are reflected in the convergence of the variability of Italian and French interest rates to that of the FRG.

A change in the process that drives exchange rate expectations suggests a 'change of regime'. If, for example, agents in financial markets had associated the abolition of exchange controls with a shift in monetary policy, we would observe a change in the process driving expectations.

As we have seen above, financial liberalization has indeed been accompanied by a 'regime change'. It is as if the authorities had realized that once exchange controls are gone, realignments become virtually impossible, since the mere possibility of a realignment could stir up an unsustainable speculative attack. The commitment to fixed exchange rates then becomes the only alternative to abandoning the EMS and letting exchange rates float freely.

3. The 'old' EMS

We now address the problems arising in the transition from the 'old' EMS equilibrium to a new situation developing as a result of a policy shift in the weaker members of the system. To sharpen the comparison, we shall to some extent caricature the features of the old system. This does not apply to its broad characterization, which, as we have mentioned above, is one of frequent, and especially frequently expected, realignments. But it does apply to our description of the system as one in which realignments followed, or were expected to follow, a crawling-peg pattern so as to keep the real exchange rate constant in the presence of persisting inflation differentials. For our purposes, however, this caricature is not a misrepresentation, in spite of the fact that the disciplinary effects of the EMS in the past depended precisely on less than full accommodation of inflation differentials. When the differential, though still persisting, has already narrowed considerably, it may be expected that periodic small realignments will be tolerated, at home and abroad. We further use the assumption of constant real exchange rates for simplicity: what really matters is that parity changes did occur and were expected to occur.

The policy shift is signalled by the resolve of the authorities of the high-inflation country to stick to the existing central parity from now on, and to resist market pressures for a realignment. Over time, the authorities' commitment acquires credibility, and agents' expectations shift.

The transition from crawling-peg to fixed exchange rates is normally associated with a contraction of output due to a loss of competitiveness. We shall instead argue that, when we allow for freedom of capital movements and integration of financial markets, a commitment to the existing parity will initially produce an undesired expansionary stimulus to domestic demand: this effect is undesired because it frustrates the effort to eliminate the inflation differential via the contraction of total demand induced by the real appreciation.

Let us first consider equilibrium in the 'old' EMS. Domestic absorption depends positively on income, on the real interest rate and on the stance of domestic fiscal policy. The current account depends positively on the relative price of home goods, and negatively on the level of income.[3] Solving for income, total demand for home goods can be written as

$$y_t = -\beta r_t + \alpha \lambda_t + \gamma f_t, \qquad [1]$$

where y denotes the logarithm of domestic demand, $\lambda \equiv e + p^* - p$ the logarithm of the real exchange rate, r_t the level of the real interest rate, and f_t is an index of fiscal stance.

Prices are predetermined: the rate of increase of prices between period t and period t+1 is a function of excess demand in period t and of past inflation:

$$p_{t+1} - p_t = [(1-\mu)/(1-\mu L)](p_t - p_{t-1}) + \theta\, y_t, \qquad [2]$$

where μ $(0 < \mu < 1)$ is the parameter of the distributed lag function of past inflation and L is the lag operator. Equation [2] is consistent with wage contracts where wages for period t+1 are set in period t, based on current conditions in the labour market and on past inflation – either because expectations follow an error-correction rule, or because of the presence of overlapping contracts. Equation [2] also assumes that firms passively set prices based on current wages, and, more importantly, rules out any forward-looking behaviour in the labour market. Our motivation for making this assumption is that we wish to concentrate on the effects on aggregate demand of a shift in exchange rate expectations: we thus overlook the effects of exchange rate expectations on the supply side of the economy.[4]

Domestic financial assets (denominated in the domestic currency) are imperfect substitutes for foreign financial assets, and capital flows depend on the uncovered interest rate differential.

Abroad prices are constant and the nominal, and real, rate of interest is fixed at i^*. In the initial equilibrium domestic output is at the full-employment level (normalized to zero), and the inflation rate is positive, but constant. The central bank lets the nominal exchange rate depreciate at a rate equal to the rate of inflation – which is the crawling-peg assumption – and keeps the domestic real rate of interest equal to i^*. Here $\lambda_t = \bar{\lambda} = 0$, and $f_t = \bar{f} = 0$ keep the goods market and the current account in equilibrium – assuming for simplicity that $i^* = 0$.[5] The initial equilibrium is depicted in Fig. 4.4, where we plot the real interest rate and the real exchange rate along the axes. Along the locus GG, y = 0 and on the locus CA the current account is in equilibrium. The equilibrium at E is independent of the rate of inflation, as the nominal exchange rate depreciates with inflation, and the real interest rate is constant at i^*.

4. A change of regime with unchanged expectations

We now suppose that the authorities resolve to eliminate the inflation differential with the foreign country and that, to do so, they decide to abandon the crawling-peg

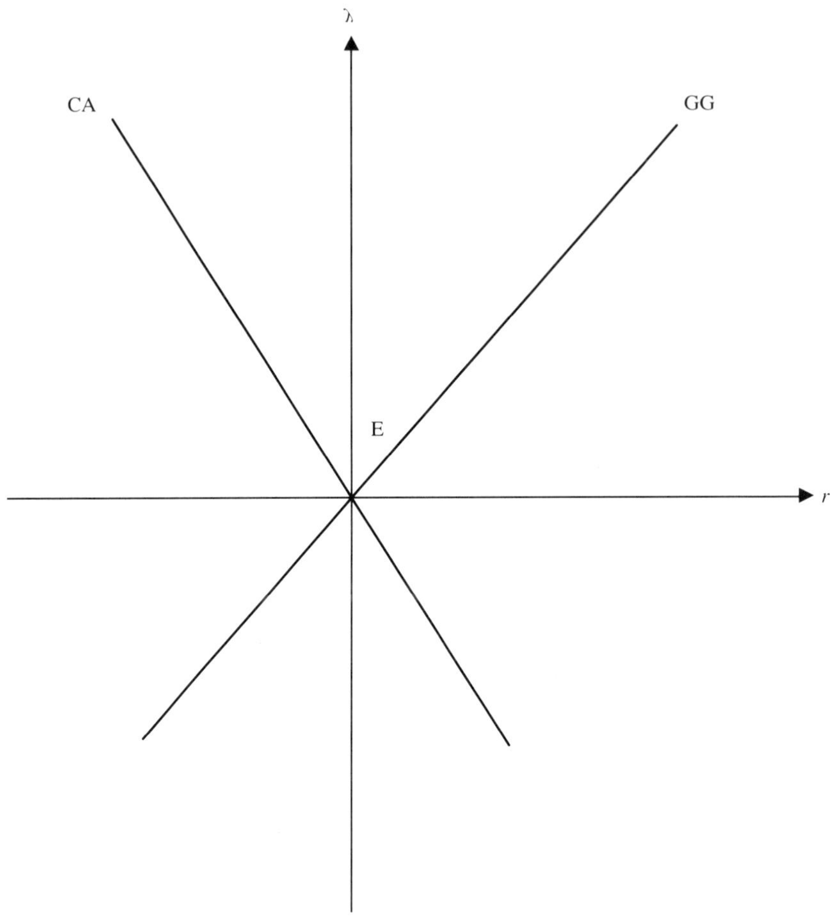

FIG. 4.4 Equilibrium real exchange rate and real interest rate

regime which has, until then, validated that differential. With a stable nominal exchange rate, the real exchange rate will appreciate over time as long as inflation persists.

We are not concerned here with the effects of real appreciation on the sacrifice ratio – or output cost – of the disinflation.[6] We want to see how disinflation is brought about by real appreciation, and how this process is affected by a shift in exchange rate expectations.

Consider first a disinflation that takes place in the presence of a constant real rate of interest. The loss of competitiveness will cause a shift away from domestic goods, and hence a fall in total domestic demand – as the current account worsens, while a constant real rate of interest keeps domestic absorption unchanged. As demand falls, the inflation rate declines, as shown by equation [2]. The real appreciation will continue as long as a positive inflation differential persists, and will be followed by real depreciation when the differential turns negative to restore the initial level of competitiveness at a constant nominal exchange rate. The dynamic path of the economy from the old to the new steady state is described by

$$\begin{vmatrix} p_{t+1}-p_t \\ \lambda_t \end{vmatrix} = \begin{vmatrix} 1-\Theta\,\alpha & (1-\mu)\,\Theta\,\alpha \\ -1 & 1 \end{vmatrix} \begin{vmatrix} p_t-p_{t-1} \\ \lambda_{t-1} \end{vmatrix} . \qquad [3]$$

The economy will converge to the new steady state provided:

$$\begin{aligned} &1-\Theta\,\alpha\,\mu < 1, \\ &4-\Theta\,\alpha\,(1+\mu) > 0, \\ &\Theta\,\alpha\,(1-\mu) > 0. \end{aligned} \qquad [4]$$

The first condition[7] requires $\mu\Theta\alpha > 0$, and is satisfied for positive values of the three parameters. The third condition requires $\mu < 1$ and the second $\alpha < 4/[\Theta\,(1-\mu)]$. Thus, for reasonable and plausible values of the parameters the process converges.

In the new steady state prices are constant, and the real exchange rate is back to equilibrium ($\bar{\lambda} = 0$). With an unchanged real rate of interest, output will also have returned to equilibrium, as absorption has remained constant throughout the adjustment, and the current account is back to equilibrium. In the process, however, the country will have incurred a series of current account deficits. Whether and to what extent these deficits will be financed by private capital flows, or by a fall in official reserves, depends on what has happened to exchange rate expectations. If we assume $(e_{t+1}-e_t)^E = p_{t+1}-p_t$, official reserves have borne the entire burden.

5. The effects of a shift in expectations

The assumption that exchange rate expectations are unaffected by the regime shift appears unwarranted. Even if the authorities are not immediately and wholly credible in their resolve to maintain and defend the central parity, experience will teach agents to be less than certain about the regular occurrence of parity realignments. To allow for this we assume that realignments are expected to occur with probability π, and that each realignment is expected to offset the current inflation differential:

$$(e_{t+1}-e_t)^E = \pi(p_{t+1}-p_t) \quad 0 \leq \pi \leq 1. \qquad [5]$$

The probability assigned to a realignment, π, depends on the agents' perception of the policy followed by the authorities. This perception reflects past behaviour in exchange rate management: the regime the agents believe they are in is thus influenced by the number and the frequency of realignments which have occurred to date. When realignments occur at (more or less) regular intervals to prevent a real appreciation of the currency, as under the crawling-peg regime, we would have $\pi = 1$.

As a result of the policy change, however, no realignment occurs at the expected dates. 'Expected dates' do not of course mean precise calendar dates: under the 'old' regime, when the time for a parity change was ripe, the formal decision would be taken in connection with specific events – like a meeting of the finance ministers, or the adoption of a policy package at home – or would be taken in cold blood to anticipate market expectations. Now, however, the authorities signal their resolve to maintain the existing parity by forgoing occasions propitious to realignments and by resisting speculative pressures at times when the markets, on the basis of past experience, expect them. Over time the commitment to fixed (or less variable) central parities becomes gradually more credible, and the probability assigned to realignments begins to fall.

If and when this happens, and if the domestic real interest rate is kept unchanged at the foreign level, the difference between the domestic nominal interest rate and the foreign rate plus the expected exchange rate depreciation, $(1-\pi)(p_{t+1}-p_t)$, will turn positive as π falls below 1. This will stimulate capital inflows which, depending on the degree of asset substitutability, may over-finance the current account deficit.

This, however, is not the only or the most relevant effect of the change in expectations. Another, more relevant, effect becomes apparent once we take a closer look at what determines the real cost of borrowing, on which domestic absorption depends. The situation we consider is one of increasing, though not complete, freedom of capital movements and of growing integration of financial and credit markets. Both enable domestic residents to borrow not only in domestic currency at the domestic interest rate, but also in foreign currency, at a cost which depends on the foreign interest rate and on the risk of depreciation of the domestic currency. The opportunity to borrow in the foreign currency, however, is not open to all agents in the economy. Small borrowers, typically households, have limited or no access to foreign credit, because of the small size of their loans relative to the fixed transaction costs involved in foreign borrowing, the market power of domestic banks, lack of information. Larger-size borrowers, typically firms, can instead turn to foreign credit and financial markets, if borrowing there costs less than borrowing at home.

Thus for 'households' the real cost of borrowing will be

$$r^{\mathrm{h}} = i - (p_{t+1} - p_t), \tag{6}$$

where i is the domestic nominal cost of borrowing, while for 'firms' it will be

$$r^{\mathrm{f}} = \min \begin{cases} i - (p_{t+1} - p_t), \\ i* + (e_{t+1} - e_t)^{\mathrm{E}} - (p_{t+1} - p_t) \end{cases}$$

Let 'household' borrowing represent a fraction (1-k) of total borrowing by domestic residents, while the fraction borrowed by 'firms' is k.

Expenditure decisions depend on the real cost of borrowing. In view of the fact that some residents have access to foreign credit, the real cost of borrowing, which affects expenditure, is a weighted average of the real cost of borrowing in domestic and foreign currency:

$$r = kr^{f} + (1-k)(i - (p_{t+1} - p_t) + k[i^{*} + (e_{t+1} - e_t)^{E} - (p_{t+1} - p_t)]. \qquad [7]$$

With exchange rate expectations as in [5][8] and the domestic real interest rate at the foreign level:

$$r = i^{*} - k(1 - \pi)(p_{t+1} - p_t). \qquad [7']$$

In the 'old' crawling-peg regime, $\pi = 1$ and $r = i^{*}$, as can be easily verified. As π falls below unity, however, this 'probability shock' causes a fall in r, in spite of the fact that the central bank pegs the domestic real interest rate. This means that, while real appreciation reduces the foreign component of total demand, the fall in the effective real borrowing rate provides an expansionary stimulus to domestic demand, which is not bargained for by the authorities and which seems to undo the disinflationary effects of real appreciation. In terms of Fig. 4.4, while real appreciation moves the system to the left of the locus $y = 0$, as expected and desired by the authorities, the decline in r caused by the probability shock shifts it below the locus: which of the two effects will prevail cannot be said *a priori*. Even if we knew, we still would have no information on how the fall in π affects the disinflation process. We must therefore take a closer look at the dynamics of the system.

The transition matrix now becomes

$$\begin{bmatrix} \dfrac{1 - \mu\Theta\beta k(1-\pi) - \Theta\alpha}{1 - \Theta\beta k(1-\pi)} & \dfrac{(1-\mu)\Theta\alpha}{1 - \Theta\beta k(1-\pi)} \\ -1 & 1 \end{bmatrix}. \qquad [8]$$

The first two stability conditions ensuring that the dynamic path leads to a new steady state now become

$$\alpha > [(1-\mu)/\mu]k\beta(1-\pi), \qquad [9]$$
$$\alpha < [4/\Theta(1+\mu)] - 2k\beta(1-\pi), \qquad [9']$$

while the third of the conditions in [4] condition ($\mu < 1$) remains unchanged. We can safely assume that the second condition in [9] is satisfied, although it is more stringent than for $k(1-\pi) = 0$. The first condition (which is derived from the requirement that the determinant be smaller than unity) has a clear economic interpretation: it is required that the effect on demand of a change in the real cost of borrowing, βk, *be sufficiently small* relative to the effect of a change in the real exchange rate. As $k(1-\pi)$ rises, because the probability assigned to a realignment declines, and/or because the number of unconstrained borrowers increases, the required value of α/β increases.

We must, however, be aware of a catch in the formal analysis of convergence in this case. The availability of foreign currency loans to unconstrained agents in the economy reduces the average cost of borrowing and stimulates domestic demand as long as the inflation rate is positive. At a zero inflation rate, borrowing in domestic or foreign currency becomes a matter of indifference, because the real cost is i^* in both cases. As inflation becomes negative, however, the average real cost of borrowing cannot rise above i^*, as shown by [5] above. Foreign currency borrowing takes place as long as its cost is less than i^*: with negative inflation domestic borrowing becomes more convenient and will be 100 per cent of total borrowing. Thus condition [9] is necessary only for positive inflation rates, while the less stringent condition $(\Theta\, \alpha\, \mu) > 0$ holds in the periods of negative inflation. True, if [9] holds it implies also $\Theta\, \alpha\, \mu > 0$, so that the ceiling set to the behaviour of r at $r = i^*$ should not jeopardize stability. However, the discontinuity implied by the fact that, as inflation turns negative, k falls to zero, makes a precise formal analysis of the whole dynamic process unmanageable.

More importantly, while it is relevant to establish that the process is stable, this, by itself, does not provide an answer to our earlier questions of how credibility and financial integration, as captured by positive values of $k(1 - \pi)$, affect the disinflation process initiated by foregoing parity changes. The formal analysis of stability only tells us that, if $k(1 - \pi) > 0$, the conditions on α/β are somewhat more stringent. Therefore, we do not even attempt a precise analysis of the dynamic process with switching parameters, and consider instead how the change in expectations affects the first phase of the disinflation, after the authorities have abandoned the crawling peg.

A turn of expectations (a fall of π below unity), caused by a growing perception of, and an increasing confidence in, the shift in policy regime produces remarkable effects, which are greater the greater is the integration of financial markets.

At the early stagès of the process, when the rate of inflation is still high and the real exchange rate not far yet from its equilibrium level, the expansionary effects of the fall in the cost of borrowing on domestic demand will always prevail on the initial contractionary effects of real appreciation. Following the policy shift, credibility results in a higher inflation rate than the authorities were expecting. It may even be the case that initially, as $k(1 - \pi)$ becomes positive, inflation *rises* above its previous level: this happens if $\alpha < \beta k\,(1 - \pi)$, which is compatible with $\alpha > \beta k\,(1 - \pi)\,(1 - \mu)/\mu$, the stability condition, if μ, the error correction term, is not too low. As time goes by, however, the contractionary effects are bound to prevail, as to higher inflation in one period corresponds greater real appreciation in the following period. As inflation begins to fall, with $k(1 - \pi) > 0$, the process becomes cumulative, for the real borrowing rate begins to rise again, reaching, as we saw above, its initial level i^* at zero inflation. True, the expectations of a parity change may decline further, and recourse to foreign currency borrowing may increase. Note, however, first that the possible rise of $k(1 - \pi)$ is bounded by $\pi = 0$, $k = 1$, while the decline of λ finds a limit only when the inflation reaches zero; second, if the inflation rate is falling, the higher $k(1 - \pi)$, the faster the rise in r.

Even though the effects of a fall in the expectation of a parity change do not prevent the eventual decline in the inflation rate, the authorities may still be worried by the initial bulge of demand and inflation. If they take a short view, they see that the very purpose of their policy appears to be defeated by that policy's credibility. In any case, they have reason to ask whether, owing to this, disinflation will be a more lengthy and more costly process than expected.

If fiscal policy is given, the authorities have two means at hand to prevent the expansionary effects analysed above. First, the domestic nominal interest rate can be raised so as to match the consequences of the decline in the expected depreciation. It can immediately be seen from [7] that this increase should be equal to the fall in expected depreciation times the ratio of unconstrained to constrained borrowers. Second, they could let the currency appreciate within the fluctuation band provided by the EMS, especially in countries like Italy and Spain with relatively wider bands. Whereas an appreciation of the central parity implies a formal decision, which may be difficult to adopt while the current balance is deteriorating, a movement within the band requires only that the central bank abstain from intramarginal interventions. Suppose then the central bank allows the currency to appreciate by, say, x per cent. As the commitment is to defend the central parity, but not whatever departure from the central parity which may occur within the band, it will be expected that the appreciation above the parity will be reversed, and this will increase the cost of foreign borrowing. The choice may also be a mix between the two options: some rise in the domestic interest rate and some appreciation within the band will always allow to prevent the initial fall in r.

But do the authorities really have to worry? Is it wise to raise the domestic interest rate and to allow a nominal appreciation in order to prevent the fall in the average cost of borrowing caused by the cheapening of foreign borrowing? The answer is negative on both counts.

Somewhat paradoxically, it turns out that the initial fall in r and the resulting bulge in domestic demand make the disinflation process shorter and less costly in terms of both output and current account deficits.

This is easily seen by solving for $p_{t+1} - p_t$:

$$p_{t+1} - p_t = [(1 - \Theta\,\beta\;k(1-\pi))]^{-1}\;\{[1 - \mu\,\Theta\,\beta\,k(1-\pi) - \Theta\,\alpha]\;(p_t - p_{t-1}) \\ - \{\,\Theta\alpha(1-\mu)\,\lambda_{t-1}\,\}. \qquad [10]$$

In the initial steady state, $\bar{\lambda} = 0$. Remembering that $\lambda_{t-1} = \lambda_t + (p_t - p_{t-1})$ and setting $(p_{t+1} - p_t) = 0$, we obtain

$$\lambda_t = -\frac{1 - \mu\Theta\alpha - \mu\Theta\beta k\,(1-\pi)}{(1-\mu)\Theta\alpha}\,(p_t - p_{t-1}). \qquad [11]$$

Thus, when disinflation has been achieved, real appreciation will be smaller the higher is $k\,(1-\pi)$. Since:

$$\lambda_t = -\sum_{1}^{t}(p_s - p_{s-1}) = -(p_t - p_0) \qquad [12]$$

the other side of this conclusion is that cumulative inflation during the process of disinflation will be less, and the price index at the end of the disinflation will be lower, the greater credibility and integration. Disinflation must then be quicker, and its output costs lower, for higher values of $k(1-\pi)$. Further, as the cumulated inflation and appreciation are lower, the cumulated current account deficit incurred in the process will be lower.

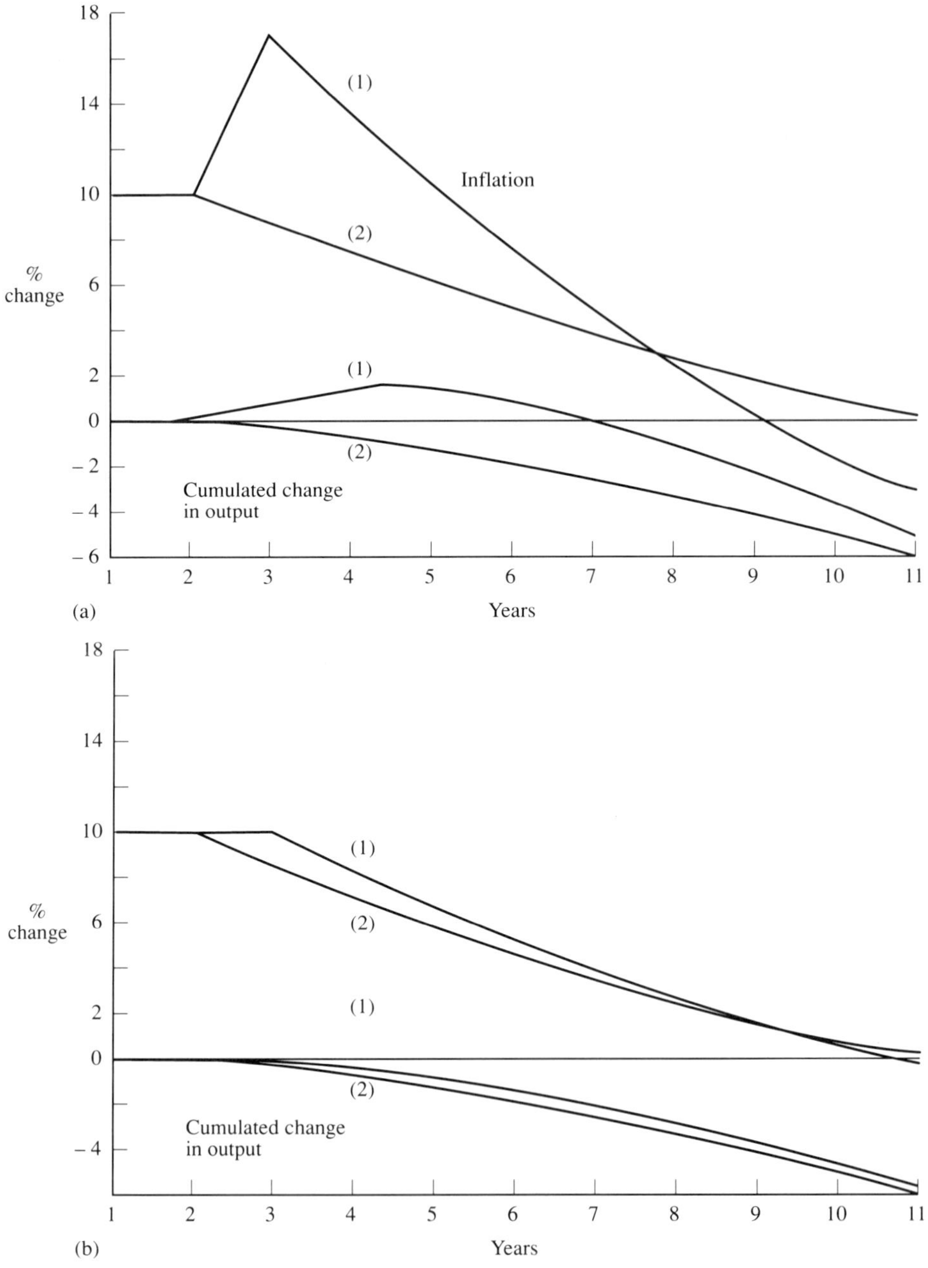

Fig 4.5 Disinflating with a fixed exchange rate. Parameter values:
(a) $\alpha = 0.2$, $\beta = 0.7$, $\mu = 0.9$, $\theta = 0.7$; (1) $k(1-\pi) = 1$, (2) $k(1-\pi) = 0$;
(b) $\alpha = 0.2$, $\beta = 0.2$, $\mu = 0.9$, $\theta = 0.7$; (1) $k(1-\pi) = 1$, (2) $k(1-\pi) = 0$

Figure 4.5a, b shows two examples obtained by simulating our model with two different sets of parameter values. In both cases inflation crosses the zero line sooner (and the cumulated output loss is smaller), the higher is $k(1 - \pi)$.

The intuition for this result is that credibility and financial integration, by raising demand, and possibly accelerating inflation at the beginning of the process, shift the loss of competitiveness towards the early stages of the disinflation. This early loss of competitiveness is carried on throughout the process and thus accelerates the convergence to zero inflation.

6. Conclusions

In this chapter we have attempted to provide an interpretation of the developments which have occurred as the EMS has evolved from a system of adjustable, and frequently adjusted, parities, where capital controls provided a shelter to weaker currencies, to one where this shelter is being removed while 'an understanding that [exchange rate realignments] would be made only in exceptional circumstances' seems to have been reached, in advance of stage two of the *Delors Report* (Delors Committee 1989). Our findings are at odds with the expected consequences of a shift to more fixed exchange rates when inflation differentials persist and there are no capital controls.

In section 2 we set forth some stylized facts, with particular reference to the experience of Spain and Italy. The change in exchange rate regime, far from inflicting hardships and imposing discipline, has been accompanied by an expansionary stimulus to domestic demand. The resulting current account deficits have been over-financed by capital inflows, while the removal of controls, contrary to what could be expected, has been followed by a reduction in the volatility of offshore rates. Our explanation of these facts is based on the effects of the change of expectations, induced by the shift in exchange rate policy, on the average cost of credit in a situation of growing integration of capital and credit markets.

As disinflation is the target of the policy change, the authorities may be worried by the unexpected and undesired expansion of domestic demand caused by the very credibility of their new stance. It is, however, our contention, and our counter-intuitive finding, that credibility and financial integration, while causing difficulties in the short run, become important assets in the longer run. If the authorities keep steady, a growing credibility in their commitment and increasing financial integration speed up the process and reduce the output cost of disinflation.

This conclusion must, however, be qualified by at least three warnings. First, credibility and financial integration make the formal condition ensuring the stability of the system more stringent than when the effects of both are neglected: if the sensitivity of aggregate demand to the average real cost of credit is too high with respect to the sensitivity to the real exchange rate, the outcome may be unstable.

Second, the process we have analysed is not without costs. Quicker disinflation is bought at the price of greater current account deficits, and hence of greater foreign indebtedness: what has been saved now may therefore have to be paid later.

Finally, any adverse shock may jeopardize the completion of the process. If the shock requires an adjustment of real wages, the market may anticipate an incentive to enforce this outcome through exchange rate depreciation, as nominal wage adjustment would be a difficult and lengthy process. Thus, under a shock, the credibility of the authorities' commitment to fixed exchange rates may quickly fade away: financial integration would then strengthen this adverse movement by lending more ammunition to speculative attacks against the currency.

A 'commitment technology' may help avoid this latter risk. A commitment to fixed parities which was the result of a broader *institutional* change, and not only the unilateral, and therefore more easily reversible, decision of one national authority would contribute to sustain the credibility of the system.

Notes

1. For an analysis of the effects of divergent growth rates of domestic demand on intra-European Community (EC) trade balances see Bini Smaghi and Vona (1988). Between 1984 and 1988 the overall current account position of the EC deteriorated by 0.3 per cent of total gross domestic product (GDP), while that of the FRG improved by 2.4 per cent. The FRG's total trade surplus rose from 3.1 per cent to 6.1 per cent of GDP; the trade surplus with EC countries rose from 1.5 per cent to 3.8 per cent. The fall in the German trade surplus with the USA, after the peak of 1986, was more than offset by the rise in the surplus towards Europe.
2. Many economists (see e.g. Barro 1988) argue that nominal interest rate targeting seems a reasonable description of central banks' activities.
3. In defining the current account we assume that foreign income is exogenous, and we neglect interest payments on net foreign assets.
4. Fischer (1988) addresses similar questions in a model where expectations affect both demand and supply.
5. Note that internal and external equilibrium require an appropriate level both of the real exchange rate *and of* fiscal policy.
6. The problem is discussed by Fischer (1988), who, unlike De Grauwe (1989), shows that the answer is ambiguous.
7. The conditions correspond to the requirement that the determinant of the state transition matrix be smaller than 1, the sum of 1 plus the trace plus the determinant be positive, and the sum of 1 plus the determinant minus the trace be also positive.
8. Note that, as π does not exceed unity (parity changes allowing a real depreciation are ruled out), and as long as the level of the real interest rate at home does not fall below the foreign level, the real cost of borrowing abroad will never exceed that of domestic borrowing.

References

Barro R. (1988) Interest rate smoothing, *NBER Working Paper* No. 2581.

Bini Smaghi, L. and **Vona S.** (1988) La Coesione dello SME e il Ruolo dei Fattori Esterni: un'Analisi in Termini di Commercio Estero, *Banca d'Italia, Temi di Discussione*, No. 103.

Committee for the Study of Economic and Monetary Union in the European Community (the Delors Committee) (1989) *Report on Economic and Monetary Union in the European Community (the Delors Report)* (with Collection of Papers), Office for Official Publication of the European Communities, Luxembourg, April.

De Grauwe, P. (1989) The Cost of Disinflation and the European monetary system, *CEPR Discussion Paper* No. 326.

Deutsche Bundesbank (1989) *Monthly Report of the Deutsche Bundesbank*, various issues.

Fischer, S. (1988) Real balances, the exchange rate, and indexation: real variables in disinflation, *Quarterly Journal of Economics*, 103, 1.

CHAPTER FIVE

Asymmetries and realignments in the EMS

Michele Fratianni and Jürgen von Hagen

1. Introduction

The creators of the European Monetary System (EMS) envisioned an island of monetary stability in Europe, not built upon the dominance of a single country. Having learnt their lessons from the breakdown of the Bretton Woods system, they aimed at a 'democratic' rather than an 'autocratic' arrangement (van Ypersele 1979). The EMS was to be a new kind of exchange rate arrangement: sufficiently *flexible* to accommodate different inflation trends among member countries and sufficiently *symmetric* to distribute equally among low- and high-inflation countries the burden of adjustment to regional external imbalances.

The principles of flexibility and symmetry were incorporated in the institutional design of the EMS. To emphasize the common point of reference, central parities and intervention limits were defined in terms of the European Currency Unit (ECU), a weighted basket of all participating currencies, rather than a grid of bilateral parities. The indicator of divergence was added to foster the convergence of economic policies within the EMS by signalling to low-inflation countries the need to loosen monetary policy, and to high-inflation countries the need to exercise more monetary discipline. The credit facilities ensured that the low-inflation countries would contribute to the symmetric adjustment process. The Bundesbank's early opposition to these features of the system indicates that it was well understood at the time that convergence in the EMS did not necessarily mean convergence at a low level of inflation (Vaubel 1980).

Realignments, changes in central parities, were designed as the principal element of flexibility in the EMS. When low- and high-inflation countries found it impossible or inconvenient to converge, they would resort to realignments to hold on to their own, preferred, inflation trend. In deference to the principle of symmetry, realignments would have to be implemented with the consent of all participants. Beyond realignments, several member countries have resorted to capital and exchange controls to shelter their domestic money markets from international forces and satisfy their demand for additional short-run flexibility.

* We would like to thank our discussant, Jacques Melitz, for valuable comments and suggestions.

Today, the prevailing view of the EMS among economists and policy-makers rejects this vision. In sharp contrast to the original intentions, the EMS is regarded as an asymmetric arrangement, in which the German Bundesbank dominates monetary policy-making and limits the policy choices available to the other members. We will call this view the German dominance hypothesis (GDH). According to GDH, the EMS is regarded as a disciplinary device, forcing the other members to follow the rigid, low-inflation rule of the Bundesbank. For these countries, EMS membership has resulted in the surrender of their monetary policy autonomy to the Bundesbank. Hence, the principles of flexibility and symmetry have both failed.

The purpose of this chapter is to reassess these issues, focusing on the empirical characteristics of the EMS. In section 2 we address the role of the Bundesbank in the system. First, we review the widely held explanation that the other members have accepted and even sought German dominance because of the Bundesbank's reputation as a central bank committed to price stability. We then go on to present in section 3 an empirical analysis of the structure of the monetary policy game in the EMS. We devise an empirical test of GDH and show that the data reject the hypothesis. While some aspects of the EMS look as if GDH were true, the strongly asymmetric and hierarchial structure of the EMS implied by GDH is not compatible with the data. Having rejected German dominance, we turn to an analysis of the empirical nature of realignments in section 4. We find that realignments are generally largely anticipated in size and direction by the market. Market predictions of realignments have improved over the history of the EMS, but realignments remain uncertain events. Flexibility in the EMS carries the cost of uncertainty about changes in central parities.

2. Bundesbank credibility

The second half of the 1980s has witnessed a growing consent among economists and policy-makers that monetary policy in the EMS has been dominated by the German Bundesbank. For example, Sarcinelli (1986: 58–59) sees 'Germany which participates in an exchange rate arrangement with other European countries, [being] concerned primarily with the DM–dollar exchange rate. This objective requires the "dominant" country to keep its growth rate in line with the nth country, and, consequently, requires the "dominated" economies to keep in step.' Katseli (1987) claims that 'within Europe, domestic central banks have chosen to lose some of the "economic effectiveness" of domestic monetary policy and accept the leadership of the Bundesbank.' Fischer (1987: 41) describes the EMS as 'an arrangement by France and Italy to accept German leadership, imposing constraints on their domestic monetary and fiscal policies'. Giavazzi and Giovannini (1987: 237) assert that 'Germany is the centre country and runs monetary policy for the whole system'. Charles Goodhart (1989: 5) describes the Deutsche Bundesbank as having played a 'central, hegemonic role within the EMS' and 'a significant political influence on the impetus for EMU'. Similarly, Russo and Tullio (1988: 332) conclude that: 'After 1983 an implicit agreement on inflation emerged, namely to converge towards the German inflation rate and to let Germany determine the "anchor" inflation rate of the system.' Gros and Thygesen (1988: 62) state flatly that 'the EMS has thus become a hierarchic and asymmetric system'. And finally, the *Delors Report* (Delors Committee 1989: para. 5) reckons that the Deutschmark (DM) is an 'anchor' for monetary policies in the EMS.

The same view has also been adopted by the press. The *Economist* (19 September, 1987) speaks of 'no parity of power in the EMS' and (21 September, 1985) predicts that '[if] sterling does join, the biggest change will be the transfer of responsibility for Britain's monetary policy from the Bank of England to Germany's Bundesbank, which, as the central bank keenest on sound money, sets the pace for others to follow'. Dale (1987) in the *International Herald Tribune* (28 September, 1987) asks 'whether Germany will continue to dominate European policy-making through its leadership of the European Community's eight-nation currency block'.

The contention of German dominance in the EMS leads to the obvious question of why the other members have accepted the unintentional asymmetry of the system. After all, each country has retained the option of leaving the arrangement, should its consequences run counter to its own goals of monetary policy. The common answer to this question has been developed in the growing game-theoretic literature on the EMS (e.g. Giavazzi and Giovannini 1987, 1988, 1989; Giavazzi and Pagano 1988; Melitz 1988; Artus 1988; Collins 1988). The basic argument is that countries with traditionally high inflation rates seek to benefit from the Bundesbank's reputation as a central bank committed to price stability. By pegging their exchange rates with the DM, they are forced to follow the Bundesbank's policy standard. This loss in policy autonomy is rewarded by a gain in credibility of their own commitment to fighting inflation, which lowers the cost of disinflation to their own economies compared to the alternative of announcing and pursuing an autonomous stabilization programme.

A MODEL OF THE EMS AND GERMAN DOMINANCE

The asymmetric view of the EMS hinges on the ability and willingness of the Bundesbank to supply credibility to the rest of the system. As a *quid pro quo,* the high-money-growth central banks accept the dominance of the Bundesbank. Let us investigate this issue first theoretically with a simple two-country model adapted from Canzoneri and Henderson (1988). In this model, shown in Table 5.1, the private sector sets money wages at the beginning of the period on the basis of the expected money supply, leaving the monetary authorities with the opportunity to generate monetary surprises. These authorities behave in the manner described by Barro and Gordon (1983); namely, they have employment targets, $\tilde{n}$ and $\tilde{n}^*$, which differ from the natural employment levels – equal to zero in the logs. By assumption, the Italian central bank has a higher employment target than the German central bank: $\tilde{n}^* > \tilde{n} > 0$. The private sector is aware of the authorities' preferences and, since no precommitment is assumed to be possible, sets expectations so as to eliminate the incentive for

TABLE 5.1 A simple two-country model

There are two identical economies described by (1) a short-run production function, (2) a demand for labour function, (3) a money market and (4) an aggregate demand function for goods and services:

$$y = y^n + (1-\alpha)\,n \qquad y* = y^n + (1-\alpha)\,n* \qquad [1]$$
$$w - p = -\alpha n \qquad w* - p* = -\alpha n* \qquad [2]$$
$$m - p = y - y^n \qquad m* - p* = y* - y^n \qquad [3]$$
$$y^d = \gamma^{-1} r + \gamma y* + (1-\gamma) y \qquad y*^d = -\delta^{-1} r + \gamma y + (1-\gamma) y* \qquad [4]$$

where high-inflation, low-credibility Italy is denoted by an asterisk, and low-inflation, high credibility FRG without.Variables are expressed in natural logarithms with the meaning:

y = output
y^n = ln $(1/(1-\alpha))$
w = nominal wage rate
p = price level of domestic output
n = employment level
m = the money stock
y^d = demand for output
r = real exchange rate = nominal exchange rate $+ p* - p$

The consumer price levels are defined as $q = p + \gamma r$ and $q* = p* - \gamma r$. With initial conditions $q_{-1} = q_{-1}* = 0$, q and $q*$ are equivalent to the FRG and Italian inflation rates. Their reduced-form solutions are:

$$q = m + (\varepsilon + \alpha - 1)(m - m^e) - \varepsilon(m* - m*^e) \qquad [5]$$
$$q* = m* + (\varepsilon + \alpha - 1)(m* - m*^e) - \varepsilon(m - m^e)$$

where $\varepsilon = \gamma^2\delta\,(1 - \alpha)$. The authorities aim at target values of employment and the overall price level according to the preference functions:

$$2U = -[\sigma\,(n-\tilde{n})^2 + q^2] \qquad 2U* = -[\sigma\,(n-\tilde{n}*)^2 + q*^2] \qquad [6]$$

---

monetary surprises. With independent monetary policies in both countries, the sub-game perfect Nash equilibrium, denoted by the subscript N, becomes:

$$m_N = q_N = \sigma\tilde{n}/(\varepsilon + \alpha); \qquad m_N* = q_N* = \sigma\tilde{n}*/(\varepsilon + \alpha). \qquad [7]$$

In equilibrium, Italy's inflation rate is higher than that of the FRG because the Banca d'Italia has a higher employment target than the Bundesbank. Substituting [7] into equation [6] of Table 5.1 we obtain the associated utility levels:

$$2U_N = -\sigma\tilde{n}^2[1 + \sigma/(\varepsilon + \alpha)^2],$$
$$2U_{N^*} = -\sigma\tilde{n}^{*2}[1 + \sigma/(\varepsilon + \alpha)^2]. \qquad [8]$$

In equilibrium, inflation yields no employment benefits. The mere fact that the authorities aim at employment levels different from the natural ones translates into an inefficiency. The authorities would be better off if they would commit themselves to credible non-inflationary policies.

Can Italy improve on [8] by fixing the price of the lira to the DM? Giavazzi and Giovannini (1987) and Giavazzi and Pagano (1988) argue for such a strategy on the ground that Italy can borrow credibility from the Bundesbank and achieve disinflation at a lower cost than through a purely domestic policy. To prove this point these authors compare Italy's utility in [8] with the utility attainable under fixed exchange rates, taking the FRG's policy in [7] as given. Italy's welfare, under these circumstances, would increase by:

$$\sigma^2[(\tilde{n}^{*2} - \tilde{n}^2)/(\varepsilon + \alpha)^2] > 0. \qquad [9]$$

But this conclusion rests on the flawed premise that German policy would not change. This is unrealistic, because the very fact that Italy adopts the exchange rate target alters the Bundesbank's policy constraint so that the policy described by [7] is no longer optimal for the FRG. Specifically, the fixed exchange rate lowers the domestic inflation cost of a German monetary surprise, since part of the German price-level effect can be exported to Italy. This implies an increase in the German employment–inflation trade-off (see Canzoneri and Henderson 1988 and Fratianni and von Hagen 1990a). Consequently, the Bundesbank has a higher incentive for monetary surprises under fixed exchange rates. The private sector recognizes this change and will set m^e accordingly. The subgame perfect Nash equilibrium under the EMS denoted by the subscript E is:

$$m_E = q_E = m_E = q_{E^*} = \sigma\tilde{n}/\alpha > \sigma\tilde{n}/(\varepsilon + \alpha). \qquad [10]$$

The Bundesbank's 'brand name' as an inflation fighter loses credibility under the EMS. In turn, this loss affects the utility levels of both countries:

$$2U_E = -\sigma\tilde{n}^2(1 + \sigma/\alpha^2); \qquad 2U_{E^*} = -\sigma[\tilde{n}^{*2} + \sigma\tilde{n}^2/\alpha^2]. \qquad [11]$$

HIGH-INFLATION COUNTRY INCENTIVES

The above equilibrium condition raises two issues. First, it is not clear that Italy gains from the arrangement. It will be beneficial to this country if $\alpha/(\varepsilon + \alpha) > \tilde{n}/\tilde{n}^*$, a condition that is satisfied if the pre-inflation biases are sufficiently different, and the degree of economic integration between Italy and the FRG is small in the sense that the income elasticity of imports, δ, is small and the relative price elasticity $1/\delta$ of imports is large. That is, the rise in the German employment–inflation trade-off arising from EMS membership must be smaller than the decline in Italy's inflation bias. In sum, the EMS need not be a superior solution for the high-inflation country even within the context of credibility.

Second, what makes markets believe in Italy's commitment to an exchange rate target when a commitment to a monetary target is reputed impossible? The importance of this question stems directly from the fact that EMS membership is not a subgame perfect strategy for Italy. Once expectations, and hence wages, have been set according to [10], Italy has a clear incentive to break the arrangement. Thus, what makes it more costly to renege on an exchange rate target than the money target? Melitz (1988) answers this question by introducing an exogenous cost to the monetary authority associated with leaving the EMS. Such an additional cost presumably intends to capture the political cost of breaking an international agreement, such as a loss of votes. The superiority of the EMS – from the viewpoint of the high-inflation country – can be likened to having introduced a *deus ex machina* in the form of a political threat: the EMS is ultimately justified by the institutional inefficiency or deficiency of the high-inflation country's political sector that impedes credible commitment to a domestic monetary target. But the practical importance of international agreements on such abstract issues as exchange rate arrangements in electoral decisions is very much in doubt. It assumes that voters pay more attention to their government's commitment to foreigners than to the domestic electorate.

The important implication of the time-consistency consideration is that Italy's low-inflation, EMS monetary policy will be credible only if the public perceives that breaking EMS agreements is sufficiently costly to the authorities. This has a bearing on the approach to monetary union proposed by the *Delors Report* (Delors Committee 1989). This would like to give the EMS a more formal, hence more visible, institutional structure only during 'stage two' of the process. It is plausible to assume that such increased visibility of the EMS would raise the members' political cost of deviating from EMS commitments. Credibility arguments therefore would favour a relatively early entry into 'stage two' to enhance monetary discipline in the EMS.

LOW-INFLATION COUNTRY INCENTIVES

Equation [10] poses the additional problem that the FRG loses from an EMS arrangement because of its higher equilibrium inflation rate. The model, therefore, cannot explain German membership in the EMS. The Bundesbank's incentive in supplying credibility must be found elsewhere. There are three ways to make the case for German membership in the EMS. The first stresses the cooperative element of the system, that is, the EMS as a mechanism for policy coordination – a feature pointed out, among others, by Canzoneri and Gray (1985), Laskar (1985), Melitz (1985) and Fratianni and von Hagen (1990b). This interpretation is based on the notion that the EMS can substitute for explicit policy coordination, internalizing the spill-over effects of domestic monetary policy under flexible exchange rates. The problem with this answer is that the cooperative interpretation can explain the EMS for all parties. Hence, the need to appeal to credibility is less important.

The second explanation is grounded on the potential conflict of interest existing between the Bundesbank and the German federal government. German law places the authority to join exchange rate arrangements with the Ministry of Finance. One may thus argue that EMS membership was imposed on the Bundesbank. The historical evidence is clear on this point: Chancellor Helmut Schmidt had to work very hard to overcome the opposition of the central bank to join the system. Norbert Kloten (1988: 3), a member of the Bundesbank Council, flatly states that 'the Bundesbank never wanted a dominant role in Europe's monetary policymaking . . . She was forced to accept that role.' According to this view, the German government uses the EMS to weaken the independence of its central bank (Vaubel 1980). But this only redirects the question: why would the Federal Government accept the higher rate of inflation incurred as a result of EMS membership? In the context of the credibility argument, the government should prefer a strong, independent Bundesbank to reduce the inefficiency of an inflation bias.

Melitz (1988) implicitly models such a strategy by enlarging the range of the German authorities' preferences, perhaps to resolve the conflict between the Ministry of Finance and the Bundesbank concerning the desired rate of the real appreciation of the DM. The authorities, in addition to their employment and inflation goals, have also a preferred value for the ratio of traded to non-traded goods in domestic output. This ratio rises with a real depreciation of the home currency and an increase of the price of non-traded goods relative to traded goods' prices. The addition of the traded goods ratio in the loss function of the authorities makes the low-inflation country willing to accept less monetary discipline than in the alternative scenario where this ratio is absent. Again, a *deus ex machina,* in the form of the government having an independent real exchange rate target, is needed to solve (and not altogether successfully) the puzzle.

But by so doing, one weakens the reason for the high-inflation country to participate in the EMS. As Melitz (1988: 67) himself puts it: 'Analysis shows that this welfare benefit now remains as vague as before. While France's traded-goods objective must bring the country closer to zero inflation, it must also lead to a lower ratio of traded goods. Germany contributes to both good and bad effect, the good one on inflation and the bad one on competitiveness.' More simply, the very reason for raising the FRG's incentive to be part of the EMS lowers that of the high-inflation country. Furthermore, the traded-goods objective raises doubts about the sustainability of the EMS. If the FRG's incentive to join the system lies in a permanent real devaluation of the DM, the system would produce permanent trade imbalances among the members and, hence, not be sustainable. As markets realize this, speculative attacks on the EMS parities would follow (Wyplosz 1986). The traded-goods objective therefore does little to explain the lasting existence of the EMS.[1]

A second objection is, why would the German federal government find it easier to weaken the Bundesbank's independence through the EMS rather than by proposing a change in the law?[2] It should be kept in mind that the Bundesbank – albeit a reluctant EMS player – retains full independence as to the size of exchange interventions and the degree to which these are sterilized. In sum, the conflict-of-interest view cannot reconcile the alleged aims of the government to be more inflation prone than those of the Bundesbank with the independence accorded to the central bank with respect to the management of interventions.

The third explanation underlying German interest in the EMS has to do with the Bundesbank itself accepting a higher inflation rate, implied by the EMS, in exchange for greater financial integration. Historically, the FRG has borne the brunt of speculative capital flows originating in the dollar area (Giavazzi and Pagano 1985). Under the EMS speculative capital flows would be more evenly distributed among European countries. The difficulty with this hypothesis is that the FRG benefits from financial integration and not from an exchange rate arrangement that permits France and Italy to maintain pervasive capital controls.

To sum up, the arguments in support of German dominance in the EMS are weak or, at best, based on *ad hoc* theorizing. This conclusion, by itself, cannot settle the issue. The asymmetric view of the EMS is so entrenched that it needs to be tested in some detail before it can be dismissed. This we do in section 3 in two alternative ways: first by considering the interdependence of short-term domestic interest rates and, subsequently, the interdependence of the growth of monetary bases.

3. A test of German dominance

Empirically, the claim of German dominance in the EMS seems to be based primarily on the reduction and convergence of inflation rates in the EMS since 1979. This evidence, presented in Table 5.2, appears to prove the point quite clearly. Average inflation rates in the EMS, measured in terms of the consumption price index (CPI), peaked in 1980 at 11.6 per cent, and declined from then on steadily to 2.2 per cent in 1987. At the same time, the standard deviation of inflation rates among the members fell from 6.2 to 1.9 per cent, a first indication of convergence. Since the German rate of inflation was always at the lower end of the group's inflation rates, this evidence has been interpreted as showing that EMS inflation rates were pulled closer to the German rate. Supporters of GDH have concluded that the Bundesbank must be the price leader of the system.

On a closer look, however, the data are less convincing. The lower part of Table 5.2 shows the rates of inflation for a group of non-EMS countries in the Organization for Economic Cooperation and Development (OECD) during the same period. Their inflation performance was similar to that of the EMS in the 1970s and the 1980s (Ungerer *et al.* 1986; Fratianni 1988). Average inflation in this group peaked in 1980, too, and declined from then on to about 3 per cent in 1987. As in the EMS, there is a notable convergence of inflation rates at the low level: the standard deviation of inflation rates declined from 5.1 to 2.1 per cent. Disinflation and convergence, thus, is by no means a special characteristic of the EMS. Dornbusch (1989) and Fratianni and von Hagen (1990b) show that EMS membership has not yielded a lower cost of disinflation in comparison to other countries either.

TABLE 5.2 CPI inflation rates: EMS and non-EMS countries (%)

	1977	1978	1979	1980	1981	1982	1983	1984	1985	1986	1987	1988
EMS												
Belgium	7.1	4.5	4.5	6.6	7.6	8.7	7.7	6.3	4.9	1.3	1.5	1.2
Denmark	11.1	10.1	9.6	12.3	11.7	10.1	6.9	6.3	4.7	3.6	4.0	4.6
France	9.4	9.1	10.7	13.8	13.4	11.8	9.6	7.4	5.8	2.5	3.3	2.7
FRG	3.7	2.7	4.1	5.4	6.3	5.3	3.3	2.4	2.2	–0.2	0.2	1.2
Ireland	13.6	7.6	13.2	18.2	20.4	17.1	10.5	8.6	5.4	3.8	3.1	2.2
Italy	17.0	12.1	14.8	21.2	17.8	16.5	14.7	10.8	9.2	5.9	4.7	—
Netherlands	6.5	4.2	4.2	6.5	6.7	5.9	2.8	3.3	2.2	0.1	0.0	0.8
Average	8.8	5.9	8.5	11.6	11.2	10.0	7.9	6.0	4.9	2.6	2.2	
Standard deviation	4.9	5.3	4.4	6.2	4.6	4.4	4.4	3.2	2.7	1.7	1.9	
Non-EMS												
Australia	12.3	7.9	9.1	10.1	9.7	11.1	10.1	4.5	6.7	8.7	8.6	7.2
Austria	5.5	3.6	3.7	6.4	6.8	5.4	3.3	5.7	3.2	1.7	1.4	1.9
Canada	8.0	9.0	9.1	10.2	12.4	10.8	5.8	4.3	4.0	4.1	4.4	4.0
Finland	12.7	7.8	7.5	11.6	12.0	9.3	8.4	7.1	5.9	2.9	4.1	—
Greece	30.5	44.1	45.5	58.5	50.6	49.1	86.1	30.8	32.0	23.0	16.4	—
Japan	8.0	3.8	3.6	8.0	4.9	2.6	1.8	2.3	2.0	0.6	0.0	0.7
Switzerland	1.3	1.1	3.6	4.0	6.5	5.7	3.0	2.9	3.4	0.7	1.4	1.9
UK	15.8	8.3	13.4	18.0	11.9	8.6	4.6	5.0	6.1	3.4	4.2	4.9
USA	6.5	7.6	11.3	13.5	10.4	6.2	3.2	4.3	3.6	2.0	3.6	4.0
Average	7.7	7.0	9.6	12.43	9.7	6.4	3.9	4.2	3.8	2.3	3.2	
Standard deviation	4.1	3.7	4.7	5.1	4.1	4.2	7.2	2.3	2.7	2.3	2.1	
Average without USA	9.3	6.2	7.3	10.9	8.7	6.7	4.8	4.1	3.6	2.7	2.7	
Standard deviation	6.0	9.9	6.5	7.7	6.2	6.4	11.0	3.5	4.6	3.5	3.6	

Source: IMF, *International Financial Statistics*; averages and standard deviations are weighted with the following 1982 real GNP-based weights. EMS: Belgium 4.55, Denmark 2.97, France 28.84, FRG 34.42, Ireland 0.99, Italy 21.07, Netherlands 7.22. Non-EMS: Australia 3.08, Austria 1.23, Canada 5.61, Finland 0.94, Greece 0.71, Japan 20.03, Switzerland 1.79, UK 8.98, USA 57.63.

There are at least two alternative interpretations of the data in Table 5.2 that give credit to neither GDH nor to the EMS. One is that all industrial countries, whether or not in the EMS, have responded to common external shocks and constraints during the 1980s that facilitated disinflation, such as the tightening of US monetary policy in the early years of the decade, and the decline in oil prices. The other is that policy-makers inside and outside the EMS, dissatisfied with the stagflationary consequences of active demand management policies pursued in the 1970s, adopted more disinflationary policies in the 1980s (Chouraqui and Price 1984). Both alternative hypotheses have the same implication for the inflation performance of the EMS: they predict that inflation rates decline and converge at the lower level. They are therefore observationally equivalent to the credibility argument and, in particular, to GDH with respect to the data presented in Table 5.10. This implies that it is impossible to infer or test GDH empirically on the basis of the inflation performance of the EMS.

TESTABLE IMPLICATIONS OF GERMAN DOMINANCE IN THE EMS

In view of this observational equivalence, we propose to test GDH empirically by focusing on monetary policy actions rather than inflation rates which reflect the outcomes of monetary policy actions. Our test is based on the premise that GDH implies a specific structure of central banks' 'reaction functions' in the EMS. Let DY be the 7×1 vector of variables summarizing all the central banks' actions in the EMS, DX a matrix representing changes in domestic variables believed to influence the behaviour of the monetary authorities, and DW the 7×1 vector representing changes in 'world' variables also believed to influence the EMS countries' monetary authorities. The latter can be modelled as a system of linear dynamic equations:

$$A(\mathrm{L})DY_t = b + B(\mathrm{L})DX_t + C(\mathrm{L})DW_t + e_t, \qquad [12]$$

where $A(\mathrm{L})$, $B(\mathrm{L})$ and $C(\mathrm{L})$ are polynomial matrices in the lag operator L, b is a fixed intercept vector; and e_t is a vector of residuals with properties:

$$E(e_i) = 0,\ E(e_i^2) = \sigma_{ii},\ i = country\ 1, \ldots, 7,$$
$$E(e_t\, e'_t) = diag(\sigma_{ii}) \text{ for } i = 1, \ldots, 7 \text{ and } E(e_t\, e'_{t*}) = 0 \text{ for } t \neq t*.$$

Furthermore, the leading coefficient of $a_{ii}(\mathrm{L})$ is set equal to unity. These restrictions force the entire set of interactions among EMS monetary policies to take place within the matrix $A(\mathrm{L})$. The test of German dominance, consequently, focuses to a large extent on the properties of this matrix.[3]

FOUR HYPOTHESES

German dominance consists of four separate hypotheses: world insularity, EMS insularity, independence from German policy and German policy independence. Let us see what the four hypotheses imply individually and jointly. First, German dominance implies that other EMS countries do not react directly to monetary policies occurring outside the EMS. The world at large can influence other EMS countries only through its impact on German monetary policy. Defining country 1 as the FRG, world insularity can be stated as:[4]

H1: World insularity $c_i = 0,\ i = 2, \ldots, 7$.

A rejection of H1 signifies that monetary policies in other EMS countries are influenced directly by what goes on outside the EMS, over and beyond what is implied by the German rule.

Second, German dominance implies that each EMS country reacts only to German and not to other members' policies:

H2: EMS insularity $a_{ij} = 0,\ i \neq j,\ i, j = 2, \ldots, 7$.

A rejection of H2 signifies that EMS countries interact independently with one another and do not exclusively follow the German rule.

Third, German dominance implies that monetary policy in a member country must depend critically on German policy and we must *reject*:

H3: independence from the FRG $a_{i1} = 0,\ i = 2, \ldots, 7$.

Fourth, German dominance implies that the FRG itself is not influenced by the monetary policy actions taken by other members:

H4: German policy independence $a_{1i} = 0,\ i = 2, \ldots, 7$.

THE CHOICE OF POLICY VARIABLES

Central banks in the EMS commonly express and assess their short-run actions in terms of the resulting changes in domestic money market interest rates. On a weekly and monthly frequency, money market interest rates embed a high degree of policy exogeneity. Thus money market interest rates are appropriate variables to represent all monetary policy actions in the short term. Beyond this horizon, changes in interest rates incorporate the endogenous response resulting from changes in economic activity and inflation rates. Over the medium term – say a quarter – the growth rate of the monetary base is a more appropriate policy variable. We shall test [12] using both monthly changes in interest rates and quarterly percentage changes in the monetary base.

There are differences in the specification of [12] depending on the choice of the policy variable. These differences are imposed by data availability and the time series properties of the left-hand-side variables. In the interest rate version of [12], *DX* consists of domestic inflation rates – measured in terms of CPI – and growth rate of output – measured in terms of the index of industrial production. Changes in the US money market rate of interest represent policy actions outside the EMS.[5] To reduce the number of free parameters in the system, the following additional restriction is imposed on $A(L)$:

$$\Phi_j a_{ij} = \Phi_k a_{ik} \; i \neq k, j; \quad j, \; k = 4, \ldots, 7; \quad i = 1, \ldots, 7, \qquad [13],$$

where Φ_j are country j's share in regional gross national product (GNP) and the group of countries 4, . . ., 7 consists of Belgium, the Netherlands, Ireland and Denmark. Condition [13] states that in the equations for the FRG, France and Italy we use a weighted average of the interest rates of these four countries, rather than each interest rate individually. Within that group, we use a weighted sum of the remaining three countries. The German, French and Italian interest rates are left unrestricted.

In the monetary base version of [12], *DX* consists of a trend, seasonal dummies and government budget deficits as a proportion of the lagged monetary base; *DW* consists of a weighted average of the monetary base growth of the USA, the UK, Canada and Japan.[6] Here as well, we reduce the number of free parameters in the system by imposing the following additional restriction on *A*(L):

$$\Phi_j a_{ij} = \Phi_k a_{ik} \; i \neq k, j; \quad j, k = 2, \ldots, 7; \quad i = 1, \ldots, 7. \qquad [14]$$

Condition [14] restricts the off-diagonal polynomials of the matrix *A*(L) so that the FRG reacts to a weighted average of the monetary base growth of the other six countries, whereas each of the six countries reacts to the FRG and a weighted average of the remaining five countries.

STRONG AND WEAK FORMS OF GERMAN DOMINANCE

We have stated German dominance in such a way as not to allow any short-run deviation from the path prescribed by Bundesbank policy. We call this the strong form of the hypothesis. A less restrictive, and for that matter a more realistic view of German dominance, is to allow short-run deviations from the Bundesbank rule, but not long-run deviations. The weak form of German dominance can be formally written as

$$\begin{array}{ll} \text{H1W} \; g(c_i) = 0, & i = 2, \ldots, 7, \\ \text{H2W} \; g(a_{ij}) = 0, & i \neq j, \; i, j = 2, \ldots, 7, \\ \text{H3W} \; g(a_{i1}) = 0, & i = 2, \ldots, 7 \\ \text{H4W} \; g(a_{1i}) = 0, & i = 2, \ldots, 7. \end{array} \qquad [15]$$

where g(·) defines the sum of all coefficients of the lag polynomial c_i(L) or a_{ij}(L).

EMPIRICAL FINDINGS

Our empirical strategy was first to estimate a 'broad' specification – allowing for several lags – and later to eliminate variables that had contributed 'little' to the explanatory power of the model. The selection process had to satisfy the twin criteria that the eliminated variable would neither lower the information value of the structure, as measured by the Akaike AIC statistic, nor generate serial correlation. The shrunken version of the model was then estimated with 3SLS and used for testing GDH.

All tests were conducted as *F*-tests, imposing the relevant restrictions on the entire system. For hypotheses H1–H3 the restrictions were imposed both at the country level – that is, leaving the other equations of the system unaltered – and at the system level, that is, restricting all six equations jointly. The interest rate results are presented in Table 5.3 and those for the monetary base in Table 5.4. Table 5.3 reports findings for the period 1983.4–1988.4[7]. To save space we are leaving out the results of the earlier period, which are not substantively different from those of Table 5.3. Table 5.4, instead, refers to the longer sample period 1979.11–1988.11.

Consider Table 5.3, first. Independence from German policy is rejected for all countries except Italy and Denmark, and for the EMS system as a whole. This would suggest that Bundesbank actions influence other member countries. But the latter also respond to each other and to US interest rates. In other words, the hypo-

TABLE 5.3 Test of German dominance: monthly onshore interest rates. Period: 1983.4–1988.4

	Strong form				Weak form			
	H1	H2	H3	H4	H1	H2	H3	H4
FRG	—	—	—	4.31**	0.38	—	—	3.03*
				(8)				(03)
Belgium	0.99	2.58**	4.41**	—	1.31	2.33	5.47**	—
	(2)	(8)	(3)		(1)	(3)	(1)	
Denmark	0.63	2.24*	1.12	—	0.59	2.61*	1.10	—
	(2)	(6)	(3)		(1)	(3)	(1)	
France	7.42**	3.70*	7.92**	—	0.74	0.20	20.4**	—
	(2)	(2)	(4)		(1)	(1)	(1)	
Ireland	3.94**	5.94**	4.26**	—	1.53	4.89**	0.63	—
	(3)	(7)	(3)		(1)	(3)	(1)	
Italy	2.44*	4.48**	2.18	—	6.51**	8.61**	0.12	—
	(4)	(4)	(3)		(1)	(2)	(1)	
Netherlands	4.97**	4.78**	5.04**	—	1.23	1.52	13.47**	—
	(3)	(8)	(3)		(1)	(1)	(1)	
EMS	3.24**	3.94**	4.39**	—	2.06	3.32**	7.00**	—
	(14)	(35)	(19)		(6)	(15)	(6)	

Note: H1 refers to world insularity; H2 to EMS insularity; H3 to independence from German policy; H4 to German policy independence. Entries are values of the *F*-tests based on 3SLS estimates. Numbers in parentheses are numerator degrees of freedom. Denominator degrees of freedom are 612 for all tests.

** Significance at the 1% level.
* Significance at the 5% level.

TABLE 5.4 Test of German dominance: quarterly percentage changes of the monetary base. Period: 1979.11–1988.11

	Strong form				Weak form			
	H1	H2	H3	H4	H1	H2	H3	H4
FRG	—	—	—	2.9*	—	—	—	3.50
				(2)				(1)
Belgium	0.90	3.1*	0.90	—	0.20	6.2*	0.00	—
	(2)	(2)	(5)		(1)	(1)	(1)	
Denmark	12.4**	0.30	0.70	—	2.60	0.60	1.00	—
	(2)	(2)	(5)		(1)	(1)	(1)	
France	12.1**	0.20	3.4**	—	12.1**	0.30	0.00	—
	(2)	(2)	(5)	—	(1)	(1)	(1)	
Ireland	6.4**	2.8	4.9**		9.7**	2.10	4.0*	—
	(3)	(2)	(5)		(1)	(1)	(1)	
Italy	6.88**	9.3**	9.7**	—	4.9*	20.7**	19.5**	—
	(2)	(3)	(5)		(1)	(1)	(1)	
Netherlands	6.5**	3.0*	2.6*	—	12.9**	5.9*	1.10	—
	(3)	(2)	(5)		(1)	(1)	(1)	
EMS	8.7**	3.9**	4.7**	—	7.1**	5.9**	5.0**	—
	(13)	(13)	(30)		(6)	(6)	(6)	

Note: H1 refers to world insularity; H2 to EMS insularity; H3 to independence from German policy; H4 to German policy independence. Entries are values of the F-tests based on 3SLS estimates. Numbers in parentheses are numerator degrees of freedom. Denominator degrees of freedom are 174 for all tests.

* significance at the 5% level.
** significance at the 1% level.

theses of world and EMS insularity are rejected. The Bundesbank itself reacts to the actions taken by other EMS central banks. Clearly, the strong version of German dominance is rejected. The weak form of German dominance stands up better than the strong form. Belgian, Dutch and French monetary policies react to Bundesbank actions, but not to actions taken by other EMS countries and the USA.[8] Italy, on the other hand, behaves in the opposite way: it appears independent from the FRG but not from other member countries and the USA. As to the FRG, its interest rates still respond to interest rate changes elsewhere in the EMS.

What emerges from Table 5.3 is a pattern not at all consistent with the view of the FRG dominating monetary policy-making in the EMS. The FRG, to be sure, is a significant player, but so are other central banks, particularly the Banque de France and the Banca d'Italia. More to the point, monetary policy in the EMS is interactive and not hierarchical. There is another aspect of the evidence that needs to be highlighted. According to the weak form of German dominance, only Italy responds to US interest rates; the hypothesis of world insularity for the entire system cannot be rejected. By itself, this finding could be interpreted as supporting German leadership in preventing other countries from reacting independently to interest rate movements outside the EMS. However, the fact that German independence and EMS insularity for some countries are rejected shows the limits of this interpretation.

Let us now move to Table 5.4 where we present the evidence from quarterly percentage changes in the monetary base. The results for testing the strong form of the hypothesis of Table 5.4 are qualitatively similar to those of Table 5.3. According to the results of testing the weak form of GDH in Table 5.4, the FRG does not react to other EMS countries. In contrast, the other members interact with one another and respond to both German and outside world policy actions. This is consistent with the view that the Bundesbank pursues an independent monetary policy in the longer run. But German policy independence in the EMS does not prevent other member countries from interacting independently with one another and reacting to the rest of the world. Hence, one conclusion suggested by Table 5.4 is that the FRG carries an independent monetary policy but does not exert leadership. From our perspective, Table 5.4 confirms the findings emerging from the short-run orientation of the interest rate data: monetary policy within the EMS is interactive rather than hierarchical.[9]

OTHER EVIDENCE ON GERMAN DOMINANCE

De Grauwe (1988) has recently presented an alternative approach to testing GDH. His test asks whether expected exchange rate devaluations of an EMS member country against the DM affect short-term interest rates only in this country—as GDH would suggest—or both in the FRG and the depreciating country. He finds that the German interest rate does not respond to expected devaluations of the Belgian franc (BF), the French franc (FF), and the Italian lira. However, interest rates in these three countries do not fully adjust either. It follows that capital controls and dual exchange rate systems were critical in isolating domestic money markets from international forces. For the Netherlands, where there are no capital controls, De Grauwe finds that interest rate adjustments are shared between the FRG and that country, a result which is consistent with ours. De Grauwe concludes that his findings provide no support for GDH.

Cohen and Wyplosz (1989) test GDH for a subgroup of EMS countries using vector autoregressions of domestic interest rates and monetary base growth rates. They find that German interest rates and base growth have significant impacts on the same variables in other EMS countries, but the opposite is also true. A similar outcome for base growth is reported by Mastropasqua *et al.* (1988). Again, GDH fails the empirical test.

Another group of authors have looked at central bank interventions in the EMS. Bofinger (1988), Camen (1986), Mastropasqua *et al.* (1988) and Roubini (1988) all estimate sterilization coefficients for the Bundesbank's interventions. The common result is that sterilization is very high, suggesting that the Bundesbank can pursue her own policy objectives independently of the EMS. However, this conclusion is erroneous because it fails to account for important institutional characteristics of Bundesbank monetary policy. Von Hagen (1989) shows that interventions have significant effects on German monetary base growth, but not immediately. Due to the design of the Bundesbank's operating procedure, these effects manifest themselves within a period of four to six months.

A third argument in support of GDH comes from the observation that in a fixed exchange rate system only one country can independently choose the exchange rate *vis-à-vis* an outside currency. German dominance could, therefore, consist of the imposition of a dollar policy on the EMS by the Bundesbank (Sarcinelli 1986). Evidence of the Bundesbank's engagement in the G5 policy coordination efforts since the 1985 Plaza Agreement (Dominguez 1990; von Hagen 1989) would then be interpreted as evidence of German dominance.[10] The crucial question here is: how independent of EMS considerations was the FRG's role in the G5 coordination process. Funabashi's (1988) detailed account of the process stresses three points. First, the Bundesbank was very reluctant to participate in coordinated intervention to stabilize the dollar and was sceptical about its success. Second, the FRG's reservations were predominantly due to EMS considerations, the fear that by manipulating the value of the dollar it would create tensions within the EMS. Finally, the Bundesbank and the Banque de France, which is also part of G5, consulted and informed other EMS member central banks throughout the process. The historical events, thus, give no reason to believe that the Bundesbank unilaterally enforced a dollar policy on the EMS.

Countries of the EMS can always escape from Bundesbank dominance through two safety valves: exchange and capital controls and realignments. The role of capital and exchange controls has been discussed by Giavazzi and Pagano (1985) and Wyplosz (1986). Wyplosz attributes to capital controls a stabilizing property in the sense that they prevent anticipated parity realignments from generating balance-of-payments crises. De Grauwe (1988: 23) corroborates the Wyplosz thesis when he concludes that

> in the offshore markets speculative shocks have usually forced the interest rates of the weak currencies to increase by the full amount of the expected realignments, leaving the DM-interest rate unaffected. The countries of these weak currencies, however, managed to (almost) completely insulate their domestic interest rates from these speculative crises. They achieved this by capital controls and other instruments of market segmentation.

4. Realignments

The importance of realignments is that they permit countries to set their long-run money growth independently of the FRG. The creators of the EMS wanted a flexible system and realignments were intended to be an important instrument of this flexibility. Critical in the analysis is whether or not realignments precipitate balance-of-payments crises. It is clear that the market has anticipated a devaluation of the FF and Italian lira relative to the DM from the very beginning of the EMS. If the devaluation timing were known, a speculative attack could destabilize the EMS by forcing an earlier devaluation of the currency. But if the realignment timing were uncertain, speculative attacks need not arise. Hence, we need to distinguish between timing and size of realignments.

Three issues deserve particular attention:

1. Did German interest rates move less than other interest rates around realignments?
2. Were realignments largely anticipated and, if so, was the size more accurately anticipated than the timing?
3. What were the size and sign of the forecast error of the spot exchange rates?

INTEREST RATE MOVEMENTS

De Grauwe (1988) presents evidence that during periods of speculative crises, identified by large numerical values of the forward premia, French and Italian offshore interest rates have moved more than German interest rates, evidence taken as supporting the asymmetric hypothesis. In the absence of capital and exchange controls the same pattern should hold for onshore interest rates.[11] We do not pursue this line of inquiry but pose instead a different question: suppose that French and Italian offshore interest rates rise more than German offshore interest rates before realignments, would this be evidence in favour of asymmetry? The rise in the differential i–i^* reflects the anticipation of the realignment; after the realignment i and i^* fall, with i falling more than i^*. This pattern of observations would not be consistent with asymmetric behaviour. The rise in the differential i–i^* is momentary and signals an anticipated realignment. In turn, the realignment provides the necessary slack in the system.[12]

Table 5.5 reports averages of weekly observations of the one-month Eurocurrency rates of interest for three separate periods: the four-week period before realignments, the four-week period after realignments and the remainder, which we call between realignments. The sample period goes from 16 March, 1979 to 6 February, 1987, and thus encompasses the 11 realignments that have taken place since the inception of the EMS (see Table 5.10). We distinguish two subperiods, EMS I and EMS II, characterized by relatively high and low inflation rates and interest rates respectively. Furthermore, the two subperiods differ in their response to realignments.

In a general sense interest rates in EMS I tend to rise in the pre-realignment period to then fall in the post-realignment period.[13] Most changes are not statistically significant. However, French interest rate changes are, and rise on average by 600 basis points before realignments. After realignments, however, they fall by 650 basis points. The French–German interest rate differential follows approximately the same pattern and, since the change in German rates is not statistically significant, its movement can be completely attributed to French interest rates.

TABLE 5.5 One-month Eurocurrency interest rates. Period averages % per annum

	Levels			Differentials relative to FRG		
	Between R	R–4	R+4	Between R	R–4	R+4
Period: 16.3.79–18.3.83						
Belgium	12.46	12.93	13.69*	4.23	4.15	4.32
France	14.07	20.15**	13.72*	5.81	11.38**	4.35*
Italy	18.24	19.45	17.55	10.00	10.64	8.20
Netherlands	8.91	9.04	10.19‡	0.65	0.26	0.83
UK	13.21	12.92	13.21	4.95	4.14	3.84
USA	12.73	12.99	13.86‡	4.46	4.21	4.50
FRG	8.27	8.78	9.37			
Period: 25.3.83–9.1.87						
Belgium	9.22	7.92**	8.53	4.18	3.17**	4.11*
France	10.40	9.22*	9.11	5.36	4.47*	4.69
Italy	13.64	11.95**	11.69	8.60	7.21**	7.27
Netherlands	5.77	5.86	5.19**	0.73	1.12**	0.77
UK	9.97	10.54‡	10.09‡	4.93	5.79*	5.67
USA	8.50	6.86**	6.97	3.46	2.12**	2.55
FRG	5.04	4.74*	4.42**			

Source: Harris Bank, Foreign Exchange Weekly Review, various issues.
Note: R–4 signifies the four-week period before realignment; R+4 the four-week period after realignment; between R signifies all other observations.
* statistically significant at the 5% level. (two-tailed t-distribution).
** statistically significant at the 1% level. (two-tailed t-distribution).
‡ statistically significant at the 10% level. (two-tailed t-distribution).

Things change in EMS II: interest rates in the pre- and post-realignment period decline relative to between-realignment periods. This is statistically the case for Belgium, France, Italy, the Netherlands and the FRG.[14] The same holds for differentials with respect to the German interest rate, reflecting a larger decline in non-German interest rates. The evidence seems to suggest a change in the nature and size of the anticipations. Realignments are more orderly and more anticipated in EMS II than in EMS I. The pre-realignment periods of EMS II take the expected realignment by actually reducing the size of the anticipated appreciation of the DM.

ANTICIPATION OF REALIGNMENTS

To stress the distinction between the timing and the size of realignments in the EMS, we can think of exchange rate anticipations in the system as a product of anticipations about the discrete event of realignments and anticipations about exchange rate changes given that a realignment takes place or not. Formally, there are two possible states of the world in each period: state R, where a realignment takes place, and state N, where no realignment occurs. Let $E_t^{\mathrm{R}}S_{t+4}$ and $E_t^{\mathrm{N}}S_{t+4}$ be the expected DM exchange rate of an EMS currency given that R or N occurs, and let $\beta_{t,t+4}$ be the probability perceived at time t of a realignment during the next four weeks. Then, the unconditional expectation, not knowing which state will prevail, of the period $t + 4$ exchange rate is

$$E_tS_{t+4} = (\beta_{t,t+4})E_t^{\mathrm{R}}S_{t+4} + (1 - \beta_{t,t+4})E_t^{\mathrm{N}}S_{t+4}. \qquad [16]$$

Assuming that open interest rate parity holds in the Eurocurrency markets and that the assets traded are perceived to be perfect substitutes, we can solve interest rate differentials for the expected exchange rate:

$$E_tS_{t+4} = i_t - i_t^* + S_t \qquad [17]$$

Taking first differences yields

$$E_tS_{t+4} - E_{t-1}S_{t+3} = \Delta i_t - \Delta i_t^* + \Delta S_t. \qquad [18]$$

Table 5.6 reports these changes in expectations before and between realignments. For France and Italy, the expected exchange rate rises significantly before a realignment, indicating that the market correctly anticipates the forthcoming event. In contrast, changes in expected exchange rates are close to zero between realignments. The size of the revision of expectations is larger in the second subperiod.

We inquire further into the time pattern of expectations with the aid of transfer functions. The dependent variable is changes in expectations, the left-hand-side variable of [18], and the transfer inputs are the pre-alignment dummy R–4 and the interaction dummy (R–4)*EMS II, to check whether or not expectation revisions were different in the two subperiods. Table 5.7 reports the basic statistics. The moving-average representation can be easily justified in terms of the construction itself of the dependent variable which implies a three-week overlapping period. The large body of evidence that changes in the exchange rate follow a random walk argues against an autoregressive component. It is true for all countries, except for Italy, where an AR 1 emerges very significantly.

TABLE 5.6: Weekly changes of the one-month expected DM exchange rate. Period averages % per annum

	Between R	R–4
Period: 16.3.79–18.3.83		
Belgium	1.42	0.96
France	1.15	3.98‡
Italy	1.24	4.87*
Netherlands	–0.03	1.26
UK	–0.82	9.40**
USA	–2.15	2.89
Period: 25.3.83–9.1.87		
Belgium	0.15	1.65
France	0.27	4.30**
Italy	0.56	5.49**
Netherlands	0.17	–0.69
UK	1.19	1.43
USA	0.97	7.76

Source: Harris Bank, *Foreign Exchange Weekly Review*.
Note: R–4 signifies the four-week period before realignment; R+4 the four-week period after realignment; between R signifies all other observations.
[‡] statistically significant at 10% level, (two-tailed *t*-distribution)
[*] statistically significant at 5% level (two-tailed *t*-distribution)
[**] statistically significant at 1% level (two-tailed *t*-distribution)

The results of Table 5.7 confirm with more precision the message contained in Table 5.6. For example, the average annual expected devaluation of the FF–DM exchange rate was 0.66 percentage points between realignments and 4.58 percentage points before realignments. The structure of expectations did not change from EMS I to EMS II. This characterization holds, not only for France, but for all countries covered in Table 5.7.[15]

In so far as France and Italy are concerned, it appears as if the markets have revised significantly the size of the depreciation before realignment. Indeed, for these two countries the size of the R–4 coefficient of Table 5.7 multiplied by 11 – the number of realignments – is not statistically different from the cumulative bilateral parity changes (see Table 5.10). In sum, the realignments were largely anticipated, with the bulk of the anticipations shaped in the four weeks before realignments. This pattern did not change between EMS I and EMS II.

TABLE 5.7 Transfer functions. Dependent variable = weekly changes of the 1-month expected DM exchange rage (% per annum)

	Constant	R–4 dummy	(R–4) *EMS II interaction dummy	AR1	MA1	MA2	MA3	SEE	DW	Q(12)
Period: 16.3.79 – 6.2.87										
Belgium	0.78	0.03	0.84		–0.10	–0.02	0.12	6.43	2.00	11.09
	[2.33]	[0.02]	[0.44]		[–2.01]	[–0.37]	[2.35]			
France	0.66	3.92	–0.12		–0.04	–0.08	–0.06	6.18	1.99	14.40
	[2.47]	[3.53]	[–0.07]		[–0.79]	[–1.70]	[–1.28]			
Italy	0.92	4.57	–0.35	0.73	–0.81			6.44	1.97	7.29
	[3.58]	[3.86]	[–0.19]	[5.93]	[–7.48]					
Netherlands	0.10	0.99	–1.91		–0.45	0.08	–0.11	5.05	2.01	20.32
	[0.67]	[1.49]	[–1.85]		[–9.10]	[1.56]	[–2.27]			
UK	0.21	9.21	–8.43		0.07	0.09	–0.01	15.55	2.00	21.38
	[0.23]	[2.75]	[–1.57]		[1.43]	[1.88]	[–0.10]			
USA	–0.59	3.47	5.49		0.05	–0.02	–0.04	20.25	2.00	13.91
	[–0.57]	[0.86]	[0.85]		[0.96]	[–0.49]	[–0.80]			

Source: Harris Bank, *Foreign Exchange Weekly Review*.
Note: R–4 signifies the four-week period before realignment; EMS II is a dummy equal to one for the period 25.3.83–6.2.87 and zero otherwise. *Q*(12) is the Ljung-box *Q*-Statistic which is treated as a chi-square with 12 degrees of freedom. The levels of significance are 14.85 (25%), 18.55 (10%), 21 (5%) and 23.3 (2.5%).

FORECAST ERROR OF THE EXCHANGE RATE

Given the assumptions above, the unconditional exchange rate expectation error can be computed from the data as

$$\begin{aligned} S_{t+4} - E_t S_{t+4} &= S_{t+4} - (i_t - i_t^* + S_t) \\ &= S_{t+4} - E^{R} S_{t+4} - (1 - \beta_{t,t+4})\, E_t^{N} S_{t+4} - E_t^{R} S_{t+4}) \\ &= S_{t+4} - E_t^{N} S_{t+4} + \beta_{t,t+4}\, (E_t^{N} S_{t+4} - E_t^{R} S_{t+4}). \end{aligned} \quad [19]$$

It is plausible to assume that $E_t^{N} s_{t+4} < E^{R} S_{t+4}$, if the realignment entails a devaluation of the currency. Assume that the conditional forecasts $E_t^{R} S_{t+4}$ and $E_t^{N} S_{t+4}$ are unbiased, and suppose that we collect data for the expectation error around realignments, so that the *ex post* true state of the world was R. Then the second line of equation [19] tells us that the average unconditional forecast error should be positive unless $\beta_{t,t+4} = 1$. Conversely, the average forecast error between realignments should be negative unless $\beta_{t,t+4} = 0$. As long as there is uncertainty about the timing of the realignment, the average unconditional forecast error will not be zero, even though the average conditional forecast errors are.

Table 5.8 reports the average unconditional forecast errors for the four EMS currencies and two non-EMS currencies. The average error is negative between realignments and positive before realignments. The switch in sign is statistically significant for the BF, the FF and the Italian lira in EMS I and the latter two in EMS II. The difference in the absolute values of the two columns of Table 5.8 is consistent with the interpretation that between realignments the probability of a realignment during the next four weeks is very small, approaching zero. In contrast, around realignments the probability of realignment rises but is still less than unity. Thus, shortly before realignments the timing remains substantially uncertain.

TABLE 5.8: Four-week forecast error of exchange rate changes; period averages, % per annum

	Between R	R–4
Period: 16.3.79–18.3.83		
Belgium	–1.72	18.98**
France	–2.93	16.65**
Italy	–6.08	13.36**
Netherlands	0.29	0.49
UK	–3.55	–2.30
USA	–10.82	–7.39
Period: 25.3.83–9.1.87		
Belgium	–2.98	–4.68
France	–3.80	10.54**
Italy	–5.45	10.77**
Netherlands	–0.49	–2.90
UK	–0.78	26.16**
USA	–0.81	51.86**

Source: Harris Bank, *Foreign Exchange Weekly Review*.
Note: R–4 signifies the four-week period before realignment; R+4 the four-week period after realignment; between R signifies all other observations.
[*] statistically significant at 5% level (two-tailed *t*-distribution)
[**] statistically significant at 1% level (two-tailed *t*-distribution)

TABLE 5.9 Transfer functions. Dependent variable = forecast error of exchange rate changes (% per annum)

	Constant	R–4 dummy	EMS II	(R–4) * EMS II Interaction dummy	AR1	MA1	MA2	MA3	SEE	DW	$Q(12)$
Period: 16.3.79–6.2.87											
Belgium	–2.44	20.82	0.26	–28.72		0.86	0.79	0.75	6.46	2.07	13.04
	[–1.68]	[8.90]	[0.13]	[–7.42]		[25.97]	[21.46]	[22.69]			
France	–4.15	18.80	2.59	–15.55		0.92	0.65	0.60	6.78	2.06	15.86
	[–2.88]	[7.93]	[1.26]	[–3.97]		[23.08]	[12.36]	[14.74]			
Italy	–7.38	17.78	2.46	–6.22		0.23	0.20	0.13	17.44	2.00	1.80
	[–3.63]	[3.94]	[0.87]	[–0.85]		[4.49]	[3.88]	[2.48]			
Netherlands	0.11	–1.63	–0.49	–0.89	–0.39	0.96	0.93	0.82	5.41	2.03	9.07
	[0.12]	[–0.85]	[–0.36]	[–0.28]	[–6.45]	[26.28]	[29.51]	[27.15]			
UK	–7.95	–7.81	5.93	14.60	0.13	0.99	0.96	0.96	16.13	2.06	19.59
	[–2.14]	[–1.23]	[1.33]	[1.44]	[2.62]	[67.39]	[53.33]	[66.36]			
USA	–5.24	–5.35	5.75	25.89		0.98	1.03	1.02	19.94	1.89	9.34
	[–2.30]	[–0.67]	[1.08]	[1.98]		[6134]	[104.23	[109.21			

Source: Harris Bank, *Foreign Exchange Weekly Review.*

Note: R–4 signifies the four-week period before realignment; EMS II is a dummy equal to one for the period 25.3.83–6.2.87 and zero otherwise. $Q(12)$ is the Ljung box Q-statistic which is treated as a chi-square with 12 degrees of freedom. The levels of significance are 14.85 (25%), 18.55 (10%), 21 (5%) and 23.3 (2.5%).

Table 5.9 looks in more detail at the structure and significance of the forecast error by fitting transfer functions, using as inputs three dummy variables: R–4, EMS II and its interaction. Again, as in the case of Table 5.7, the construction of the dependent variable implies serial correlation, which we have captured with a third-order, moving-average process. An autoregressive component emerged in the Dutch and British cases. The results of Table 5.9 corroborate the 'first impressions' of Table 5.8. Taking France as an example, the FF experienced an actual average depreciation of 4 percentage points which is lower than the expected value. This entire sample negative forecast error stands in sharp contrast to a positive forecast error of approximately 14 percentage points in the pre-realignment period of EMS I and a negative forecast error of approximately 1 percentage point in the pre-realignment period of EMS II. Belgium behaves qualitatively like France. Italy behaves quantitatively like France only for EMS I. The pre-realignment average forecast error of the lira in EMS II remains approximately 10 percentage points. The guilder–DM exchange rate shows a zero average forecast error. The £–DM and the US$–DM rates suffer from a roughly constant negative average forecast error – roughly because there is some evidence of a positive error in the pre-realignment period of EMS II.

TABLE 5.10: Parity realignments in the EMS

Date	DM	HFL	FF	BF	Lira	DKR	IR£
24.9.79	2					–2.9	
30.11.79						–4.8	
23.3.81					–6		
5.10.81	5.5	5.5	–3		–3		
22.2.82				–8.5		–3	
14.6.82	4.25	4.25	–5.75		–2.75		
EMS I	11.75	9.75	–8.75	–8.5	–11.8	–10.7	0
21.3.83	5.5	3.5	–2.5	1.5	–2.5	2.5	–3.5
22.7.85	2	2	2	2	–6	2	2
7.4.86	3	3	–3	1		1	
4.8.86							–8
12.1.87	3	3		2			
EMS II	13.5	11.5	–3.5	6.5	–8.5	5.5	–9.5
Total	25.25	21.25	–12.3	–2	–20.3	–5.2	–9.5

The general picture that emerges from Tables 5.8 and 5.9 is that EMS currencies behave differently from non-EMS currencies. Realignments are events producing drastic changes in expectations and prediction errors. The change in average prediction errors affects Belgium, France and Italy. The Netherlands, the UK and the USA are largely unaffected. Our interpretation is that realignments, even though partly anticipated by the market, are discrete events bound to generate noise.

Revision of the realignment probability

Rewrite [18] as

$$\begin{aligned} E_tS_{t+4} - E_{t-1}S_{t+3} = {} & E_t^{\mathrm{N}}S_{t+4} - E_{t-1}^{\mathrm{N}}S_{t+3} \\ & + \beta_{t-1}\,(E_t^{\mathrm{R}}S_{t+4} - E_{t-1}^{\mathrm{R}}S_{t+3} - E_t^{\mathrm{N}}S_{t+4} + E_{t-1}^{\mathrm{N}}S_{t+4}) \\ & + (\beta_t - \beta_{t-1})\,(E_t^{\mathrm{R}}S_{t+4} - E_t^{\mathrm{N}}S_{t+4}). \end{aligned} \quad [20]$$

This states that the revision of expectations consists of two components: revisions of expected exchange rates for each possible state, R or N, and revisions of the probability of a realignment. Assume that, shortly before realignments, changes in the realignment probability are the dominant source of revisions of exchange rate expectations, i.e. newly arriving information mostly concerns the timing of the next realignment, and not so much the exchange rate level in either state. The revision [20] then is approximately

$$(\beta_t - \beta_{t-1})\,(E_t^{\mathrm{R}} S_{t+4} - E_t^{\mathrm{N}} S_{t+4}).$$

Next, consider the average unconditional forecast error [19]. If the conditional exchange rate forecast of a realignment is unbiased, the average expectation error around realignments is

$$(1 - \beta_t)\,(E_t^{\mathrm{R}} S_{t+4} - E_t^{\mathrm{N}} S_{t+4}).$$

Consequently, the ratio of [20] to [19] is approximately equal to

$$\frac{\beta_{t,t+4} - \beta_{t-1,t+3}}{1 - \beta_{t,t+4}} = \frac{-\Delta(1 - \beta_{t,t+4})}{1 - \beta_{t,t+4}} \qquad [21]$$

Equation [21] yields a measure of how fast markets revise downwards the chance of a non-realignment, or the complement of the average relative change in the realignment probability during the four weeks before a realignment. For France and Italy, the countries showing significant changes in expectations around realignments, the average relative change in the non-realignment probability turns out to be

	EMS I	EMS II
France	–0.24	–0.41
Italy	–0.36	–0.51

Not only the revisions go in the correct direction – i.e. realignments become increasingly likely over the period – but the speeds of revision also rise between EMS I and EMS II. Furthermore, the relative changes are well below unity in absolute value, a result that is consistent with a stable learning process.

5. Summary and conclusions

The dominant interpretation of the EMS is that it is an enlarged DM area. We have challenged this interpretation, both at the theoretical and empirical level. Theoretically, it is hard to justify simultaneously both the interest of the low-inflation FRG in supplying credibility and the high-inflation countries in accepting the discipline implied by a fixed exchange rate commitment. Empirically, we have found no evidence that the FRG has dominated monetary policy-making in the EMS. Of course, the rejection of German dominance does not imply that the system works perfectly symmetrically. There is evidence that the FRG has pursued an independent monetary policy, but that should not be mistaken as German leadership in the EMS.

What is the mechanism through which EMS members can disengage their monetary policies from the restrictive course pursued by the Bundesbank? There are two safety-valves for countries that do not want to adhere to the discipline of the Bundesbank: capital and exchange controls and realignments. Capital and exchange controls shelter domestic from international money and capital markets and manifest themselves in positive differentials between offshore and onshore interest rates. These differentials have become much smaller since 1983, a reflection of the diminished importance of capital and exchange controls. Realignments serve to preserve the member countries' freedom to choose long-run monetary trends independently of the Bundesbank. The existence of these safety valves represents the embodiment of flexibility principle wanted by the creators of the EMS and makes this system operate without being a DM area.

Our evidence is consistent with this flexible view of the EMS. The data suggest that the markets were not caught totally unprepared about the size and the timing of the realignments. At realignments, there were significant changes in interest rates, evidence in support of the hypothesis that realignments did act as a safety-valve.

The uncertain timing of realignments generated non-zero average forecast errors of the exchange rate, where expectations are measured according to open interest rate parity. The sign of the error changes and its size increases dramatically in the four-week period before realignments. While these results suggest that markets learn, the learning is incomplete and obfuscated by the uncertain timing of the realignments. Discrete and sizeable jumps in the exchange rates may provide less information to market participants than continuous changes. The fundamental question of whether the EMS arrangement contributes to the average error by trading off lower short-run variability of the exchange rates for longer run uncertainty remains quite open.

At a more general level, we conclude that the importance of the EMS – and the role of the FRG within the EMS – in the disinflation process of the 1980s has been overstated. The convergence of inflation rates in Europe at the current low levels has more to do with the growing consensus among policy-makers in the region that inflation trends had to be reversed than it has to do with the EMS. But credibility considerations do have a role for the future of the EMS. To the extent that the political cost of monetary activism will be raised by a more formal structure of monetary policy coordination, the strengthening of the EMS proposed by the *Delors Report* (Delors Committee 1989) may be able to lock in the gains for the future, should this consensus disappear.

Notes

1. Jacques Melitz pointed out to us that his model was built with the purpose of highlighting the potential failures of an EMS grounded on traded-on goods objectives.
2. An ordinary law, and not a constitutional law, would be needed to change the autonomy of the Bundesbank.
3. A more detailed explanation of the test can be found in Fratianni and von Hagen (1990a) and von Hagen and Fratianni (1989).
4. We define $a_{ij} = 0$ and $c_i = 0$ to mean $a_{ij}(\mathrm{L}) = 0$ and $c_i\,(\mathrm{L}) = 0$.
5. The data come from the IMF tape of the *International Financial Statistics*. Money market interest rates are measured by line 60b, the index of industrial production by line 66c, the index of consumer prices by line 64. With the exception of domestic output, all data are seasonally unadjusted.
6. The monetary base is measured by line 14 and the budget deficit by line 80 in the *International Financial Statistics*. The weights underlying the construction of the world monetary base are based on GNP: 0.626 for the USA, 0.097 for the UK, 0.06 for Canada and 0.215 for Japan.
7. More precisely, the results are based on estimates from the entire sample, 1979.3–1988.4, but incorporate parameter changes at an assumed break point at 1983.3, where applicable.
8. This should be interpreted loosely. Technically, the evidence on weak dominance for Belgium, the Netherlands and France rejects H3, but fails to reject H1 and H2.
9. There are two notable differences between the results of the weak form of Tables 5.3 and 5.4. The first difference is that we could reject German independence according to the weak form of Table 5.3, whereas the opposite holds for Table 5.4. The second difference has to do with Italy which, contrary to the interest rate results, is the only country whose monetary base path has been linked to the FRG. The strong reaction of H3 for the system is attributable entirely to the Italian rejection. Testing H3 jointly for the other five countries yields an F–statistic of 1.8, a value below the 10 per cent significance level. Such differences need not be contradictory, as the findings of Table 5.3 have a more short-term orientation and pertain to the recent experience of the EMS, whereas the findings of Table 5.4 have a longer-term orientation and encompass the entire EMS experience.
10. This interpretation was suggested to us by Allen Meltzer.
11. Capital and exchange controls affect the difference between offshore and onshore interest rates, difference which rises around realignment. In the first part of the EMS – what we call EMS I – the differentials were quantitatively more important than in the latter part, a reflection of the diminished importance of exchange and capital controls. See on this point Radaelli (1989) who questions the weight usually assigned to capital controls on the stability of exchange rates on the ground that such controls distort trade flows and hence influence the pattern of trade more than exchange rate gyrations.

12. It is interesting to note that in Melitz (1988) the frequency of realignments has the opposite interpretation. Infrequent realignments signal weak rather than strong price discipline because they lead to more accommodation of inflation differentials.

13. The significance tests indicated in Tables 5.5, 5.6 and 5.8 refer to the following t–statistic:

$$t = (x_1 - x_2)/[\mathrm{std}(1/n_1 + 1/n_2)^{1/2}],$$

where std = $[(n_1{*}\mathrm{var}_1 + n_2{*}\mathrm{var}_2)/(n_1 + n_2 - 2)]^{1/2}$, x_1 and x_2 are the sample averages of the second period, var_1 and var_2 the sample variances, and n_1 and n_2 the number of observations.

14. The UK and the USA have been added to Table 5.5 to compare results between EMS and non-EMS countries.

15. We also investigated but rejected the possibility that the level of the expected exchange rate may influence its revision. The potential importance of the level occurs in cases when forecasts that have produced an 'excessively' appreciated currency are likely to be followed by a string of forecasts going in the opposite direction.

REFERENCES

Artus, **P**. (1988) The European Monetary System, exchange rate expectations and the reputation of the authorities, paper presented at the Conference on International Economic Policy Coordination, Aix-en-Provence, 24–25 June 1988.

Barro, **R**. and **Gordon**, **D** (1983) Rules, discretion and reputation in a model of monetary policy, *Journal of Monetary Economics* **12** (July), pp. 101–21.

Begg, D. and **Wyplosz, C.** (1988) Why the EMS? Dynamic games and the equilibrium policy regime, in Bryant, R. C. and Portes, R. (eds) *Global Macroeconomics*, London, Macmillan.

Bofinger, **P.** (1988) Das Europaische Wahrungssystem und die geldpolitische Kooperation in Europa, *Kredit und Kapital*, **21**, pp. 317–45.

Camen, **U**. (1986) FRG monetary policy under external constraints, 1979–84, *Working Paper 21*, CEPS Brussels.

Canzoneri, **M**. and **Gray**, **J. A**. (1985) Monetary policy games and the consequences of non-cooperative behavior, *International Economic Review*, **26**, pp. 547–64.

Canzoneri, **M**. and **Henderson**, **D**. (1988) Is sovereign policymaking bad?, in Brunner, K. and Meltzer, A. H. (eds), Carnegie-Rochester Conference Series on Public Policy, vol. 28, North-Holland, Amsterdam, pp. 93–140

Chouraqui, **J. C.** and **Price, R. W. R.** (1984), Medium-term financial strategy: the co-ordination of fiscal and monetary policies, *OECD Economic Studies*, **2**, 7–49.

Cohen, **D**. and **Wyplosz**, **C**. (1989) The European Monetary Union: an agnostic evaluation, typescript.

Collins, S. (1988) Inflation and the European Monetary System, in Giavazzi F., Micossi S. and Miller M. (eds), *The European Monetary System*, Cambridge, Cambridge University Press.

Committee for the Study of Economic and Monetary Union (*the Delors Committee*) (1989) *Report on Economic and Monetary Union in the European Community*, (*the Delors Report*) (with Collection of Papers), Office for Official Publications of the European Communities, Luxemburg

Dale, R. (1987) Bonn's EMS partners seek larger economic say-so, *International Herald Tribune*, 28 September.

De Grauwe, P. (1988) Is the European Monetary System a DM-zone?, typescript, October.

Dominguez, K. (1990) Market responses to coordinated Central Bank intervention, in Meltzer A. H. and Plossers C. (eds) *Carnegie–Rochester Conference Series on Public Policy*, vol. 32, North-Holland, Amsterdam.

Dornbusch, R. (1989) Credibility, Debt and Unemployment: Ireland's failed stabilization, *Economic Policy*, **8**.

The Economist (1987) No parity of power in the EMS, *Economist* 19 September.

Fischer, S. (1987) International macroeconomic policy coordination, *NBER Working Paper 2244*.

Fratianni, M. (1988) The European Monetary System: how well has it worked? A return to an adjustable-peg arrangement, *Cato Journal*, pp. 477–501.

Fratianni, M. and **von Hagen, J.** (1990a). German dominance in the EMS: the empirical evidence, *Open Economies Review*, January, pp. 67–87.

Fratianni, M. and **von Hagen, J.** (1990b) The European Monetary System ten years after, in Meltzer A. H. and Plossers C. (eds) *Carnegie-Rochester Conference Series on Public Policy,* vol. 32.

Funabashi, Y. (1988) *Managing the Dollar: From the Plaza to the Louvre*. Institute for International Economics, Washington, D.C.

Giavazzi, F. and **Pagano, M.** (1985) Capital controls and the European Monetary System, in *Capital Controls and Foreign Exchange Legislation*, Euromobiliare, Occasional Paper 1, June.

Giavazzi, F. and **Pagano, M.** (1988) The advantage of tying one's hands: EMS discipline and central bank credibility. *European Economic Review* , **32**, pp. 1055–82.

Giavazzi, F. and **Giovannini, A.** (1987) Models of the EMS: is Europe a greater deutschmark area?, in Bryant R. C. and Portes R. (eds.) *Global Macroeconomics*, St. Martin's Press, New York, pp. 237–65.

Giavazzi, F. and **Giovannini, A.** (1988) The role of the exchange-rate regime in a disinflation: empirical evidence on the European Monetary System, in Giavazzi, F., Micossi, S. and Miller, M. (eds) *The European Monetary System*, Cambridge University Press. Cambridge, pp. 85–107.

Giavazzi, F. and **Giovannini, A.** (1989) *Limiting Exchange Rate Flexibility: The European Monetary System*. MIT Press. Cambridge, Mass.

Goodhart, C. (1989) The *Delors Report*: was Lawson's reaction justifiable?, London School of Economics, typescript.

Gros, D. and **Thygesen, N.** (1988) Le SME: performances and perspectives, *Observations et Diagnostics Economiques 24*, Banque de France, pp. 55–80.

Harris Bank (various issues). International money market and foreign exchange rates, *Weekly Review*. Chicago.

International Monetary Fund (various issues) *International Financial Statistics*, Washington, D.C.

Katseli, L. T. (1987) Macroeconomic policy coordination and the domestic base of national economic policies in major european countries, paper presented at the Conference on the Political Economy of International Macroeconomic Policy Coordination, 5–7 November, Andover, Mass.

Kloten, N. (1988) Die Europäische Währungsintegration: Chancen und Risken in *Deutsche Bundesbank Auszüge aus Pressartikely* **81** pp. 1–7

Mastropasqua, C. Micossi, S. and **Rinaldi, R**. (1988) Interventions, sterilization and monetary policy in the EMS countries (1979–1987). In Giavazzi, F., Micossi, S. and Miller, M. (eds), *The European Monetary System*, Cambridge, Cambridge University Press, pp. 252–87.

Melitz, J. (1985) The welfare cost for the European Monetary System, *Journal of International Money and Finance*, **4,** 485–506.

Melitz, J. (1988), Monetary discipline, Germany and the European Monetary System: a synthesis, in Giavazzi, F., Micossi, S. and Miller, M. (eds) *The European Monetary System*, Cambridge University Press, Cambridge, pp. 51–79.

Micossi, S. The intervention and financial mechanisms of the EMS and the role of the ECU, *Banca Nazionale del Lavoro Quarterly Review*, (December), pp. 327–345.

Organization for Economic Cooperation and Development (1988). OECD, *Why Economic Policies Change Course: Eleven Case Studies*, Paris.

Radaelli, G. (1989) Stabilita' dello SME, controlli sui movimenti di capitale e interventi sui mercati di cambi. *CEEP Economia*, N.1, pp. 1–36.

Roubini, N. (1988) Sterilization policies, offsetting capital movements and exchange rate intervention policies in the EMS, PhD dissertation, Harvard University, Ch. 4.

Russo, M. and **Tullio, G**. (1988) Monetary policy coordination within the European Monetary System: is there a rule? In Giavazzi, F., Micossi, S. and Miller, M. (eds) *The European Monetary System*, Cambridge University Press, Cambridge, pp. 41–82.

Sarcinelli, M. (1986) The EMS and the international monetary system: towards greater stability. Banca Nazionale del Lavoro *Quarterly Review* (March), pp. 57–83.

Tsoukalis, L (1987) The political economy of the European Monetary System, paper presented at the Conference on the Political Economy of International Macroeconomic Policy Coordination, November, 5–7. Andover, Mass.

Ungerer, H., Evans, O., Mayer, T. and **Young, P**. (1986) *The European Monetary System: Recent Developments*, December, International Monetary Fund. Washington, D.C.

van Ypersele, J. (1979) Operating Principles and Procedures of the EMS in Trezise, P.M. (ed) *The EMS: its Promise and Prospects*, Brookings, Washington, D.C.

Vaubel, R. (1980) The return to the new EMS, in Brunner, K. and Meltzer, A.H.(eds), *Monetary Institutions and the Policy Process*, Carnegie-Rochester Conference, vol. 13, North-Holland, Amersterdam, pp. 173–221.

von Hagen, J. (1989) Monetary targeting with exchange rate constraints – the Bundesbank in the 1980s, Working Paper, Federal Reserve Bank of St Louis and Italian International Economic Center.

von Hagen, J. and **Fratianni, M**. (1989) German dominance in the EMS: Evidence from interest rates, Working Paper, Federal Reserve Bank of St Louis and Italian International Economic Center.

Wyplosz, C. (1986) Capital controls and balance of payments crises, *Journal of International Money and Finance*, **5**, pp. 167–79
Wyplosz, C. (1988) Monetary policy in France: monetarism or Darwinism ?, *Finanzmarkt und Portfolio Management*, **2**, pp. 56–67.

Comment: Jacques Melitz

There have been recent efforts to correct the possibly exaggerated emphasis on German leadership in the EMS (see, *inter alia*, De Grauwe 1989, Cohen and Wyplosz 1989). But the effort to redress the balance now poses a serious danger of going too far in the opposite direction. I find this danger particularly clear in Fratianni and von Hagen's (F–vH) chapter, as in a previous work of theirs (Fratianni and von Hagen 1989), where they present the thesis of German leadership in the EMS as an extreme and totally untenable position. According to F–vH, this position states that the Germans act totally independently of the rest, even though such German behaviour would be contrary to optimizing principles in the light of the high degree of economic interdependence between the FRG and the others. Further, F–vH posit that the argument of German dominance in the EMS implies that the non-German members of the system completely abandon their monetary independence and let the Bundesbank dictate their monetary policy for them, whereas the record of inflation differentials, realignments and capital controls in the EMS makes this view almost impossible to defend.

The trouble, of course, is that this does not make for very interesting debate. Many live advocates of German leadership, for example, are prone to think that the Germans would have disinflated less if the other members had pursued a more expansionary monetary policy since 1982. Yet F–vH would interpret any evidence in favour of this view as implying more symmetry in the system than the advocates of Geman dominance pretend by mere virtue of the fact that the Germans respond at all to the rest. This is worth remembering, however, even if the FRG may have little to do with a Stackelberg leader in the EMS. A Stackelberg leader responds to the follower but is a leader none the less. Because of this debating strategy, F–vH's challenge to the partisans of an asymmetric interpretation of the EMS seems to me to be more limited than it might have been. I will confine myself to the grounds for this reaction to their chapter.

As a starting-point, it should be observed that F–vH fail to tell us how far they would go in denying asymmetry in the EMS. More specifically, would they oppose the usual modelization of the system as one where the Germans control their money supply in between realignments while the others defend the parities? Indeed the system was not supposed to work this way at all at the outset and the efforts to avoid it by the non-Germans led to the famous indicator of divergence. This same effort by the others reasserted itself recently at the Nyberg meeting (1987) where the Bundesbank was induced to accept some of the burden of intervention within the margins. Would F–vH now wish to argue, in line with these events, that the usual modelization is wrong and the EMS should really be interpreted as a system where the burden of intervention between realignments is essentially shared? I gather that they do not, but only because of discussion at the conference itself, not from reading the paper. Yet considerable importance can properly be assigned to this point, since in any international game where one party controls his money supply and the other participates in fixing the exchange rate, the two will respond differently to many shocks (Giavazzi–Giovannini 1984).

The most sensitive issue as regards the question of German leadership and the presence of asymmetry in the EMS is whether the system has promoted monetary discipline outside of the FRG while benefiting the FRG nevertheless. F–vH take issue with this view. Let me explain why I do not find them very convincing.

The argument that the EMS has promoted monetary discipline has always centred on French and Italian behaviour. There has never been any effort to argue that Switzerland or Austria, for example, would have displayed greater monetary discipline if they had joined the system. Yet many observers view the international evidence of a general disinflationary tendency in the OECD in the 1980s as casting serious doubt on the hypothesis of monetary discipline in the EMS. Why is this the case? Why should any policy hypothesis about the effect of entry into an organization by specific nations be settled by a sampling of as many different OECD countries as possible without drawing any distinction between them? Suppose one were to argue that a particular corporation responded strongly to a tax incentive for specific reasons. Would it be useful to oppose this view on the grounds of the lack of a similar response by a large number of corporations chosen at random? I believe the analogy to be fair. The statistical evidence that has served to put into question the monetary discipline hypothesis has not even distinguished between non-members of the EMS who kept their exchange rate fixed in relation to some other currency or currency basket in the 1980s, as opposed to others who adopted a policy of a flexible exchange rate. Thus, the Austrian example, concerning a country which kept its exchange rate fixed relative to the DM, has been cited (Collins 1988: note 13, and F–vH, Table 5.10) as arguing against the tendency of membership in the EMS to foster monetary discipline in France and Italy. Yet surely the question is how France and Italy would have behaved if, unlike Austria, they had floated rather than followed the DM outside the EMS. Indeed, if we limit the focus to the non-EMS countries outside the OECD who adopted a flexible exchange rate policy in the 1980s, we will find that these countries include those few, like Sweden and Australia, who tried to buck the general disinflationary trend at some stage. But this is not my main point, which is the more general one that international tests based on the largest possible number of countries cannot be the final arbiter of policy hypotheses about specific countries.

One of my principal dissatisfactions with F–vH's treatment of the monetary discipline hypothesis is that they ignore the emphasis of the advocates of the position on the limited conditions under which the hypothesis can be expected to be correct. The essential argument has been that the right conditions for the hypothesis have stood but cannot be expected to last. Thus, according to this literature, the EMS probably never had much of a future if monetary discipline was to remain a fundamental pillar for it. Yet F–vH, like Vaubel in a recent review article (1989), consider the dynamic instability of the EMS, based on the hypothesis, as itself an argument against it. But do social arrangements never arise if they contain the seeds of their own destruction? Must the evolution of the EMS towards monetary unification in recent years necessarily mean that the 'monetary discipline' interpretation was never correct or has no further application? I would suggest that F–vH will at least need to entertain these questions in order to allow adequate scope for genuine debate.

Finally, I find that F–vH simply raise too many objections to the monetary discipline hypothesis based on an unsympathetic choice of modelization. The most natural thing to do, if one is trying to model the EMS as an arrangement fostering monetary discipline because of German behaviour, is to treat the Germans as possessing monetary discipline to the hilt, thus as capable of obtaining a zero-inflation reputational equilibrium in or out of the EMS. This means allowing the Germans sufficient sensitivity to the future penalities of succumbing to the temptation to inflate in the present. What F–vH do instead is to model the situation as one where the sole German distinction is to place less weight on current output relative to current inflation than the rest. As the Germans are no more sensitive to the future than anybody else in the conception, the inevitable result is that they inflate for the same short-sighted reasons as the others, but simply do so less. Of course, in this case, the FRG will inflate more inside the EMS than outside it, as F–vH say, on the familiar Rogoff ground that inflation at home (of producer prices) costs less in terms of consumer inflation under fixed exchange rates. Admittedly, if this is the right view to take, the EMS looks rather flawed as a mechanism for promoting monetary discipline. But is it the right view to take? Has the EMS really induced the FRG to inflate more? Do we not know how to model the EMS so as to avoid the problem?

I have a similar reaction to F–vH's criticism of the treatment of the German advantage of membership by those who view the system as asymmetric. Their tendency has been to treat this German advantage as one of competitiveness. In other words, they argue that the higher inflation rates of the other members of the system make German goods more competitive between realignments. This leaves open the sizeable problem of modelling why competitiveness increases German welfare. One way to handle the issue is to introduce imported raw materials (Giavazzi-Giovannini 1986). Another is to recognize protective measures which tend to promote excessive levels of non-traded and sheltered goods relative to traded and exposed goods. A third is to admit a problem of inadequate aggregate demand during the adjustment to a past shock or policy mistake (Viñals 1988). Because of the importance of keeping theory simple, every modeller has contented himself with one of these avenues. However, F–vH merely address one of their choices, dismiss it, and thereby pretend to have disposed of the general argument. Yet is it really so difficult to construe the EMS as an arrangement where the Germans gain competitiveness while the others get monetary discipline? How general is F–vH's complaint? The particular advantage of competitiveness that F–vH dismiss so lightly, I would like to add, involving the presence of interferences with trade keeping the exposed sector too small, is a particular one that the European Commission has recently emphasized in arguing for the benefits of 1992 (the Cecchini Report on *The Costs of Non-Europe*).

There is some solid empirical work in F–vH's chapter which would tend to show that the Germans are not insensitive to the behaviour of the other members of the system, and that the non-Germans have retained some monetary independence in the system. I only neglect this merit of their chapter because the issue of symmetry or asymmetry in the EMS seems to me essentially independent. Even if the EMS is not a 'greater Deutschmark area' and everyone in it acts in response to everybody else, there can be major asymmetries in the system. More distinctions are necessary. Let me cite a recent review article by Portes (1989) as a good indication of the range of major factors that set the FRG apart in the EMS even if there are certain limits to German dominance which need to be kept in mind.

References

Cohen, D. and **Wyplosz, C.** (1989) The European Monetary Union: an agnostic interpretation, *CEPR Discussion Paper*, No. 306, April.

Collins, S. (1988) Inflation and the European Monetary System, in Giavazzi, F., Micossi, S. and Miller, M. (eds) *The European Monetary System*, Cambridge University Press, Cambridge

De Grauwe, P. (1989) Is the European Monetary System a DM-zone? *CEPR Discussion Paper* No. 297, March

Fratianni, M. and **von Hagen, J.** (1989) The European Monetary System after ten years, prepared for the Carnegie–Rochester Conference, 21–22 April.

Giavazzi, F. and **Giovannini, A.** (1984) The dollar and the European Monetary System, University of Manchester conference (organized by Michael Artis), September.

Giavazzi, F. and **Giovannini, A.** (1986) Monetary policy interactions under managed exchange rates, *Economica*, **56**, pp. 199–214.

Portes, R. (1989) Macroeconomic policy coordination and the European Monetary System, *CEPR Discussion Paper* No. 342, September.

Vaubel, R. (1989) Image and reality of the European Monetary System – a review, *Weltwirtschaftliches Archive* **125**, (2), pp. 397–405.

Viñals, J. (1988) Discussion, in Giavazzi, F., Micossi, S. and Miller, M. (eds) *The European Monetary System,* Cambridge University Press, Cambridge, pp. 79–84.

CHAPTER SIX

Monetary and exchange rate policy in the EMS with free capital mobility

Lorenzo Bini Smaghi and Stefano Micossi*

1. Introduction

This chapter reviews the functioning of the exchange rate mechanism (ERM) of the European Monetary System (EMS) in recent years. Its main purpose is to discuss the consequences and implications of increased (full) capital mobility for exchange rate management and monetary policies. In particular, section 2 examines the evolution of exchange rate management in the short term and the changing role of interventions, interest rates and official facilities. Section 3 discusses monetary policies in the ERM; after reviewing the debate on the model of monetary coordination that has prevailed in the early years of the EMS, it considers the claim that the degree of symmetry of the system may be increasing. Sections 4 and 5 discuss the implications for the ERM of increasing capital mobility, both as regards the long-term viability of the system (section 4) and the policy requirements in short-term management (section 5). Section 6 summarizes the main conclusions.

2. Recent developments in the EMS

Macroeconomic performance in the ERM area has improved in the second part of the 1980s. Growth has picked up, led by buoyant investment; average inflation has continued to decline until 1987, and has increased slightly since then; the consolidation of fiscal imbalances has proceeded further, although at a slow pace. On the external front, the area as a whole has gone to an average surplus in current payments of about 1 per cent of gross domestic product (GDP).

*We wish to thank H. Dalgaard, N. Karamouzis and the participants to the conference for their helpful comments, D. Porciani for valuable research assistance and V. D'Ambrosio for editing the numerous versions of this chapter. The authors are solely responsible for the opinions expressed.

TABLE 6.1 Indicators of nominal convergence of ERM countries*

	1980	1981	1982	1983	1984	1985	1986	1987	1988	1989
Consumer prices										
Lowest annual % change	5.8	6.0	4.7	2.8	2.4	2.1	–0.5	–0.7	0.7	1.3
Highest annual % change	20.2	21.2	17.0	15.1	11.1	9.2	5.9	4.7	5.0	6.5
Average annual % change	11.2	11.7	10.2	7.8	6.3	4.8	2.2	2.1	2.4	3.1
Dispersion in relation to average	5.6	5.8	4.5	3.9	2.9	2.2	2.2	2.0	1.7	1.6
Unit labour costs										
Lowest annual % change	5.0	2.7	3.1	–0.2	–2.9	0.4	1.8	–0.8	–0.1	–1.1
Highest annual % change	19.6	22.3	16.5	15.5	8.5	8.1	5.8	10.3	4.3	4.4
Average annual % change	10.9	9.9	8.3	6.3	3.2	3.4	3.4	3.0	1.6	1.9
Dispersion in relation to average	5.8	6.3	4.7	5.3	3.5	2.4	1.4	3.6	1.7	1.8
Broad money stock†										
Lowest annual % change	5.0	6.1	6.3	5.1	3.9	4.7	0.2	2.7	3.2	2.2
Highest annual % change	12.7	20.4	18.0	19.4	19.4	13.5	14.5	12.2	11.4	9.1
Average annual % change	8.4	10.4	11.4	11.0	10.1	8.3	7.2	6.5	7.0	6.2
Dispersion in relation to average	2.9	4.8	3.8	4.7	4.9	3.0	4.3	3.2	2.9	2.4
General government balances (% of GDP)										
Highest surplus or lowest deficit	0.3	–1.8	–1.2	1.6	2.9	5.8	6.0	5.2	5.4	5.6
Lowest surplus or highest deficit	–12.7	–13.2	–13.7	–11.6	–11.5	–12.5	–11.4	–10.5	–10.1	–9.9
Average performance	–4.6	–7.4	–7.4	–6.4	–5.3	–4.6	–4.1	–3.7	–2.9	2.7
Dispersion in relation to average	4.8	4.6	4.6	4.7	4.8	6.0	6.4	5.4	4.7	4.8
Current account (% of GDP)‡										
Highest surplus or lowest deficit	–0.6	2.2	3.2	3.1	4.1	4.1	4.4	3.9	4.1	4.3
Lowest surplus or highest deficit	–11.8	–14.7	–10.6	–7.0	–6.1	–4.7	–5.5	–3.0	–2.0	–1.8
Average performance	–3.8	–3.3	–2.6	–1.0	–0.7	–0.3	–0.3	0.7	1.1	1.2
Dispersion in relation to average	3.8	5.4	4.4	3.2	3.3	3.2	3.4	2.1	2.2	2.2
Memorandum items										
Real GDP										
Highest annual % change	4.0	2.3	3.0	2.6	4.8	4.3	3.4	4.1	4.5	4.2
Lowest annual % change	–0.4	–1.3	–1.4	–0.6	1.6	0.9	–0.4	–0.7	–0.2	1.0
Average annual % change	1.9	0.1	0.9	1.1	3.1	2.5	2.2	2.0	3.1	3.1
Unemployment (% of civ. labour force)										
Lowest annual % change	0.7	1.0	1.3	1.6	1.8	1.7	1.4	1.6	1.4	1.3
Highest annual % change	9.1	11.1	13.7	14.8	16.2	17.7	18.1	18.8	18.5	17.9
Average annual % change	6.0	7.7	9.1	10.1	10.5	10.4	10.1	10.3	10.1	9.8

Source: Committee of Governors of the EEC (1987).

* Averages and standard deviations are unweighted.
† National definitions.
‡ For Belgium and Luxembourg BLEU data.

Convergence of performances has evolved unevenly (Table 6.1). The rise in inflation in 1988–89 has not impeded a further contraction of inflation differentials, and the dispersion of price and unit cost increases is now at the minimum of the decade. The picture is more mixed for macro-policies. Convergence of monetary aggregates growth has improved; on the fiscal side, however, the reduction in the average deficit, in per cent of GDP, has gone along with a persistently high dispersion of performances. The dispersion also remains high for current external payments; bilateral imbalances within the area have widened, with growing deficits in Italy, France and Spain (and the UK) and surpluses in the Federal Republic of Germany (FRG), the Netherlands and Belgium.

As for the international environment, monetary policy in the US remained easy through 1986 and most of 1987, and – despite the Louvre Accord – the dollar continued to depreciate; during 1987, dollar depreciation was increasingly resisted with official interventions (Gaiotti *et al.* (1989)). Subsequently, monetary policy turned restrictive in the USA and the dollar started to appreciate[1], reaching in early June 1989 peaks of 2.05 Deutschmarks (DM) and 151 yen.

The EMS has withstood the oscillations of the dollar well. Central rates between the main ERM currencies, that had been left unchanged since March 1983, were realigned in July 1985 (lira) and April 1986 (French franc (FF)). Thereafter turbulence was limited to end 1986–early 1987, when a small realignment of central rates was implemented (on 12 January), and to some periods of pronounced dollar decline in 1987. Since January 1987 the currencies of the ERM have rarely touched the band limits (Fig. 6.1).

Nominal exchange rates have continued to maintain pressure on relative prices, notably in the case of Italy, Ireland and France (Fig. 6.2). On balance, however, this does not seem to have led to major distortions of competitive positions.[2]

The stability of exchange rates within the ERM has been altogether remarkable, especially if one considers that since 1986 France and Italy have dismantled many of their restrictions on capital transactions. At present (the end of 1989), all financial transactions on assets with maturity above 18 months and most trade-related operations are free.[3] Contrary to expectations, the opening of financial markets has been accompanied by strengthening exchange rates. In particular, after the reform of foreign operations legislation entered into effect in October 1988, the lira appreciated markedly, moving back in early 1989 into the narrow fluctuation band (Fig. 6.1). It is therefore interesting to examine in some detail how management techniques have evolved during this period.

It may be recalled, first of all, that in September 1987 the EMS central banks agreed in Basle to adapt the system's management techniques.[4] Access to the very-short-term facility (VSTF)[5] was made possible for intramarginal interventions, under certain conditions, and the 50 per cent limit on the obligation to accept European Currency Units (ECUs) in settlements of debts was *de facto* lifted; the availability and flexibility of the system's financing facilities were thus considerably expanded.

This, however, was the visible, but perhaps less important aspect of the agreement. The important aspect was an understanding that participating central banks would be prepared to make fuller use of the fluctuation band and at the same

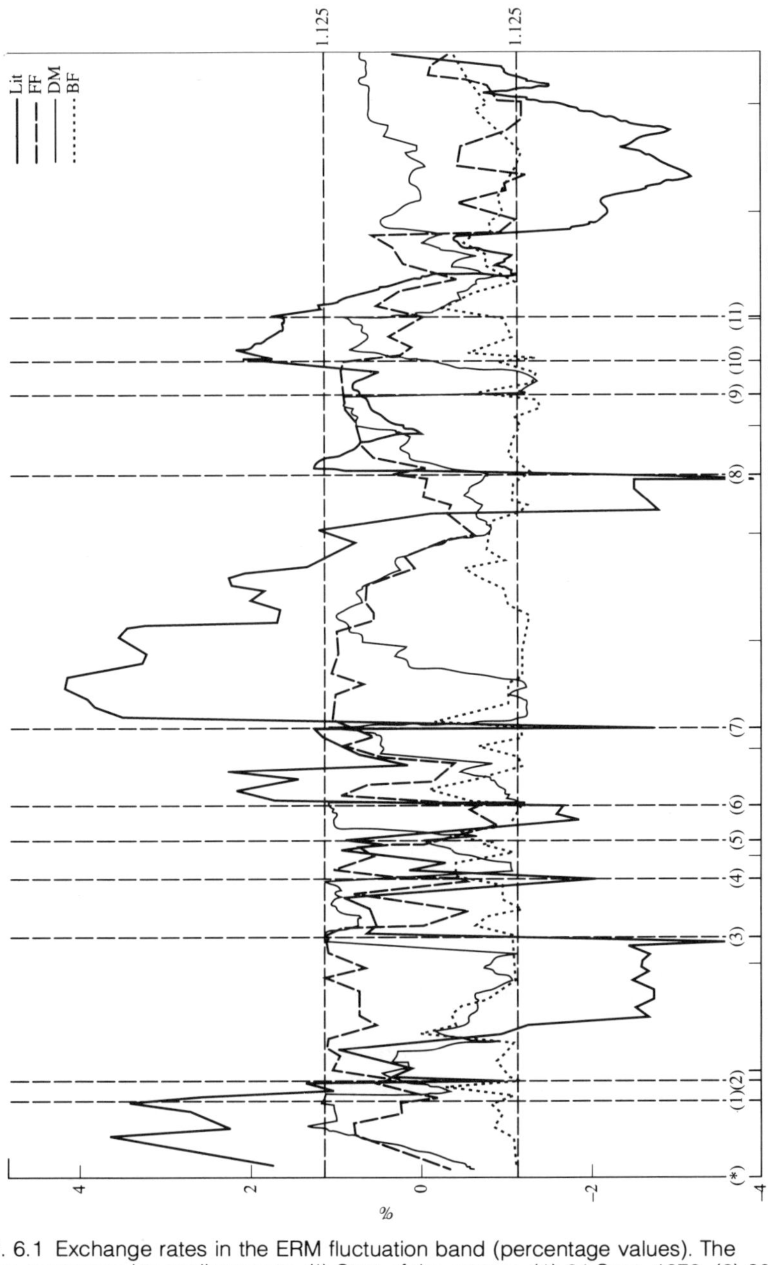

FIG. 6.1 Exchange rates in the ERM fluctuation band (percentage values). The notes correspond to realignments. (*) Start of the system. (1) 24 Sept. 1979, (2) 30 Nov. 1979, (3) 23 Mar. 1981, (4) 5 Oct. 1981, (5) 22 Feb. 1982, (6) 14 June 1982, (7) 22 Mar. 1983, (8) 22 July 1985, (9) 7 Apr. 1986, (10) 4 Aug. 1986, (11) 12 Jan. 1987. *Source*: Bank of Italy

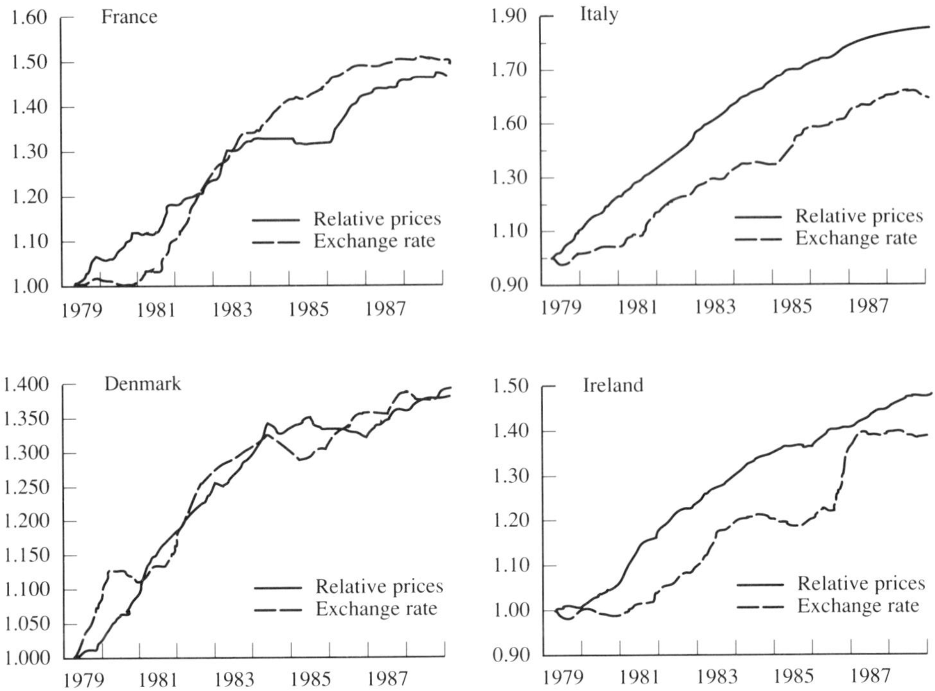

FIG. 6.2 Relative prices and exchange rate with respect to the FRG (indices 1979, I = 100). Relative prices are measured in terms of producer prices

time to adjust interest rates more readily in response to incipient pressures in exchange markets; as a consequence, there was a clear implication that resort to official intervention would be reduced.[6]

Table 6.2 summarizes foreign exchange interventions of ERM countries. The period 1986–87 stands up as that of heaviest intervention since the EMS was set up; weakness of the dollar is reflected in the large share of dollar purchase (above one-fifth of the total). Quite high also is the share of interventions in Community currencies (above 70 per cent, mostly in DM); the prevalence of sales over purchases is a reflection, once again, of the often noted asymmetric effect of the dollar in the ERM currencies, whereby a weak dollar leads in the short run to a stronger DM within the ERM (Micossi and Padoa-Schioppa 1984; Giavazzi and Giovannini 1989). Figure 6.3 shows that these sales fell almost entirely on central banks other than the Bundesbank. It is also apparent that these central banks took upon themselves a large share of interventions in dollars. Funabashi (1988) has documented that this was to an extent the result of explicit agreement among ERM central banks, designed to limit the repercussions of dollar interventions stemming from the Louvre Accord on the system's cohesion.

TABLE 6.2 Foreign exchange interventions of ERM countries

		1979–82*		1983–85		1986–7		1988–89†	
		(a)	(b)	(a)	(b)	(a)	(b)	(a)	(b)
$	P	31.4	16.5	22 .1	15.1	40.4	20.9	5.3	8.1
	S	107.3	56.3	56.3	38.4	13.3	6.9	24.2	37.0
ERM currencies									
At the margin ‡		20.5	10.7	15.4	10.5	22.3	11.6	0.9	1.4
Intramarginal	P	10.6	5.5	29.0	19.8	42.6	22.1	23.1	35.3
	S	18.6	9.7	19.6	13.4	71.1	36.9	9.3	14.2
Others	P	0.1	0.1	3.2	2.2	1.4	0.7	2.0	3.1
	S	2.2	1.2	0.9	0.6	1.8	0.9	0.6	0.9
Total gross		190.7	100	146.5	100	192.9	100	65.4	100
Total net §		–86.0	45.1	–22.5	15.4	–1.8	0.9	–3.7	5.7
Memorandum items									
Recourse to VSTF ¶		17.1	9.0	15.3	10.4	34.3	17.8	—	—
ECU spot settlement of intervention		6.4	3.4	1.5	1.0	0.8	0.4	—	—

Sources: EMCF, BIS.
(a) Flows in billion dollars; (b) percentage of total gross interventions.
P = purchases S= sales.

* For 1979, March–December.
† For 1989, January–June.
‡ Purchases or sales.
§ Minus sign denotes net sales.
¶ Very-short-term financing

Interventions at the margin were substantial ($22 billion or 11 per cent of the total); however, they were mostly undertaken just before the January 1987 realignment. Recourse to the VSTF was also substantial and larger than compulsory interventions; following the Basle–Nyborg Agreement, the VSTF was used in some occasions to finance intramarginal interventions (notably in the autumn of 1987). Use of the ECU in settlements remained modest; the ECU mobilization facility was activated by Italy and Belgium, but the balances of intervention currencies thus made available were not used. Finally, large gross interventions corresponded, for the system as a whole, to a net balance close to zero ($–1.8 billion), showing the decreasing importance of interventions in the financing of external payments imbalances. The intervention pattern that has been described is reflected in the large increase of dollar holdings by ERM countries (and, for that reason, also of ECUs) and the virtual stability of balances in ERM currencies (Table 6.3).

FIG. 6.3 Interventions by the ERM countries and effective exchange rate of the DM. The effective exchange rate of the DM is calculated with respect to all countries and to ERM countries. Increases in the index (1980 = 100) indicate an appreciation of the exchange rate.

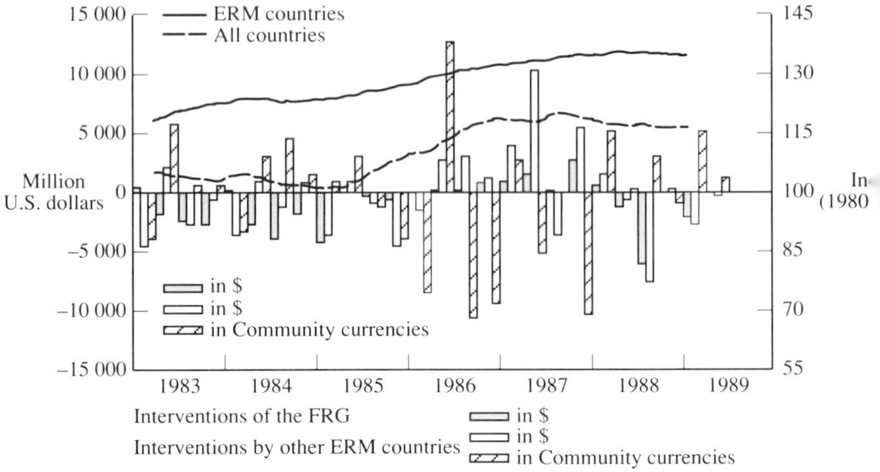

TABLE 6.3 Official net reserves of ERM countries*

	1979	1983	1985	1987	1988	1989†
Convertible currencies	39.0	59.9	67.0	102.0	97.0	99.3
Dollars	35.3	46.5	42.4	71.6	60.7	58.7
EMS currencies	3.2	10.2	19.7	21.6	29.3	34.5
Others	0.5	3.2	4.9	8.8	7.0	6.1
ECUs	26.6	49.9	43.5	60.0	49.7	42.7
Net position on the IMF‡	7.3	14.2	14.1	15.8	14.1	12.6
Others §	–4.4	–16.7	–16.2	–25.7	–24.9	–28.8
Total	68.5	107.3	108.4	152.1	136.0	125.7
Memorandum item						
Euromarket deposits ¶	—	28.7	37.1			

Source: BIS Monthly Statistical Series.

* Outstanding amounts in billions of US dollars at the end of the period (excluding gold holdings).
† End of May.
‡ Including SDRs.
§ Other assets minus official short-term liabilities.
¶ Monetary authorities' net liabilities reported to the BIS (not available for Ireland).

In 1988–89 we saw a return to the pattern of intervention typical of periods of dollar strength, with increasing shares of dollar sales and purchases of ERM currencies (DM), in a context of much lower gross interventions. No recourse was made to the system's official facilities; net interventions were again modest ($–3.7 billion) relative to the gross total. At the end of the period the share of dollar holdings in total reserves was about 60 per cent; that of ERM currencies had reached its historical maximum of 28 per cent, a consequence of the DM playing increasingly the reserve-currency role in the system.

Against this background, more detailed information on the evolution of management techniques of the ERM is presented in Tables 6.4 (exchange rates) and 6.5 (interest rates). We have adopted here a different period classification, to highlight changes that in fact date back to the January 1987 realignment. Increased cohesion of exchange rates within the band is mirrored in the uniform decline of daily mean (percentage) changes *vis-à-vis* the DM. Moreover, it may be seen that currencies have on average remained closer to their DM central rate than in any previous period since the EMS inception (cf. the column 'Position in the ERM band' in Table 6.4). As noted above, since the beginning of 1989 the lira has joined the other currencies in the narrow band.

On the other hand, the day-to-day (unconditional) variability of bilateral exchange rates in relation to the DM, remained relatively high in 1987–89 in all cases except for the Dutch guilder, with increasing values for the lira and the FF. Thus, it seems confirmed that countries were defending their currency rates more flexibly in day-to-day operations.

The data on interest rate variability also confirm that in the lastest period there has been no significant decrease in the relative variation of domestic interest rates, notably in France and Italy.[7] This suggests that, while in the past interest rate changes had provided little support in meeting exchange rate tensions in the early years of the EMS (see also Mastropasqua *et al.* 1988, De Grauwe 1989a and Giavazzi and Giovannini 1989), they have become more important as capital restrictions were dismantled.

Figure 6.4a, b offers evidence on the changing roles of interventions and interest rates in meeting exchange market pressures in selected periods. In the first two episodes (February–March 1983 and February–March 1984) we observe interventions in an increasing scale continuing for four to five weeks, and interest rate changes coming to help rather late (in 1983) or not at all (1984). In the January 1987 realignment episode interventions were more concentrated, and interest rate differentials tended to adjust earlier to counteract pressures. In the other three episodes (1987 and 1988), in an environment of higher capital mobility, we observe large interventions only initially, while interest rate differentials open up more promptly and exchange rates are allowed to adjust within the fluctuation band. Central banks, in sum, seem to have become aware of the destabilizing effect of large-scale interventions, once they become known to the markets, and tend to use them with more determination when incipient pressures develop in exchange markets, while partly absorbing them on the exchange rate; interventions, however, subside rather soon and interest rate differentials widen to increase the cost of open positions in foreign exchange.

A final aspect concerns realignments. In this regard, for some time the

TABLE 6.4 Variability of exchange rates within the ERM*

	Percentage changes *vis-à-vis* the DM		Absolute value of percentage changes *vis-à-vis* the DM		Position in the ERM band†	
	Mean	Standard deviation	Mean	Standard deviation	Mean	Standard deviation
Lira						
Mar. 79–Mar. 83	0.02	0.28	0.12	0.25	0.58	1.82
Apr. 83 –Dec 86	0.01	0.13	0.08	0.10	1.74	1.72
Jan. 87–June 89	0.00	0.16	0.09	0.13	–1.19	1.21
FF						
Mar. 79–Mar. 83	0.01	0.24	0.13	0.20	0.67	0.58
Apr. 83–Dec. 86	0.01	0.12	0.08	0.09	0.66	0.45
Jan. 87–June 89	0.00	0.12	0.07	0.09	–0.23	0.54
HFL						
Mar. 79–Mar. 83	0.003	0.17	0.09	0.14	0.50	0.61
Apr. 83–Dec. 86	0.001	0.11	0.07	0.09	0.28	0.73
Jan. 87–June 89	0.00	0.04	0.03	0.03	0.65	0.53
BF						
Mar. 79–Mar. 83	0.02	0.22	0.12	0.18	–0.98	0.37
Apr. 83–Dec. 86	0.004	0.14	0.09	0.11	–0.91	0.22
Jan. 87–June 89	0.002	0.06	0.04	0.05	–0.55	0.24
DKR						
Mar. 79–Mar. 83	0.02	0.27	0.16	0.22	0.31	0.65
Apr. 83–Dec. 86	0.01	0.13	0.10	0.09	0.35	0.71
Jan. 87–June 89	0.00	0.12	0.09	0.08	–0.13	0.65
IR£						
Mar. 79–Mar. 83	0.01	0.24	0.16	0.18	–0.12	0.60
Apr. 83–Dec. 86	0.01	0.14	0.10	0.10	0.49	0.58
Jan. 87–June 89	0.00	0.12	0.08	0.09	0.18	0.56
DM						
Mar. 79–Mar. 83					–0.09	–0.12
Apr. 83–Dec. 86					0.26	0.49
Jan. 87–June.89					0.42	0.18

Source: Banca d'Italia, daily data (%)
We have excluded the data of the days immediately preceding and following realignments.
† Calculated from daily maximum spreads from central rates; (–) sign indicates depreciation

TABLE 6.5 Interest rate variability

	Domestic Market rates*		Euro-Rates†		Differential with DM		Differential with Euro-DM	
	Mean	Standard deviation	Mean	Standard deviation	Mean	Standard deviation	Mean	Standard deviation
Italy								
Mar. 79–Mar. 83	0.13	1.03	0.11	2.43	8.39	2.60	12.12	3.63
Apr. 83 –Dec. 86	–0.18	0.45	–0.12	0.97	8.95	1.88	9.38	2.06
Jan. 87–June 89	0.03	0.43	0.03	0.63	5.58	0.73	6.58	0.92
France								
Mar. 79–Mar. 83	0.00	0.92	0.26	2.21	4.05	2.03	7.31	5.04
Apr. 83–Dec. 86	–0.09	0.24	–0.10	1.18	4.87	1.41	6.16	2.16
Jan. 87–June 89	0.01	0.32	–0.03	0.39	3.79	0.83	3.94	0.95
FRG								
Mar. 79–Mar. 83	–0.11	0.67	–0.10	0.62	—	—	—	—
Apr. 83–Dec. 86	–0.01	0.19	0.00	0.00	—	—	—	—
Jan. 87–June 89	0.07	0.39	0.07	0.37	—	—	—	—
Denmark								
Mar. 79–Mar. 83	0.10	3.40	n.a.	n.a.	6.30	4.22	n.a.	n.a.
Apr. 83–Dec. 86	–0.13	1.94	n.a.	n.a.	4.74	1.56	n.a.	n.a.
Jan. 87–June 89	–0.09	0.35	n.a.	n.a.	4.48	1.70	n.a.	n.a.
Ireland								
Mar. 79–Mar. 83	0.02	0.91	n.a.	n.a.	5.63	2.54	n.a.	n.a.
Apr. 83–Dec. 86	–0.01	1.08	n.a.	n.a.	6.94	1.53	n.a.	n.a.
Jan. 87–June 89	–0.17	0.58	n.a.	n.a.	4.69	2.35	n.a.	n.a.
Belgium								
Mar. 79–Mar. 83	–0.03	0.89	–0.02	1.07	4.57	1.55	4.88	1.56
Apr. 83–Dec. 86	–0.08	0.46	–0.08	0.46	4.29	1.03	4.29	1.03
Jan. 87–June 89	0.02	0.31	0.02	0.28	2.66	0.61	2.63	0.61
Netherlands								
Mar. 79–Mar.83	–0.19	0.85	–0.17	0.83	0.10	1.52	0.37	1.39
Apr. 83–Dec. 86	0.02	0.29	0.02	0.28	0.60	0.50	0.72	0.44
Jan. 87–June 89	0.04	0.33	0.04	0.33	0.88	0.48	0.83	0.47

Source: IMF, International Financial Statistics, monthly data.
* (Three months) money market rates (first differences).
† Three-months Euro deposit rates (first differences).

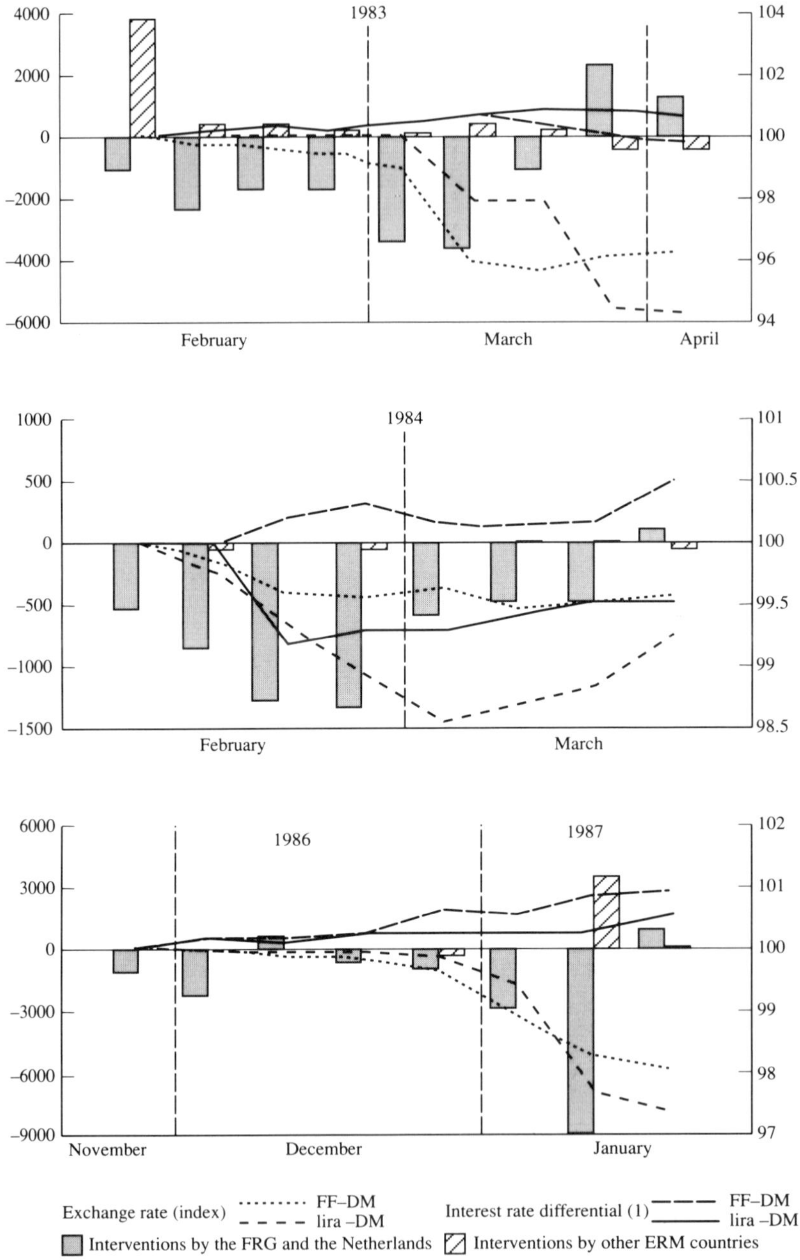

FIG. 6.4a ERM – interventions, exchange rate and interest rate differentials in selected periods. Three months domestic money market rate, difference in percentage points from beginning of the period (+ 100).

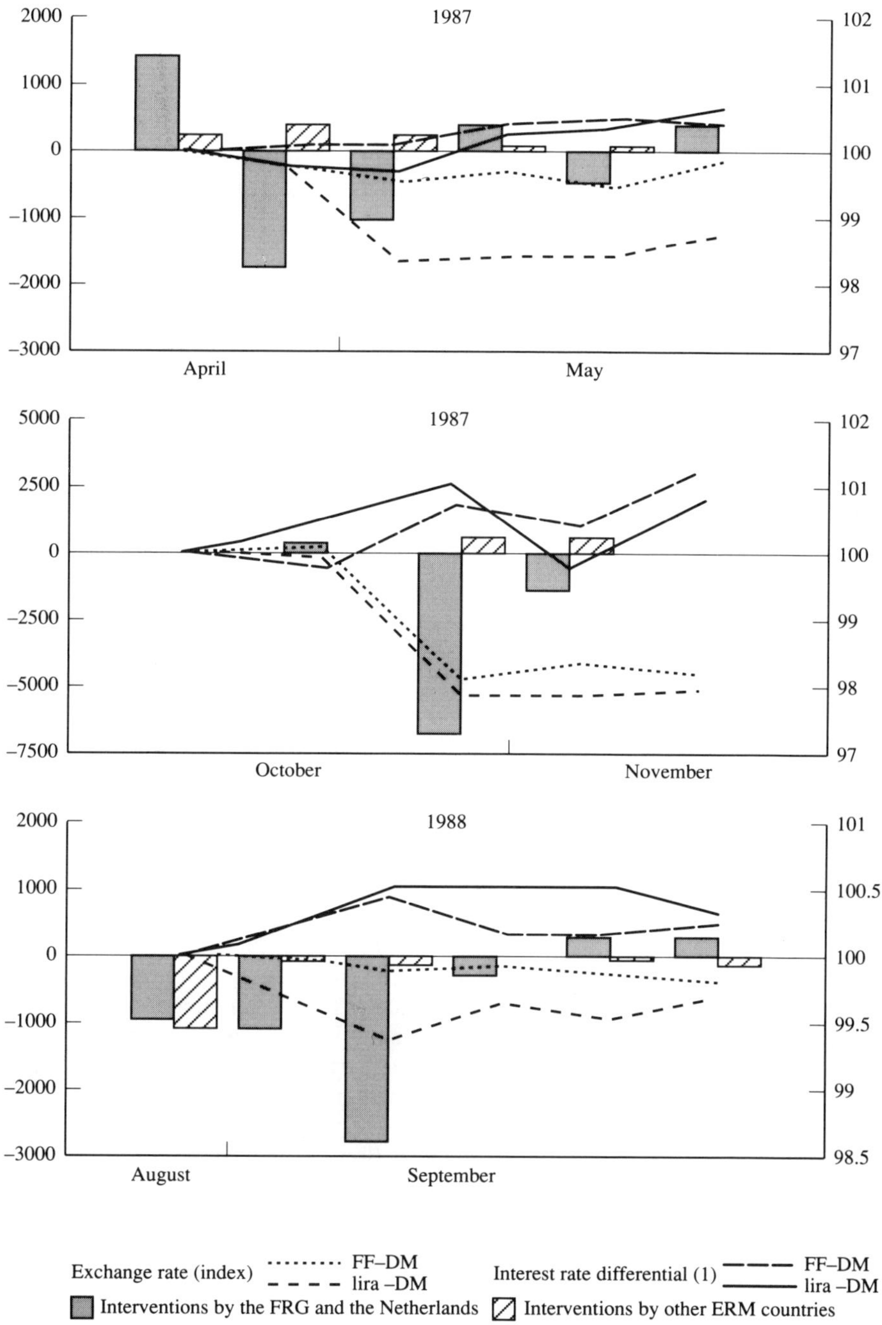

FIG. 6.4 continued

Realignments	24.9.79	23.3.81	5.10.81	14.6.82	22.3.83	22.7.85	7.4.86	12.1.87

DM/lira – central rates – market rates Dollar/lira	– 2.0 – 0.6 – 0.1	– 6.0 – 2.1 – 0.6	– 8.0 – 3.3 – 0.9	– 6.7 – 1.5 – 2.5	– 7.6 0.07 – 0.5	– 7.8 – 3.2 – 4.1	– 3.0 – 0.7 – 1.5	– 2.9 0.5 – 1.1

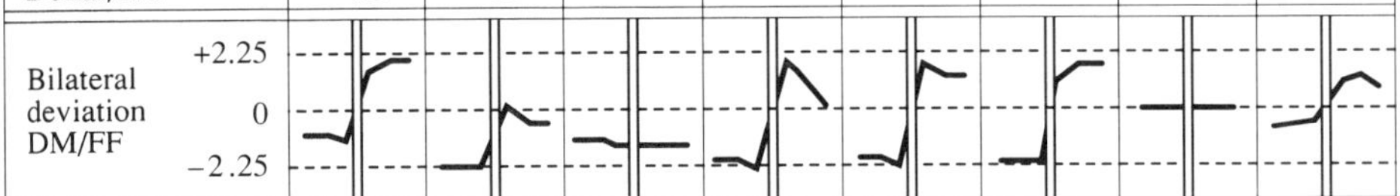

DM/lira – central rates – market rates Dollar/FF	– 2.0 – 0.3 0.2	— 0.2 – 2.8	– 8.0 – 4.4 – 2.0	– 9.6 – 5.5 – 6.5	– 7.6 – 3.5 – 4.0	— 0.1 – 0.8	– 5.8 – 3.4 – 4.3	– 2.9 0.2 – 0.9

FIG . 6.5 Exchange rate changes at realignments (percentage values). Percentage change between the day preceding and that following the realignment. A negative change indicates a depreciation of the currency in the denominator; the dates indicate the first days of the new central rates

experience of the lira showed that tensions can be greatly reduced if market rates are not allowed to change much around realignment. As Fig. 6.5 shows, central rate changes always led to a jump in the FF–DM market rate in the first 10 realignments, but not in the case of the lira–DM market rate;[8] in some cases the lira rose in the first market-day after the realignment. With the January 1987 realignment, the principle that central rate changes should not exceed the band width or entail jumps in market rates seems to have become a guiding rule of the system.[9] And yet, it is also understood that realignments should be infrequent, with more emphasis on their exceptional nature.

In summary, liberalization of financial flows within the EMS has been accompanied by increased flexibility in exchange rate management within the fluctuation band and a strengthened commitment to limit realignments and to bend short-term monetary policy management to the requirements of ERM cohesion. This has favoured exchange rate stability in the system and has facilitated smooth transition towards an environment of high capital mobility.

3. Monetary policies: symmetry and the nominal anchor yet again

For many years it was accepted wisdom that the EMS has worked as an asymmetric system,[10] meaning:

1. That the burden of intervening in foreign exchange markets and moving interest rates to keep exchange rates within agreed margins has been unequally shared among participating central banks; and/or
2. That the medium-term stance of monetary policy has been set by the Bundesbank, with the other central banks more or less 'following' and occasional realignments providing some leeway of monetary independence.

Some empirical evidence supporting the hypothesis of asymmetry is available, albeit not terribly strong; it mainly concerns short-term management. Mastropasqua *et al.* (1988) show that participation by the Bundesbank in ERM-related intervention operations was always minimal, and the data in section 2 confirm it for recent years. Their estimates of central bank reaction functions for the FRG, France, Italy and Belgium display the expected ordering of sterilization coefficients of the foreign creation of a monetary base (with values closer to minus one than to zero for the FRG, to zero than to minus one for Belgium and the other two countries falling in between).

These results have been criticized on grounds that there are 'optimal' central bank policies that do not entail asymmetric behaviour and that, under a wide range of domestic and foreign disturbances, would none the less lead to a pattern of estimated coefficients indicating asymmetry (Roubini 1988b). This implies that estimated sterilization coefficients cannot by themselves prove (or disprove) the asymmetry hypothesis. They could still be considered an *ex post* measure of sterilization behaviour conditional on the knowledge that the actual policies followed by ERM central banks did imply asymmetry.

The evidence from the behaviour of interest rates in national markets is mixed. Giavazzi and Giovannini (1989) find that the volatility of unanticipated interest rate movements[11] in domestic markets in the FRG is about half that of France, but more or less equal to that of Italy (who maintained extensive controls on international capital flows through 1985). De Grauwe (1989a), on the other hand, finds that there is no significant difference in interest rate volatility in the three countries.

De Grauwe (1989a) and Fratianni and von Hagen (1989) present evidence respectively that interest rates and monetary base 'innovations' in the FRG are affected by innovations in these variables in other ERM countries, which they consider evidence of a symmetric working of the system. It may be recalled that similar evidence for money base innovations had already been identified by Bekx and Tullio (1987) and Mastropasqua *et al.* (1988). This last paper, as well as that of Russo and Tullio (1988), points to the role of the DM as intervention currency in the ERM as an alternative explanation that would make this evidence consistent with asymmetry. Dudler (1988) makes clear, in this regard, that the Bundesbank always reacts gradually to short-term disturbances on monetary-base growth, making it possible that DM interventions by other ERM countries show up for some time in monetary base creation in the FRG; and Russo and Tullio (1988) were able to conclude, from detailed analysis of the liquidity effects in the FRG of DM interventions during the life of the EMS, that these effects were temporary in every year except 1979 and 1981.

In discussing this issue, Thygesen (1988) was careful to point out that asymmetry would in any event be far from complete and that there are instances when the Bundesbank did intervene or change its monetary course in view of exchange rate considerations.[12] We do know, however, that up until 1985 the FRG always met its yearly monetary targets; that Italy and France have increasingly constrained their monetary policies to the requirements of stability in nominal exchange rates; that Belgium, the Netherlands, Denmark and Ireland have pegged their currencies to the DM rather rigidly since the EMS was set up.

Failure to confirm empirically the asymmetric model of coordination could thus be seen as casting doubt more on the specification and testing of the hypothesis than on the hypothesis itself. It is important to note that in most cases the specification of empirical tests entails the existence of a systematic and more or less automatic response by central banks to monetary and exchange rate disturbances. In practice, however, we know that central banks make little resort to automatic pilots and rather prefer manual sailing; their responses reflect judgement and discretion much more than optimal feed-back rules.[13]

In this regard, there seems to be a consensus that in recent years the system has become more symmetric than it used to be. The data on interest rate variability in Table 6.5 offer some support to this contention; so does the evidence that the process of convergence may have slowed, if not come to a halt, in the past two to three years, and that current account deficits have been 'easily financed – rather, over-financed – by capital flows' (Spaventa 1989). To the extent that, as noted by Wyplosz (1989), asymmetry was the systemic consequence of a reserve constraint, removal of this constraint may help explain increased symmetry.

Against this background, a fair question to ask is whether the model of monetary coordination of the ERM has continued to perform satisfactorily from the standpoint of providing the system with a stable monetary anchor. Indeed, the FRG has not been immune to the general acceleration of inflation since 1987, and in this regard does not seem to have placed restrictive pressure with monetary policy on the rest of the system; it was noted in section 2 that the resurgence of inflation has gone along with increased convergence of inflation rates between ERM participants.

Since 1986 monetary targets were systematically exceeded in the FRG, and both in 1986–87 and in 1988–89 the real rate of growth of money (M2) was high by historical standards. In the first period the main impulse to monetary expansion came from the foreign component, in the second the slow-down in the foreign component was largely (not entirely) compensated by an acceleration in the domestic component (see also Fig. 6.6).

Developments in 1986–87 reflect interventions in the dollar market (see Fig. 6.4) and loosening monetary conditions by the Bundesbank related to increased resistance to the depreciation of the dollar, in the presence of a large and growing current external surplus (Gaiotti *et al.* 1989). An acceleration of (nominal and real)

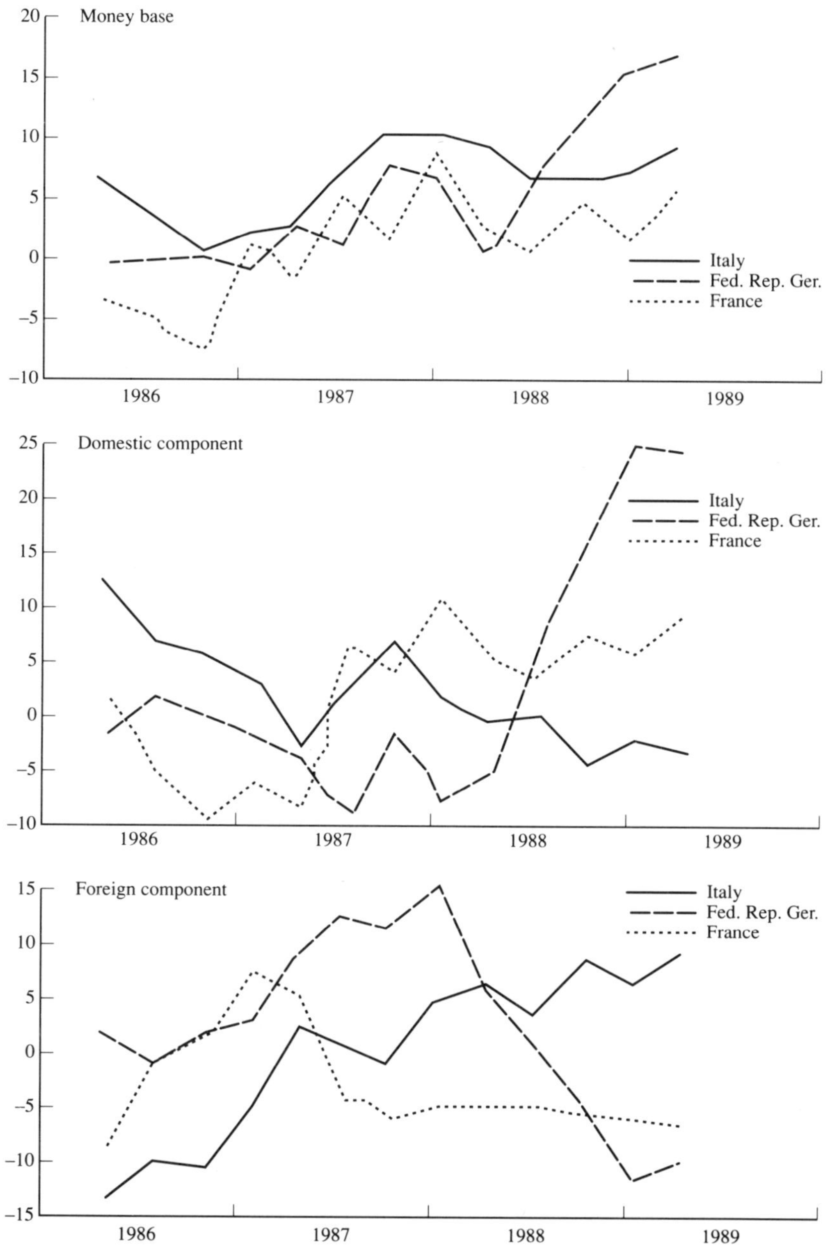

FIG. 6.6 Growth of monetary base and components (percentage changes). The domestic and foreign components are calculated as a contribution to (real) monetary base growth, as follows: $(C_t - C_{t-4})/BM_{t-4}$, where C is the relevant monetary base component.
Source: IMF, *International Financial Statistics*, quarterly data, various issues.

monetary growth is also observed in both France and Italy (in the former case pushed by the domestic component, in the latter case by the foreign component). These developments would seem to confirm that when an external (dollar) exchange rate objective is superimposed on the ERM, notably when the dollar is weak, the system's monetary discipline is loosened (Kregel 1989). Participation by the FRG in dollar stabilization efforts can be explained by its increasing dependence of net exports, notably towards non-EC countries, as a source of growth.[14]

In 1988–89, however, real monetary growth has remained buoyant in the FRG, and the money base has accelerated considerably, despite the dollar appreciation and a sizeable negative contribution of the foreign sector. Since mid-1988 M2 has expanded more rapidly in the FRG than in either France or Italy (Fig. 6.6). It is no wonder, therefore, that the system has been perceived as less constraining and that the requests for more symmetry in monetary management have subsided. The performance of the DM in the ERM can be plausibly related to these developments in relative monetary conditions.

An explanation in terms of exchange rate competitiveness objectives is obviously less compelling in this case. The reason, instead, could be found in the consequences of increased monetary and financial integration within the EMS area.

With high (full) capital mobility and strengthened expectations of exchange rate stability, capital flows increasingly from low to high-yield, high-inflation countries, as the experience of Italy, but also of Spain and in certain periods the UK, clearly shows. As a result, the external component of money base creation is systematically positive in high-inflation countries, reducing the perception of the external constraint on domestic policies; typically, the monetary effects of these inflows are less than fully sterilized. At the same time, close to full sterilization continues to prevail in the centre country, as clearly reflected in the strong acceleration in the domestic base in the FRG. As a result, monetary policy in the aggregate becomes more expansionary.

The above discussion would suggest that, with increasing capital mobility, the existence of inflation differentials within the area and the requirement for higher-inflation countries to maintain more restrictive monetary policies, may actually lead the system to converge towards the highest, rather than the lowest, inflation if 'collective' monetary management is not modified. One suggestion[15] is to set targets for the domestic component of monetary aggregates along the lines of the earlier literature on monetary policy cooperation under fixed exchange rates (see, e.g. McKinnon 1977).

4. Free capital movements and long-term viability of the EMS

At the latest by 1 July, 1990, all remaining restrictions on monetary transactions should be removed in France and Italy, making capital fully free to move around in most of the EMS area.[16] This raises issues on the one hand of long-term viability of the ERM of the EMS, on the other of adequacy of existing rules and arrangements for exchange rate management within the system. We will take up the long-term aspects in this section and discuss the implications for exchange rate management within the ERM in section 5.

In our view the issue of long-term viability of the EMS with free capital movements has been overemphasized, for a number of reasons. To start with, once we rule out the possibility of an insolvent government, there is little doubt that under any circumstances of practical relevance there will exist appropriate monetary policies that will sustain a system of managed exchange rates;[17] the only question is whether countries will be willing to adopt and maintain such policies. The decision to concur in the liberalization directive already provides an indication of their intention to do so; it may be argued, however, that countries are underestimating the costs implicit in this commitment.

While this may well be so, a convincing case that full liberalization of capital will raise substantially the costs of membership in the ERM has not been made. Some authors have argued that with fully free capital it will become more difficult to meet the government solvency constraint, since inflation-prone countries will have to accept a lower-than-optimal rate of inflation from the standpoint of tax policy and reduced revenues from seigniorage.[18] In addition, the real rate of interest may have to go up and the growth rate to go down as a result of the policies required to sustain the exchange rate and foster disinflation.

This conclusion is far from obvious. First of all, the above models are based on *ad hoc* assumptions on the optimizing behaviour of fiscal authorities, and ignore the possibility that inflation may in fact be the result of the latter's inability to reach a socially desirable optimum because of externalities.[19] In addition, Dornbusch himself recognized, in his comment to Grilli (1989), that equilibrium seigniorage rules out inflation as a strategic coordination problem. Even if one was willing to accept that governments indeed try to set inflation optimally, it strains credibility that private agents would not react to the perception of such a policy, with adverse implications for inflation, real interest rates, the tax base and the entire macroeconomic picture.

Secondly, the loss of revenues from seigniorage would tend to be compensated by a reduction in the (real) cost of government borrowing stemming from enhanced credibility of the government both as a debtor and an inflation-fighter.[20] Enhanced credibility of stability-oriented economic policies would also encourage capital inflows, at least initially, thus facilitating the financing of the public debt and of the current external deficit, and reducing their cost. Lower inflation in the context of increased economic integration could entail higher, rather than lower, real growth as a result, among other things, of larger inflows of foreign direct investment, as indeed seems to be confirmed by the experience of the 1980s in Europe.

In the long run a problem of 'sustainability' can arise to the extent that, over time, foreigners become less willing to accumulate claims on deficit countries. However, economic theory has not provided us with definite answers on this issue. The upper bound on net foreign indebtedness can be very large for a country that maintains 'sound' financial policies. At the same time, standard portfolio models (Hooper and Morton 1982) do predict that widening real interest rate differentials in

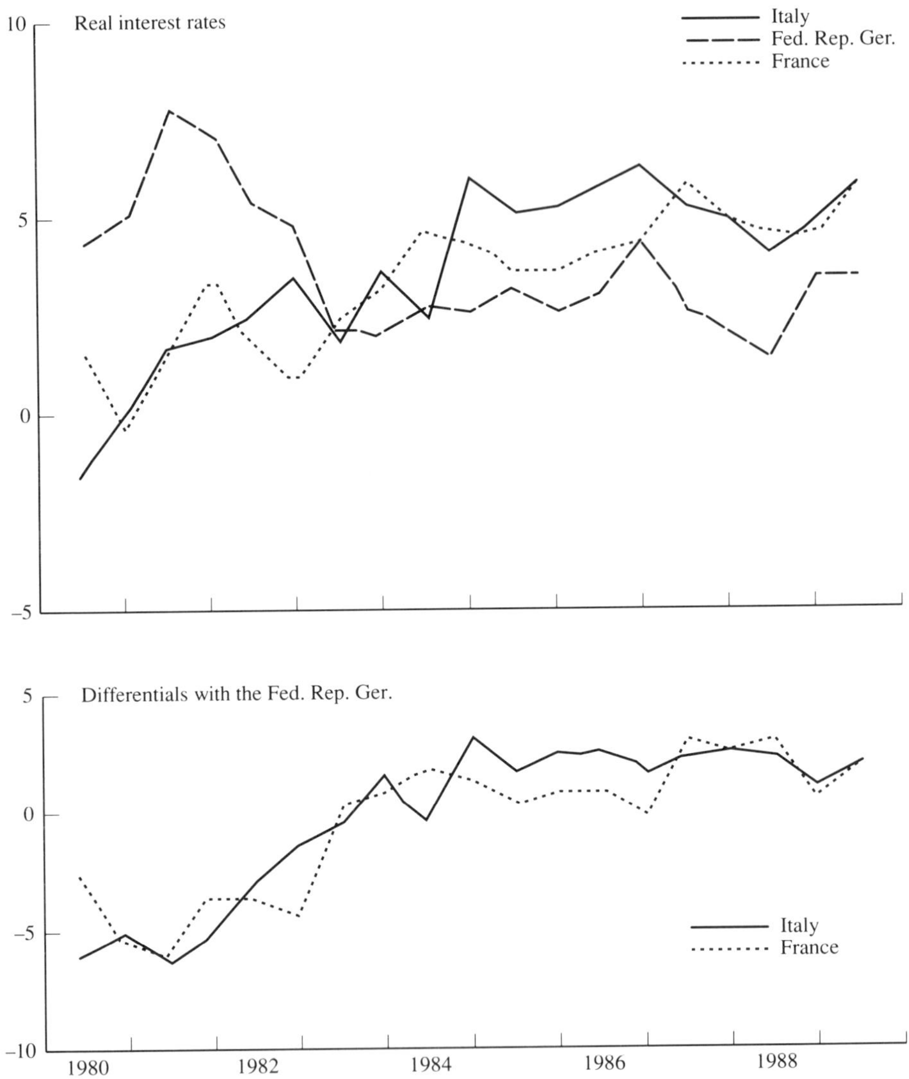

FIG. 6.7 Real interest rates and interest rate differentials in selected ERM countries. Money market (three months) interest rates deflated with inflation rate forecasts of the OECD outlook for the coming semester. *Source*: BIS

favour of deficit countries would be required to offset the resulting changes in net relative supplies of assets denominated in ERM currencies. On the other hand, to the extent that integration of capital markets – in the context of increasingly fixed exchange rates – makes assets denominated in different currencies good (close-to-perfect) substitutes, problems of sovereign risk may loose relevance within the area; the creditworthiness of individuals and firms could increasingly become the only criterion relevant in determining the cost of borrowing and risk premiums. A plausible case could thus be made for accelerating, rather than slowing liberalization, in the presence of widening current imbalances, and for tightening up at the same time the exchange rate constraint.

As an empirical matter, nominal interest rate differentials *vis-à-vis* the FRG have declined considerably since 1983; real differentials, however, have been higher, on average, in 1986–87 and 1988–89 than they had been at any time since the EMS inception; in France they have gone further up in 1988–89, and they are now higher than in Italy. Since mid-1988, in particular, real interest rates have increased in all three countries, but more in France and Italy than in the FRG (Fig. 6.7).

A number of factors may explain these developments. In 1986–87 the dollar depreciated considerably, placing pressure on 'weak' currencies within the EMS;[21] domestic demand has tended in general to grow more rapidly in France and Italy. Italy also has larger public sector deficit and debt, and higher cost and price increases; this, however, is no longer true of France, where all these variables are now closely in line with those in the FRG (but where perhaps higher real interest rates were precisely the cost to be paid to achieve full convergence of nominal magnitudes). On the other hand, during most of 1987–89 monetary policy has been lax in the FRG, with real interest rates going down to the minimum of the decade.

However, the turnaround in countries' net foreign positions during the EMS stands out as a potential explanation. Italy and France were in (current account) surplus in 1979 but have now substantial deficits (between 0.5 and 1 per cent of GDP); their net foreign position has worsened in the past 10 years by some \$30 billion. The opposite has happened in the FRG, that now has large current surpluses and net asset position *vis-à-vis* some ERM countries, and in the other DM-group countries in northern Europe, Belgium, Denmark and the Netherlands (Bini Smaghi 1989a).

If the above argument is considered relevant the only way to reduce real interest differentials – barring a large (once-and-for-all?) realignment that today does not seem feasible – is to tighten the exchange rate constraint so as to reduce differences in risk premiums on the various currencies. Financial liberalization would also contribute to ease the external financing constraint (see section 5).

On the other hand, we should keep in mind that the dismantling of restrictions has taken place under considerable market pressure, in the sense that financial innovation was increasingly eroding their effectiveness. Halting, or worse, reversing the liberalization process may prove in practice very difficult and costly now that firms, households and financial intermediaries have started to learn to operate in sophisticated open markets. Considerable political costs would also be involved for a country taking such a course, since that would require resort to a safeguard clause under a Community procedure.

These considerations bring us back, in the end, to the fundamental issue of the role of capital controls in the panoply of instruments available to maintain exchange rate cohesion within the ERM. The experience of the 1970s has taught us that controls cannot avoid reserve losses or depreciations if monetary policy accommodates inflation systematically.

On the contrary, capital controls can contribute to smooth the adjustment in a phase of disinflation, by reducing the volatility of interest and exchange rate changes.

A simple aggregative model that displays properties consistent with this view is presented in the Appendix. The model is solved to derive the real interest rate and output path during disinflation under alternative policy regimes of monetary targeting (floating exchange rates) and fixed exchange rates ('the ERM'). It is shown that capital controls can tilt the balance in favour of the ERM regime since they reduce the required increase in interest rates, hence the output loss, along the path of disinflation.

This explanation of the interest of inflation-prone countries in joining the ERM offers an alternative to the 'credibility' hypothesis (Giavazzi and Pagano 1988; Rogoff 1985), that has been criticised increasingly as logically unconvincing.[22] It also points to an interpretation of controls on capital transactions within the ERM as a complement to appropriate monetary policies rather than a substitute. Micossi and Rossi (1989) present evidence that in Italy the shift to non-accommodative monetary policy after the inception of the EMS gradually eased the pressure on barriers to international capital flows, so that these barriers had on average already ceased to 'bite'[23] – in the sense of impeding *net* outflows that would otherwise take place – when they were removed. Controls were used to ease the transition to lower inflation and reduce its output costs; they were never conceived as a device to sustain a systematic divergence in inflation and monetary policy relative to the FRG.

Indeed, it is now recognized as a general requirement for monetary policies in the EMS that the medium-term path of nominal variables should not entail devaluations at regular intervals or, stated alternatively, that monetary policies should not accommodate inflation differentials.[24] Realignments, then, could still occur in response to unanticipated real shocks, but they would not be a systematic, hence foreseeable, feature of the system. A system that did not meet this requirement would always be exposed to the risk of collapsing under speculative attacks; the considerations developed above make it clear, however, that this requirement cannot be considered a novel feature of the system, although the leeway for short-run deviations from the prescribed policy course will be reduced with the removal of remaining restrictions.

5. Capital mobility and short-term management of the ERM

It is useful to recall, first of all, that the ERM is an agreement to stabilize nominal exchange rates within narrow margins. Central rate changes were invariably decided under strong market pressure; they were not planned in advance and there is no rule of objective criteria agreed upon to determine when the time is ripe. This strengthens the contention (cf. section 4) that the ERM was not conceived and has not been operated as a crawling peg designed to accommodate systematic divergences in inflation and monetary policies.

In this context, it has been argued above that capital controls may have helped to reduce the output cost of disinflation. In addition controls have performed two other functions. The first one, well recognized in the literature (Giavazzi and Pagano 1985; De Grauwe 1989b; Micossi and Rossi 1989), was that of reducing pressure in foreign exchange markets, and associated changes in interest rates, when expectations of a realignment developed. The second function was that of facilitating exchange rate management within the band in the time interval between realignments. This is a straightforward implication of asset market theories of exchange rate determination: sterilized interventions tend to be more effective with low capital mobility.[25]

This role of controls was especially relevant for Italy which maintained wide fluctuation margins: in this case capital controls worked to reduce capital inflows[26] when expectations on the lira were stable, thereby avoiding exchange rate changes in a direction opposite to that of 'fundamentals'. The Bank of Italy then was able to decide when and to what extent to arrange an orderly descent of the lira within the band, consistent with its objectives on inflation on the one hand, on competitiveness on the other.[27]

Bearing in mind these considerations on the nature of the ERM agreements, we can turn to consider the implications of increasing (full) capital mobility for the short-term management of the system.

A first general requirement for monetary policy – that it should not accommodate inflation differentials – has been noted in section 4. With full capital mobility, however, sticking to that policy may be tantamount to renouncing realignments since the conditions of pressure in foreign exchange markets that usually justified changing central rates are not likely to develop (Spaventa 1989). A decision to loosen monetary policy with the explicit objective of provoking a realignment, on the other hand, may entail serious risks of destabilizing foreign exchange markets and set in motion giant flows of capital. Thus, realignments may have to be decided and implemented not only by surprise, but also to a large extent independently of market developments or the position of currencies in the band. That such a decision would not be likely to happen too often is quite obvious.

Further requirements will have to be met in the management of interest and exchange rates in day-to-day operations, that basically boil down to doing some more of what has already been done following the Basle–Nyborg Agreement of September

1987 (see section 2). Central banks should never provide systematic opportunities for profit to speculators by pegging prices in the domestic money market and the foreign exchange market at the same time: exchange rates should be allowed to oscillate within the band in response to incipient market pressure, the monetary effects of interventions should not be sterilized and interest rates should be allowed to respond even more flexibly to incipient market pressures. Such a policy would not entail systematic deviations of monetary policies from their medium-term course as long as the general requirement of non-accommodation stated above was met.[28] It would also not necessarily entail in practice a large increase in interest rate volatility. For one thing, higher capital mobility would imply stronger stabilizing speculation (higher interest rate elasticity) in response to 'virtuous' interest rate changes, once the credibility of the ERM was strengthened by renouncing controls (Gros and Thygesen 1988).

Two further issues should be noted. First, full capital mobility may indeed complicate the management of monetary policy to the extent that currency substitution undermines the stability of the demand for monetary base.[29] Attempts to change monetary conditions in one country will more rapidly and extensively spill over to the others. Given the size of financial intermediation and monetary base in France and Italy, the FRG cannot consider itself immune from this implication of free capital. Beyond short-term responses, coordination of monetary targets becomes necessary, as argued by Caranza *et al.* (1988).

Second, the issue arises whether official financing facilities of the EMS – notably the VSTF – can still be considered adequate in the new environment. What has been said already provides part of the answer. To the extent that monetary policies adapt more readily to the requirements of exchange rate management within the ERM, official reserve movements and recourse to the system's financing facilities are likely to be small (and indeed we saw it decreasing over time). If, on the other hand, monetary and intervention policies became mutually inconsistent, then the amount of private capital that could be set in motion would be virtually unlimited and no official facility, however large, would be sufficient to meet it. In a way, therefore, the issue becomes less relevant than it was with capital controls, when some countries on occasion made substantial resort to the system's facilities to resist pressure on their currency.

The last issue that should be addressed is the stringency of the exchange rate constraint, that is the width of the fluctuation band. In section 4 it was pointed out that a narrow band may entail benefits of a reduction of risk premiums on weak currencies because of enhanced credibility of government policies.

However, the issue still arises whether from the standpoint of short-term management full capital mobility would require more or less exchange rate flexibility (wider or narrower band). A wider band for all member countries has been advocated (Masera 1988 and Kenen 1988) on grounds that financial shocks would be more likely and could be more readily absorbed on the exchange rate, thus limiting the need for interest rate changes.

The counter-argument stresses the role of the band width on expectations: a credibly defended smaller band reduces the potential gains from speculation and, therefore, can cut at the root the likelihood of speculative attacks.[30] Marris (1989) also points to the benefit of a narrow band in minimizing the risk of capital flows driving the exchange rate away from fundamentals, and thus becoming a source of real shocks in the system. If narrowing the band reduces the scope for exchange-rate-induced shocks, it can also lessen the need for interest rate changes. To the extent that risk premiums reflect currency instability, a tighter exchange rate constraint would also contribute to reducing them.

The issue, of course, cannot be settled *a priori*: optimal (exchange rate) policies will in general depend on the structure of disturbances that are likely to affect the economy (Henderson 1984). In the Appendix we show that indeed under certain shocks (real or risk premium shocks) there can be a trade-off between exchange rate and interest rate variability; on the other hand, the variability is reduced for both variables under pure monetary shocks.

Artis and Taylor (1988) present high-technology empirical evidence of a reduction of variability for both interest rates and exchange rates during the life of the EMS, which would seem to confirm a prevalent stabilizing role of the exchange rate constraint. This, of course, was also in general a period of reduced instability in the real sector of the economy and sharply decelerating inflation.

In Fig. 6.8 we have plotted the variances of exchange rates and interest rates since mid-1987 for France and Italy; during this period the liberalization of capital has been accelerating in both countries. As can be seen, in the case of France there is not only a trend reduction in the variability of both variables, but also a distinct tendency for the two to move together (positive covariance). Italy, on the other hand, seems to display both a pick-up in the variances and a negative correlation between them, which may indicate that indeed exchange rate flexibility has helped to moderate interest rate variability.

More empirical work is clearly needed on this issue. What can be said, however, is that liberalization does tilt the balance of choice in favour of more exchange rate stability or of a narrowing of the fluctuation band. If, on the other hand, the real sector cannot be made more stable – say, by means of improved fiscal policies – then the choice may be one between two evils: greater exchange rate flexibility may make it easier to absorb shocks stemming from the real sector, but the country will be more exposed to financial shocks both in the foreign exchange and the domestic financial (government debt) market.

6. Conclusions

In recent years the ERM has functioned remarkably well, both in periods of dollar weakness and dollar strength, not least because of important improvements in management techniques following the Basle–Nyborg Agreement of September 1987. Far from weakening exchange rate cohesion within the ERM, increased capital mobility may have helped to strengthen it, especially since inflation differentials have been sharply reduced. Monetary policies have responded more readily to the requirements

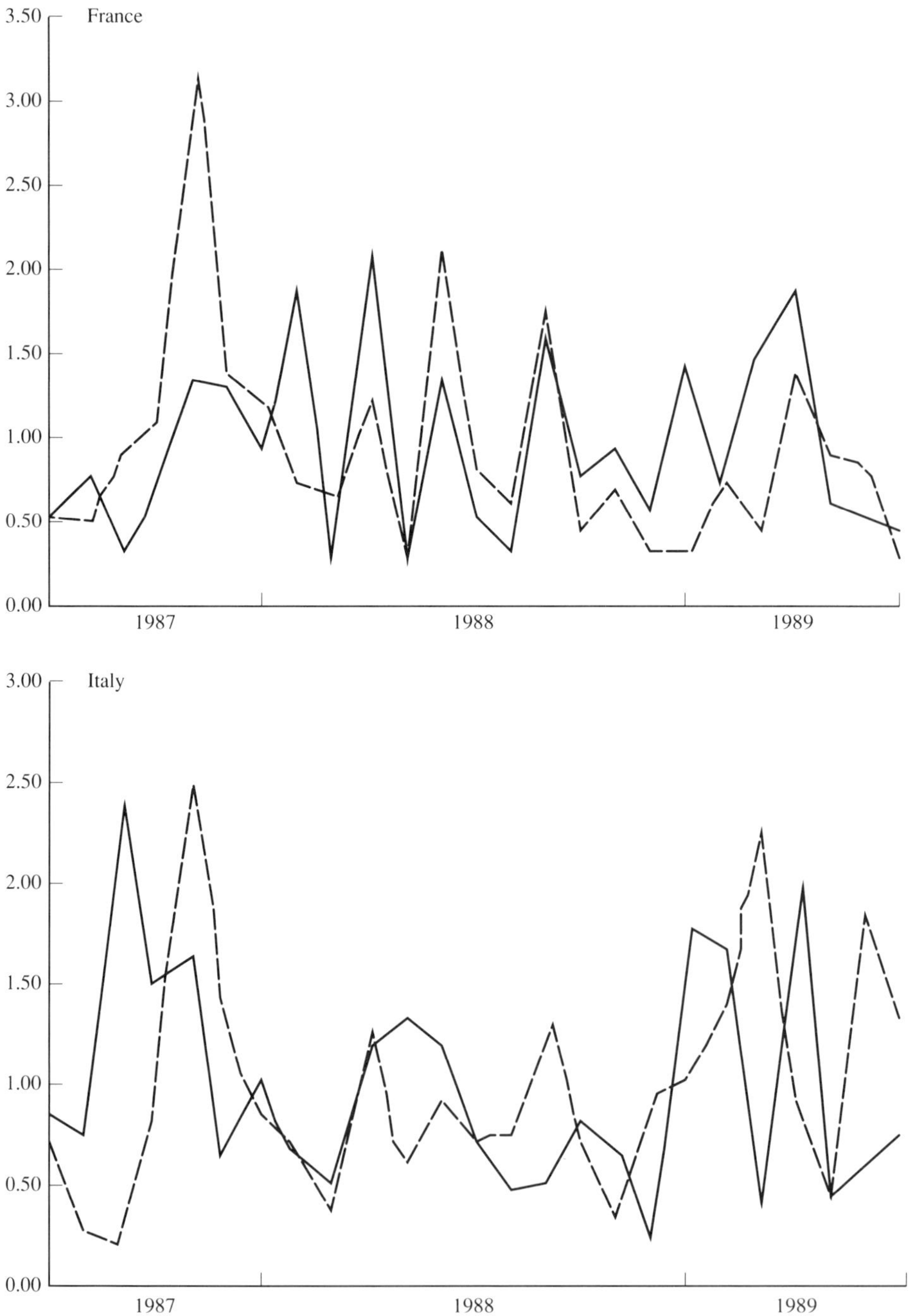

FIG. 6.8 Exchange rate and interest rate variances (daily data). Variances are normalized with their means; (——) interest rates, (----) exchange rates

of exchange rate stability in inflation-prone countries and have been relatively lax in the centre country, thus helping reduce the perception of an asymmetric working of the system. Widening current account imbalances within the EMS have gone along with widening real interest rate differentials between France and Italy, on one side, and the FRG on the other, raising questions as to the real (growth) cost of full economic and monetary integration in Europe.

In this regard, however, there seems to be no convincing argument that full freedom of international capital flows will contribute to raise these costs or threaten the long-term viability of the system *per se*. On the contrary, improved credibility of stability-oriented policies may help reduce the (real) cost of government borrowing and the external financing constraint, thanks to the expanded inflow of foreign capital.

With free capital, the short-term management of the system will require even stricter adhesion to the principles of the Basle–Nyborg Agreement, entailing further losses of monetary autonomy by ERM countries. The full liberalization of monetary transactions will make it more difficult to manage monetary aggregates at national level because of currency substitution. We have also discussed the possibility that monetary discipline in the system may have loosened as a direct consequence of superimposing free capital on the asymmetric model of coordination that had served the EMS so well during the phase of disinflation. The need for coordination may extend from short-term management to the setting of targets and medium-term objectives.

Free capital would also seem to require that the exchange rate constraint in the ERM be tightened in the sense both of (gradually) renouncing realignments and of narrowing the fluctuation band, notably for countries that maintain a wide oscillation band: this is basically a consequence of the need to limit, in the new environment, expected changes in exchange rates and, hence, the opportunities for speculative position-taking in the foreign exchange market.

Appendix

In this appendix we compare, through the use of a simple model by Flood (1981), the adjustment paths for the main macroeconomic variables resulting from two disinflation strategies, one based on monetary targeting, the other on an exchange rate objective.

THE MODEL

Assume a small open economy described by the following equations:

$$m_t^{\mathrm{d}} - p_t = -(1/\lambda)i_t + v_t, \quad v_t \sim N(0,\sigma_v^2), \qquad \text{[A.1]}$$

$$y_t^d = \delta(e_t - p_t) - \sigma(i_t - ({}_tp_{t+1} - p_t)), \qquad [A.2]$$

$$y_t^s = y, \qquad [A.3]$$

$${}_{t-1}y_t^d = y_t^s = \bar{y}, \qquad [A.4]$$

$$i_t = i_t^* + \beta({}_te_{t+1} - e_t) + w_t \quad 0<\beta<1;\ w \sim N(0, \sigma_w^2), \qquad [A.5]$$

$$i_t^* = \bar{i}^* + u_t, \quad u \sim N(0, \sigma_u^2). \qquad [A.6]$$

All coefficients are positive. Equation [A.1] represents the demand for money; v_t is a random money demand disturbance, normally distributed with zero mean and finite variance. Equation [A.2] defines aggregate demand as a function of the real exchange rate $(e_t - p_t)$ and the real interest rate $(i_t - ({}_tp_{t+1} - p_t))$, with ${}_tp_{t+1}$ denoting current price expectations for the next period. By equation [A.3] aggregate supply is constant at its steady state. Equation [A.4] defines the price adjustment process: prices are assumed to be set by agents so as to clear goods markets based on expectations of one period ahead and are therefore (temporarily) 'rigid' in response to unexpected shocks.[31] Equation [A.5] illustrates the interest parity conditions, with the coefficient ß reflecting the degree of capital mobility (when ß=0, markets are 'segmented' by capital controls); w_t represents a risk premium, which is assumed to be a random variable normally distributed, with zero mean and finite variance. The foreign interest rate is defined in equation [A.6] as the sum of a constant i^* (for simplicity set equal to zero) and a stochastic term u_t, which represents a real disturbance; like v_t and w_t, u_t is a random variable normally distributed with zero mean and finite variance.

DISINFLATION POLICIES

Initially, the economy's nominal variables (i.e. money supply, price level and exchange rate) are all assumed to be varying at a constant rate μ. This situation has been prevailing for some time and is expected by market participants to continue $({}_tp_{t+1} = (1+\mu)p_t;\ {}_tm_{t+1} = (1+\mu)m_t)$.

We consider two alternative strategies that the authorities can follow to reduce inflation (to zero). The first consists in deciding (and announcing) at time t to bring money supply growth down to zero.

$$\begin{aligned} m_t &= m_{t-1}, \\ m_{t+1} &= m_{t-1}(1+\mu), \\ m_{t+j} &= m_{t+1} \qquad all\ j > 1. \end{aligned} \qquad [A.7]$$

The rate of growth of money supply is brought down to zero at time t and is kept equal to zero afterwards, except that in period $t+1$ an additional amount μm is supplied to maintain unchanged the real quantity of money and eliminate the need for a price level reduction at time $t+1$.

The second strategy consists of fixing, at time t , the exchange rate at its $t\!-\!1$ level, and adjusting afterwards, once and for all, for purchasing power parity.

$$
\begin{aligned}
&e_t = e_{t-1}, \\
&e_{t+1} = e_{t-1}(1+\mu), \qquad\qquad [A.8] \\
&e_{t+j} = e_{t+1} \qquad \textit{all } j > 1.
\end{aligned}
$$

The exchange rate is adjusted at time $t+1$ to eliminate the real appreciation that develops at time t; subsequently it is maintained constant at e_{t+1}.

Both strategies are announced at time t and are assumed to be credible. We also assume for the time being that there are no other shocks in the economy (w_t, v_t, u_t = 0). We can solve the model to obtain the adjustment path for the endogenous variables (e, i, y). The first strategy ('monetary targeting') leads to the following exchange and interest rate dynamics:

$$
\begin{aligned}
&e_t = [1+\mu - \lambda\mu/\beta]\, e_{t-1}, \\
&e_{t+1} = (1+\mu)\, e_t \qquad\qquad [A.9]
\end{aligned}
$$

$$
\begin{aligned}
&i_t = \lambda\mu m_{t-1}, \\
&i_{t+1} = 0. \qquad\qquad [A.10]
\end{aligned}
$$

Aggregate demand expands as follows:

$$
\begin{aligned}
&y_t = [\delta\lambda\mu/\beta - \sigma\lambda\mu]\, m_{t-1}, \\
&y_{t+1} = \overline{y} = 0. \qquad\qquad [A.11]
\end{aligned}
$$

In the second strategy ('exchange rate targeting') the exchange rate is an exogenous variable while money supply becomes endogenous. The dynamics of adjustment are as follows:

$$
\begin{aligned}
&i_t = \beta\mu\, m_{t-1}, \\
&i_{t+1} = 0, \qquad\qquad [A.12]
\end{aligned}
$$

$$
\begin{aligned}
&m_t = [1 + \mu(1-\beta)/\lambda]\, m_{t-1}, \\
&m_{t+1} = (1+\mu)\, m_{t-1} \qquad\qquad [A.13]
\end{aligned}
$$

Aggregate demand behaves as follows:

$$
\begin{aligned}
&y_t = [\delta\mu+\sigma\beta\mu]\, m_{t-1}, \\
&y_{t+1} = \overline{y} = 0. \qquad\qquad [A.14]
\end{aligned}
$$

Comparing the two equilibrium paths (Fig. 6A.1), it can be seen that the steady state (at period $t+1$) of all variables is the same in the two cases: this reflects the long-run neutrality property of the model.

During the transition to zero inflation (at time t) the interest rate response to the two disinflation strategies depends on the size of the ß and λ coefficients (cf. equations [A.10] and [A.12]). The coefficient ß, which represents the degree of capital mobility, can be reduced by capital controls: with ß approaching zero, domestic interest rates only rise very little during the disinflation strategy based on exchange rate targeting; as a consequence, the output cost of disinflation is reduced. On the

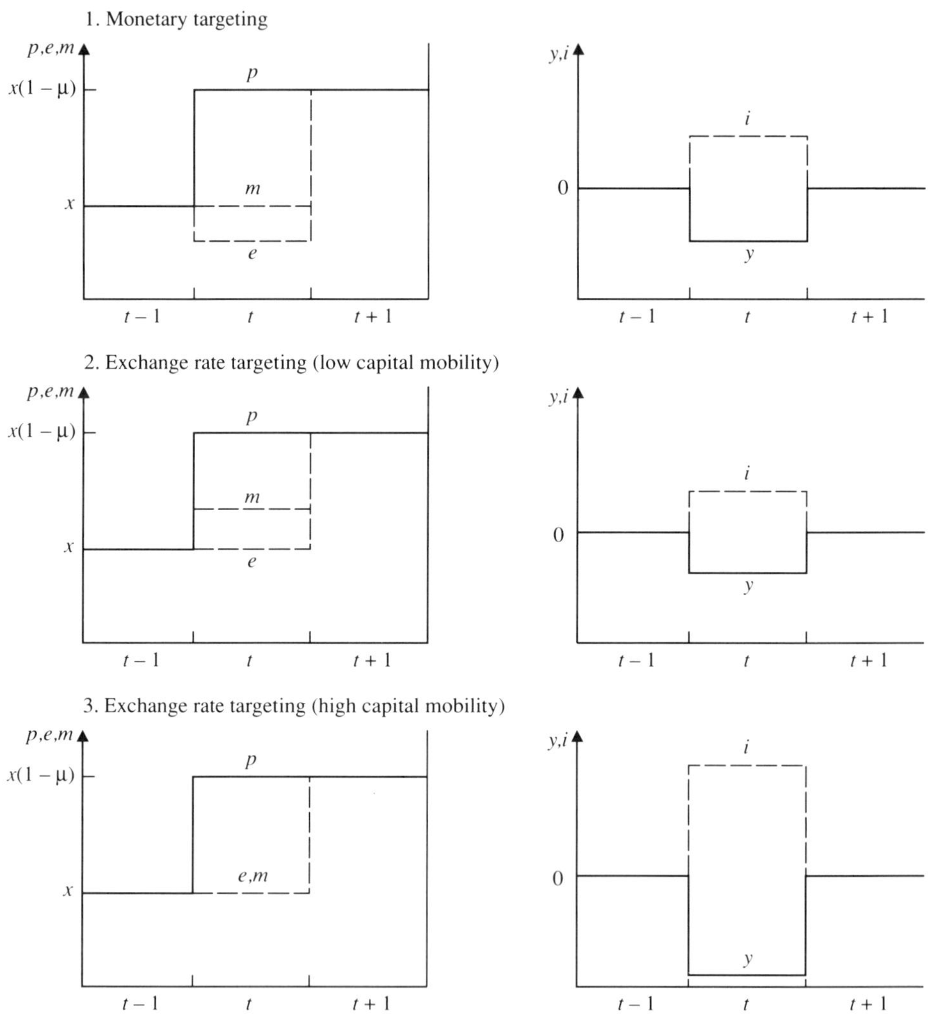

FIG 6A.1 Adjustment paths under alternative strategies

other hand, with high capital mobility exchange rate targeting becomes very costly in terms of interest rate change and output cost.

This simple model tends thus to suggest that an optimal strategy for disinflation is that of targeting the exchange rate, and at the same time limiting capital mobility. This intuitive result is in line with the previous literature on this subject, in particular Begg and Wyplosz (1987) and Bini Smaghi (1990).

THE VARIABILITY OF EXCHANGE RATES AND INTEREST RATES WITH RANDOM DISTURBANCES

The model above can be used to examine the effects of alternative shocks, under a monetary or an exchange rate target rule, on the variability of the exchange and the interest rate.

The money supply process can be modelled as follows:

$$m_t + m_{t-1} + \alpha({}_te_{t+1} - e_t), \qquad [A.15]$$

where the parameter α represents the degree of flexibility allowed for the exchange rate around its steady-state non-shock level. If α is zero the exchange rate is floating and free to move in response to exogenous disturbances; if α is infinite, the exchange rate is fixed (at its steady-state level) and the money supply becomes endogenous.

By solving the system of equations [A.1–A.6] and [A.15] with the method of undetermined coefficients we obtain the following:

$$\begin{aligned} e_t &= m_{t-1} + \lambda\pi v_t + \pi w_t + \pi u_t, \\ i_t &= -\pi\beta\lambda v_t + \pi\lambda\alpha w_t + \pi\lambda\alpha u_t, \end{aligned} \qquad [A.16]$$

where $\pi = 1/(\lambda\ \alpha + \beta) > 0$.

This result has some interesting implications. For increasing values of α, the exchange rate is decreasingly affected by exogenous shocks (for $\alpha \rightarrow \infty, \pi \rightarrow 0$). What happens to the interest rate then depends on the nature of the exogenous shocks; for rising values of α the interest rate response to monetary shocks (v >0) increases, while it diminishes in the presence of real (u_t) and risk premium (w_t) shocks.

We can calculate the variances of the exchange rate and the interest rate:

$$\begin{aligned} var(e) &= \pi^2\ [\lambda^2\sigma_v^2 + \sigma_w^2 + \sigma_u^2\ ], \\ var(i) &= (\pi\lambda)^2\ [\beta^2\sigma_v^2 + \alpha^2\sigma_w^2 + \alpha^2\sigma_u^2\ ]. \end{aligned} \qquad [A.17]$$

By differentiating var(e) and var(i) with respect to α, we obtain

$$\frac{\partial\, var(e)}{\partial\alpha} = \pi^3\ [-2\lambda\sigma_v^2 - \sigma_w^2 - \sigma_u^2\ ],$$

$$\frac{\partial var(i)}{\partial\alpha} = \pi^3\ [-\beta^2\lambda^2\sigma_v^2 + \beta\sigma_w^2 + \beta\sigma_u^2\ ]. \qquad [A.18]$$

It can be seen that as α increases in the presence of monetary shocks we observe a reduction in the variability of both the exchange and the interest rates; in the presence of real or financial risk premium shocks, instead, as α rises the decrease in exchange rate variability is associated with an increase in interest rate variability. The obvious implication is that capital controls can be used to limit the 'transfer' of shocks from the foreign exchange to the domestic money market when real or risk premium shocks prevail: from equation [A.18] it can be seen that as β goes to zero the sensitivity of the exchange rate variability to an increase in α also goes to zero. What is less obvious is that when pure monetary shocks are likely to prevail, increasing 'rigidity' in exchange rate pegging will also help reduce the variability of interest rates: in equation [A.18] the impacts of σ_v^2 on var(e) and var(i) have the same sign.

Notes

1. The turning-point was represented by the 'bear squeeze' of early 1988, an episode of concerted intervention in support of the dollar that caught markets by surprise leading to heavy losses on short-positions in dollars, (Marris 1989).
2. If international competitiveness is measured in terms of unit labour costs, since the inception of the EMS a systematic depreciation of the DM is only apparent *vis-à-vis* the lira (by some 15 per cent); the DM rate of the FF is now close to its 1979 level, and appreciations of the DM are observed vis-à-vis all the other ERM currencies, including the Irish pound (IR£). (BIS 1989; 179).
3. At the end of 1989 limits remained on the possibility of taking short positions and hedging in foreign exchange, and of lending to non-residents.
4. Committee of Governors of the EEC (1987) and Dini (1988). The agreement was endorsed shortly afterwards by the Council of Finance Ministers (ECOFIN) gathered in Nyborg.
5. For a description of the EMS mechanisms and facilities see Micossi (1985) and Mastropasqua *et al.* (1988).
6. The Basle–Nyborg Agreement reflected more than anything else awareness of the policy conflicts that had led to the January 1987 realignment. On that occasion the dollar came under strong selling pressure in December 1986, pushing the DM up in the ERM band. The Banque de France intervened heavily in rigid defence of the market rate, and raised interest rates; the Bundesbank, however, also let its money market rates edge up to slow liquidity creation in response to its dollar purchases, and did not participate in ERM-related interventions. The perception of a policy conflict, made acute by public recriminations, set in motion huge capital flows; in early January the Banque de France suddenly let the DM rate go to the limit, forcing the Bundesbank to intervene and drawing heavily on the VSTF. In a few days the Bundesbank was confronted with monetary base flows, owing to DM interventions, equivalent to some 20 per cent of its targeted increase for the year.

All this happened at a time when there was a consensus among EMS monetary authorities that there was no 'fundamental' reason for a realignment.

7. Increased values of the coefficients of variation go hand in hand with a decline in standard deviations, as will be seen (see Fig. 6.8).
8. Bini Smaghi and Masera (1987). The lira devaluation of July 1985 stands out as an exception: as may be recalled, however, in that case the lira was devalued 'by surprise' without very heavy market pressures.
9. And as such is incorporated in Committee of Governors of the EEC (1987) in their report to the ECOFIN Council that is the basis of the Basle–Nyborg Agreement.
10. Giavazzi and Giovannini (1987). Efforts to model the EMS as a strategic game, such as Giavazzi and Pagano (1988) and Melitz (1988) typically emphasize monetary discipline (that entails asymmetry) in the explanation of the interest of inflation-prone countries in joining the system.
11. Obtained as the residual from forecasting regressions that include as dependent variable a time trend, seasonal dummies and four lags of the dependent variable. See Giavazzi and Giovannini (1989: Ch. 4, 73–7).
12. An example is that of October 1987 when the FRG and France agreed on a coordinated interest rate change of opposite sign.
13. This feature of policy coordination within the ERM has been recognized and explicitly modelled by Begg and Wyplosz (1987): in their model of 'bounded rationality', the rules of the system only extend to the choice of a 'loose' policy regime, within which a lot of room remains for the (cooperative or non-cooperative) setting of policy instruments.
14. Contrary to most other EC countries, the share of German exports towards the EC has stagnated during the 1980s, at about 50 per cent of total exports. Further insight on the vulnerability of the German economy to real exchange rate appreciation can be found in Mayer (1989): 'the paper illustrates how labour market rigidities and regulations are likely to combine with protectionist policies to generate an environment in which an appreciation of the exchange rate is a serious threat to economic growth and employment'.
15. See for instance Caranza, *et al.* (1988), Russo and Tullio (1988), Bini Smaghi (1989b).
16. Ireland, Spain, Greece and Portugal will still enjoy transitional regimes until 1992–93.
17. Buiter (1986) has shown that in the absence of a foreign liquidity (reserves) constraint the collapse of a managed exchange rate can only be brought about by expectations of government default. In a more realistic setting where there is a foreign liquidity constraint (reserve cannot be borrowed without limit), then a viable managed exchange rate also requires that the domestic credit component does not grow, along the steady-state path, more rapidly than the demand for money. See also Driffill (1988).
18. Cf. Dornbusch (1988), Grilli (1989) and Giavazzi and Giovannini (1989: Ch. 8). Canzoneri and Rogers (1989) argued that the relevance of the optimal taxation arguments increases with the relative share of the 'black economy', where the need for cash for transactions is higher.
19. This had been argued by Aizenman (1989). In this context an exchange rate agreement or monetary unification are a way to remove such externality.

20. See Gros and Thygesen (1988) and De Grauwe (1989b). In the case of Italy, for instance, a 1 per cent reduction in the average cost of government debt, as a result of lower risk premium, would lead to reduced interest payments roughly equivalent to the entire yearly revenues from seigniorage (that are at present of the order of 1 per cent of GNP).
21. The well-known observed asymmetric response of ERM currencies to the fluctuations in the dollar exchange rate entails rising interest rate differentials *vis-à-vis* the DM when the dollar is falling.
22. Begg and Wyplosz (1987) note (i) that the formal setting of the EMS did not specify that one currency would assume a special role (no announcement effect); (ii) that if a country is able to take the decision to join the EMS to disinflate, why then should it not be able to appoint domestically the conservative central banker that is needed for 'credibility'.
23. They were 'biting', as documented by Giavazzi and Pagano (1985), in the periods immediately preceding realignments, thus reducing the need for (larger) interest rate changes. This 'temporary' function of controls, however, is conceptually different from that of making it possible to sustain a 'permanently' divergent stance of monetary policy relative to ERM partners. See Micossi and Rossi (1989).
24. Cf. Obstfeld (1988a) and Driffill (1988); they note that a monetary policy rule that entailed anticipated discontinuities in asset prices would be inconsistent with conventional assumptions on efficient (and perfectly integrated) capital markets. The only alternative, with 'divergent' monetary policies, would really be a system of 'soft' bands that would be adjusted automatically whenever a currency hit the edge; such a system would not be qualitatively different from one of floating exchange rates.
25. For a recent restatement see Obstfeld (1988b).
26. This aspect is recognized by Giavazzi (1989:19) who notes the role of the ceiling on banks' net foreign indebtedness in preventing capital inflows in periods of calm in the system.
27. There are, we believe, almost no instances of central banks of the ERM actively pushing exchange rates up or down in the band; interventions in foreign exchange markets were typically 'leaning into the wind'.
28. Provided, of course, ERM countries were not intervening collectively to peg their dollar exchange rate. See section 3.
29. See Gros and Thygesen (1988). The problem of stability of the demand for money base will be aggravated by 'structural' shifts in countries where monetary base is more heavily taxed.
30. Krugman (1988) has explicitly modelled, in a seminal paper, the stabilizing role of the band on exchange rate expectations. The literature on 'smooth pasting' has rapidly expanded; see Krugman (1989), Flood and Garber (1989), Froot and Obstfeld (1989). An important factor influencing the credibility of the band is the size of the monetary authorities' foreign exchange reserves.
31. A similar price adjustment mechanism is used by Flood (1981).

References

Aizenman, J. (1989) Competitive externalities and the optimal seigniorage, *NBER Working Paper*, No. 2937, April.

Artis, M. J. and **Taylor, M. P**. (1988) Exchange rates, interest rates, capital controls and the European Monetary System: assessing the track record, in Giavazzi F., Micossi, S. and Miller, M. (eds), *The European Monetary System*, Cambridge University Press, Cambridge, pp. 185–206.

Begg, D and **Wyplosz, C**. (1987) Why the EMS? Dynamic games and the equilibrium policy regime, in Bryant, R. and Portes, R. (eds), *Global Macroeconomics: Policy Conflict and Cooperation,* St Martin's Press, New York.

Bekx, P. and **Tullio, G**. (1987) The European Monetary System and the determination of the DM-US dollar exchange rate, mimeo, Commission of the EEC.

Bini Smaghi, L. (1989a), Fiscal prerequisites for further monetary convergence in the EMS, *Banca Nazionale del Lavoro Quarterly Review*, No. 169, pp. 165–89.

Bini Smaghi, L. (1989b) Progressing towards European monetary union: selected issues and few proposals, mimeo, Banca d'Italia.

Bini Smaghi, L. (1990) Target zones vs real exchange rate rules: comparative dynamics, *European Journal of Political Economy*, f. **50**

Bini Smaghi, L. and **Masera, R. S.** (1987) L'evoluzione degli Accordi di Cambio dello SME, in *L'unificazione monetaria e lo SME*, Il Mulino, Bologna, pp. 133–96.

BIS. (1989) *59th Annual Report*, Basle.

Buiter, W. H. (1986) Fiscal prerequisites for a viable managed exchange rate regime: a non-technical eclectic introduction, *CEPR Discussion Paper*, No. 129, September.

Canzoneri, M. and **Rogers, C.** (1989) Is Europe an optimal currency area?, mimeo, NBER.

Caranza, C., Papadia, F. and **Zautzik, E**. (1988) Liberalizzazione valutaria e politica monetaria, mimeo, Banca d'Italia.

Committee of Governors of the EEC (1987) *Report on the Strengthening of the EMS*, BIS, September.

Cohen, D. and **Wyplosz, C**. (1989) The European Monetary System: an agnostic evaluation, *CEPR Discussion Paper*, No. 306, April.

De Grauwe, P. (1989a) Is the European Monetary System a DM-zone, *CEPR Discussion Paper*, No. 297, March.

De Grauwe, P. (1989b) *Liberalization of Capital Movements and the EMS*, paper presented at the Conference on the EMS, Ten Years Later, Bergamo, 5 May.

Dini, L. (1988) A new phase in the European Monetary System: introductory statement, in Giavazzi, F., Micossi, S. and Miller, M. (eds), *The European Monetary System*, Cambridge University Press, Cambridge, pp. 385–88.

Dornbusch, R. (1982) PPP Exchange-rate rules and macroeconomic stability, *Journal of Political Economy*, February, **90** pp. 158–65

Dornbusch, R. (1988) The European Monetary System, the dollar and the yen, in Giavazzi, F., Micossi, S. and Miller, M. (eds), *The European Monetary System,* Cambridge University Press, Cambridge, pp. 23–41.

Driffill, J. (1988) The stability and sustainability of the European Monetary System with perfect capital markets, in Giavazzi, F., Micossi, S. and Miller, M. (eds), *The European Monetary System*, Cambridge University Press, Cambridge, pp. 211–28.

Dudler, H. (1988) Monetary policy and exchange market management in Germany, in *Exchange Market Intervention and Monetary Policy*, BIS, March, Basle, pp. 65–96.

Flood, R. (1981) Explanation of exchange rate volatility and other empirical regularities in some popular models of the foreign exchange market, Carnegie Conference Series on Public Policies, **15**, pp. 219–50.

Flood, R. and **Garber, P.** (1989) The linkage between speculative attacks and target zones models of exchange rates, *NBER Working Paper*, No. 2918, April.

Fratianni, M. and **Von Hagen, J**. (1989) The European Monetary System ten years after, *Indiana University Discussion Paper*, No. 419.

Froot, K. and **Obstfeld, M**. (1989) Exchange rate dynamics under stochastic regime shifts: a unified approach, *NBER Working Paper*, No. 2835, January.

Funabashi, Y. (1988) *Managing the Dollar: From the Plaza to the Louvre*, Institute for International Economics, Washington, D.C.

Gaiotti, E., Giucca, P. and **Micossi, S**. (1989) Cooperation in managing the dollar (1985–87): interventions in foreign exchange markets and interest rates, *Temi di Discussione del Servizio Studi*, No. 119, Banca d'Italia, June.

Giavazzi, F. (1989) The EMS Experience, Paper presented at the Conference on 'The EMS: Ten Years Later.', Bergamo, 5 May.

Giavazzi, F. and **Giovannini, A**. (1987) Models of the EMS: is Europe a greater Deutschmark area?, in Bryant, R. and Portes, R. (eds), *Global Macroeconomics: Policy Conflicts and Cooperation*, St. Martin's Press, New York, pp. 237–76.

Giavazzi F. and **Giovannini A.** (1989) *Limiting Exchange Rate Flexibility: The European Monetary System*, MIT Press, Cambridge, Mass.

Giavazzi, F. and **Pagano, M**. (1985) Capital controls and the European Monetary System, *Euromobiliare Occasional Paper*, No. 1, May.

Giavazzi, F. and **Pagano, M**. (1988) The advantage of tying one's hands: EMS discipline and central bank credibility, *European Economic Review*, June, **32**, pp. 1055–82.

Grilli, V. (1989) Seigniorage in Europe, in De Cecco, M. and Giovannini, A. (eds), *A European Central Bank*, Cambridge University Press, Cambridge.

Gros, D. and **Thygesen, N.** (1988) The EMS achievements: current issues and directions for the future, *CEPS Paper*, No. 35, March.

Henderson, D. W. (1984) Exchange market intervention operations: their role in financial policy and their effects, in Bilson, J. and Marston, R. (eds), *Exchange Rate Theory and Practice*, University of Chicago Press, Chicago, pp. 357–406.

Hooper, P. and **Morton, J**. (1982) Fluctuations in the dollar: a model of nominal and real exchange rate determination, *Journal of International Money and Finance*, April, pp. 39–55.

Kenen, P.B. (1988) Reflections on EMS experience, in Giavazzi, F., Micossi, S. and Miller, M. (eds), *The European Monetary System*, Cambridge University Press, Cambridge, pp. 388–93.

Kregel, J.A. (1989) The EMS, the dollar and the world economy, paper presented at the Conference on the EMS, Ten Years Later, Bergamo, 5 May.

Krugman, P.R. (1988) Target zones and exchange rate dynamics, *NBER, Working Paper*, No. 2481, January.

Krugman, P. R. (1989) *Target zones with limited reserves*, mimeo, NBER.

Marris, S. (1989) *Deficits – and surpluses – forever?*, mimeo, June.

Masera, R.S. (1988) European currency: an Italian view, in Giavazzi, F., Micossi, S. and Miller, M. (eds), *The European Monetary System*, Cambridge University Press, Cambridge, pp. 393–404.

Mastropasqua, C., Micossi, S. and **Rinaldi, R.** (1988) Interventions, sterilisation and monetary policy in European Monetary System countries, 1979–87, in Giavazzi, F., Micossi, S. and Miller, M. (eds), *The European Monetary System*, Cambridge University Press, Cambridge, pp. 252–87.

Mayer, T. (1989) Economic structure, the exchange rate and adjustment in the Federal Republic of Germany, *IMF Staff Papers*, **36**, (2), pp. 435–63.

McKinnon, R. (1977) Beyond fixed parities: the analytics of international monetary agreements, in Aliber, R. (ed), *The Political Economy of Monetary Reform*, Macmillan, London, pp. 42–56.

Melitz, J. (1988) Monetary discipline and cooperation in the European Monetary System: a synthesis, in Giavazzi, F., Micossi, S. and Miller, M. (eds), *The European Monetary System*, Cambridge University Press, Cambridge, pp. 51–79.

Micossi, S. (1985) The intervention and financing mechanism of the EMS, *Banca Nazionale del Lavoro – Quarterly Review*, December, **155**, pp. 327–45

Micossi, S. and **Padoa-Schioppa, T.** (1984) Short-term interest rate linkages between the United States and Europe, *Tensi di Discussione del Servizio Studi*, **33**, Banca d'Italia.

Micossi, S. and **Rossi, S.** (1989) Restrictions on international capital flows: the case of Italy, in *European Factor Mobility: Trends and Consequences*, Macmillan, London, pp. 195–214.

Obstfeld, M. (1988a) Competitiveness, realignment, and speculation: the role of financial markets, in Giavazzi, F., Micossi, S. and Miller, M. (eds), *The European Monetary System*, Cambridge University Press, Cambridge, pp. 232–47.

Obstfeld, M. (1988b) The effectiveness of foreign-exchange interventions: recent experience, *NBER Working Paper*, No. 2796, December.

Rogoff, K. (1985) Can exchange rate predictability be achieved without monetary convergence? Evidence from the EMS, *European Economic Review*, June–July, **28**, pp. 93–115.

Roubini, N. (1988a) Sterilization policies, offsetting capital movements and exchange rate intervention policies in the EMS, Ch. IV of unpublished Ph.D. dissertation, Harvard University.

Roubini, N. (1988b) Offset and sterilization under fixed exchange rates with an optimizing central bank, *NBER Working Paper*, No. 2777, November.

Russo, M. and **Tullio, G.** (1988), Monetary policy coordination within the European Monetary System: is there a rule?, in Giavazzi, F., Micossi, S. and Miller, M. (eds), *The European Monetary System*, Cambridge University Press, Cambridge, pp. 292–356.

Spaventa, L. (1989) The new EMS: symmetry without coordination, paper presented at the Conference on Managing the EMS in an Integrated Europe, Madrid, 11–12 May.

Thygesen, N. (1988) Introduction, in Giavazzi, F., Micossi, S. and Miller, M. (eds), *The European Monetary System*, Cambridge University Press, Cambridge, pp. 1–20.

Vona, S. and **Bini Smaghi, L.** (1988) Economic growth and exchange rates in the European Monetary System: their trade effects in a changing external environment, in

Giavazzi, F., Micossi, S. and Miller, M. (eds), *The European Monetary System*, Cambridge University Press, Cambridge, pp. 147–78.
Wyplosz, C. (1989) Asymmetry in the EMS: intentional or systemic, *European Economic Review*, March, **33**, pp. 310–20.

Comment: Henning Dalgaard

My task of commenting on the chapter by Bini Smaghi and Micossi has been complicated by the fact that I find myself basically agreeing with the main conclusions.

My comments will, therefore, be concentrated on my experience from Denmark and from our exchange rate cooperation in the EC on the operational effects of the increased capital flows.

Fortunately, I do not need to argue in favour of capital liberalization in general – this discussion has been brought to a happy conclusion in the EC. But I should like to stress – based on our Danish experience – that full liberalization does not necessarily create problems for the exchange market provided you follow a reasonable economic policy.

In fact our experience has been that when capital movements have been liberalized to a certain extent (trade credits, direct investments and portfolio investments) there is little merit in retaining the remaining restrictions. As long as some restrictions are retained you are stuck with problems of administration and control but, nevertheless, most major market participants will be able to take the positions they want – although perhaps not in the way they would prefer. The idea that it would be valuable to maintain restrictions on short-term capital transactions overlooks the fact that at present most capital transactions are – or can be changed into – short-term transactions.

When Denmark liberalized the remaining restrictions last autumn nothing happened – which was exactly as expected.

Another point which I should like to stress is that capital flows have been increasing not only because of liberalization, but for many other reasons such as the following:

1. The increase in international trade and direct investments;
2. The improvement of capital markets and the development of new financial instruments;
3. The increasing awareness in companies and institutions of the importance of movements in financial markets; and
4. The education of thousands of financial experts.

Consequently, capital flows have increased dramatically everywhere – whether or not there are restrictions.

In today's world a developed country will have to allow for some capital movements, at least those linked to foreign trade and direct investments, and they will make possible enormous capital flows. A country will, therefore, have to develop an economic policy which can control net capital flows – and if such a policy is in place, some further liberalization will make little difference.

The problem to be studied should, therefore, not be limited to the consequences of capital liberalization, but should rather be the problems resulting from the ever increasing capital flows.

These capital flows are at present much more important than current account balances in deciding the development of exchange rates. Fortunately, it is in principle quite simple to control capital flows. You just have to ensure the right balance between interest rate differentials and expectations of changes in exchange rates.

The decision taken by the EC central bank governors on the technique to be used in the management of exchange rate cooperation – known as the Basle–Nyborg Agreement – was important, not only because it contained new ideas, but because more central banks used the well-known technique more skilfully. Basically the idea is to influence exchange rate expectations through modest changes of the exchange rate within the margins, and to compensate for remaining variations in expectations through changes in interest rate differentials.

For example, when capital began to flow out of Denmark just before Easter this year, the outflow was stopped completely by a rise in the level of interest rates by 0.5 per cent. There have been many similar examples.

The effect of interest rate changes on the exchange rates is obvious, but the effect of movements of the exchange rate within the band is more complex.

Many central banks thought originally that it would create speculative pressures if the exchange rate was allowed to approach the limit because it would increase expectations of an imminent realignment. That may have been true at the time. But in periods when a realignment is not expected – as has now been the case for a long time – the situation is different. The closer the rate gets to the limit, the smaller the chances of a further gain on the exchange rate and the bigger the risk of a loss.

It is important to note that it is not only the wording of the EMS agreement which is relevant. Confidence in the agreement has been established because it has been demonstrated in practice that realignments are considered to be serious decisions which are used only when no other method is available.

Therefore, you can see the same effect outside the EMS, if confidence has been established. For example, this makes it possible for Austria to keep a practically stable rate for the schilling against the DM without too much effort. On the other hand where confidence in the exchange rate is lacking, very big changes in exchange rates are often necessary to equilibrate markets.

Central banks have often been worried about the rapid development of the international financial markets. It is interesting that this development also has had positive effects. For example the fact that the time horizon of the market has shortened has been helpful in certain respects. The market now mostly looks to the very near future, and it is much easier to convince the market that your exchange rate will be unchanged for a week than for half a year.

Previously many companies did not follow the foreign exchange market closely. Therefore they would not normally change their positions much, but when they heard rumours of a realignment they tended to panic. Now more and more companies are following the market every day and adjusting their position according to circumstances. As a consequence the adjustments are more gradual and rational.

In conclusion, there is reason for optimism with regard to the possibilities for stabilizing exchange rates despite the increasing capital flows.

But of course there is another side to the coin. To the extent that you use interest rate changes to influence capital flows – and thereby exchange rates – the possibility of using interest rate changes for domestic purposes is limited. As the markets are not perfect, there is, however, a little leeway, and to some extent you can trade your position in the EMS band against a change in interest rates.

The possibility of following an independent interest rate policy has been tested recently by Spain and Italy, where interest rates have been clearly too high for the foreign exchange market. It has, however, proved to be possible to maintain orderly foreign exchange markets by letting the rates rise within the band and by substantial intervention purchases. This is not a new situation in the EMS. As pointed out by Giavazzi and Spaventa (Chap.4.) it was the same development we saw in Denmark in the years 1984–85.

It was also mentioned that the disciplinary effect from the current account has been weakened, now that almost any deficit can be financed so easily.

It is true that easy financing results in fewer crises in the foreign exchange markets. But there are still plenty of indicators showing potential problems, and the absence of crises gives time for an orderly adjustment.

It would be a problem in the long run if countries attempted to avoid all realignments – including those which would have been useful. However, this does not now seem to be a problem in the EMS. There are no tensions indicating a need for a realignment, and indeed if you are looking at the development in real effective exchange rates since the last realignment, you see only minor changes.

My conclusions are as follows:

1. Large movements of capital are here to stay;
2. A country cannot reduce problems from capital movements significantly with restrictions – unless it is willing to sacrifice its effective participation in the international economy;
3. Countries, therefore, have to accept the policies necessary to control net capital flows; and
4. This could be done, but it does mean that certain instruments – in particular interest rates – will have to be reserved mainly for this purpose.

Comment: Nicholas Karamouzis

L. Bini Smaghi and S. Micossi have presented a very interesting chapter focusing on three main topics: (a) an overview of major developments in the EMS since 1985; (b) a summary of empirical evidence for and against the hypothesis that the model of monetary coordination in the EMS has been asymmetric; and (c) the implications of increased capital mobility for the short-term management of the EMS and for the long-term viability of the system.

In the first part of the chapter, concerning the main developments in the EMS since 1985, I agree broadly with most of the analysis and conclusions of the authors and the comments by Henning Dalgaard. I have, however, two general criticisms. First, recent experience with the functioning of the EMS has shown that a flexible interest rate policy along with the full use of the band should play a central role in the short-term management of the system. This is an important point that needs to be strongly emphasized. Though interventions in the foreign exchange markets would be useful and effective under certain circumstances, timely and swift adjustments of short-term interest rates have proved to be the most effective means of defending the parities and countering speculation, especially in an environment of liberalized capital flows. Second, in the more distant past, dollar weakness was usually accompanied with tensions in the EMS, mainly because capital movements away from dollar-denominated assets were mostly channelled into DM-denominated assets, putting upward pressure on the DM against the other currencies participating in the exchange rate mechanism of the EMS. This phenomenon is not so evident in the recent past where the EMS seems to be considerably more resilient to a weakening dollar. Such a development could be attributed, in my judgement, to better macroeconomic convergence among ERM countries, especially in the areas of money growth and inflation, improved credibility of the policies of central banks and the adoption of more flexible and coordinated interest rate policies following the Basle–Nyborg Agreement.

On the subject of asymmetry in the EMS as regards the burden of interventions, interest rate adjustment and the setting of monetary policy, Bini Smaghi and Micossi review several studies mainly concerning the short-term management of the system. Though the empirical evidence on this issue is mixed, the authors seem to be leaning on the side of accepting the hypothesis of asymmetry in the EMS stating that 'failure to confirm empirically the asymmetric model of coordination, thus, could be seen as casting doubt more on the specification and testing of the hypothesis than on the hypothesis itself' (p. 134). I have some doubts whether additional empirical work would resolve this debate. Moreover, I would find it rather unnecessary because the EMS had to be asymmetric the way it developed in recent years, especially in the setting of the medium-term stance of monetary policy, if the exchange rates were to be kept fixed but adjustable and the convergence process to be advanced. On this issue I would agree with similar views expressed by Professors Gros and Thygesen on another occasion. The system has benefited from the role played by the DM as an 'anchor' for monetary stability and for participants' monetary and intervention policies. An alternative model of cooperation would have required the establishment of a common European monetary policy and much closer monetary policy coordination which were premature in the early 1980s, especially in view of the significant macroeconomic divergences that prevailed among participants in the system.

The authors wonder if the recent experience with the Bundesbank's monetary policy (p. 134) perhaps shows that exchange rate objectives relative to the rest of the world are taking up an increasing importance in shaping up the FRG's monetary policy to the detriment of domestic price stability and the function of the DM as nominal anchor of the EMS. In my view, experience with the Bundesbank's monetary policy, particularly in the 1988–89 period, in no way corroborates the hypothesis that policy has been lax. Official and market interest rates have been rising since it became evident that inflationary pressures were building up in the economy. Interest rates at the end of 1989 were more than twice as high compared with their levels a year and a half earlier, while a further rise in official interest rates was anticipated by market participants. Nominal and real money growth rates have recently been decelerated with a reasonable time-lag following the interest rate hikes. In addition, I would be reluctant to rely solely on money growth alone as an indicator of the stance of monetary policy, especially in an environment of liberalization of capital flows and financial deregulations and innovations. Overall, I do not find strong evidence that when the dollar is weakening the system's monetary discipline is loosened, and the most recent experience does not provide any support to this hypothesis.

On the issue of capital liberalization and the long-term viability of the EMS, I would agree with Bini Smaghi and Micossi that today we do not have convincing evidence that full liberalization of capital movements will raise substantially the cost of membership in the EMS. However, I would add that this cost would depend on the degree of progress towards monetary and fiscal convergence that a candidate country has achieved before full membership. I am also in agreement with the authors' contention that capital controls are ineffective and they have not averted the loss of foreign exchange reserves or exchange rate pressure. Our experience in Greece with capital controls supports such a conclusion. But capital controls have perhaps a role to play in the short term and on a temporary basis, when monetary policy is aiming at too many targets without sufficient support from other policy instruments, especially fiscal policy. The recent experience of Spain with the imposition of capital controls to contain capital inflows and domestic liquidity expansion is indicative of the case.

Bini Smaghi and Micossi present a simple aggregative model that shows formally that capital controls can tilt the balance in favour of the ERM regime since they reduce the required increase in interest rates, and hence the loss of output, along the path of disinflation. I am rather sceptical on the extent to which capital controls would lower the output loss of disinflation. Despite questions as regards their effectiveness, a distinction should be drawn in the model between short-term and long-term interest rates. Capital controls may reduce the magnitude of short-term interest rate increases, but the relevant interest rate to assess the output loss should be the long-term interest rate. A credible anti-inflationary policy is usually accompanied by an inversion of the yield curve, thus, the output loss is unlikely to be greater than otherwise, unless we assume that capital controls lower long-term interest rates. In addition, increases in short-term interest rates aiming at defending the currency, and discouraging speculation, are usually of short duration and it is unlikely that they would filter into long-term interest rates to have a significant effect on output. Conversely, pursuing such a policy in a consistent manner could have a beneficial effect by lowering long-term interest rates.

It has been shown that when the financial system is subjected to certain types of shocks there is a trade-off between interest rate and exchange rate variability in the context of exchange rate management of the EMS. An interesting issue worth exploring is to assess the welfare and economic costs of increased interest rate variability *vis-à-vis* increased exchange rate variability and the factors that determine such costs. The Federal Reserve, for instance, appears to assign greater importance to short-term interest rate smoothing, except during the 1979–82 period of non-borrowed reserve targeting, based on the notion that excessive interest rate volatility is costly. However, interest rate smoothing has resulted in 'base drifting' and laxity of monetary control in some countries, while the evidence on the costs of short-term interest rate volatility is weak.

Finally, on the issue of the width of the fluctuation band, it would be interesting to examine alternative theoretical arguments in the context of the recent experience of Spain's participation in the ERM with a wide band, especially the implications for monetary policy and macroeconomic management had the peseta joined the ERM with the narrow band.

CHAPTER SEVEN

Seigniorage and EMS Discipline

Daniel Gros*

1. Introduction

The implications for public finances of participation in a low-inflation European Monetary System (EMS) are widely recognized. It has even been argued that for some countries participation in such an EMS would not be advisable because of the loss of seigniorage. This chapter analyses, therefore, the issue of seigniorage and EMS discipline, both from an empirical and a theoretical point of view.

The basis for any discussion about the importance of seigniorage has to be a careful measurement of the amount of seigniorage that would be lost through participation in a low-inflation EMS. The data presented below suggest that the countries which have relied most on seigniorage (Greece, Portugal) would have to give up about 2 per cent of gross domestic product (GDP) in seigniorage revenue if their inflation rates were to converge to the current German rate. For Italy and Spain the loss would be lower. These values are somewhat lower than other estimates because in Italy, Spain and Greece central banks pay substantial interest on required reserves.

The data presented below also suggest that for Italy and Spain most of the loss of seigniorage has already materialized with the disinflation of the last five years. The remaining loss of revenue for these two countries would therefore be below 1 per cent of GDP.[1]

The realization that participation in the EMS would lead to this loss of seigniorage revenue has led some observers (see for example Dornbusch 1987) to claim that it would not be advisable for these 'fiscally weak' countries to link themselves to a low-inflation policy via the EMS. These countries should therefore, if they wish to remain in the EMS, adopt a crawling-peg policy that would allow them a rate of inflation of about 8 – 10 per cent.

This chapter disputes this view. The view that the loss of seigniorage should be avoided rests on the implicit assumption that outside the EMS these countries would choose the optimal amount of seigniorage. However, there are strong reasons to believe that this is not the case. Indeed this chapter suggests that participation in a low-inflation EMS might be a second-best option – even from a purely public finance point of view – that is much closer to the optimum than an independent, excessively inflationary policy.

The intuition behind this result can be easily seen if one realizes that a large public debt, assuming it is sold at fixed nominal interest rates, creates an incen-

* I wish to thank Paul De Grauwe for comments and suggestions.

tive for the government to use surprise inflation to reduce the real interest rate it pays on the debt. This chapter therefore takes into account that both anticipated and unanticipated inflation can be used as a source of revenue. Although unanticipated inflation cannot be used systematically, the mere existence of the temptation to use surprise inflation can lead (see Barro 1983a) to an equilibrium with excessive inflation.

This chapter therefore argues that the view that countries with large fiscal deficits and large public debts need the revenue from seigniorage, does not take into account the consideration that countries in which the level of public debt, relative to gross national product (GNP), is high face an inefficiency which would make EMS discipline more desirable. The authorities in countries with high levels of debt would have a strong incentive to use surprise inflation to reduce the real burden of servicing this debt. The public perceives this incentive and comes to anticipate higher inflation rates. If the authorities are not able to bind themselves to a credible non-inflationary policy this then implies that inflation would be too high in countries with high levels of public debt.

Since the inefficiency associated with the incentive to use surprise inflation is proportional to the public debt, this chapter comes to the conclusion that, in particular, countries with high public debt might find it optimal to participate in a zero-inflation EMS, although for these countries it would be optimal to use at least some revenue from seigniorage.

Barro (1983a) and Giavazzi and Giovannini (1988) also refer to the revenue gain for the government from unexpected inflation, however, they do not link this to the seigniorage issue as done here. Obstfeld (1989) also considers the revenue from surprise inflation, but does not make welfare comparisons.

The chapter does not discuss explicitly why the EMS would have a low common inflation rate. This could be rationalized by assuming that the EMS works asymmetrically and that the centre country, presumably the Federal Republic of Germany (FRG), has an efficient tax-collection system, a low public debt and a strong aversion against inflation and would therefore set a very low inflation rate. Other countries with less efficient tax-collection systems and higher public debts would like the FRG to choose a higher inflation rate to allow them to use some seigniorage. Fiscally weak countries would therefore have an incentive to join the EMS and then argue for higher inflation rates inside the EMS.

The conclusion of this chapter that the high-inflation countries considered here would gain from participation in the EMS is a direct consequence of the fact that the potential revenue from surprise inflation is much more important than the revenue from seigniorage, because in most countries the interest-bearing public debt is much larger than the monetary base.

Implicit in and crucial for this analysis is the idea that a crawling-peg type participation in the EMS would not be credible. The public would not believe a government that promises to use only anticipated inflation and never surprise inflation. The analysis is therefore based on the assumption that the authorities have a choice only between a full commitment to the EMS or a discretionary national monetary policy. Also implicit in this analysis is that government debt is not indexed or denominated in foreign currency; this is indeed the case for most EMS countries.

The chapter is organized as follows: section 2 describes the government budget constraint and provides some figures for the potential seigniorage effects of a full participation in the EMS. Section 3 uses the standard framework in which both taxes and inflation involve welfare costs and analyses the inflation rates that result if policy-makers have the incentive to use surprise inflation. Section 4 shows under what conditions it would be in the interest of a country with a weak fiscal system to adhere to a zero-inflation EMS. Section 5 applies this model to data from the high-inflation countries and suggests that these countries would indeed benefit from joining a zero-inflation EMS and that the welfare gain would be substantial. Section 6 considers the incentives for a country that has joined the EMS to argue inside the EMS for higher inflation rates. Section 7 contains some concluding remarks.

2. Seigniorage effects of the EMS

Consider the usual flow government budget constraint:

$$D(b_t) = (g_t - q_t) + b_t\,[\cap + E_t(p_t) - p_t\,] - D(M_t)/P_t, \qquad [1]$$

where the left-hand side represents the change in the debt to GDP ratio, b_t. The right-hand side of this equation gives the sources of the increase in the debt to GDP ratio:

1. The net of interest deficit as a percentage of GDP (spending, g_t, minus taxes, q_t, expressed as a percentage of GDP);
2. Interest payments on the debt, the *ex post* real interest rate is equal to the real rate, $\cap$, plus expected inflation, $E_t(p_t)$ (assuming, as usual in this type of model, a constant real rate), minus actual inflation, p_t;
3. Seigniorage revenue, which is equal to the increase in the monetary base, $D(M_t)$, divided by the price level, P_t.

Real growth would also affect the growth rate of the debt to GDP ratio, but is not taken into account in equation [1] because it would only clutter the model and its inclusion would not change any of the conlusions.[2]

Table 7.1 provides some data about seigniorage in five EC member countries, the four with the highest inflation rates plus the FRG. Seigniorage is measured as the increase in the monetary base minus interest payments on reserves divided by the GDP deflator. Table 7.1 suggests that seigniorage was an important source of revenue in the early 1980s in Portugal and Greece, amounting to over 5 per cent of GDP in Portugal in 1979–81. The table also shows that seigniorage is a rather erratic source of revenue, mainly because of shifts in money demand, which are assumed away in most models.

TABLE 7.1: Seigniorage implications of the EMS

	Portugal	Greece	Italy	Spain	FRG
1979–81	5.29	3.28	1.37	1.32	0.00
1982	5.86	3.39	1.45	1.87	0.48
1983	2.70	–0.02	1.49	2.01	0.50
1984	0.63	3.48	1.39	7.51	0.35
1985	1.07	0.56	1.81	0.59	0.30
1986	1.62	0.22	0.60	0.88	0.56
1987	2.85	3.09	0.69	1.28	0.84
1988	2.19	0.57	0.65	–0.36	1.01
1989	1.61	1.96	0.77	0.91	0.52
1990	1.45	1.70	0.86	0.87	0.52
1991	1.29	1.44	0.81	1.00	0.52
1992	0.96	1.17	0.76	0.96	0.52
1993	0.80	0.90	0.75	0.91	0.52

Data from IMF, *International Financial Statistics* and national sources.

Note: The implications of the EMS for seigniorage are calculated assuming the growth rate of GDP of all countries converges linearly from the value in 1988 to 5% in 1993. This allows for 2–3% real growth and 2–3% inflation, both about the current values for the FRG. It is also assumed that the current ratios of reserves to GDP and of currency to GDP are constant. In Italy, Spain and Greece the interest rate on reserves is assumed to go linearly from the current values to zero in 1993. The assumption of constant reserves and currency to GDP ratios are needed to isolate the effects of financial market integration from the effects of lower inflation. For further details see Gros (1989).

Spain and Italy seem to rely less on seigniorage. This is also a consequence of the substantial interest payments made by their central banks on required reserves of commercial banks. In the three years 1979–81, that is, before the EMS started to be a constraint for Italy, seigniorage revenue amounted to only 1.37 per cent of GDP. It is interesting to note that although Italy still has higher inflation rates than the FRG it had less revenue from seigniorage over the last three years. The reason for this is the apparent upward shift in the demand for base money over the last years in the FRG.[3] Even for Spain, which joined the EMS only very recently, the disinflation of the 1980s has already reduced seigniorage revenue considerably.

To obtain an estimate of the likely fall in seigniorage revenue that would result from 'full EMS discipline', Table 7.1 also provides simulations for the period 1989–1993. These simulations are based on the assumption that these four countries gradually converge to the current EMS average in terms of inflation by 1993 and that the current monetary base to GDP ratios do not change. The last assumption might be questionable because the financial market integration under the 1992 programme would certainly put pressures on the central banks in Italy and Spain to reduce the currently rather high required reserve ratios. Gros (1989) provides some estimates of the combined effect of financial market integration and the EMS.

The effects of EMS discipline (without financial market integration) measured in Table 7.1 vary considerably across these four countries. For Italy and Spain the adjustment seems already to have taken place; a further reduction in inflation to about 2–3 per cent coupled with an elimination of interest payments on reserves would even raise seigniorage slightly in these two countries. In Portugal seigniorage would have to fall by 1.4 per cent of GDP – from about 2.2 per cent of GDP to about 0.8 per cent. In Greece seigniorage has been very erratic: compared to 1988 there would be a big increase in 1989; compared to the average for 1986–88 there would be a fall of about 0.5 per cent of GDP.

The loss of seigniorage revenue (from EMS discipline alone) appears therefore to be substantial (potentially more than 3–4 per cent of GDP) for Portugal and Greece, if one compares full EMS convergence to the extremely inflationary time around 1980. However, since all these countries have already disinflated considerably in the meantime the residual loss of revenue would be minor, zero for Italy and Spain and only 1–1.5 per cent of GDP for Greece and Portugal.

A comparison with the results in Gros (1989) shows that financial market integration would lead to a further reduction in seigniorage. For Italy and Spain this would amount to about 1 per cent of GDP, for four to five years, leading to negative seigniorage up to 1993.

3. The model

Section 2 has measured the loss of seigniorage revenue from EMS discipline. This section discusses whether the loss of seigniorage revenue from EMS discipline also represents a welfare loss.

Before going into welfare considerations it is necessary to rewrite the budget constraint [1] in terms of inflation rates. Using the usual assumption that demand is proportional to income this yields:[4]

$$D(b_t) = g_t - q_t + b_t\,[\cap + E_t(p_t) - p_t\,] - p_t\sigma, \qquad [2]$$

where σ is the constant ratio of monetary base to GDP.

This section uses the standard model of taxes and inflation that cause deadweight losses to discuss the choice between inflation and taxes. The rationale for these deadweight losses has been extensively discussed in the literature; it is therefore sufficient at this point to assume without further justification that there exists a social loss function of the following form:[5]

$$L_t = \int_0^\infty [\tau q_s^2 + \alpha p_s^2 + \beta\,(\Phi - g_s)^2\,]\, N_s \exp \cap\, (t-s)\, ds. \qquad [3]$$

The social loss arising from given inflation rates or taxes is proportional to output. This is compatible with the idea that the social losses from inflation and distortional taxes arise in the production of income. The total loss caused by a certain inflation rate and tax revenue depends therefore on the size of the economy which has to operate with these distortions.

The parameter α represents the relative weights attached to inflation in the loss function. The parameter τ represents the weight attached to distortional taxes; a high value of this parameter indicates that it is difficult for the government to obtain tax revenue. A fiscally 'weak' country is defined as a country in which raising a certain tax revenue, q_t, involves a relatively high social loss; that is, a fiscally weak country has a high value of τ.

The only innovation in the loss function [3] is that it acknowledges, in contrast to other discussions, that government expenditure is undertaken because society derives some benefit from it. The specific functional form used in equation [3] implies that there is an optimal level of government spending, equal to ϕ. Divergences of the actual spending, g_s, from this optimum cause losses that are quadratic in the divergence between the optimum and actual spending levels. The parameter β measures the relative weight in the social loss function given to achieving the optimal amount of government spending.

In a *discretionary regime*, where the government is not able to bind itself credibly to a certain inflation rate, the problem for the government is to minimize the total social loss [3] by choosing the optimal time paths for the tax rate, q_t, and the inflation rate, p_t, subject to the budget constraint [2].

Normalizing the initial level of income to one, the maximization problem for the government can be written formally as:

$$Min\ L_t = \int_0^\infty [\tau q_s^2 + \alpha p_s^2 + \beta(\Phi - g_s)^2\,] \exp(-\cap)\,(s-t)\, \mathrm{d}s, \qquad [4]$$

$$s.t.\ 0 = g_s + b_s\,[\,\cap + E_s(p_s) - p_s\,] - q_s - p_s\sigma - D(b_s),$$

where the minimization is done over time paths of the inflation rate, p_t, expenditure, g_t, and tax revenue, q_t, given the initial value of the debt to GNP ratio and the inflationary expectations of the public, $E(p_t)$. Denoting the shadow value of the budget constraint by Ω_t, the first-order conditions for an optimum and the Euler equation can be written as

$$2\tau q_t \exp(-\cap)\, t - \Omega_t = 0, \qquad [5]$$

$$2\alpha p_t \exp(-\cap)t - (\sigma + b_t)\,\Omega_t = 0, \qquad [6]$$

$$-2\beta(\Phi - g_t) \exp(-\cap)t + \Omega_t = 0, \qquad [7]$$

$$\Omega_t\,(\cap + E_t(p_t) - p_t) = -\,\mathrm{D}(\Omega_t). \qquad [8]$$

Combining equations [5] and [6] shows that at each point in time the marginal cost of raising revenue from taxation or inflation must be the same. This yields the following relationship between tax revenue and inflation:

$$q_t\,\tau\,(\sigma + b_t) = \alpha p_t. \qquad [9]$$

This equation implies that, for a given debt, both taxes and seigniorage should be used.[6] But this equation also implies that the higher the debt the higher is the inflation rate associated with any tax rate. This effect is due to the increased temptation for the government to use surprise inflation to reduce the debt service burden. The importance of this temptation increases with the level of the debt and since this temptation is correctly taken into account by the public the expected inflation rate is given by [9]. This implies that for any given tax revenue the public expects higher inflation rates to be associated with higher levels of the public debt, and that fiscally weak countries can be expected to have higher inflation rates for given values of government debt:

$$E_t\,(p_t) = q_t\,(\sigma + b_t)\,\tau/\alpha. \qquad [10]$$

Combining the first-order conditions [5] and [7] yields a simple linear relationship between expenditure and tax rates:

$$\tau q_t = \beta\,(\,\Phi - g_t). \qquad [11]$$

The discussion so far has only determined certain relationships that have to hold at each point in time. The time path of these variables can be found by using the law of motion of the shadow value and the fact that rational expectations imply that expected inflation equals actual inflation. The Euler equation [8] then implies that the time path of Ω_t is given by

$$\Omega_t + \Omega_0 \exp(-\cap\,)t. \qquad [12]$$

Substituting this result into the first-order condition [5] yields the result that the optimal tax rates are constant over time:

$$2\tau q_t = \Omega_0. \qquad [13]$$

The initial value of the shadow price of the budget constraint depends on the initial value of government debt and the parameters of the model. However, whatever this initial condition, equations [13] and [11] imply that tax revenue and expenditure are constant over time. The only instrument the government would like to vary over time is the inflation rate.

To avoid the computational complications that arise from an inflation rate that varies over time the remainder of this section focuses on the special case of a government that has decided on a programme to stabilize the debt to GNP ratio. In this case $D(b_t)$ is identically equal to zero and b_t is equal to a constant denoted by b_{SS}. This assumption has the additional advantage that the present value of future losses in equation [3] collapses to $(1/\cap)$ times the constant loss per unit of time. (The general case of a varying debt to GNP ratio is considered in Gros 1988.) For the special case of a constant debt to GNP ratio the inflation rate (actual and expected) becomes a constant, proportional to the steady-state tax revenue, q_{SS}:

$$p_t = p_{SS} = q_{SS}\, \tau\, (\sigma + b_{SS})/\alpha. \qquad [14]$$

This result can be substituted back into the government budget constraint [2] with $D(b_t) = 0$ and $b_t = b_{SS}$. Combining this with the relationship between tax revenue and expenditure yields an explicit solution for the equilibrium inflation rate as a function of the parameters of the model and the value at which the debt to GNP ratio is stabilized:

$$p_{SS} = \frac{\tau(\sigma + b_{SS})\,[\,\Phi + b_{SS}\,]}{\alpha\,[1 + (\tau/\beta) + \tau\sigma(\sigma + b_{SS})/\alpha\,]} \qquad [15]$$

This result implies that the steady state inflation rate is an increasing function of the steady state debt to GNP ratio and the parameter, Φ, which indicates the propensity of the government to spend.[7]

Since the steady-state inflation rate is also an increasing function of the parameter τ this framework predicts that, in a discretionary regime, inflation would be higher in fiscally weak countries; and that inflation would be especially high in countries characterized by a combination of large public debts and an inefficient tax-collection system. However, this does not necessarily imply that a fiscally weak country is also better off with this high inflation rate compared to the alternative of joining a low-inflation EMS, as discussed in section 4.

4. Discretionary equilibrium versus EMS discipline

To determine whether a country would benefit from joining a low-inflation EMS it is necessary to compute the total loss for the country under the discretionary regime discussed so far and the loss that would result if the inflation rate is given exogenously by the EMS. Under the discretionary regime the inflation rate would be higher but tax revenue could be lower, and consequently the distortion from collecting taxes would be lower. It is therefore unclear *a priori* which regime is preferable.

The total loss under the discretionary regime can be calculated most conveniently by rewriting the loss function as

$$L = q^2 \, [\tau + \alpha \, (p/q)^2 + \beta((\Phi - g)/q)^2 \,]. \qquad [16]$$

Starting with this equation the subscript ss is omitted as it only clutters the equations. It is understood that the variables q, g, b and p are all evaluated under the condition that the debt to GNP ratio has to be constant. After substituting out from equations [9] and [11], the loss under discretion (times $\cap$) denoted by L_{d}, is equal to

$$L_{\text{d}} = \frac{[\,\Phi + b\cap\,]^2 \, \tau \, [1 + (\tau/\beta) + \tau(\sigma + b)^2/\alpha\,]}{[1 + (\tau/\beta) + \tau\sigma(\sigma + b)/\alpha\,]^2} \qquad [17]$$

If the country belongs to the EMS, its inflation rate is exogenously given and is denoted by π_{EMS}. The total loss (times $\cap$) under the EMS can then be calculated by setting p_t equal to π_{EMS} in the expression for the loss [16] and by calculating the value for q_t from the government budget constraint. Using condition [11] that relates spending to tax revenue yields

$$L_{\text{EMS}} = \frac{\tau[\,\Phi - \sigma\pi_{\text{EMS}} + b\cap]^2}{[1 + (\tau/\beta)]} + \alpha\pi_{\text{EMS}}{}^2. \qquad [18]$$

A country has an incentive to join the EMS if the EMS regime yields a lower loss, that is, if $L_{\text{d}} - L_{\text{EMS}} > 0$. To simplify the algebra it is assumed that the EMS implies an inflation rate of zero. The Appendix shows that a country would benefit from joining a zero-inflation EMS if

$$b > \sigma \, \frac{1 + (\tau/\beta) + \sigma^2(\tau/\alpha)}{1 + (\tau/\beta) - \sigma^2(\tau/\alpha)}. \qquad [19]$$

This condition implies that a country without any public debt would have no interest in joining the EMS from the public finance point of view analysed in this framework. Such a country would not benefit from the EMS because it does not have to deal with the inefficiency that obtains under a discretionary regime where policy-makers are tempted to use surprise inflation to lower the debt service burden. For such a country the discretionary inflation rates (and consequently also the tax rates) represent an overall optimum. However, a country with a high public debt would be likely to benefit from the EMS discipline since the disadvantage of not being able to choose the inflation rate would be more than offset by the fact that this constraint also eliminates a source of inefficiency. Inspection of condition [19] also reveals that the right-hand side is an increasing function of τ.[8] This is the formal expression of the argument that fiscally weak countries need the inflation tax, the more costly the tax-collection system is the higher has to be the debt to GNP ratio for the country to benefit from joining a zero-inflation EMS.

5. Welfare gains from EMS discipline

The argument that the EMS has indeed been a disciplinary device for some member countries (see, e.g., Giavazzi and Giovannini (1988)) implies that a country like Italy would have been in a discretionary equilibrium prior to the creation of the EMS. Observation of the actual inflation and tax rates in 1978/79 should therefore yield some information about the relative magnitudes of the parameters on the right-hand side of equation [19] and thus also about the critical debt to GDP ratio which would make it optimal for a fiscally weak country (like Italy) to join a zero-inflation EMS.

To obtain a numerical estimate for the critical value of b for Italy it is necessary to have estimates of σ, τ/β and τ/α. The remainder of this section shows how these estimates could be obtained using Italy as an example.

Information on the value of τ/β could be obtained from the first order condition equating the marginal utility of expenditure and the marginal cost of taxation; however, since the optimal expenditure ratio, Φ, is not directly observable it is not possible to obtain a direct estimate of τ/β from observations about tax and expenditure rates alone. But an *upper bound* on the critical debt to GDP ratio can be obtained by setting τ/β equal to zero (i.e. by setting β equal to infinity) since the right-hand side of equation [19] is an increasing function of β.

Finally, information on the value of τ/α can be obtained indirectly from observations about inflation and tax rates through equation [9] which implies that if Italy was in a discretionary equilibrium in 1979 the value of τ/α should be given by $p_t/q_t(\sigma + b_t)$. The relevant figures for Italy in 1979 were as follows:

p_t = inflation (GDP deflator) : 16 per cent,
q_t = central government revenue : 34 per cent of GDP,
b_t = debt to GDP ratio : 0.54,
σ = monetary base : 20 per cent of GDP.[9]

This yields an estimate of τ/α equal to 0.64. Inserting these values into the right-hand side of equation [19] implies that for Italy in 1979 an upper bound on the critical debt to GDP ratio would be given by

$$0.2\,\frac{1 + 0.04*(0.64)}{1 - 0.04*(0.64)} = 0.2\ (1.025/0.975) \approx 0.21 \qquad [19A]$$

With a debt to GDP ratio of about 0.54 it was therefore in the interest of Italy, from the public finance point of view, to join the EMS in 1979 and thus 'tie the hands' of the monetary authorities (Giavazzi and Pagano 1986). Given that the debt to GDP ratio is now about one in Italy it is apparent that the benefits from EMS discipline should be even greater today than they were in 1979.

Inspection of equation [19] suggests that in general the critical debt to GDP ratio is about equal to the monetary base to GDP ratio because σ is usually a small fraction and appears squared in the term that multiplies σ in equation [19]. For all EC member countries that are perceived as fiscally weak the debt to GDP ratio is several times as big as the monetary base to GDP ratio, as shown in Table 7.2. Since tax revenues (relative to GDP) and inflation rates in these countries are of the same order of magnitude this implies that all fiscally weak EC member countries should gain from joining a zero-inflation EMS.

TABLE 7.2: Macroeconomic data

	Debt/GDP	Monetary base/GDP	Government* revenue/GDP	Inflation (GDP deflator)
Belgium	125.1	8.0	45.0[85]	1.3
Denmark	58.4	3.4	42.1	5.0
FRG	43.9	9.9	29.6	2.1
Greece	66.7	19.6	35.6[85]	29.4[86]
Spain	48.1	19.3	26.4[84]	11.1[86]
France	36.7	6.2	40.1	2.8
Ireland	119.8	10.2	42.6[84]	5.6[86]
Italy	92.6	15.2	36.1	5.6
Luxembourg	14.9		43.6[84]	1.6[86]
Netherlands	75.0	8.1	51.6	–1.1
Portugal	67.6	16.9	34.6[85]	21.6[85]
UK	53.2	3.4	37.9[85]	4.4
EUR12	59.2			

Source: Commission of the European Communities, *Annual Economic Report 1988–89;* and *International Financial Statistics*. 1987 data, except where indicated.
* Central government revenue, 1986 data, except where indicated.

Given the values for σ and (τ/α) it is also possible to calculate the benefit from EMS discipline as the proportional reduction in the welfare loss a country like Italy would experience if it went from a discretionary regime to a zero-inflation EMS. The proportional change in welfare from such a switch in regime is equal to $[(L_d/L_{EMS}) - 1]$ and can be calculated using equations [17] and [18]. The Appendix shows how the resulting expression can be simplified. Substituting $\sigma = 0.2$, $(\tau/\beta) = 0$, $b = 0.54$ and $(\tau/\alpha) = 0.64$ in equation [A.3] yields the result that in a zero-inflation EMS the social loss is about 7 per cent lower than under a discretionary regime. However, assuming that the parameters of the social loss function that describe the aversion to inflation and the fiscal structure of the economy have not changed in the meantime, with the current debt to GDP ratio (of about one) the gain from EMS discipline is much larger – about 20 per cent of the loss under discretion.

6. Incentives within the EMS

However, even a country that would benefit from joining a zero-inflation EMS would still have an incentive to argue for higher inflation rates inside the EMS. This can be seen by considering the fact that the inflation rate for the EMS as a whole that would minimize the total loss for the country in question would not be equal to zero, since it would always be optimal for any country to use both taxes and seigniorage. Formally, this can be shown by computing the optimal inflation rate in a regime in which the government can credibly bind itself to a certain inflation rate. In this case the loss function is minimized if the marginal costs of using seigniorage and of using taxes are equalized, that is, if

$$\tau\sigma q_t = \alpha p_t. \qquad [20]$$

This condition, which determines only the ratio of seigniorage receipts to tax receipts, is independent of the level of the steady state government debt, b_{SS}. However, the value of b_{SS} still determines the absolute value of q and p via the budget constraint [2]. It can then be shown that for a country that belongs to the EMS the social loss is decreasing in the EMS inflation rate as long as this rate is lower than the optimal inflation rate implicit in equation [20]. The change in the social loss of belonging to an EMS with a given inflation rate π_{EMS}, can be calculated by taking the derivative of equation [18] with respect to π_{EMS}:

$$[d(L_{EMS})/d(\pi_{EMS})\,] = 2[-q(\pi_{EMS})\,\tau\sigma + \alpha\pi_{EMS}], \qquad [21]$$

where the notation $q(\pi_{EMS})$ indicates that the value of q depends on π_{EMS} since it is equal to the first term on the right-hand side of equation [18]. The right-hand side of equation [21] is negative as long as the actual inflation rate in the EMS, π_{EMS}, is lower than the optimal inflation rate in a non-discretionary regime, as given by equation [20]. The EMS inflation rate which would be optimal for the country in question is given by the value of π_{EMS}, denoted by π^*_{EMS}, for which the right-hand side of equation [14] is equal to zero, that is, if

$$\tau\sigma q(\pi^*_{EMS}) = \alpha\pi^*_{EMS}. \qquad [22]$$

The tax rate, $q(\pi^*_{EMS})$, that is implicit in this inflation rate, can be calculated from condition [8] where the debt to GNP ratio has to be constant. Using the budget constraint with $D(b_t) = 0$ and $b_t = b$ yields:

$$\pi^*_{EMS} = \frac{[\Phi + b\cap]\,(\tau\sigma/\alpha)}{[1 + (\tau/\beta) + (\tau\sigma^2/\alpha)]}. \qquad [23]$$

Comparing the results for the discretionary steady-state inflation rate p_{SS} in equation [15] and the optimal EMS inflation rate π^*_{EMS} in equation [23] shows that the optimal EMS inflation rate (which is equal to the optimal inflation rate in a non-discretionary regime) is lower than the discretionary inflation rate as long as the government has a positive debt. The EMS inflation rate that would be optimal for the home country depends on the parameter, τ, which indicates the relative efficiency of the tax system. The higher is τ, i.e., the lower the efficiency of the tax system, the higher is the EMS inflation rate that would be optimal for the home country. In this sense 'fiscally weak' countries would have an incentive to join a low-inflation EMS and to argue inside the EMS for a higher inflation rate.

Some information about the order of magnitude of the EMS inflation rate that would be optimal for a country like Italy can be obtained by using the values for σ, b and τ/α calculated above. Inspection of the right-hand side of equation [23] reveals that the computation of π^*_{EMS} seems also to require information about $\cap$, Φ and (τ/β). However, for realistic values of $\cap$ the expression in square brackets in the numerator is practically equal to Φ since the other term (i.e. $\cap b$) is the product of a fraction times a number that would be < 0.05, whereas the optimal expenditure ratio, Φ, can be assumed to be between 0.2 and 0.5.

The only important parameter that remains to be determined is therefore Φ, which is not observable. However, it turns out that, given the observed expenditure and tax ratios in Italy in 1979, varying the value of the optimal expenditure ratio between 20 and 50 per cent of GDP does not lead to widely differing results for the optimal EMS inflation rate for Italy. If Φ is assumed to be 0.4, π^*_{EMS} is equal to 4.4 per cent, for Φ equal to 0.5, π^*_{EMS} increases only to a little over 5.5 per cent. Given that the Italian inflation rate is over 5 per cent at present this result implies that the reduction in inflation and therefore also seigniorage Italy has experienced so far has increased welfare – even taking into account that some positive inflation would be desirable in Italy from a public finance point of view.

These welfare calculations are, of course, meant to be only illustrative. They illustrate the general result that a high level of debt has two opposing effects on the incentives for a fiscally weak country: a high debt means that the country should gain from joining a low-inflation EMS, but a high debt also implies that the country would gain from an increase in the EMS inflation rate, once it has joined.

7. Concluding remarks

The optimal use of the revenue from inflation (i.e. seigniorage) is in general given by the condition that the marginal cost from inflation should equal the marginal cost of using other taxes that are also distorting. This consideration has been used to argue that 'fiscally weak' countries such as Italy and Spain should not accept German inflation rates by pegging through the EMS rigidly to the DM, but should opt for a crawling peg that allowed them a higher inflation rate. If the public did believe a policy announcement that the authorities are aiming for a constant rate of depreciation against the DM, it might indeed be optimal for these countries to opt for a crawling peg inside the EMS.

However, it is highly unlikely that such a policy would command much credibility with the public. The mere announcement of such a policy would constitute an admission of 'fiscal weakness' which might lead the public to expect higher deficits and larger future debts. But the decisive problem inherent in such a policy would be given by the discretionary (and discrete) nature of the realignment process which would make it difficult for the public to believe that the government would be using only seigniorage and would not be tempted to use surprise inflation to reduce the burden of servicing a large public debt. A government that announces that it is going to use the revenue from anticipated inflation, but never that from unanticipated inflation faces some inherent credibility problems, especially if the debt to GNP ratio is very high.

The idea underlying this chapter is that the inefficiency associated with this credibility problem might be important enough to override the public finance aspect that would otherwise make higher inflation rates the optimal policy.[10]

Actual inflation rates are, of course, not determined exclusively by public finance considerations; the purpose of this chapter is to show only that 'fiscally weak' countries do not have an obvious interest in retaining the full liberty of determining their own inflation rates. Participating fully and credibly in a low-inflation EMS might be in the interest of countries with large public debts, even if this implies a need to raise taxes and reduce expenditure. Some very simple calculations suggest that all of the EC countries that are considered as fiscally weak should benefit from EMS discipline and that the welfare gains from joining a low-inflation EMS might be substantial.

The result that a 'fiscally weak' country would have an incentive to argue for higher inflation rates inside the EMS might be behind the call in the *Delors Report* (Delors Committee 1989) that some constraints on national fiscal policies would be necessary at an advanced stage of monetary integration. The goal of price stability for Europe would be difficult to achieve if fiscal conditions vary too widely across member countries.

Appendix

To obtain the result [19] note that both [17] and [18] contain the terms $\tau\,[\,\Phi-\sigma\mu+b_{ss}\,(\cap-\mu)]^2$ if $\pi_{EMS}=0$; to calculate the sign of the difference between [17] and [18] this term can be neglected. Participation in a zero-inflation EMS leads therefore to a lower loss if

$$\frac{L_{d(iscretion)}}{L_{EMS}}-1 \qquad [A.1]$$

$$=\frac{[1+(\tau/\beta)+\tau(\sigma+b_{ss})^2/\alpha]\,[1+(\tau/\beta)]-[1+(\tau/\beta)+\tau\sigma(\sigma+b_{ss})/\alpha]^2}{[1+(\tau/\beta)+\tau\sigma(\sigma+b_{ss})/\alpha]^2}>0.$$

Multiplying out the square term and performing some elementary cancellations yields:

$$\frac{L_{\mathrm{d}}}{L_{\mathrm{EMS}}} - 1 = [1+(\tau/\beta)+\tau\sigma(\sigma+b_{\mathrm{ss}})/\alpha]^{-2} \qquad [A.2]$$
$$\times \{ [1+(\tau/\beta)]\tau(\sigma+b_{\mathrm{ss}})^2/\alpha - 2\sigma(1+(\tau/\beta))\tau(\sigma+b_{\mathrm{ss}})/\alpha - \sigma^2[\tau(\sigma+b_{\mathrm{ss}})/\alpha]^2\}.$$

After pulling the term $\tau\ (\sigma + b_{\mathrm{ss}})/\alpha$ out of the curled brackets and some further simplifications this yields:

$$\frac{L_{\mathrm{d}}}{L_{\mathrm{EMS}}} - 1 = [1+(\tau/\beta)+\tau\sigma(\sigma+b_{\mathrm{ss}})/\alpha]^{-2}\ \tau(\sigma+b_{\mathrm{ss}})/\alpha \qquad [A.3]$$
$$\times \{ (1+(\tau/\beta))\, b_{\mathrm{ss}} - \sigma[1+(\tau/\beta)] - \sigma^2\tau(\sigma+b_{\mathrm{ss}})/\alpha \}.$$

Collecting terms in b_{ss} and pulling out the term $[1 + (\tau/\beta) - (\tau\sigma^2/\alpha)]$ yields finally:

$$\frac{L_{\mathrm{d}}}{L_{\mathrm{EMS}}} - 1 = [1+(\tau/\beta)+\tau\sigma(\sigma+b_{\mathrm{ss}})/\alpha]^{-2}\ \tau(\sigma+b_{\mathrm{ss}})/\alpha \qquad [A.4]$$
$$\times [1+(\tau/\beta)-(\tau\sigma^2/\alpha)] \times \left\{ b_{\mathrm{ss}} - \frac{\sigma[1+(\tau/\beta)+(\tau\sigma^2/\alpha)]}{[1+(\tau/\beta)-(\tau\sigma^2/\alpha)]} \right\}.$$

It is apparent from this equation that the loss under a discretionary policy regime exceeds the loss with a zero-inflation EMS if the expression in the curled brackets is positive; which corresponds to the inequality in [19] (under the implicit assumption that the term $[1 + (\tau/\beta) - (\tau\sigma^2/\alpha)]$ is positive).

Notes

1. For a similar view see Buiter (1987).
2. See Gros (1988) for an analysis that takes into account real growth.
3. Gros (1989) also calculates another measure of seigniorage, the interest rate savings on the monetary base that is less dependent on shifts in money demand. According to this measure, Italy has more seigniorage than the FRG.

   An implicit assumption in this chapter (as in general in the literature on the optimal inflation tax) is that no interest is paid on required reserves. If full market interest were paid on reserves only currency should be counted in the monetary base. A conceptual problem arises if less than full market interest is paid on reserves. This problem is ignored here, and in the calculations using data from Italy the 5.5 per cent interest paid on reserves is neglected. This could make the case for using seigniorage stronger than it is in reality.
4. See Gros (1988) for a derivation.
5. See Mankiw (1987) for a similar formulation that does not consider the determinants of government spending. A social loss from inflation is difficult to

justify on purely economic welfare grounds in models, like this one, that incorporate a constant velocity money demand function. In the standard economic welfare analysis the loss from a tax is given by the triangular areas under demand and supply functions; with a constant velocity money demand function there is no such triangle since the demand function becomes a vertical line. This chapter should therefore be viewed as a contribution to the literature on the optimal inflation tax, which uses the assumption of a constant velocity for computational convenience and is therefore forced to assume only that inflation causes a social loss for unspecified reasons.

6. In Mankiw (1987) inflation is proportional to taxes (in the special case of a quadratic loss function) only because he does not take into account the revenue from surprise inflation.
7. To see this divide the denominator and nominator of [15] by ($\sigma + b$); the resulting expression is obviously increasing in b.
8. To see this divide the denominator and the nominator of [19] by τ, the resulting expression is increasing in τ.
9. This value is used here for σ despite the fact that in Italy some interest (5.5 per cent) is paid on required reserves so that the non-interest-bearing part of the monetary base, which is the part on which the government earns seigniorage, was actually lower.
10. The framework presented here implies that the first best option for any government facing a credibility problem associated with its public debt would be to issue only indexed securities or denominate all debt in foreign currency. However, the use of this type of instrument has always been very limited in countries with moderate inflation rates and developed domestic financial systems. A recourse to indexed or foreign currency denominated public debt seems therefore very unlikely given the situation in the current and prospective member countries of the EMS. Moreover, to have an impact on the incentive to use surprise inflation, the recourse to indexed or foreign currency denominated debt would have to be very large. As suggested by inequality [19], the remaining domestic currency debt would have to be about the same order of magnitude as the monetary base. For a country like Italy this would imply that over four-fifths of the total debt would have to be reissued, indexed for foreign currency.

References

Barro, R. J. (1983a) Inflationary finance under discretion and rules, *Canadian Journal of Economics*, No. 1, February pp. 1–16.

Barro, R. J. (1983b) Rules, discretion and reputation in a model of monetary policy, *Journal of Monetary Economics*, **12**, pp. 101–21.

Buiter, W. (1987) The current global economic situation, outlook and policy options, with special emphasis on fiscal policy issues, *CEPR Discussion Pape*r No. 210.

Committee on the Study of Economic and Monetary Union (the Delors Committee) (1989) *Report on Economic and Monetary Union in the European Community* (with Collection of Papers), Office for Official Publications of the European Communities, Luxemburg.

Dornbusch, R. (1987) The EMS, the dollar and the yen, paper prepared for the Conference on the EMS, Perugia, 16–17, October.

Giavazzi, F. (1987) The exchange rate question in Europe, paper prepared for the Macroeconomic Policy Group organized by CEPS and the EC.

Giavazzi, F. and **Giovannini, A**. (1988) *Limiting Exchange Rate Flexibility: the European Monetary System*, MIT Press, Cambridge, Mass..

Giavazzi, F. and **Pagano, M**. (1986) The advantage of tying one's hand, EMS discipline and central bank credibility, *CEPR Discussion Paper*, No. 135.

Gros, D. (1988) Seigniorage versus EMS discipline: some welfare considerations, *CEPS Working Document* No. 38, Centre for European Policy Studies, Brussels, September.

Gros, D (1989) *Seigniorage in the EC: The Implications of the EMS and Financial Market Integration*, International Monetary Fund, IMF WP/89/7, Washington, D.C.

Mankiw, G. N. (1987) The optimal collection of seigniorage, theory and evidence, *Journal of Monetary Economics*, **20**, pp. 327–41.

Obstfeld, M. (1989) Dynamic seigniorage theory: an exploration, *NBER Working Paper*, No. 2869.

Comment: Louka Katseli

According to much of the recent literature (Dornbusch 1988; Giavazzi and Pagano 1988) some countries cannot afford joining a European monetary union (EMU) or for that matter the EMS. These countries are those where the money base is relatively large and where the public debt is high so that its servicing requires a significant tax pressure provided through 'seigniorage'. Taxing the money base essentially through an inflation tax lessens the burden of servicing the debt. If nominal interest rates remain unchanged, this can be achieved through anticipated or 'surprise inflation' so that the *ex post* real interest rate is effectively reduced.

In this chapter Gros shows that if the public anticipates the temptation of the government to use surprise inflation to reduce the burden of the debt, a higher than optimal inflation rate results, creating an inefficiency that would be eliminated by participation in a low-inflation EMS. Under such conditions, for a 'fiscally weak' country such as Greece, Gros argues that participation in the EMS would be a 'second-best' policy that is much closer to the optimum than an independent, excessively inflationary policy. The first best option would be to issue only indexed securities or denominate all debt in foreign currency. So, according to Gros, it is precisely countries which need seigniorage that are prone to end up with higher than optimum inflation. In these cases, the potential revenue from surprise inflation is more important than the revenue from seigniorage as the interest-bearing public debt is larger than the monetary base.

Gros's conclusion is analytically equivalent to the general point made by Sargent and Wallace (1981) who argued that if the foreseen path of government deficits violates its budget constraint, the public should rationally anticipate the possibility of an eventual pick-up in money growth and inflation. Under such circumstances, they argued, inflation accelerates immediately.

In section 2, Gros provides some estimates for past seigniorage revenue for Portugal, Greece, Italy, Spain and the FRG, as well as simulations for the period 1989–93 under the assumption of full EMS discipline. In doing so, he assumes that the current monetary base to GDP ratios will not change, a dubious assumption as he himself admits, since financial integration and the pressure of competition will reduce the money base substantially. Is seignorage loss important? It is if one compares recent years with the 1979–81 period as Gros does. The choice of 1979 as a base year is questionable, however, since the second oil-price shock raised inflation substantially for supply reasons and therefore seigniorage–revenue losses are substantially overestimated. We could, however, accept Gros's conclusion that full participation in the EMS would lead to a 2–4 per cent loss of seigniorage revenue as a percentage of GDP at least for the high money-base countries. This is consistent with recent estimates provided by other authors (Cohen and Wyplosz 1989).

In section 3, Gros uses a social loss function to show that the loss of seigniorage revenue is also a welfare loss. According to his specification, there are social losses from inflation, from discretionary taxes and finally from deviations from an 'optimal' level of government spending. What constitutes an 'optimal level of government spending' and why divergences of actual spending from this optimal level create social losses are not discussed. Gros furthermore, defines a 'fiscally weak' country as a country which has a relatively high aversion to taxes. It is not clear, according to this definition, why Greece should be considered more 'fiscally weak' than the UK or the FRG. The weight attached to distortionary taxes in the social loss function is likely to be affected by the desirable level and composition of social expenditures that would be financed by taxes and hence could be lower for a developing country. 'Fiscal weakness' should instead reflect inefficiencies in the tax-collection system and could instead be modelled as the level of resources (e.g. government spending) required to obtain the same level of taxes. The reorganization of fiscal authorities and the effective monitoring of tax returns in countries with a high proportion of self-employed or agricultural workers is inherently difficult and requires resources.

By minimizing the social loss function relative to the government budget constraint, the first-order condition implies that the marginal cost of raising revenue from taxation or inflation must be the same, and that the higher the debt the higher is the inflation rate associated with any tax rate due to the incentive of the government to use surprise inflation. Expected inflation is higher the higher the debt and the more fiscally weak the country. This is the 'discretionary' regime that Gros discusses, and by calculating the total loss function under this regime, in contrast to the EMS regime where inflation is exogenously determined, he derives the level of debt to GDP ratio that would enable a country to benefit from joining a zero-inflation rate EMS. For Italy, this ratio turns out to be about 20 per cent. Given that the debt to GDP ratio is much higher, he concludes that it was in the interest of Italy, from a public finance point of view, to join the EMS in 1979. He infers from this that other high-debt countries face a similar inefficiency and should follow the same policy option.

A major point is in order here: for this conclusion to hold, inflation must come as a surpise so that nominal interest rates do not compensate fully for its effect. The degree of indexation of public debt and the term structure of debt are important considerations. Giavazzi and Pagano (1988) provide some estimates of short-term debt and the average maturity of debt for EC countries. Greece and Portugal, both non-EMS countries, have a high proportion of short-term indexed debt. Thus, at least for non-EMS countries, the benefits of surprise inflation are, I would argue, very limited and one should not rest the argument of EMS entry on the inefficiency of surprise inflation. Furthermore, according to most econometric evidence (Alogoskoufis 1986, 1988), it is not at all clear that the monetary model fares well in these types of economies. Cost–push considerations, exchange rate policy, including the variance of exchange rate changes (Katseli 1988) or productivity changes, all prove to be important determinants of domestic inflation.

This raises a fundamental question for external and internal adjustment in these types of economies: what is the optimal real exchange rate path for an open economy whose domestic costs are rising faster than its competitors, if it wants to disinflate with the minimum cost to employment and output? Fixing the nominal exchange rate will increase the burden of adjustment substantially, especially if a contractionary monetary policy stance is adopted as well. The loss of seigniorage revenues, the increase in interest rates and the decline of growth will increase the rate of public debt accumulation and lead to pressures for a considerable decline in the only flexible part of the budget, namely public investment, with negative implications for long-term growth. Maintaining some flexibility in exchange rate management during the period of adjustment will provide instead some degree of freedom to national governments to decide upon the income distribution consequences of disinflation.

Finally, in view of 1992, and its asymmetric effects on national economies, it will probably be optimal to maintain some exchange rate flexibility as opposed to forcing a joint monetary policy upon countries which face different adjustment paths.

The decision to enter the EMS should thus be based on these types of strategic considerations as opposed to the 'seigniorage' or 'surprise inflation' arguments that are raised in Gros's chapter. Despite these reservations as to its policy relevance, this chapter is an important contribution to the relevant literature.

References

Alogoskoufis, G. (1986) On the determinants of consumer price inflation in Greece, *Greek Economic Review*. **8**; pp. 245–66.

Alogoskoufis, G, (1988) Macroeconomic policy and the external constraint in the dependent economy: the case of Greece, *Discussion Paper in Economics*, 89/3, Birkbeck College, February.

Cohen, D. and **Wyplosz C.** (1989) The European Monetary Union: an agnostic evaluation, *CEPR Discussion Paper*, No. 306, April.

Dornbusch, R. (1988) The EMS, the dollar and the yen, in Giavazzi, F., Micossi, S. and Miller, M. (eds), *The European Monetary System*, Cambridge University Press, Cambridge, pp. 23–41.

Giavazzi, F. and **Pagano, M.** (1988) The advantage of tying one's hands: EMS discipline and central bank credibility, *European Economic Review*, **32**, pp. 1055–82.

Katseli, L. (1988) On the effectiveness of discrete devaluation in balance of payments adjustment, in Marston, R.C. (ed.), *Misalignment of Exchange Rates: Effects on Trade and Industry*, University of Chicago Press, Chicago, 192–210.

Sargent, T. and **Wallace, N.** (1981) Some unpleasant monetarist arithmetics, *Federal Reserve Board of Minneapolis Quarterly Review*. Fall, pp. 1–17.

CHAPTER EIGHT

Exchange rate volatility and international trade:the effect of the European Monetary System

André Sapir and Khalid Sekkat*

1. Introduction

Advocates of freely floating exchange rates have generally emphasized the gains from greater flexibility as compared to fixed exchange rates. Flexible rates have been viewed as enabling countries, by insulating them from outside disturbances, to retain a degree of autonomy in the pursuit of domestic macroeconomic objectives.

Ever since the shift from fixed to flexible exchange rates in the early 1970s, however, there has been an increase in exchange rate instability. This has given rise to concern about the costs of flexible rates, particularly on trade. Some authors have recently argued that the evidence of the 1980s suggests that the disadvantages of floating rates now outweigh their advantages. For instance, despite his avowed long-held belief that flexible exchange rates represented the best system available, Paul Krugman (1989: 1) has stated that: 'I have now changed my mind: based on the view I now have of how floating rates work in practice, I am now an advocate of an eventual return to a system of more-or-less fixed rates subject to discretionary adjustment'.

The concern about flexible exchange rates relates to two forms of instability: volatility and misalignment. 'Volatility' refers to short-term fluctuations of nominal or real exchange rates, while 'misalignment' designates important deviations of the actual real exchange rate from its equilibrium state.

The international monetary system now proposed by Krugman and others is broadly similar to the European Monetary System (EMS) which has prevailed in Europe for the past decade. One of the clear achievements of the EMS has been a significant reduction in the degree of nominal exchange rate volatility among the participating European countries. This is illustrated in Table 8.1.

* We are very grateful to Marie-Cristine Adam, Ulrich Camen, Mathias Dewatripont, André Farber, and especially Anne-Marie Gulde for helpful discussions during early stages of the research. We have also benefited from comments and suggestions by Paul De Grauwe and other participants at the Conference on the European Monetary System in the 1990s held at the Bank of Greece, Athens.The Commission of the European Community kindly supplied the data on trade prices.

The purpose of this chapter is empirically to investigate the impact of exchange rate instability on trade, drawing on the experience of the EMS. The scope is limited to the study of volatility. Analysis of the possible impact of misalignment on trade is deferred to further research.

TABLE 8.1 Nominal exchange rate volatility*
German Mark against selected EMS and non-EMS currencies (1973–78 and 1979–87)

Currency	1973–78	1979–87
EMS currencies		
BF	0.96	0.94
HFL	1.25	0.56
FF	2.13	1.21
Lira	3.42	1.10
Average	1.94	0.95
Non-EMS currencies		
£	3.04	2.95
Japanese yen	3.04	3.11
US$	3.68	3.48
Average	3.25	3.18

*Computed as the standard deviation of monthly percentage changes in bilateral nominal exchange rates over the relevant period.

The chapter is organized as follows: section 2 reviews the existing literature on exchange rate variability and trade, sections 3 and 4 present the methodology and the empirical results, and section 5 summarizes the main results and draws the conclusion.

2. Exchange rate variability and trade: old and new views

Economic research on exchange rate variability and trade has generally focused on whether greater instability has negatively impacted international trade. This traditional approach was first pursued with respect to volatility. More recently there have also been attempts to quantify the impact of misalignment on trade.

Early research concentrated on short-term fluctuations of nominal or real exchange rates. Assuming that economic agents are risk averse, theoretical analysis generally predicted that the risk associated with volatility would result in a lower volume of trade (see, e.g., Clark 1973, Ethier 1973 and Heckerman 1973). It was also found that exchange risk could either increase or decrease trade prices depending on whether the risk is borne by exporters or importers (see Hooper and Kohlhagen 1978).

Empirical investigation, however, has been inconclusive on the influence of volatility on trade volumes. Several studies support the hypothesis that volatility has an adverse impact on trade (see, e.g., Cushman 1983, Akhtar and Hilton 1984, and Kenen and Rodrick 1986). In contrast, other researchers have failed to identify such negative influence (see, e.g., Hooper and Kohlhagen 1978, Gotur 1985, and Bailey *et al.* 1987). According to Frenkel and Goldstein (1989) the difficulty in identifying a significant association between volatility and trade might reflect the availability of hedging instruments against exchange rate risk, or the adaptability of multinationals.

Recent research has argued that the floating exchange rate regime affects trade flows not so much because of short-term fluctuations but rather because it produces medium-term swings in real exchange rates (Williamson 1983). The hypothesis here is that misalignment generates uncertainty against which there is little possibility of insurance. Empirical work along this line includes the papers by De Grauwe (1987), De Grauwe and de Bellefroid (1989) and Perée and Steinherr (1989). The evidence reported in these studies supports the hypothesis that uncertainty resulting from medium-run exchange rate movements adversely affects trade flows. In particular, De Grauwe (1987: 395), finds that '[t]he greater exchange rate stability provided by the EMS has been a source of growth of intra-EMS trade'.

The large swings in the value of the dollar in the 1980s have generated a completely *new approach* to the issue of exchange rate variability and trade which focuses on the responsiveness of import prices to exchange rate changes. It stems from the failure of the US trade deficit to improve after 1985 despite the strong fall of the dollar. The new approach investigates the role of market structure and exchange rate stability in the relationship between exchange rates and traded goods prices.

The persistence of the US trade deficit partly reflects the failure of foreign exporters to pass through exchange rate changes into dollar import prices. In recent years there has been a substantial literature on the transmission of nominal exchange rate changes to import prices in the USA, using both aggregated and disaggregated data. Most estimates of the share of exchange rate changes transmitted into total (non-oil) import prices vary between 50 and 80 per cent (see Mann 1986, Hooper and Mann 1989 and Moffet 1989). The degree of pass-through, however, appears to vary a great deal across industries (see Mann 1987, Feenstra 1987, and Knetter 1989).

Although incomplete pass-through is consistent with perfect competition under certain conditions, most of the theoretical explanations have been cast in terms of models of imperfect competition in which exporters are capable of price discrimination across markets. According to Krugman (1989), this behaviour of 'pricing to market' explains why foreign suppliers did not lower their dollar prices in the USA during the 1980–84 dollar appreciation, nor increase them during the subsequent dollar depreciation. Instead, they preferred to increase their profit margins when the dollar rose and lower them when the dollar fell. In these models incomplete pass-through is, therefore, associated with fluctuations in profit margins.

Several explanations have been provided as to why exporters price to market. The most appealing argues that sunk costs related to penetrating foreign markets and the instability of exchange rates have combined to render trade prices and volumes unresponsive to exchange rate changes (see Krugman 1989 and Dixit 1989).

The principal message of the new literature is that exchange rate instability creates an incentive for firms not to react to exchange rate changes: 'the incentive not to act is greater, the more volatile the exchange rate' (Krugman 1989: 11). Moreover, the degradation of the quality of price signals caused by fluctuating exchange rates varies according to market structure. The deterioration will be greater in more imperfectly competitive markets.

3. Methodology

This section presents a simple model to test the implication of the new approach to exchange rate variability and trade: that volatility reduces the degree of pass-through. The model also incorporates the message of the old approach, namely that volatility adds a risk premium to international trade.

Following Mann (1987), we start with the following simple model of import price determination under imperfect competition:

$$PM = C*g/E, \qquad [1]$$

where PM is the import price in domestic currency, C the marginal cost of production in foreign currency, g the mark-up and E the exchange rate (units of foreign currency per unit of domestic currency).

Log differentiation of [1] yields:

$$\mathrm{d}\ln(PM) = \mathrm{d}\ln(C) + \mathrm{d}\ln(g) - \mathrm{d}\ln(E). \qquad [2]$$

If the mark-up is constant, then exchange rate movements change import prices one-for-one, assuming foreign costs are constant. Conversely, exchange rate changes will not be fully passed through if the foreign mark-up is adjusted. For instance, a depreciation of the domestic currency (a fall in E) would not give rise to an increase of import prices if the foreign profit margin were sufficiently lowered.

The new approach described in section 2 implies that foreign mark-ups adjust to changes in the exchange rate at a speed that varies with the degree of exchange rate instability. Equation [2] therefore becomes

$$\mathrm{d}\ln(PM) = \mathrm{d}\ln(C) + c(I)*\mathrm{d}\ln(E) - \mathrm{d}\ln(E) \qquad [3]$$

where c is the extent of adjustment of the foreign mark-up. This coefficient depends on the instability of the exchange rate, which is measured by an index I. The greater the degree of exchange rate volatility, the larger the adjustment of the foreign markup. Equation [3] can be rewritten as

$$\mathrm{d}\ln(PM) = \mathrm{d}\ln(C) - [1 - c(I)]*\mathrm{d}\ln(E), \qquad [4]$$

which indicates that $c(I)$ measures the extent to which exchange rate instability lowers the responsiveness of import prices to exchange rate changes (i.e. the pass-through). The greater the volatility of the exchange rate, the lower the degree of pass-through and, therefore, the greater the degree of pricing to market.

Postulating that c is directly proportional to I, equation [3] yields the following regression model:

$$\begin{aligned}\mathrm{d}\ln(PM_{ijt}) &= a_i*\mathrm{d}\ln(C_{jt}) + b_i*\mathrm{d}\ln(E_{ijt}) \\ &\quad + c_i*I_{ijt}*\mathrm{d}\ln(E_{ijt}) + u_{ijt},\end{aligned} \qquad [5]$$

where i denotes the importing country, j the exporting country, t the time period, and u_{ijt} is a regression disturbance.

Finally, adding a risk premium in accordance with the traditional approach, the model becomes:

$$\begin{aligned}\mathrm{d}\ln(PM_{ijt}) &= a_i*\mathrm{d}\ln(C_{jt}) + b_i*\mathrm{d}\ln(E_{ijt}) \\ &\quad + c_i*I_{ijt}*\mathrm{d}\ln(E_{ijt}) + d_i*\mathrm{d}\ln(I_{ijt}) \\ &\quad + u_{ijt},\end{aligned} \qquad [6]$$

where d In I_{ijt} is a proxy for the risk premium.

The implications of the previous discussions for the coefficients in regression [6] are as follows. We expect a to be positive and close to unity, b negative, c positive, $(b + c*I)$ negative and d positive or negative depending on whether the exchange risk is borne by exporters or importers.

4. Empirical results

The purpose of this section is to test the model presented in section 3. One of the objectives is to examine whether the EMS, by stabilizing exchange rates within Europe, enables a greater responsiveness of trade prices to exchange rate changes than prevails under a regime of flexible rates.

Assuming that foreign costs pass through immediately, but that changes in exchange rates pass through with some delay, the following price equation was estimated:

$$\begin{aligned}\mathrm{d}\ln(PM_{ijt}) &= a_i*\mathrm{d}\ln(C_{jt}) + b_i*\mathrm{d}\ln(E_{ijt}) \\ &\quad + e_i*\mathrm{d}\ln(E_{ijt-1}) \\ &\quad + c_i*I_{ijt}*[\mathrm{d}\ln(E_{ijt}) + \mathrm{d}\ln(E_{ijt-1})] \\ &\quad + d_i*\mathrm{d}\ln(I_{ijt}) + u_{ijt}.\end{aligned} \qquad [7]$$

In order to capture the possibility that the pass-through varies according to market structure, the price equation was estimated separately for seven industries with different characteristics. These industries include: chemical products, metal products, agricultural and industrial machinery, office machines, electrical goods, motor vehicles and textiles and clothing.

The price equation was estimated, for each industry, over a sample of five importers (three countries inside the EMS: France, the Federal Republic of Germany (FRG), Italy, and two outside the EMS: the UK and the USA) and eight exporters (the five importers plus Belgium, Japan and the Netherlands). Due to the limited quantity of time-series data, it was necessary to pool time-series and cross-section data for all exporting countries. Estimation of equation [7] provided, therefore, 35 separate sets of parameter estimates: one for each of the 7 sectors and the 5 markets.

The most important features of the data are as follows. Import prices (*PM*) are indexes of disaggregate import unit values. The costs of a given foreign partner for a given sector (*C*) are proxied by the export price (itself an index of disaggregate export unit values) of that country's exports for the given sector to its main markets. Import and export price indexes were obtained from a data bank provided by the EC Commission. It includes prices and quantities for exports and imports on a bilateral basis among a number of industrial countries. It is disaggregated into 15 manufacturing sectors (defined at the 2-digit level of the NACE classification), of which 7 are used in the estimations. The bilateral exchange rates (*E*) are obtained using the annual average dollar rates (IFS, line rf). Finally, volatility (*I*) is measured by the standard deviation of the 12 monthly percentage changes in end-of-period exchange rates (IFS, line ae) for that year.

Table 8.2 presents the ordinary least squares (OLS) estimation results for our seven sectors. The sample period lies between 1966 and 1987, depending on data availability. The overall quality of the estimations is very good, especially for first-difference regressions. One notable exception, however, concerns equations for the US market which exhibit very low R-squares.

The estimated coefficient of the cost variable has the predicted positive sign and is significantly different from zero in nearly all cases. The degree of cost pass-through for a given sector tends to be the same across all five markets in the sample. Two categories of sectors can be distinguished according to the size of the cost coefficient. The first category comprises four sectors which display a high degree of pass-through (i.e. at least 70 per cent): chemical products, metal products, motor vehicles and textiles and clothing. In these sectors exporters seem to enjoy strong market power which enables them to pass through their cost changes to foreign buyers. In the case of the last three sectors, this situation might reflect the collusive behaviour of exporters facilitated by the imposition of voluntary export restraint (VER) arrangements.

The second category includes three sectors with a low cost pass-through (i.e. at most 40 percent): agricultural and industrial machinery, office machines and electrical goods. Here, exporters appear to have relatively little market power. This seems to be particularly true in the US market for office machines and electrical goods for which the cost coefficient is close to zero, reflecting a strong competitive environment.

TABLE 8.2: Regression results for seven sectors by import market

	France	FRG	Italy	UK	USA
Chemical products (estimation period: 1966–87)					
Cost (a)	0.860 (20.12)*	0.850 (20.06)*	0.822 (14.70)*	0.821 (15.51)*	0.742 (6.96)*
Exchange rate					
Current (b)	–0.693 (–6.29)*	–0.775 (–6.73)*	–1.175 (–7.80)*	–0.518 (–3.85)*	–0.428 (–1.71)*
Lagged (e)	0.031 (0.30)	–0.065 (–0.73)	–0.023 (–0.23)	–0.112 (–0.96)	0.088 (0.47)
Effect of volatility on:					
Pass-through (c)	–3.640 (–1.07)	2.862 (0.98)	5.167 (1.34)	–4.748 (–1.20)	–6.634 (–1.12)
Import prices (d)	–0.003 (–0.72)	0.007 (1.26)	0.004 (0.57)	–0.007 (–1.13)	–0.000 (–0.01)
R^2	0.710	0.723	0.677	0.586	0.281
Metal products (estimation period: 1972–87)					
Cost (a)	0.914 (33.01)*	1.001 (32.97)*	0.855 (14.44)*	0.954 (19.95)*	0.770 (9.76)*
Exchange rate					
Current (b)	–1.015 (–7.17)*	–1.031 (–6.22)*	–1.861 (–5.97)*	–1.324 (–4.77)*	–0.787 (–2.26)*
Lagged (e)	–0.143 (–1.13)	–0.160 (–1.20)	–0.765 (–3.49)*	–0.092 (–0.38)	–0.207 (–0.79)
Effect of volatility on					
Pass-through (c)	5.377 (1.27)	6.792 (1.58)	29.742 (3.55)*	9.704 (1.17)	1.697 (0.19)
Import prices (d)	0.000 (–0.04)	0.024 (2.21)*	0.059 (3.08)*	0.040 (1.59)	0.003 (0.14)
R^2	0.902	0.907	0.731	0.783	0.575

TABLE 8.2 *cont.*

	France	FRG	Italy	UK	USA
Agricultural and industrial machinery (estimation period: 1978–87)					
Cost (a)	0.408 (6.01)*	0.351 (6.45)*	0.417 (5.09)*	0.386 (4.80)*	0.836 (2.61)*
Exchange rate					
Current (b)	–0.869 (–4.65)*	–0.284 (–1.68)*	–0.954 (–5.06)*	–1.023 (–4.20)*	–0.796 (–1.40)
Lagged (e)	0.020 (0.12)	0.394 (3.07)*	0.043 (0.28)	–0.206 (–0.89)	–0.172 (–0.40)
Effect of volatility on:					
Pass-through (c)	–1.157 (–0.20)	–12.399 (–2.58)*	–3.544 (0-.60)	10.348 (1.41)	–1.159 (–0.01)
Import prices (d)	0.003 (0.30)	0.016 (1.49)	–0.000 (–0.04)	0.171 (0.81)	–0.016 (–0.28)
R^2	0.521	0.568	0.601	0.102	0.197
Office machines (estimation period: 1978–87)					
Cost (a)	–0.269 (3.58)*	–0.172 (2.61)*	–0.495 (5.40)*	–0.245 (3.68)*	–0.276 (–0.84)
Exchange rate					
Current (b)	–1.357 (–4.28)*	–0.077 (–0.25)	–0.913 (–2.77)*	–0.994 (–3.14)*	–1.324 (–1.51)
Lagged (e)	–0.509 (–1.76)*	0.437 (1.82)*	–0.202 (–0.76)	–0.321 (–1.08)	–1.561 (–2.25)*
Effect of volatility on:					
Pass-through (c)	13.418 (1.41)	–16.616 (–1.85)*	0.890 (0.09)	13.718 (1.45)	42.743 (1.71)*
Import prices (d)	0.004 (0.22)	0.017 (0.80)	0.070 (2.96)*	0.021 (0.74)	–0.145 (–1.59)
R^2	0.331	0.259	0.410	0.073	0.059

TABLE 8.2 *cont.*

	France	FRG	Italy	UK	USA
Electrical goods (estimation period: 1978–87)					
Cost (a)	0.371	0.366	0.305	0.340	0.194
	(4.36)*	(5.61)*	(3.59)*	(4.66)*	(0.33)
Exchange rate					
Current (b)	–0.865	–0.217	–1.422	–1.080	0.336
	(–3.01)*	(–0.92)	(–5.62)*	(–4.06)*	(0.34)
Lagged (e)	–0.113	0.365	–0.108	–0.428	0.689
	(–0.43)	(2.00)*	(–0.52)	(–1.71)*	(0.91)
Effect of volatility on					
Pass-through (c)	0.410	–20.302	5.624	14.198	–30.121
	(0.05)	(–3.04)*	(0.71)	(1.77)*	(–1.12)
Import prices (d)	–0.001	0.040	0.019	–0.004	0.000
	(–0.08)	(2.51)*	(1.06)	(–0.18)	(–0.00)
R^2	0.224	0.533	0.452	0.196	0.054
Motor vehicles (estimation period: 1978–87)					
Cost (a)	0.672	0.406	0.883	0.714	1.299
	(8.79)*	(5.25)*	(7.20)*	(9.43)*	(6.94)*
Exchange rate					
Current (b)	–0.963	–0.469	–0.842	–0.926	0.306
	(–5.96)*	(–2.59)*	(–3.98)*	(–5.47)*	(0.86)
Lagged (e)	–0.096	–0.369	–0.197	–0.127	0.369
	(–0.65)	(2.72)*	(–1.13)	(–0.80)	(1.34)
Effect of volatility on					
Pass-through (c)	6.647	–9.959	6.962	5.629	–22.569
	(1.32)	(–1.95)*	(1.06)	(1.10)	(–2.30)*
Import prices (d)	0.001	–0.014	0.006	0.007	–0.019
	(0.072)	(–1.29)	(0.38)	(0.49)	(–0.53)
R^2	0.465	0.642	0.204	0.412	0.230

TABLE 8.2 *cont.*

	France	FRG	Italy	UK	USA
Textiles and clothing (estimation period: 1966–87)					
Cost (a)	0.673 (11.86)*	0.484 (9.80)*	0.751 (10.61)*	0.671 (12.51)*	0.969 (7.32)*
Exchange rate					
Current (b)	–1.079 (–9.25)*	–0.489 (–4.62)*	–0.811 (–5.25)*	–0.863 (–7.83)*	–0.678 (–3.04)*
Lagged (e)	–0.241 (–2.19)*	–0.172 (2.06)*	–0.034 (–0.33)	–0.157 (–1.67)*	–0.305 (–1.82)*
Effect of volatility on					
Pass-through (c)	9.040 (2.52)*	–3.706 (–1.36)	–3.423 (–0.87)	1.847 (0.56)	–1.100 (–0.20)
Import prices (d)	0.000 (0.07)	0.124 (2.42)*	–0.006 (–0.80)	–0.005 (–0.97)	0.013 (1.32)
R^2	0.534	0.490	0.628	0.577	0.348

Note: Figures in brackets are *t*-statistics.
* Indicates the coefficient is significant at the 5% level.

The estimated coefficient of the current exchange rate variable has the predicted negative sign and is significantly different from zero in nearly all cases. On the other hand, the coefficient of the lagged exchange rate variable is generally not significantly different from zero. Moreover, in two-thirds of the equations, the sum of the coefficients for the current and lagged variables are not significantly different from unity. Somewhat surprisingly, the sum of these two coefficients is not significantly different from zero in three out of seven German cases (i.e. agricultural and industrial machinery, office machines and electrical goods).

The regression results indicate that volatility has generally no impact on exchange rate pass-through. Out of 35 cases reported in Table 8.2, the estimate of the coefficient *c* is significantly positive, at the 5 per cent level, in only 4 instances. There is no obvious pattern among these cases, neither in terms of sectors nor in terms of market. The behaviour on the German market is again atypical, with an unexpected negative impact of volatility in four cases.

In Table 8.3, we have computed the total exchange rate pass-through (i.e. $b + e + c^*I$), distinguishing among suppliers between EMS and non-EMS members. As expected from the previous discussion, the degree of exchange rate pass-through is generally close to unity. It is often close to zero in the German and US markets.

TABLE 8.3 Pass-through of exchange rates,* by sector and import market (1979–87)

	France	FRG	Italy	UK	USA
Chemical products					
EMS	–0.69	–0.82	–1.16	–0.74	–0.51
Non-EMS	–0.76	–0.76	–1.06	–0.74	–0.51
Metal products					
EMS	–1.11	–1.15	–2.39	–1.18	–0.95
Non-EMS	–1.01	–1.00	–1.86	–1.18	–0.95
Agricultural and industrial machinery					
EMS	–0.86	0.03	–0.94	–0.98	–0.97
Non-EMS	–0.88	–0.24	–1.00	–0.98	–0.97
Office machines					
EMS	–1.76	0.25	–1.11	–0.98	–1.76
Non-EMS	–1.49	–0.12	–1.09	–0.98	–1.76
Electrical goods					
EMS	0.97	0.02	–1.48	–1.16	0.23
Non-EMS	–0.97	–0.43	–1.38	–1.16	0.23
Motor vehicles					
EMS	–1.00	–0.16	–0.98	–0.91	0.08
Non-EMS	–0.87	–0.38	–0.85	–0.91	0.08
Textiles and clothing					
EMS	–1.25	–0.34	–0.87	–0.97	–1.01
Non-EMS	–1.06	–0.42	–0.93	–0.97	–1.01

*Computed on the basis of the coefficients reported in Table 8.2 as (b + e + c*l).

Among the 21 cases that concern markets belonging to the EMS, the degree of exchange rate pass-through is greater (in absolute value) for intra-EMS trade in 11 occurrences. However, the above results with respect to the coefficient c imply that the difference in pass-through between trade with EMS and non-EMS partners is significant in only 4 instances.

Finally, the regression results also indicate that volatility has generally no direct impact on import prices. The coefficient of the volatility variable is significantly different from zero in only five cases, three of which occur in the German market. In all these situations, volatility has a positive impact on prices, implying that the exchange risk is borne by the exporter. This would happen if trade were invoiced in the importer's currency, as may, indeed, be the case for exports to the FRG.

5. Conclusion

The purpose of this chapter was to explore the possible impact of the EMS on trade through the observed significant reduction of exchange rate volatility. This was done by estimating bilateral import price equations for five import markets and seven exporters across seven manufacturing sectors.

The results indicate that the volatility-reduction aspect of the EMS appears to have had no significant impact on import prices. Indeed, we found only negligible evidence that volatility affects import prices via either the lowering of the exchange rate pass-through or the addition of a risk premium. One explanation might be the availability of hedging instruments against exchange rate volatility.

Further research on the issue of exchange rate variability and trade should take into account three limitations of the present study. First, there is a need to use more disaggregate data. Second, the regression analysis should take into account a broader set of explanatory factors. Finally, it would be useful to go beyond volatility and consider the possible impact of misalignment on trade.

References

Akhtar, M. A. and **Hilton, R. S.** (1984) Effects of exchange rate uncertainty on Germany and US trade, *Federal Reserve Bank of New York Quarterly Review*, **9**, pp. 7–16.

Bailey, M., Tavlas, G. S. and **Ulan, M.** (1987) The impact of exchange rate volatility on export growth: Some theoretical considerations and empirical results, *Journal of Policy Modeling*, **9**, pp. 225–43.

Clark, P. B. (1973) Uncertainty, exchange risk, and the level of international trade, *Western Economic Journal*, **11**, pp. 302–13.

Cushman, D. O. (1983) The effects of real exchange rate risk on international trade, *Journal of International Economics*, **15**, pp. 45–63.

De Grauwe, P. (1987) International trade and economic growth in the European Monetary System, *European Economic Review*, **31**, pp. 389–98.

De Grauwe, P. and **de Bellefroid, B.** (1989) Long-run exchange rate variability and international trade, in Arndt, S. W. and Richardson, J. D. (eds), *Real Financial Linkages*, MIT Press, Cambridge, Mass., pp. 193–212.

Dixit, A. (1989) Hysteresis, import penetration and exchange rate pass-through, *Quarterly Journal of Economics*, **104**, pp. 205–28.

Ethier, W. (1973) International trade and the forward exchange market, *American Economic Review*, **63**, pp. 494–503.

Feenstra, R. (1987) Symmetric pass-through of tariffs and exchange rates under imperfect competition: an empirical test, *NBER Working Paper*, No. 2453, Cambridge, Mass.

Frenkel, J. A. and **Goldstein, M.** (1989) Exchange rate volatility and misalignment: Evaluating some proposals for reform, *NBER Working Paper*, No. 2894, Cambridge, Mass.

Gotur, P. (1985) Effects of exchange rate volatility on trade: Some further evidence, *IMF Staff Papers*, **32**, pp. 475–512.

Heckerman, D. (1973) On the effects of exchange risk, *Journal of International Economics*, **3**, pp. 379–85.

Hooper, P. and **Kohlhagen, S. W.** (1978) The effect of exchange rate uncertainty on prices and volume of international trade, *Journal of International Economics*, **8**, pp. 483–511.

Hooper, P. and **Mann, C.** (1989) Exchange rate pass-though in the 1980s: the case of US imports of manufactures, *Brookings Papers on Economic Analysis*, **1**, pp. 297–337.

International Monetary Fund *International Financial Statistics*, Washington, D.C., various issues.

Kenen, P.B. and **Rodrick, D.** (1986) Measuring and analyzing the effects of short-term volatility in real exchange rates, *Review of Economics and Statistics*, **68**, pp. 311–15.

Knetter, M. M. (1989) Price discrimination by US and German exporters, *American Economic Review*, **79**, pp. 198–209.

Krugman, P. (1989) *Exchange Rate Instability*, MIT Press, Cambridge, Mass.

Mann, C. (1986) Prices, profit margins and exchange rates, *Federal Reserve Bulletin*, **72**, pp. 366–79.

Mann, C. (1987) The puzzling behavior of non-oil import prices, mimeo.

Moffet, M. H. (1989) The *J*-curve revisited: an empirical examination for the United States, *Journal of International Money and Finance*, **8**, pp. 425–44.

Perée, E. and **Steinherr, A.** (1989) Exchange rate uncertainty and foreign trade, *European Economic Review*, **33**, pp. 1241–64.

Williamson, J. (1983) *The Exchange Rate System*, Institute of International Economics, Washington, D.C.

Comment: Paul De Grauwe

This paper by André Sapir and Khalid Sekkat is a useful addition to the existing literature about the effects of exchange rate volatility on international trade. Their conclusion is in line with a long series of empirical studies that have failed to detect strong effects of exchange rate volatilty on international trade.

The relationship between exchange rate volatility and international trade is a complex one. The authors, therefore, restrict their attention to one issue. They ask the question of how exchange rate variations are 'passed-through' into prices, and to what extent this pass-through is affected by the exchange rate regime. Since the authors spend relatively little time in presenting the theory, it will be useful to do this in the present comment. This will also allow us to evaluate whether the authors have succeeded in correctly setting up testable hypotheses of that theory.

Let us consider a domestic producer who operates in an imperfectly competitive environment. Let us call this producer BMW. BMW produces for the home market (Germany) and for the foreign market (America). In Figure 8.1 we present the American market for BMWs. The demand for BMWs is represented by the downward sloping curve D (MR is the marginal revenue curve). It will be assumed that BMW operates under constant returns to scale. The marginal cost of producing a BMW in Germany is C^*, which is expressed in DM. This marginal cost can be translated into dollars by dividing by the exchange rate, i.e.

$$C = C^*/E$$

where C is the dollar value of the marginal cost of producing one BMW; E is the exchange rate (the price of the dollar in units of DM).

The marginal cost curve (in dollars) is represented by the horizontal line in Figure 8.1. Equilibrium is obtained in point F (where marginal revenue equals marginal cost). BMW will export Q_1 cars to America and price it at P_1. The vertical line FB represents the mark-up and is a measure of the market power of BMW in America.

Now let the DM depreciate relative to the dollar. This is an increase in E. We show the effect in Figure 8.2. The dollar cost of a BMW declines, so that the marginal cost curve shifts downwards. The new profit maximizing point is now G (versus F in the pre-depreciation situation). BMW will therefore lower its dollar price from P_1 to P_2, however, by a lower percentage than the percentage of the depreciation of the DM.

Is there any reason to believe that BMW may not change its dollar price at all, following the depreciation ?

The answer is yes. In order to see this, let us look at the profit under two pricing strategies. One strategy is to adjust the price to its optimal level P_2. The profit realized under this flexible pricing strategy (FPS) is represented by the rectangle ECGK. A second pricing strategy is to keep the initial price P_1 unchanged. The profit is then ABCD. We can now measure the difference in profits of the two pricing strategies by the difference between the shaded rectangles α and β. In imperfectly

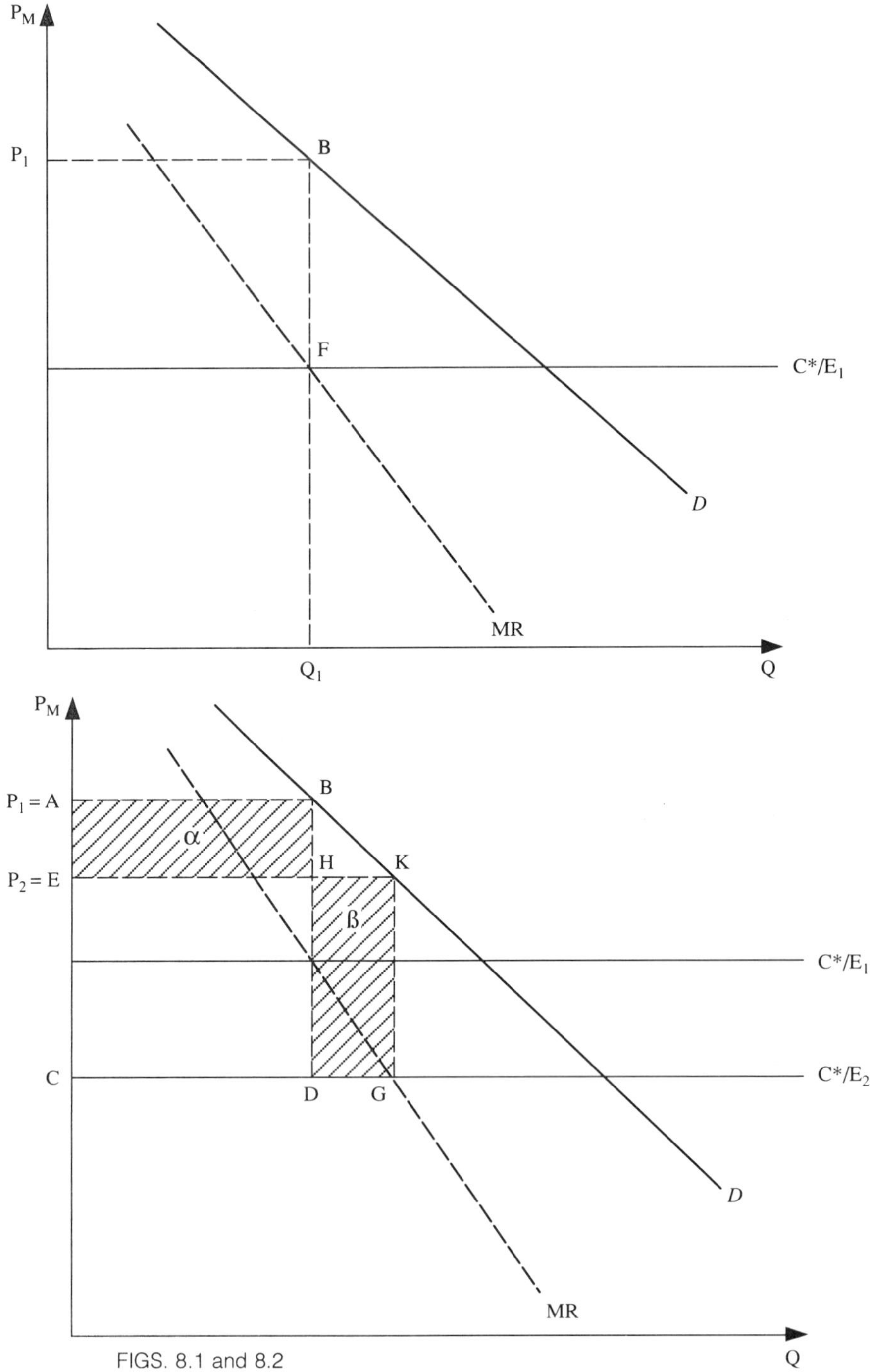

FIGS. 8.1 and 8.2

competitive markets this difference will be of a 'second order of magnitude'. In other words, the firm does not increase its profits very much by following the flexible pricing strategy after the depreciation. The intuition is clear. By reducing its price, BMW gains market share. This raises profits. However, the increased market share is achieved at the expense of a lower profit margin (KG instead of BD). The latter reduces total profits. By keeping its price unchanged, BMW forfeits the possibility of increasing its market share (and thus potential profits). However, this allows BMW to increase its profit margin, which increases total profits.

If this was all that happened, it would still be worthwile for BMW to follow a flexible pricing strategy and to lower its price, because this remains the profit maximizing response to the depreciation of the DM. In other words this strategy ensures larger total profits than the fix-price strategy. (Graphically we have that $\beta > \alpha$.)

The existence of sunk costs associated with expanding its market share may, however, lead BMW to follow the fix-price strategy. This will be the case if this sunk cost exceeds the expected increase in total profits resulting from lowering the price in America. In general, these sunk costs may be quite important in markets for differentiated products. They include, for example, the cost of increasing a commercial network. In that case we will observe fix-price strategies, i.e. firms will not adjust their prices in their export markets following exchange rate changes. This phenomenon has been called 'pricing to market'.

The previous analysis is essentially static. When deciding about its pricing strategy, BMW will also have to make a judgement about whether the observed depreciation is temporary or permanent. If it perceives the depreciation of the DM to be permanent, it will compare the once for all sunk cost of expanding its operations in America with the present value of all future gains in profits. Even if the one period gain is small, the addition of future gains may make it attractive to follow a flex-price strategy. If, on the other hand, the depreciation of the DM is perceived to be temporary, it is much more likely that BMW chooses a fix-price strategy.

We now come to an important insight which allows us to derive conclusions about the degree of price flexibility in different exchange rate regimes. In a floating exchange rate environment (like in our example of BMW exporting to America), the firms are very uncertain about the permanent or temporary nature of exchange rate changes. As a result, when a depreciation occurs, the exporting firm will have an incentive to 'wait and see' before it adjusts its price. By waiting, it keeps its options open: if the depreciation observed today happens to be permanent, the loss of waiting until next period to adjust the price is limited to a one-period smaller profit. In the next period the firm can still adjust its price. If, however, the firm immediately adjusts its price, it runs the risk of making a large loss (the sunk costs) if the depreciation turns out to be temporary. In that case it will have to increase its price in the export market again.

In a fixed exchange rate environment, like the EMS, this option value of waiting is much less likely to be important. When, for example, the FF devalues relative to the DM, this is very likely to be perceived as a permanent exchange rate change. There will be no incentive to wait in order to see whether this devaluation is not reversed in the next period. It is, therefore, more likely that 'pricing to market' will be less pronounced within the EMS than between countries that allow their exchange rates to float freely.

This theory about the differences in pricing strategies of firms in different exchange rate regimes sounds quite plausible. And yet, Sapir and Sekkat find no evidence for it. In fact they find no evidence for 'pricing to market' under either exchange rate regime. This is troublesome, as other researchers have found rather strong evidence of 'pricing to market' by Japanese and German exporters in America (See Marston (1989), Krugman (1987)).

One possible reason of the failure of Sapir and Sekkat to find evidence for 'pricing to market' could be that they relate price changes to a measure of exchange rate variability which makes no distinction between the permanent or temporary nature of the exchange rate changes. In their econometric analysis all exchange rate changes are lumped together whether they are permanent or temporary.

Marston and Krugman avoid this problem by concentrating on currencies and periods where the exchange rate changes have been largely temporary. As a result, they find significant 'pricing to market' behaviour.

In order to give the theory a fair chance it would be useful in further reseach to compare clear cases of permanent exchange rate changes (e.g. the French devaluations during 1982-83) with cases of temporary exchange rate changes that occurred mostly in floating exchange rate environments.

References

Krugman, P. (1987) Pricing to Market When the Exchange Rate changes, in Arndt, S. and Richardson, D. (eds.) *Real Financial Linkages among Open Economies*, Cambridge: MIT Press, Cambridge, pp. 49–70.

Marston, R. (1989) Pricing to Market in Japanese Manufacturing, *NBER Working Paper*, No. 2905, March.

PART TWO

A TWO-SPEED EMS IN THE 1990s?

CHAPTER NINE

The EMS, Spain and macroeconomic policy*

José Viñals

1. Introduction

As a new member of the European Community (EC) since 1986, Spain also had the option of being a full participant in the European Monetary System (EMS). The Spanish Council of Ministers decided on 16 July 1989 to exercise this option, and from the following Monday the peseta officially started obeying the rules of the Exchange Rate Mechanism (ERM) of the system.[1] Moreover, and unprecedentedly, the peseta became subject to the discipline mechanism of the EMS even before its formal inclusion in the ECU – which took place in September 1989 – although its weight in the currency basket (5.3 per cent) had already been accorded.

This chapter focuses on the issue of Spanish participation in the EMS and tries to answer the following questions. What net gains can be derived from EMS membership? Were all the required preconditions satisfied for a smooth entrance into the system? What has been the experience of the peseta so far inside the EMS? What are the main economic policy changes due to take place as a result of Spain's membership? The chapter is organized as follows: section 2 identifies and analyses the main relative advantages for Spain of EMS participation. Section 3 deals specifically with the timing and conditions of Spanish integration. Section 4 analyses how future monetary and fiscal policy should be changed to achieve stability of the peseta exchange rate inside the EMS. Section 5 looks at the recent evolution of the peseta inside the system. Finally, section 6 briefly summarizes the conclusions.

2. What can Spain expect from EMS membership?

Before making the decision regarding Spain's entrance into the EMS, Spanish economic authorities carefully examined the relative net gains to be made in going from

* The final version of this chapter was written in November 1989. The views expressed in it are those of the author and do not necessarily represent those of the Banco de España.

the former exchange rate policy of managed floating to the policy of formal explicit exchange rate targets dictated by EMS membership. Although the choice of an exchange rate policy does not, by itself, affect the external restrictions to which the economy is subject, it does affect the constraints within which economic policy operates. The basic issue was, then, to what extent could EMS membership allow Spain to improve its fundamental economic policies and, consequently, its economic performance? In what follows, the likely effects of EMS membership on Spanish economic stability, on monetary policy effectiveness and credibility and on the short-term volatility and medium-term behaviour of the peseta are analysed.

THE EXCHANGE RATE AS AN ECONOMIC STABILIZER

It is often said that fixing the exchange rate prevents this variable from helping the economy adjust in the face of macroeconomic shocks. However, even those who are in favour of allowing the exchange rate to move flexibly concede that fixing the exchange rate may be the appropriate thing to do following monetary and financial shocks. Intuitively, with a stable exchange rate, money supply and/or demand changes are automatically offset in the money market, and do not lead to changes in the real side of the economy via interest rate or exchange rate variations. The problem comes, rather, when the economy is hit by real shocks. Since these normally require adjustments in relative prices, such as the real exchange rate, and since relative national price levels are not fully flexible in the short-term, the flexibility of the exchange rate can help make easier the required change in the real exchange rate.

Ideally, one would like to have an optimal exchange rate policy that responds to the variety of shocks hitting the economy in line with the above-mentioned principles. However, this is easier said than done, since the derived optimal exchange rate rule may be too complex to be operational.

From this point of view, the EMS seems to offer an *a priori* attractive combination. In fact, by constraining the bilateral exchange rates of member countries to move within the band, the resulting macro outcome is desirable in the case of monetary and financial shocks, and also of small, transitory, short-lived, real shocks. At the same time, when real shocks are large and persistent, the system still allows changes in the nominal exchange rate – beyond the flexibility provided by the band – through suitable realignments of central rates.[2] In this regard, the survival of the EMS without major tensions in the period 1979–89 – marked by important oil-price variations, the US budget deficit problem and the October 1987 stock market fall – seems to support the *de facto* useful macroeconomic role performed by the EMS.

In sum, although the EMS may not always provide a theoretically optimal exchange rate policy,[3] it seems to provide a practically adequate exchange rate policy for its members.

EXCHANGE RATE VOLATILITY AND MISALIGNMENT

An alternative way of looking at the appropriate exchange rate policy is through the concepts of volatility and misalignment.

It is generally agreed that exchange rate instability is one of the most salient characteristics of the present floating exchange rate system. The cost of exchange rate instability can come in two forms: short-term volatility costs and medium-term misalignment costs.

The first type of cost is associated with the uncertainty introduced in price signals by the *short-term fluctuations* of the market exchange rate. However, one would expect such costs to be rather small given the existence of hedging facilities through the forward exchange market. In fact, the available empirical evidence is not conclusive regarding the trade and output effects of short-term exchange rate volatility.[4]

In this regard, although the evidence[5] points towards major nominal and real exchange rate short-term variability reductions of intra-EMS currencies since 1979 (Table 9.1) this should perhaps better be considered as a small, rather than as a major economic benefit, and mainly as an illustration of the successful mechanical functioning of the system *vis-à-vis* the 'snake'.

Misalignment costs are much more visible and important. Given that the real exchange rate is a key price in an open economy, any sustained divergence between the market exchange rate and the fundamental equilibrium exchange rate is bound to cause very significant economic problems. As Williamson (1987) has pointed out, misalignment can result in large payment imbalances, misdirected international investment flows, unnecessary shifts of resources between the tradable and the non-tradable sectors of the economy, destruction of productive capacity and protectionist threats.[6] Indeed, few people will negate that the overvaluation of the dollar during the 1980s defies a 'fundamentalist' explanation,[7] and that it had significant economic costs. The behaviour of the pound in 1980–81 is another recent example of misalignment.

However, such developments have not been apparent in EMS currencies.[8] Specifically, the tight bands established by the EMS around the bilateral central rates have prevented the exchange rate from taking off from the course dictated by the equilibrium exchange rate when this last rate has not changed. On the other hand, when the fundamentals of the economy of a member country have changed, realignments have seemed to move the central rate close to the new equilibrium rate. Although some speculative capital flows have preceded each EMS realignment so far (Table 9.2), such realignments have most likely contributed to avoid important misaligments between the currencies of member countries since 1979.

In sum, the EMS performs a useful role by reducing the size of short-term, unpredictable and self-reversing exchange rate changes, and also, and mainly, by accommodating medium-term exchange rate movements. From the Spanish viewpoint, given that about 57 per cent of our imports, and 66 per cent of our exports are currently with EC countries, and given also that a very large portion of our capital flows

TABLE 9.1 Nominal and real exchange rate variability*

	Variability of nominal exchange rates against EMS currencies		Variability of nominal exchange rates against non-EMS currencies		Variability of real exchange rates against EMS currencies		Variability of real exchange rates against non-EMS currencies	
	1974–78	1979–85	1974–78	1979–85	1974–78	1979–85	1974–78	1979–85
Belgium	11	7	18	23	12	8	19	25
Denmark	13	8	17	23	17	9	20	24
France	17	8	19	24	17	9	19	25
FRG	15	7	18	22	16	8	19	23
Italy	18	9	20	21	20	9	21	22
Netherlands	11	6	18	24	13	7	20	25
EMS average†	14	7	18	23	16	8	20	24
Japan	21	22	20	27	23	23	23	29
UK	17	21	19	24	18	24	21	28
USA	19	27	16	21	20	28	18	27
Non-EMS average†	19	23	18	24	20	25	21	28

Source: Ungerer, Evans and Nyberg (1986).

* The variability is measured by the standard deviation (×1000) of changes in the natural logarithm of average monthly bilateral exchange rates. Numbers have been rounded.
† Averages of countries shown.

TABLE 9.2: Central parity realignments in the EMS (% change)

	24.9.79	30.11.79	23.3.81	5.10.81	22.2.82	14.6.82	21.3.83	22.7.85	7.4.86	4.8.86	12.1.87
BF	0	0	0	0	–8.5	0	1.5	2	1	0	2
DKR	–2.9	–4.8	0	0	–3.0	0	2.5	2	1	0	0
DM	2.0	0	0	5.5	0	4.25	5.5	2	3	0	3
FF	0	0	0	–3.0	0	–5.75	–2.5	2	–3	0	0
IR£	0	0	0	0	0	0	–3.5	2	0	–8	0
Lira	0	0	–6.0	–3.0	0	–2.75	–2.5	–6	0	0	0
HFL	0	0	0	5.5	0	4.25	3.5	2	3	0	3

is also with the EC, avoiding misaligment costs through the EMS seemed a significant benefit.

MONETARY POLICY EFFECTIVENESS AND CREDIBILITY

One of the traditional criticisms against a regime of limited floating like the EMS is that it implies the loss of autonomy for monetary policy.[9] The basic reason is that in such a system monetary policy has to be fully devoted to achieving the desired exchange rate target, therefore losing the potential to fight unemployment.

It is not clear, however, that monetary policy should be devoted – or can even be successfully devoted – to systematically influencing real economic variables in a world where monetary illusion tends to disappear, and where, as in the case of Spain, the unemployment problem is very much linked to structural problems like the organization of labour markets,[10] etc. Monetary policy, rather, should be devoted primarily to the achievement of *sustained price stability*, leaving to fiscal and structural policies the function of removing the constraints that prevent the economy from creating jobs.

Viewed in this light, the key issue is then whether it is easier to control inflation through an autonomous monetary policy in the context of a floating exchange rate, or through the targeting of the exchange rate inside the EMS.

With respect to the first choice, monetary autonomy will be successful in helping to control inflation if the following conditions are simultaneously satisfied:

1. The authorities resist the temptation to accelerate money growth, in the face of given inflationary expectations,[11] so as to grow a bit more 'just this period';
2. Money demand and money supply functions are reasonably stable[12] (predictable);
3. Monetary policy is not severely conditioned by the financing of budget deficits or wage increases.

However, it is not obvious that these conditions will be simultaneously satisfied in many countries, and particularly in a country like Spain, where the process of financial innovation is intense, and where the financing of the budget deficit creates important problems for the achievement of the targeted money growth rates (Table 9.3).

But what are the conditions for the second choice to work adequately in the pursuit of a low and stable rate of inflation? In principle mainly two:

1. That the foreign rate of inflation that serves to anchor domestic inflation through the maintenance of a stable exchange rate be lower and more stable than the national inflation rate;
2. That the commitment of the authorities to stabilize the exchange rate through the appropriate means be fully believed.

TABLE 9.3 Differences in economic policy: EEC and Spain (%)

	Budget balance* (% GDP)		Monetary growth†		Nominal wage growth	
	EEC	Spain	EEC	Spain	EEC	Spain
1981	–5.3 (–1.6)	–3.9 (–3.1)	11.8	16.2	13.0	15.7
1986	–4.8 (0.3)	–6.1 (–2.3)	10.4	11.8	6.2	9.9
1987	–4.3 (0.7)	–3.6 (0)	11.0	14.0	5.5	6.3
1988	–3.6 (1.0)	–3.0 (0.3)	9.4	11.0	5.6	6.5
1989‡	–2.9 (1.3)	–2.7 (0.4)	—	6.5–9.5§	6.1	7.0

Source: Commission of European Communities, and Banco de España.

* The budget balance net of debt interest payments is in brackets.
† Broad money. Annual average.
‡ Forecasts of the Commission for the EEC, and forecasts of Banco de España for Spain.
§ Money targets for 1989.

Regarding the first condition, it must be noted that once Spain has joined the EMS, the effective anchor for domestic price stability is given by the German inflation rate. In fact, a reasonably realistic characterization of the workings of the EMS so far is one where the Federal Republic of Germany (FRG) sets its national policy to achieve a low and stable rate of inflation, while the other EMS members peg the exchange rate *vis-à-vis* the DM.[13] Consequently, since, as shown in Table 9.4, German inflation is lower and more stable than Spanish inflation, the first condition for the successful control of Spanish inflation within the EMS seems to be satisfied.

TABLE 9.4 Inflation in the EMS (consumer prices, annual average, in %)

	1979	1982	1987	1988	1989 *
Belgium	3.9	7.3	1.6	1.3	2.4
Denmark	10.4	10.2	4.1	4.8	3.7
FRG	4.0	4.7	0.5	1.3	2.5
France	10.4	11.2	3.2	2.7	2.7
Ireland	14.9	15.9	3.1	2.1	2.8
Italy	15.1	15.9	4.8	4.9	4.6
Luxembourg	5.2	10.8	0.6	1.4	2.2
Netherlands	4.3	5.3	–0.4	0.9	1.4
EMS	8.9	9.8	2.5	2.7	3.1
EMS–FRG differential	4.9	5.1	2.0	1.4	0.6

Source: Commission of European Communities.

* Forecasts of the Commission

Regarding the second condition, EMS membership imposes very high costs on countries that do not forcefully stabilize their exchange rate, something that will not generally be the case when exchange rate targets are pursued outside a formal system like the EMS. Clearly, the recent decision about the peseta joining the EMS proves how strong is the commitment of Spanish authorities to exchange rate stability.

In this respect, it has been argued that exchange rate targets are more credible than monetary targets.[14] This is so because, while an excessive monetary expansion can always be justified *ex post* as a needed change of money targets in the presence of portfolio disturbances, exchange rate targets automatically accommodate this type of disturbance, and can only be changed for reasons which are quite visible to the public. Exchange rate targets, therefore, make 'cheating' more obvious and, consequently, politically more costly. On the other hand, since central exchange rate realigments imply non-negligible economic, as well as political, costs for the EMS members triggering them, the credibility of EMS exchange rate targets is further reinforced.

In turn, a country with a credible exchange rate policy can find lowering inflation more feasible and economically less painful inside than outside the system. This is so because EMS membership – by altering the incentives that policy-makers have to pursue inflationary policies – can increase the credibility to the public of the anti-inflationary stance of the authorities. As is well known, when disinflationary monetary policy is more credible it works faster and with smaller output costs.

A recent body of literature has tried to rationalize the disciplinary effect of the EMS on high-inflation member countries.[15] Intuitively, if the system works such as not to let countries fully compensate the competitive losses resulting from higher inflation with an exchange rate depreciation, extra inflation will imply a competitiveness loss and, therefore, lower output. That this has indeed been the case is exemplified by the strong real exchange rate appreciation shown in Fig. 9.1 of the Irish pound (IR£), the Italian lira, and the French franc (FF) (until 1987) in relation to the German mark (DM) since the beginning of the EMS.[16]

Within such a framework, governments have an added disincentive to play the disinflation game, and this results in lower inflation without a reduction in the average output of the economy. Consequently, Spain's recent entrance into the EMS may not only consolidate and 'lock in' the inflationary gains made so far in the last decade or so, but may also help in achieving a lower and more stable inflation rate without having to bear the output costs that otherwise would emerge.

But what is the empirical evidence of this? It is obvious that testing the credibility/discipline hypothesis is not without major complications, and in fact the evidence is rather mixed. While it cannot be disputed that the EMS period has coincided with a substantial reduction in inflation and inflation differentials (Table 9.4) of member countries, it is not clear how much, if any, of this effect to attribute to the EMS itself.

Among recent empirical studies, De Grauwe (1986) and Collins (1988) cast more than a shadow of doubt on the inflation discipline virtues of the EMS. In contrast, Giavazzi and Giovannini (1988) find some weak evidence in its support, while Ungerer *et al.* (1986), and Russo and Tullio (1988) strongly support it. Another interesting study is Artis and Taylor (1988), who analyse to what extent exchange rate stability within the EMS has been purchased at the cost of increasing interest rate instability or, rather, EMS policy credibility benefits have been so large as to reduce speculative attacks on the exchange rate and consequently reduce interest rate instability. They find some evidence in support of the credibility hypothesis.

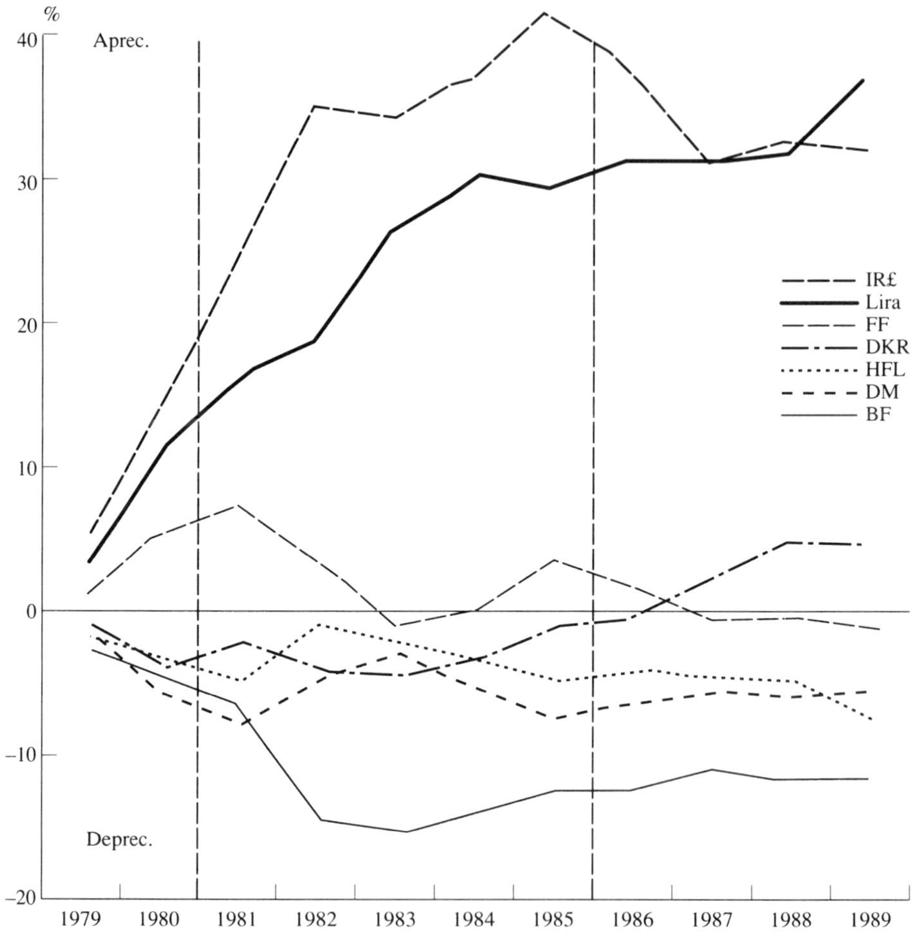

FIG. 9.1 Real exchange rates of EMS currencies. For each currency the real exchange rate is calculated (with CPIs) in relation to the rest of the EMS currencies. *Source*: EC and Banco de España

Without intending to give a final verdict on the available evidence, it seems reasonable to say that there are some indications that the EMS has helped member countries to be less inflationary, although it is true that this effect was probably not very significant until 1982. Indeed, the system seems to have prevented member countries from following policies of competitive devaluations like those observed in Sweden and Greece in the 1981–82 period, and from continuing with overly expansionary policies like those of France in 1981–83.

3. Spain's entrance into the EMS

WHY?

As suggested by the analysis in section 2, although the EMS is not a perfect exchange rate arrangement, it certainly is attractive for a country like Spain. Moreover, it happens to be the case that our managed floating exchange rate policy of recent years has informally kept the peseta moving during most of 1986, 1987 and 1988 within a ±6 per cent band with respect to EMS currencies, as shown by Fig. 9.2. Therefore, the real issue was why not also share the benefits that can be derived from formal adherence to the EMS rather than maintain the former status quo.

Three main objections were raised against Spanish membership. The first objection was that the entrance of Spain into the EMS would merely mean buying exchange rate stability at the cost of increased interest rate instability. This would not be true, however, as indicated earlier, if importing German monetary policy helps reduce – in the medium-term – the underlying instability that current Spanish policies impose on national interest rates. Indeed, it might be expected that a stable peseta–DM exchange rate will help bring future Spanish interest rates closer on average to German interest rates.[17] If this is the case, domestic interest rates will be lower and more stable in the future than they have been so far (Fig. 9.3).

The second – and very serious – objection was that the benefits from membership would likely be small – given the very substantial reduction of inflation experienced by Spain in the last 10 years (Table 9.5) – while the costs from not being able to use the exchange rate in a more discretionary manner would exacerbate the already significant unemployment problems of the Spanish economy (Table 9.5). This objection contained more than a grain of truth[18] and, indeed, it would be desirable to allow for a higher non-inflationary rate of growth in the EMS (particularly in the FRG). However, it should also be taken into account that the EMS helps to prevent the inflation gains so hardly obtained in the past from vanishing, while it also reduces output and unemployment costs associated with further decreases in inflation. It should also be pointed out here that nominal exchange rate changes are not very effective in influencing the real exchange rate in an economy as highly indexed as that of Spain. If the real exchange rate is regarded as an important economic variable, it should be taken into account that systematic improvements in competitiveness can be

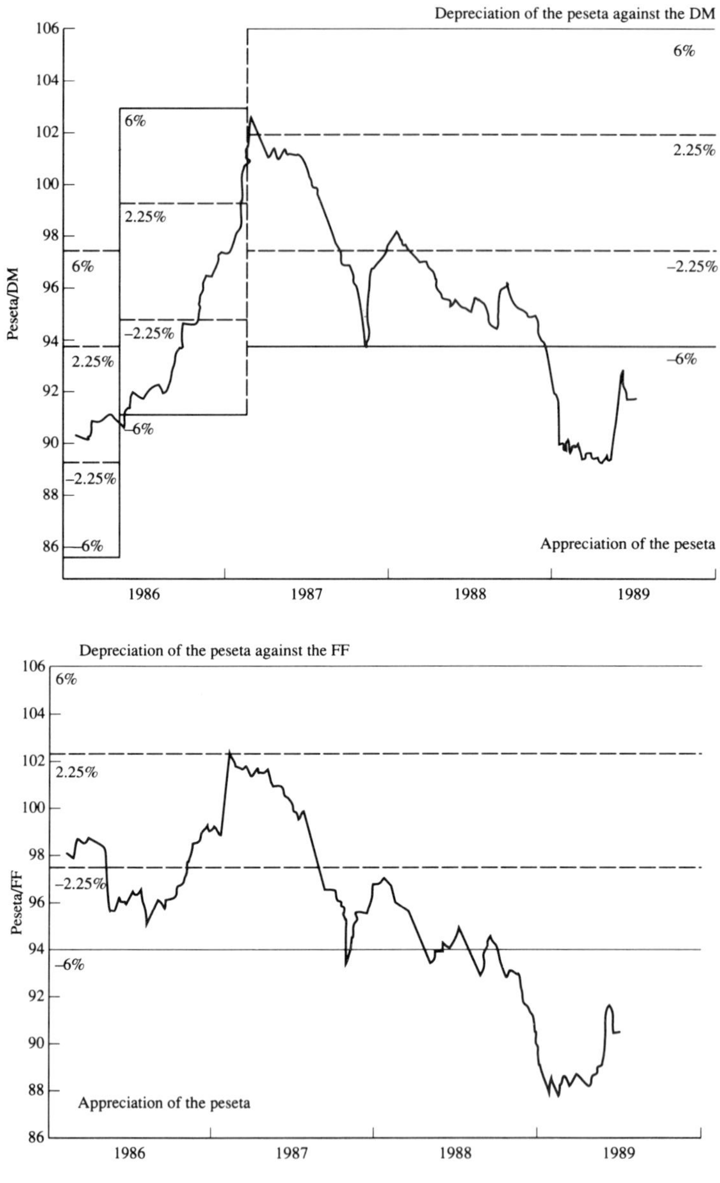

FIG. 9.2 Bilateral fluctuation of the peseta (Jan. 1986–Jun 1989) (percentages). Note: the discontinuous straight lines represent the borders of the 2.25 per cent band around computed central parities. The continuous straight lines represent the borders of the 6 per cent band around computed central parities. It is assumed that the 'shadow' central parities between the DM correspond to the peseta–DM exchange market rate observed on the day of the last EMS reaalignment of January 1987. *Source*: Banco de España

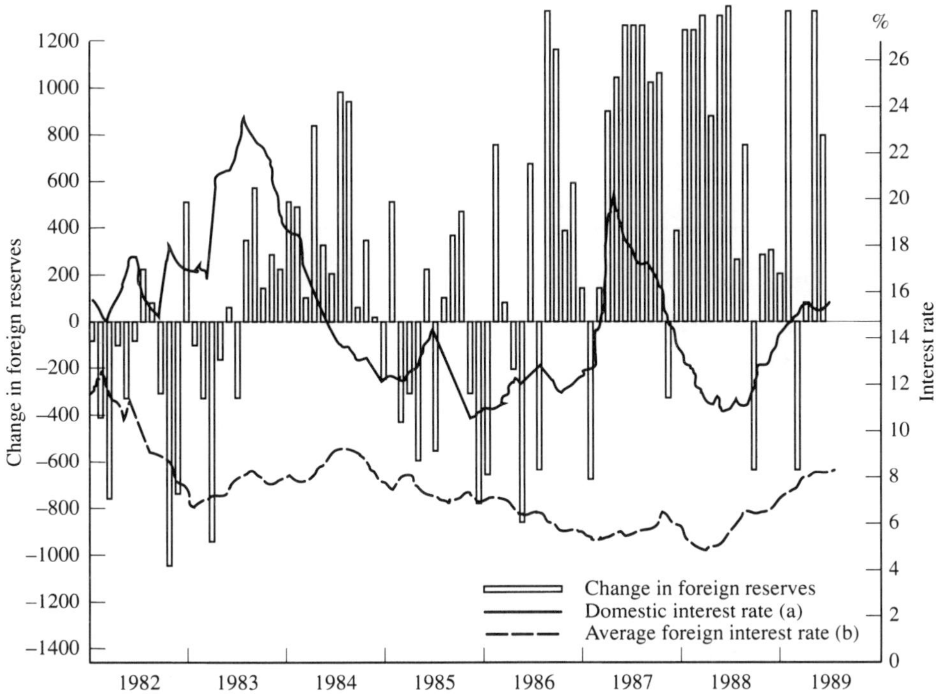

FIG. 9.3 Interest rates and foreign exchange reserves. Notes: (a) Madrid interbank three-month rate; (b) Euromarket three-month rates, weighted according to the foreign currency composition of Spain's external debt. *Source*: Banco de España

more effectively obtained by reducing the inflation differential of the Spanish economy than by the depreciation or periodic devaluation of the peseta. In other words, 'real' problems like unemployment should be fought with 'real' policies, i.e. fiscal and structural policies.

The third objection to Spanish membership was that the peseta would not be able to hold its own in a system like the EMS after the complete liberalization of intra-Community capital flows by the end of 1992, since speculative attacks will then be unstoppable. This was, perhaps, the most serious objection of the three, but it must be recalled that the system has recently been reinforced at the end of 1987 following the Basle-Nyborg Agreement.[19] Nevertheless, it must be taken into account that if speculative activity mainly comes from policy divergences between Spain and the other EMS countries, the incentive to equalize inflation rates without capital controls will be stronger than with capital controls. As a result, policy coordination will be fostered under the new situation, and smaller, less frequent realignments will be required. Moreover, by making speculative attacks less likely, capital controls will not be needed so much to defend the peseta.[20]

TABLE 9.5 Differences in macroeconomic performance: EEC and Spain (%)

	Inflation*		Unemployment		Current account balance (% GDP)	
	EEC	Spain	EEC	Spain	EEC	Spain
1981	12.0	14.3	7.7	14.4	–1.0	–2.7
1986	3.8	8.7	11.9	21.5	1.2	1.7
1987	3.4	5.4	11.6	20.6	0.6	0.1
1988	3.6	5.1	11.3	19.5	0.1	–1.1
1989†	4.8	6.5	10.9	17.4	–0.2	–3.2

Source: Commission of European Communities, and Banco de España.

* Consumer prices, annual average.
† Forecasts of the EC Commission for the EC, and of Banco de España for Spain.

WHEN AND HOW?

Among the conditions to be satisfied by the Spanish economy prior to entering the EMS, two stood out as particularly important.[21]

The first referred to the inflation differential between Spain and the EMS that should be achieved prior to entering the system. In fact, one would have liked the inflation differential between Spain and the FRG (the lowest inflation country in the EMS) to have been small enough so as not to trigger an immediate speculative movement against the peseta. This differential had been 8.9 points in 1986, 4.0 points in 1988, and is expected to be 4.0 points in 1989. Indeed, by the time of entrance Spain's inflation differential *vis-à-vis* the FRG was roughly as small as that of Italy. Therefore, judging by the Italian experience, Spain's inflation seemed to be small enough to validate the recent entrance into the system. Nevertheless, it seemed safer to enter with the 6 per cent band rather than with the 2.25 per cent band, at least during a transitory period while Spain further narrows the inflation differential.

The second condition was related to the process of opening up the trade balance that the Spanish economy has been undergoing since 1 January, 1986 as a result of its integration in the EEC.[22] As explained in section 2, in the face of major changes in the structure of effective tariffs and subsidies, and of important reductions in quotas and other non-tariff trade barriers, it is desirable to retain some degree of flexibility for the exchange rate so as to help achieve the required relative price changes, and intersectoral reallocation of resources between the tradable and non-tradable sectors. At the same time, it seems reasonable and practical to wait until the uncertainties in the balance of payments caused by this process have been substantially reduced so as to have a better idea of what peseta exchange rate could be realistically sustained in the EMS.

By the time of entrance Spain had already abolished many of the quantitative restrictions to EEC trade existing before 1 January, 1986, and had also achieved about half of the agreed reduction in the 14 per cent basic tariff (Table 9.6). The key issue was, however, if the 6.65 basic tariff points that still had to be eliminated after 1989 were consistent with the sustainability of the peseta within the 6 per cent band. Although this is a complex issue, it seemed that the transitory 6 per cent band for the peseta was probably sufficient to accommodate any remaining trade adjustments.

TABLE 9.6 Tariff reduction, Spain–EEC

		%
March	1986	10
January	1987	12.5
January	1988	15
January	1989	15
January	1990	12.5
January	1991	12.5
January	1992	12.5
January	1993	10
Total		100

Source: Viñals (1987).

In sum, both the inflation and the trade opening preconditions were satisfied by mid-1989, therefore allowing the peseta to join the EMS with a transitory 6 per cent band.

As important as the moment chosen for entering the EMS and the width of the bilateral fluctuation band was the choice of the central exchange rate *vis-à-vis* the rest of member currencies. The Spanish authorities chose a central rate of 65 pts–DM. Was this justified?

As it is well known, choosing the central exchange rate for any EMS currency is not an easy task. However, there are two factors which should guide the decision. First, the central rate should be chosen so as to be consistent with the anti-inflationary potential gains to be reaped from EMS membership, without at the same time putting too big a burden on the external competitiveness of the economy. Second, the chosen central rate should be one that remains sustainable inside the system, at least in the short term.

Standard PPP calculations seemed to show a slight overvaluation of the peseta by June 1989. However, given the existing very large interest rate differentials in favour of the peseta, it was felt that any attempt to devalue the peseta significantly would have been unjustified,[23] and rapidly offset by the market. Therefore, since it was expected that interest rate differentials would persist in the short term, the central rate chosen had to be consistent with them and, consequently, it could not be very different from the actual market rate. On the other hand, given the relatively high degree of *de facto* wage indexation in Spain, a significant devaluation would have added to wage–price pressures at a time when inflation was already rising as a result of the very high domestic demand growth. Consequently, the favourable effects on competitiveness would have been small and transitory, while the inflationary effects would have run against the anti-inflationary benefits expected from the system.

On the basis of the above considerations, a central rate of 65 pts–DM was set. This rate, in turn, was reasonably near the closing market rate of 64.3 pts–DM on 16 June.

4. Economic policy strategy

As has been stressed in section 2, Spanish entrance into the EMS has important consequences for economic policy, and especially for monetary policy. In this section we explore in some depth how Spanish future monetary policy strategy and tactics could be revised with the peseta inside the system to achieve the necessary stability of the peseta exchange rate. In this regard, there are two issues which seem particularly important.

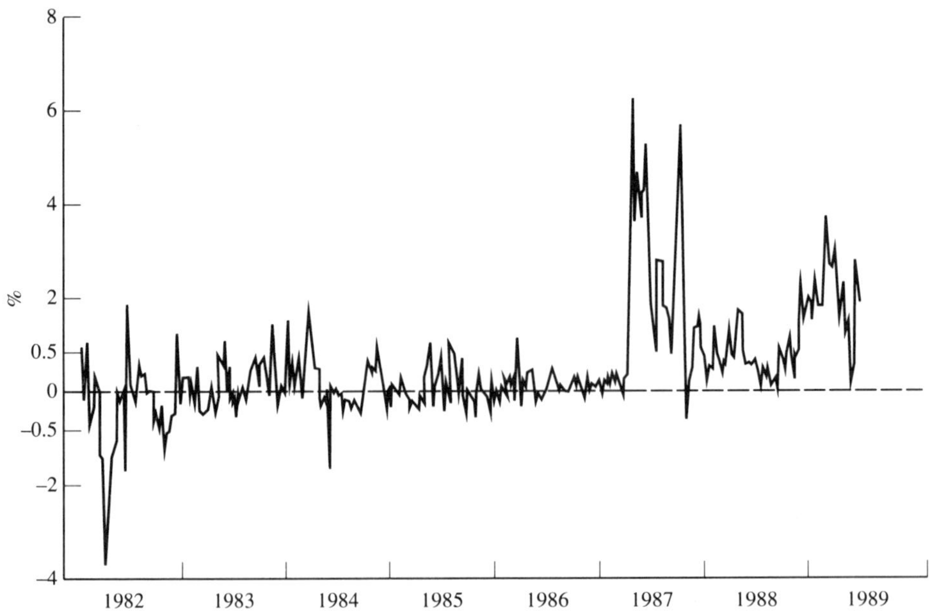

FIG. 9.4 Deviations from covered interest parity (three-month domestic– Eurodollar deposit rates)

The first is that, although the peseta had actually moved within a 6 per cent band in relation to EMS currencies in recent years, this was achieved mainly through foreign exchange intervention operations and capital controls, rather than through policy coordination, as suggested by the wide interest rate differential and the change in foreign reserves shown in Fig. 9.3, and by the deviations from covered interest rate parity in recent years shown in Fig. 9.4. Nevertheless, inside the EMS it is highly desirable to make policy coordination the prime weapon for exchange rate stability. In other words, monetary growth and exchange rate goals should be mutually consistent.

The second important issue to be addressed is that although monetary policy can contribute very substantially to achieving exchange rate stability, it cannot – should not – be the sole factor. In other words, if Spanish fiscal policy is misaligned with respect to the fiscal policies followed by EMS countries (and most notably by the FRG), monetary policy will also have to be misaligned to guarantee exchange rate goals. While in the short-term even this inappropriate mix of monetary and fiscal policy can be consistent with exchange rate targets, the situation is not sustainable, and will be even less so after the introduction of free capital mobility in the EC. Consequently, both monetary and fiscal policy have to share the burden of guaranteeing exchange rate stability through intra-EMS policy coordination.

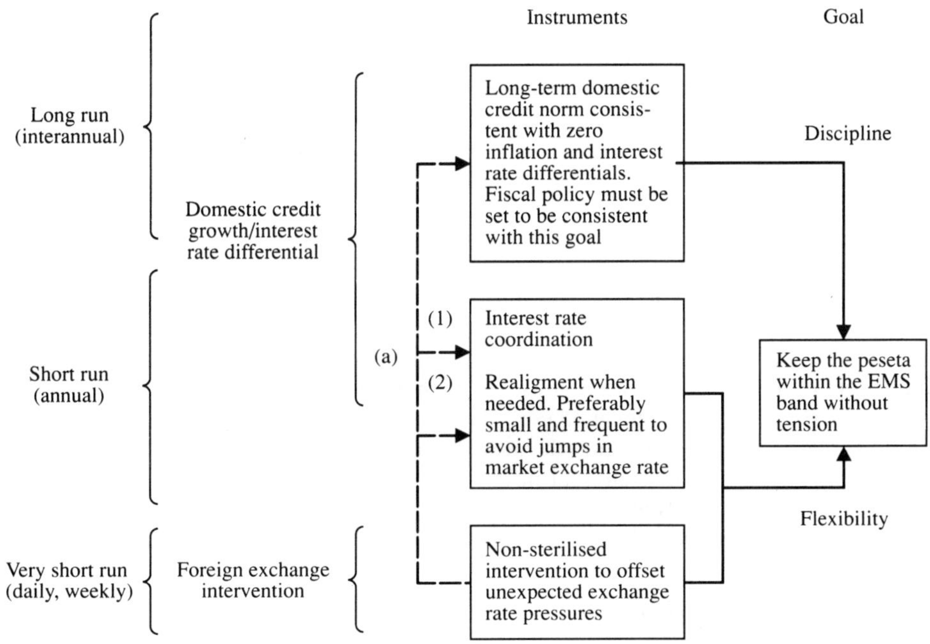

FIG. 9.5 Monetary and fiscal policy for exchange stability. (a) The observation of foreign exchange developments may lead to (1) adjustments in short-term interest differentials; (2) realignments and (3) changes in the long-term domestic credit growth norm

Having said this, in the following we analyse a benchmark case that shows how monetary and fiscal policy could be set to ensure the stability of the peseta both in the short and the long term. Fig. 9.5 provides a summary of the main elements of this policy proposal.

THE LONG TERM

Although the EMS is much more complex than a purely fixed exchange rate system, there are certain basic conditions that have to be simultaneously satisfied in the long-term in the context of free intra-Community capital flows: (a) equalization of national interest rates, (b) equalization of national inflation rates and (c) external balance.

These conditions necessarily imply that Spanish money growth (m) should be set on average to finance domestic potential output growth (n) at the chosen inflation rate (p). Taking the FRG as the anchor for price stability in the system, this means that average domestic monetary growth should be approximately equal to the sum of German inflation (p^*) plus the potential real income growth of the Spanish economy times the long-term income elasticity of money demand (k). That is:

$$m = p^* + kn. \qquad [1]$$

At the same time, since in the long-term the current account balance and the overall balance of payments must be in equilibrium, domestic credit growth (c) should be sufficient to achieve the desired money growth rate:

$$c = m. \qquad [2]$$

To give an example of the orders of magnitude involved, if Spain's potential output is realistically expected to grow between 2 and 4 per cent, and if German inflation oscillates between 1 and 2 per cent, while the long-term income elasticity of money demand[24] is approximately 1, average money growth in Spain should be roughly between 3 and 6 per cent. If we compare this long-term norm with the actual money growth figures in Table 9.3, it is clear that the long-term sustainability of the peseta in the EMS needs further doses of monetary discipline.

However, as recent theoretical developments[25] have made clear, the desired long-term monetary growth rates will only be achieved if fiscal policy is set consistently. That is, when the real interest rate is higher than the real growth rate of the economy, budget deficits[26] cannot exceed a certain magnitude if the public sector is to remain solvent. In fact, the long-term fiscal solvency condition can be formally expressed as

$$f = (r-n)b - (p+n)h \qquad [3]$$

where f is the budget balance ($f \lesseqgtr 0$), b the public debt, and h the money base, all as a fraction of income.

This familiar equation states that for the public sector to be solvent in the long-term (ie. for b and h to be bound), any sustained primary fiscal deficit ($f < 0$)

must be financed by the revenue collected from the inflation tax on bondholders at the rate [$-(r$-$n)$], and on base moneyholders at the rate [$(p+n)$]. Therefore, with (p=p*, r=r*, n, b, h) given in the long-term, equations [1 – 3] indicate that there is an (m, f) combination that is internally consistent. In other words, both fiscal and monetary policy must be set to ensure the long-term stability of the exchange rate (see Fig. 9.5).

Specifically, if we assume a between one and three percentage point differential between the real interest rate and the real growth rate of Spain, the same inflation and real growth rates as before, plus the condition that current public debt and base money (as a fraction of GDP) be kept constant at their 1988 values, the computations shown in Table 9.7 indicate that the maximum sustainable primary structural budget balance in Spain should not exceed a deficit larger than 0.1–0.7 per cent of GDP in the more optimistic growth scenario and, indeed, may actually be a surplus as high as 0.5 per cent of GDP in the less optimistic growth scenario. Since there was a primary surplus of 0.3 per cent of GDP in 1988, and since about two-thirds of the surplus is of a structural[27] nature, the actual primary structural surplus is around 0.2 per cent. Consequently, it is not clear that there are no sustainability problems now and it is therefore critical that this situation improves in the future.[28]

Summarizing, while it seems that the EMS may help its members achieve more monetary discipline, its effect on fiscal discipline is not as direct. Therefore, as the above example makes clear, Spain will need to enforce future fiscal discipline even more to guarantee the long-run stability of the peseta in the system.

TABLE 9.7: Maximum sustainable primary structural budget balance (%GDP)

		Real growth (%)	
		n = 2	n = 4
Inflation %	p = 1	–0.2 (0.5)	–0.5 (0.1)
	p = 2	–0.4 (0.3)	–0.7 (–0.1)

Source: Banco de España.

Note: Calculated from equation [3] in the text, assuming r–n=1, and taking b=32.77 and h=17.15 (1988 values). The numbers in brackets are those resulting from assuming r–n=3.
Numbers have been rounded.

THE SHORT-TERM

Although the long-term monetary and fiscal norms must be satisfied by the economy on average, there should also be some short-term monetary and fiscal flexibility to guarantee exchange rate stability in the presence of macroeconomic shocks through the appropriate coordination of interest rate movements.

For example, if at the beginning of the year the economic authorities foresee certain domestic or foreign shocks that tend to take the exchange rate away from its equilibrium level, the appropriate thing to do would be to modify the mix of annual monetary and fiscal policy in line with this goal. If the shocks are transitory in nature, and do not change the underlying values of potential growth, German long-term inflation, etc. on which the calculations of the long-term monetary and fiscal policy norms are based, there should just be a transitory deviation of monetary and fiscal policy from their norms. Only when changes are fundamental – in the sense of affecting the above mentioned underlying values – will it be advisable also to revise the norm, and/or seek a realignment of the currency (see Fig. 9.5). In other words, annual exchange rate stability should be mainly guaranteed by suitable policy adjustments (with occasional realignments), rather than by foreign exchange market intervention operations, as was recently the case in Spain.

THE VERY SHORT-TERM

In principle, the monetary and fiscal strategy described above could be expected to be sufficient to maintain exchange rate stability. It is a fact of life, however, that foreign exchange markets are continuously hit by all sorts of 'news' which, in turn, tend to alter exchange rates. In that case, it becomes necessary for the monetary authorities to intervene to keep the exchange rate on target. Consequently (non-sterilized) intervention operations have an important role to play in guaranteeing the stability of the peseta in the EMS.

In this regard, it seems that a reasonable rule would be to automatically intervene in the foreign exchange market to offset exchange rate pressures, and only think of altering monetary policy if tensions are strong and persistent.[29] Indeed, speculative capital flows will be smaller – and so will be the required policy changes – the stronger the commitment shown by the authorities to defend the parity.[30] Only in the case of a shock that significantly changes the fundamentals of the economy will a realignment be needed (see Fig. 9.5).

But will this kind of strategy require even greater intervention by Spanish authorities in the foreign exchange market now that the peseta is in the EMS? The answer is that this is not likely to happen as long as the policy recommendations made so far in this section are followed. Indeed, it is even possible that inside the EMS Spain will, on average, reduce the size of intervention operations as a result of the improved inner consistency between monetary and fiscal policy and exchange rate targets.

5. The peseta inside the EMS

At the time this chapter was written (November 1989), the peseta had already been inside the EMS for four and a half months. Overall, its performance has been satisfactory and market demand has been large enough to appreciate the peseta from 64.3 pts–DM on 16 June to 63.2 pts–DM on 2 November. The strength of the peseta has been related to the increase in the domestic short-term interest rate (three-month) from 14.97 per cent on 16 June to 15.20 per cent on 2 November, and to the decrease in the size of the risk premium that the very entrance originated. Both phenomena have slightly widened the three-month covered interest differential *vis-à-vis* the DM from 0.83 to 0.89 per cent between those two dates. Fig. 9.6 shows the recent evolution of the peseta inside the wide band of the EMS.

As has already been pointed out, achieving two goals, price and exchange rate stability, requires, at the minimum, two instruments: fiscal and monetary policy.

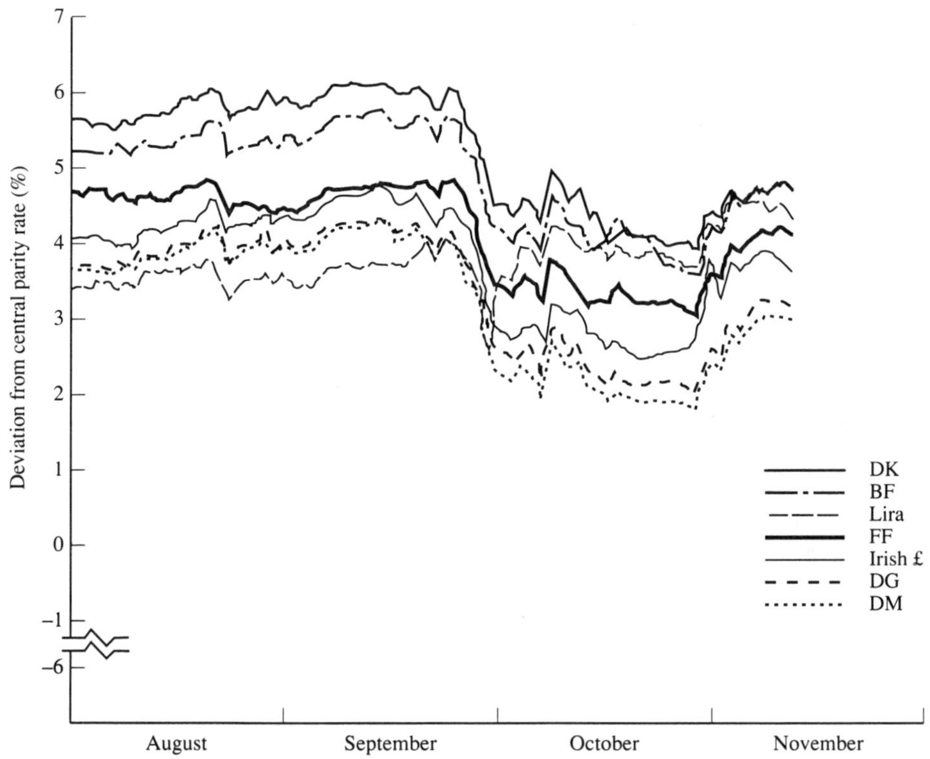

FIG. 9.6 The peseta inside the EMS (appreciation (+) and depreciation (–) of the peseta inside the wide band in relation to other EMS currencies). *Source*: Banco de España

If fiscal policy continues to be relatively expansionary in Spain, this will continue to put upward pressure on the domestic interest rate and will require 'monetary tightening cum capital controls' to preserve price and exchange rate stability, as is now the case in Spain. To solve this problem it is advisable that the policy mix in Spain be altered so that fiscal policy becomes less expansionary relative to monetary policy than is nowadays the case. This with allow the achievement of a nominal demand growth that is consistent with non-inflationary sustained output growth, and a lowering of the domestic interest rate so as to take pressure off the peseta.

However, because fiscal policy affects the relevant economic variables, especially the exchange rate and the price level, with a longer lag than monetary policy, it would be dangerous to loosen monetary policy simultaneously with the tightening of fiscal policy. Rather, monetary policy should remain tight until the effects of fiscal policy begin to be felt, and only then be gradually relaxed. Fortunately for Spain, the presence of short-term capital controls allows this policy mix adjustment process to take place while continuously preserving exchange rate stability. It is therefore advisable that the reorientation in the macro policy mix be done by the time capital controls disappear in most EC countries in July 1990.

Finally, it is important to mention that the constraints imposed by formal EMS membership have increased so much, and have been made so evident to the public, that the difficulties of continuing with the current policy mix may force future fiscal policy to move in a less expansionary direction than otherwise – a move that would probably not have happened if the peseta had remained outside the EMS.

6. Conclusions

This chapter has explicitly focused on the issue of Spanish participation in the EMS and, in so doing, has come up with tentative answers to the following questions. Is it in the interest of Spain that the peseta is inside the EMS? Were the preconditions for a smooth entrance of the peseta into the system satisfied by the Spanish economy? What are the main economic policy changes that are likely to occur in Spain as a result of EMS membership?

Several of the most important conclusions obtained are the following. First, although the choice of exchange rate policy does not, by itself, alter the external restrictions to which the economy is subject, it does nevertheless affect the constraints within which economic policy operates. In this regard, Spain's entrance into the EMS may help rationalize and make economic policy more credible: by modifying the perceived trade-offs of alternative actions by the government, by reducing the incentives that policy-makers have to pursue inflationary policies and also by allowing the authorities to introduce further complementary doses of fiscal and wage discipline. As a result, Spain's entrance into the EMS may not only consolidate and 'lock in' the disinflation benefits made so far in the last decade, but may also help to achieve a lower and more stable inflation rate in the future without having to bear the output costs that would otherwise emerge.

Second, while the EMS may not always provide the theoretically optimal exchange rate policy, it seems to provide a practically adequate exchange rate policy for its members. Specifically, the EMS performs a useful role by reducing the size of short-term, unpredictable and self-reversing exchange rate fluctuations, and also (and mainly) by accommodating medium-term exchange rate movements. Since about 57 per cent of Spanish imports and 66 per cent of Spanish exports are with EC countries, and since a large portion of registered capital flows is also with the EC, avoiding exchange rate misalignment costs through the EMS seems a rather significant benefit.

Third, at the time of joining, Spain's inflation differential *vis-à-vis* the FRG, as well as the remaining part of the trade balance opening process to the EEC, seemed small enough not to have prevented Spain from joining the EMS with the transitory 6 per cent band.

Fourth, the central peseta–DM exchange rate was set so as to give credibility to the anti-inflationary stance of the authorities and be consistent with current policies.

Fifth, the proper strategy to ensure the continued stability of the peseta in the EMS is through the pursuit of suitable monetary and fiscal policies both in the short and the long term. Rather than playing a central role, foreign exchange intervention operations should play a supporting role, specially in the very short term.

Sixth, while in the short term monetary policy is sufficiently powerful to achieve the stability of the peseta even if fiscal policy in Spain is too expansionary, this does not make such a macro policy mix desirable. Moreover, since the EMS does not only constrain current policies but also future policies, exchange rate stability will not be sustainable in the long term unless the fiscal deficit is compatible with a rate of monetary growth consistent with a zero inflation (and interest) differential between Spain and the FRG. This, in turn, calls for additional reforms to foster fiscal (and also labour costs) discipline in Spain following EMS membership.

Seven, while in the past EMS membership seems to have provided monetary but not fiscal discipline, the inclusion of the peseta in the EMS has made so evident the problems of not adequately coordinating monetary and fiscal policy that it may also increase future fiscal discipline. The difference between the case of Spain and those of other EMS countries is that nowadays the greater degree of capital mobility and the forthcoming disappearance of exchange controls greatly increase the costs to a country of foregoing fiscal discipline. Costs which, no doubt, were perceived to be much smaller in 1979 when most of the present member countries joined the EMS.

Finally, although it is true that the EMS is not without problems and that it needs to be reformed in the light of the coming European internal market[31] to sustain a higher growth rate while preserving low inflation, EMS membership was a necessary condition to achieve the full economic integration of Spain into the EEC. It could be thought, perhaps, that it would have been advisable for Spain to postpone entrance until these reforms take shape. However, it seems preferable for Spain to participate as an EMS member in the process of negotiating such reforms in order that the Spanish position on the future of the system be taken into account.

Notes

1. Although Greece and the UK have their currencies in the ECU and, therefore, are technically in the EMS, they are not subject to the discipline imposed by the exchange rate mechanism (ERM). At present, this is exactly the opposite case from the peseta.
2. When realignments are sufficiently small, changes in the central rate will not be accompanied by jumps in the market rate on the day of realignment and speculators will not be rewarded.
3. See, among others, the papers by Henderson (1985) and Marston (1985a) on the issue of optimal exchange rate policy. In Marston (1985b), it is indicated that in an exchange rate union like the EMS the adjustment to asymmetric financial disturbances may be better with some exchange rate flexibility. This may be a reason why major dollar–DM tensions – an asymmetric disturbance – have often led to EMS realignments. Still, exchange rate fixity would be preferable with symmetric financial disturbances.
4. While the IMF (1983) survey study finds no evidence of the effects of exchange rate volatility on trade flows, the studies by Cushman (1986) and De Grauwe and Verfaille (1987) find some effect. See, however, Krugman (1989) and Sapir (above, Chap. 8).
5. Table 9.1 shows a reduction in the variability of total movements in nominal and real exchange rates within the EMS. These findings are confirmed by the more sophisticated tests of Rogoff (1985b), Gros (1987a), Artis and Taylor (1988) and Russo and Tullio (1988).
6. See also the study by Baldwin and Lyons (1989) on the exchange rate hysteresis effect.
7. The recent paper by Frankel and Froot (1986) explains the behaviour of the dollar in the 1980s as an irrational speculative bubble.
8. De Grauwe and Verfaille (1987) support this conclusion. Although Artis and Taylor (1988) find that deviations from PPP exchange rates are permanent inside the EMS, they do not take into account that this may be due (in addition to misalignment) to permanent changes in real exchange rates.
9. Monetary policy will be completely ineffective in influencing real variables when there is perfect substitutability between domestic and foreign assets, and perfect capital mobility; or, alternatively, when prices are fully flexible.
10. On the structure of Spanish labour markets see Dolado and Malo de Molina (1985), Andres and García (1989), and Viñals (1990).
11. This is the well-known problem of dynamic inconsistency of optimal policies studied by Kydland and Prescott (1977), and by Barro and Gordon (1983a, 1983b).

While governments think they can get away with playing the inflationary game, in fact, people's expectations adjust so that, on average, real output is where it would be without the expansionary policies while inflation is higher.

12. This condition is stressed by Artis and Miller (1986).
13. Collins (1988) examines the variety of different theoretical models of the EMS that result depending on the different assumptions made about the degree of cooperation and symmetry of the system. On the empirical side, the asymmetry hypothesis is confirmed by Giovannini (1988), and other researchers, and disputed by De Grauwe (1989).
14. See Giavazzi and Giovannini (1988) for a more complete discussion of the credibility issue.
15. See, among others, Rogoff (1985a), Collins (1988), Giavazzi and Giovannini (1988), Giavazzi and Pagano (1987) and Melitz (1988).
16. If the measure of real competitiveness chosen is relative unit labour costs, then it is the case that both the lira and the FF show at present an appreciation *vis-à-vis* 1979, while the IR£ starts showing a depreciation relative to 1979 levels since 1987.
17. The evidence in Artis and Taylor (1988) suggests that this may indeed be the case. Even so, it is likely that national short-term interest rates will oscillate quite a lot in pre-realignment periods; oscillations that will be smaller – relative to those of Eurorates – the more intense are national capital controls.
18. Here we criticize this as an objection to membership. It is true, however, that this may be a valid reason for postponing membership as discussed later.
19. It is true, nevertheless, that the extreme austerity of German fiscal policy may act as a brake on the real growth of other EMS countries. In such case, a more expansionary fiscal stance in the FRG would be desirable.
20. For a contrast of views about the likely effects of removing capital controls see Rogoff (1985b), Driffill (1988), Gros (1987b), Gros and Thygesen (1988), Obstfeld (1988), Padoa-Schioppa (1987), Wyplosz (1988), and Viñals (1988). The last paper mentioned defends the need to make reforms that facilitate the full coordination of national economic policies to preserve exchange rate stability under the new circumstances.
21. The issue of Spanish membership has been discussed, among others, by Gil (1985), Eguidazu (1985), Kessler (1987) and Viñals (1987). The recent publication of ICE (1988) gathers a useful set of views on the subject.
22. The economic effects of Spain's entrance in the EC and of the 1992 Single Internal Market are analysed in Viñals (1990).
23. In fact, analyses of the proximate determinants of Spain's trade balance show that while the real appreciation of the peseta has had some negative effect on Spain's trade balance in recent years, most of the deterioration has been due to the high domestic demand growth and to the tariff-reduction and quantitative restrictions elimination processes associated with EC membership. See Viñals (1990).
24. See the recent estimates in Dolado (1988).
25. See, for example, the pioneering article by Sargent and Wallace (1981).
26. Specifically, primary structural budget deficits.
27. See Raymond-Bara (1983) for an econometric estimation of the cyclical and structural components of the Spanish budget deficit.

28. Giavazzi and Giovannini (1989) also apply this methodology to other European countries.
29. This strategy is the one recommended by the Working Group on Exchange Rate Market Intervention (1983).
30. See Krugman (1988), and Gros and Thygesen (1988) on this point.
31. The *Delors Report* (Delors Committee 1989) suggests a number of reforms in the monetary and fiscal spheres to sustain and improve exchange rate stability within the EMS.

References

Andrés, J. and **García, J**. (1989) Main features of the Spanish labour market facing 1992, mimeo.

Artis, M. and **Miller, M.** (1986) On joining the EMS, *Midland Bank Review*, Winter.

Artis, M., and **Taylor, M.** (1988) Exchange rates and the EMS: assessing the track record, in Giavazzi, F., Micossi, S. and Miller, M. (eds), *The European Monetary System*, Cambridge University Press, Cambridge, pp. 185–206.

Baldwin, R., and **Lyons, R**. (1989) Exchange rate hysteresis: the real effect of large vs. small policy misalignments, *NBER Working Paper* No. 2828, January.

Barro, R. J., and **Gordon, D.** (1983a) Rules, discretion and reputation in a model of monetary policy, *Journal of Monetary Economics*, **12**, July, pp. 101–21.

Barro, R. J., and **Gordon, D**. (1983b) A positive theory of monetary policy in a natural rate model, *Journal of Political Economy*, **91**, August, pp. 589–610.

Collins, S. (1988) Inflation and the EMS, in Giavazzi, F., Micossi, S. and Miller, M. (eds), *The European Monetary System*, Cambridge University Press, Cambridge, pp. 112–36.

Committee for the Study of Economic and Monetary Union (the Delors Committee) (1989) *Report on Economic and Monetary Union in the European Community* (the *Delors Report*) (with Collection of Papers), Office for Official Publications of the European Communities, Luxemburg.

Cushman, D. O. (1986) Has exchange rate risk depressed international trade? The international impact of third country exchange risk, *Journal of International Money and Finance*.

De Grauwe, P. (1986) Fiscal policies in the EMS: a strategic analysis, *International Economics Research Paper*, No. 53, Catholic University of Louvain.

De Grauwe, P. (1989) Is the EMS a DM-zone?, *CEPR Discussion Paper* no. 297, March.

De Grauwe, P. and **Verfaille, G**. (1987) Exchange rate variability, misalignment, and the European Monetary System, in Marston, R. (ed) *Misalignment of Exchange Rates: Effects on Trade and Industry*, University of Chicago Press, Chicago, pp. 77–103.

Dolado, J. J. (1988) Innovación financiera, inflación y la estabilidad de la demanda de ALP en España, *Boletín Económico*, Banco de España, April, pp. 19–36.

Dolado, J. J., and **Malo de Molina, J. L**. (1985) Desempleo y rigidez del mercado de trabajo en España, *Boletín Económico*, Banco de España, September, pp. 22–41.

Driffill, J. (1988) The stability and sustainability of the EMS with perfect capital markets, in Giavazzi, F., Micossi, S. and Miller, M. (eds), *The European Monetary System*, Cambridge University Press, Cambridge, pp. 211–28.

Eguidazu, S. (1985) El Sistema Monetario Europeo: una alternativa para la peseta, *Papeles de Economía Española*, No. 25, pp. 304–25.

Frankel, J. and **Froot, K.** (1986) Explaining the demand for dollars: international rates of return, and the expectations of chartists and fundamentalists, *Working Paper* No. 8604, University of California, Berkeley.

Giavazzi, F. and **Giovannini, A.** (1988) Interpreting the European disinflation: the role of the exchange-rate regime, in Giavazzi, F., Micossi, S. and Miller, M. (eds), *The European Monetary System*, Cambridge University Press, Cambridge, pp. 85–107.

Giavazzi, F. and **Giovannini, A.** (1989) Can the EMS be exported? Lessons from ten years of monetary policy coordination in Europe, *CEPR Discussion Paper*, No. 285, January.

Giavazzi, F. and **Pagano, M.** (1987) The advantage of tying one's hands: EMS discipline through Central Bank credibility, *European Economic Review*, **32**, pp. 1055–82.

Giovannini, A. (1988) How do fixed exchange-regimes work: the evidence from the Gold Standard, Bretton Woods and the EMS, *NBER Working Paper* No. 2766, November.

Gil, G. (1985) Aspectos monetarios y financieros de la integración española en la Comunidad Económica Europea, Banco de España, Servicio de Estudios, *Estudios Económicos*, No. 37.

Gros, D. (1987a) On the volatility of exchange rates, a test of monetary and portfolio balance models of exchange rate determination, *CEPS Working Document* No. 31, August.

Gros, D. (1987b) Capital controls in the EMS: a model with incomplete separation, *CEPS Working Document* , No. 32, August.

Gros, D. and **Thygesen, N.** (1988) The EMS: achievements, current issues, and directions for the future, CEPS Paper No. 35, Brussels, February.

Henderson, D. (1985) Exchange market intervention operations: their role in financial policy and their effects, in Bilson, J. and Marston, R. (eds), *Exchange Rate Theory and Practice*, University of Chicago Press and NBER, Chicago, pp. 359–406.

Información Comercial Española (ICE) (1988), *España y el Sistema Monetario Europeo*, No. 657, May.

International Monetary Fund (IMF)(1983) Exchange rate volatility and world trade, *Occasional Paper* No. 28, July.

Kessler Saiz, G. (1987) La peseta en el Sistema Monetario Europeo: algunas reconsideraciones, *Información Comercial Española*, February, **642**, pp. 7–26.

Krugman, P. (1988) Target zones and exchange rate dynamics, *NBER Working Paper* No. 2481.

Krugman, P. (1989) *Exchange Rate Instability*, MIT Press, Cambridge, Mass.

Kydland, F. and **Prescott, E.** (1977) Rules rather than discretion: the inconsistency of optimal plans, *Journal of Political Economy*, **85**, pp. 473–93.

Marston, R. (1985a) Stabilization policies in open economies, in Kenen, P. and Jones, R. (eds) *Handbook of International Economics*, vol. 2, North-Holland, Amsterdam.

Marston, R. (1985b) Some general characteristics of exchange rate unions, mimeo, University of Pennsylvania, February.

Melitz, J. (1988) Germany, discipline, and cooperation in the European Monetary System, in Giavazzi, F., Micossi, S. and Miller, M. (eds), *The European Monetary System*, Cambridge University Press, Cambridge, pp. 51–79

Obstfeld, M. (1988) Competitiveness, realignment, and speculation: the role of financial markets, in Giavazzi, F., Micossi, S. and Miller, M. (eds), *The European Monetary System*, Cambridge University Press, Cambridge, pp. 232–49.

Padoa-Schioppa, T. (1987) *Equity, Efficiency and Growth*, Oxford University Press, Oxford.

Raymond-Bara, J. L. (1983) El saldo del presupuesto coyuntural y estructural en España, *Papeles de Economía Española*, No. 23, pp. 28–35.

Rogoff, K. (1985a) The optimal degree of commitment to an intermediate monetary target, *Quarterly Journal of Economics*, **100**, 4.

Rogoff, K. (1985b) Can exchange rate predictability be achieved without monetary convergence? Evidence from the EMS, *European Economic Review*, June–July, **28**, pp. 93–115.

Russo, M. and **Tullio, G**. (1988) Monetary policy coordination within the EMS: is there a rule?, in Giavazzi, F., Micossi, S. and Miller, M. (eds), *The European Monetary System*, Cambridge University Press, Cambridge, pp. 292–56.

Sargent, T. and **Wallace, N.** (1981) Some unpleasant monetarist arithmetic, *Federal Reserve Bank of Minneapolis Quarterly Review*, Fall., **5**, pp. 1–17.

Ungerer, H., **Evans, O.** and **Nyberg, P.** (1983) The European Monetary System: The experience 1979–1982, *Occasional Paper*, No. 19, International Monetary Fund, May.

Ungerer, H., **Evans, O.** and **Nyberg, P.** (1986) The European Monetary System: recent developments, *Occasional Paper*, No. 48, International Monetary Fund, December.

Viñals, J. (1987) La incorporación de España al Sistema Monetario Europeo y sus consecuencias para la política monetaria, in *La política monetaria en España*, FEDEA, pp. 63–106.

Viñals, J. (1988) El SME y el Mercado Unico de 1992: perspectivas de futuro, *Boletín Económico*, Banco de España, June, pp. 51–75.

Viñals, J. (1990) Spain and the 'EEC cum 1992' shock, in Bliss, C. and Braga de Macedo, J. (eds), *Unity with diversity in the European economy*, Cambridge University Press, Cambridge.

Viñals, J. and **Domingo, L.** (1987) La peseta y el SME: Un modelo del tipo de cambio peseta-marco, *Revista Española de Economía*, **4**, (1), pp. 93–110.

Williamson, J. (1987) Exchange rate management: the role of target zones, *American Economic Review*, **77**, (2), May, pp. 200–4.

Working Group on Exchange Rate Market Intervention (1983) *Jurgensen Report*, March.

Wyplosz, Ch. (1988) Capital flows liberalization and the EMS: a French perspective, in *European Economy*, No. 36, pp. 85–103.

CHAPTER TEN

Portugal, the EMS and 1992: stabilization and liberalization

Francisco S. Torres*

1. Introduction

After having joined the European Community (EC) in 1986, Portugal faces now the challenge posed by the creation of a European internal market by 1992. Political commitment to this objective has exerted pressure for domestic liberalization and stabilization. This process has, however, been hampered and partly neutralized by persistent fiscal imbalances, which led to an unsustainable path of public debt growth (from 40 per cent of gross domestic product (GDP) in 1980, public debt rose to 74 per cent in 1988), high inflation rates and cyclical external disequilibria. The need for an integrated stabilization package is therefore a necessary condition for a non-disruptive process of integration.

In this chapter we discuss the possible macroeconomic adjustment to the real shock of 1992. The European Monetary System (EMS) is here considered as a unique device to reduce the output costs of disinflation and adjustment. The high level of Portuguese public debt reinforces the importance of the role of the EMS during the process of stabilization and liberalization. Moreover, it is argued that the process of gradual external liberalization will further enhance the credibility of the adjustment.

Section 2 describes the disciplinary role of the EMS with particular emphasis on 'fiscally weak' countries. Section 3 provides a brief description of the recent Portuguese debt accumulation experience; its sustainability is discussed in the light of progressive reduction of implicit taxation. Section 4 deals with the problem of external liberalization, namely its effects on domestic stabilization. Section 5 stresses the usefulness of the EMS as a disciplinary device in the process of convergence. Finally, section 6 provides some concluding remarks.

* I thank Miguel Beleza, Paul De Grauwe, Daniel Gros and Jorge Braga de Macedo for comments and suggestions and Miguel Rosa, Norberto Rosa and Maria José Vidal for statistical evidence; the ideas expressed in the paper are however my sole responsibility.

2. EMS discipline and the public debt trap

Concerning the selection of an appropriate exchange rate regime, policy-makers in small countries may be tempted to join an area of monetary stability where the tone of the monetary stance is given by a credible (anti-inflation) leader; the authorities 'tie their hands' in search of a solution for the internal consistency problem – too high a level of inflation resulting from the non-cooperative game with the private sector. Such an explicit external commitment to an exchange rate rule works domestically as a reputational constraint.

By analysing the trade-off between the benefits of monetary (exchange rate) policy flexibility and the costs associated with dynamic inconsistency (as was done for the EMS case by Giavazzi and Pagano 1988) it is possible to discuss the potential impact of the EMS on both a country's economic stability and performance and its authorities' policy effectiveness and credibility.

Given the current structure of the system, one can weigh the advantages and disadvantages of adhering to the EMS. On the one hand, by joining, high-inflation countries of the EC confer more credibility on their policy-makers: the competitiveness losses incurred by inflating the economy enforce domestically the rules of the system. On the other hand, if the punishment costs are too high the EMS may be a welfare-deteriorating arrangement for the joining country. These costs depend on the characteristics of the specific country.

The question of flexibility should be weighted against the credibility/stability problem and translates into the following. To what extent is a stable exchange rate regime compatible with large and persistent external shocks or large structural asymmetries which would require adjustments in relative prices?

As is well known, when shocks asymmetrically hit the different countries in an exchange rate union, the arrangement is suboptimal, as it imposes the same monetary policy on countries facing different problems; as stressed by Giavazzi and Giovannini (1987), in the presence of cross-country asymmetries in the intermediate input–wage–price transmission mechanism, common exogenous shocks are transmitted asymmetrically to different countries. The evidence for Europe presented by these authors confirms the suboptimality of irrevocably fixed exchange rates. Moreover, for a country facing a process of trade liberalization it may be optimal to adjust relative prices through exchange rate changes. Throughout this chapter we disregard this problem since realignments in the EMS allow for some adjustment to external shocks.

We shall then concentrate on the problem of structural asymmetries, namely the structural weakness of some fiscal and financial systems.

'Fiscally weak' countries (with relatively inefficient tax-collection systems and high public debt levels) may need revenue from seigniorage to finance their rigid expenditures. Therefore, it has been argued (see Dornbusch 1988 and Giavazzi 1989) that too quick a convergence to the present EMS average inflation rate may shift the entire fiscal burden on to explicit taxes which cannot absorb it, at least in the short-term, without causing more distortions to the existing tax system (namely, by raising marginal tax rates). In fact, evidence suggests (see Fig. 10.1) that one currency area Europe is not optimal, at least in the short–medium term, from a fiscal viewpoint.[1] It has been argued, therefore (see Dornbusch 1988), that southern countries should adopt a more flexible policy in the form of a crawling-peg *vis-à-vis* the 'northern' members of the EMS; this would allow for a higher inflation rate and the 'optimal' level of seigniorage.

(a) Seigniorage as percentage of total revenues;

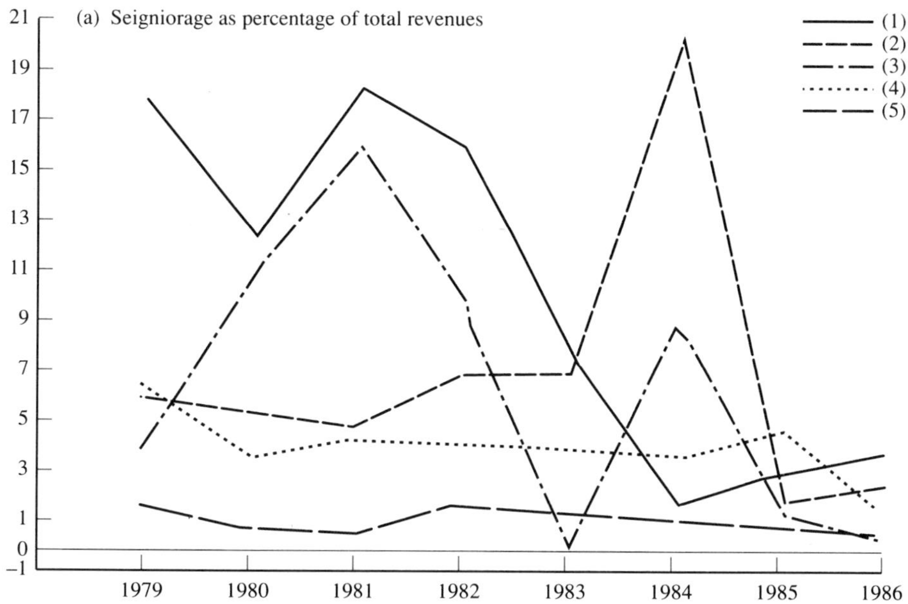

FIG. 10.1 The North–South fiscal asymmetry. (1) Portugal, (2) Spain, (3) Greece, (4) Italy, (5) ERM countries (except Italy). *Sources and definitions*: seigniorage is the change in monetary base (IMF, *International Financial Statistics* (line 14); OECD, *Main Economic Indicators*; Bank of Portugal, *Monetary and Financial Statistics*). For Greece, Italy and Spain, where considerable interest payments on reserves are paid, various national sources were used to compute the appropriate measure of seigniorage (the change in monetary base minus interest paid on reserves); data are from Gros (1990). Total revenues include seigniorage and total explicit taxation as reported from the OECD, *Tax Revenue Statistics of OECD Member Countries*, 1987. Central banks' claims on the government are as in line 12a of IMF, *International Financial Statistics*.

FIG. 10.1 continued

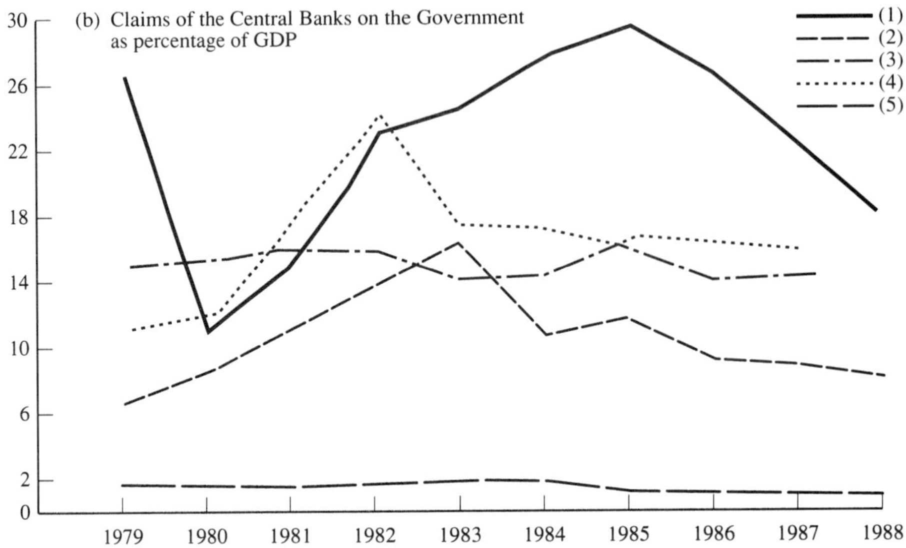

(1) Portugal (2) Greece (3) Spain (4) Italy (5) ERM

This argument is especially important for countries with high public debts and can be illustrated by a conventional government budget constraint:

$$D(B_t) = (G_t - T_t) + r\, B_t - D(H_t)/P_t \qquad [1]$$

where B stands for public debt, G for government expenditure, T for government taxes, H for monetary base and P for the price level; r is the real interest rate and D a difference operator such that $D(B_t) = dB_t/dt$.

Dividing equation [1] by GDP(Y_t) we obtain:

$$D(b_t) = (g_t - t_t) + (r - n)b_t - D(H_t)/P_t\, Y_t \qquad [2]$$

where n stands for the real GDP growth rate and all lower-case letters (except the real interest rate, r) for variables expressed as ratios to real income.

Equation [2] can then be read as follows: the time path of public debt as a share of GDP ($D(b_t)$) is equal to the primary deficit (government expenditure, g_t, minus taxes, t_t) as a percentage of national income plus the debt service ratio (the implicit real rate of interest, r, net of GDP growth, n, times the ratio of outstanding debt to GDP, b_t) minus seigniorage revenue (measured as the change in the monetary base, $D(H_t)$) as a proportion of national income. When the government is unable to generate primary surpluses (i.e. $g_t - t_t > 0$), a reduction of seigniorage revenues (a lower $D(H_t)/P_tY_t$) implies a faster debt accumulation: higher interest payments, due to tight money and newly issued debt, feed back into higher budget deficits, which in turn require new bond issuance. This spiral (equation [2] is unstable when $r > n$) then translates into future inflation taxes to service the debt (again a higher $D(H_t)/P_tY_t$).[2] Let the private sector anticipate the whole process from the outset, and the demise of the stabilization programme will be triggered by speculative attacks on the currency intended to be stabilized.

For 'fiscally weak' countries, where fiscal authorities cannot help in the disinflation process, the solution would then be to resort to standard seigniorage revenue or other hidden taxation schemes coupled with strict exchange controls.

However, even for a country with a relatively loose money stance, accommodated by a crawling-peg *vis-à-vis* tight money countries, the credibility argument still holds: in countries with a large non-indexed public debt, the incentive to use surprise inflation as a means of finance (by reducing the real interest rate paid on outstanding debt) may further increase the resulting inflation rate. This is because the private sector rationally anticipates the government's temptation.[3] As put forward by Gros (1990), the public would not believe a government that promises to use only an 'optimal' anticipated inflation rate; it would, on the contrary, expect the authorities to use surprise inflation as a consistent policy towards their assumed fiscal weaknesses. The resulting inflation rates would then be far above the 'optimal' level.

For countries with various administrative controls, as Portugal, other forms of implicit taxation might constitute a more important source of revenue than the seigniorage immediately derived from a high inflation rate (as suggested in Beleza and Macedo 1988). In this case some loss of implicit tax revenues will come independently from EMS discipline, given the need to liberalize domestically in view of the coming external liberalization.[4] It remains then to be discussed at which pace the domestic financial liberalization, fiscal discipline and disinflation should be implemented and coordinated in order to minimize the further distortion of the existing tax system and to avoid the failure of the stabilization/liberalization attempts in view of the political objective of 1992.

Given the above arguments, our problem returns to the following question. Under which conditions can EMS discipline enhance the sustainability and/or reduce the output costs of a stabilization programme[5] coupled with a process of domestic liberalization and financial integration?

3. Exchange controls, seigniorage and public debt in Portugal

EXCHANGE RATE AND MONETARY POLICY

After the breakdown of the Bretton Woods System, the Portuguese currency (escudo) followed an adjustable peg to the US Dollar (from 1971 to 1977). In February 1977, the escudo was devalued by 15 per cent in effective terms. Six months later, Portugal adopted a crawling-peg regime. The average monthly rate of the escudo has since then been adjusted in relation to a basket of currencies weighted according to their importance in Portugal's international merchandise trade; the rate of the crawl is pre-announced. The system was primarily designed to maintain Portugal's external competitiveness, as measured by relative unit labour costs, interest rate differentials and inflation differentials. The initial monthly rate of the crawling peg was fixed at 1 per cent, while at the same time another 4 per cent discrete devaluation took place.

The crawling-peg regime was followed up, with many changes in its pre-announced monthly rate and several discrete exchange rate changes, until the end of 1985; the Portuguese government decided then to suspend it for four months in order to moderate inflationary expectations.[6] By 1 April 1986, the crawling peg was resumed at a decreasing rate. Since July 1988, the effective monthly rate of devaluation of the escudo has been 0.25 per cent. Figure 10.2 depicts the evolution of the escudo exchange rate.

This managed exchange rate system, coupled with capital controls, quantitative credit controls and administratively set interest rates, has allowed the government to collect substantial implicit revenues from the productive sector. This distorted

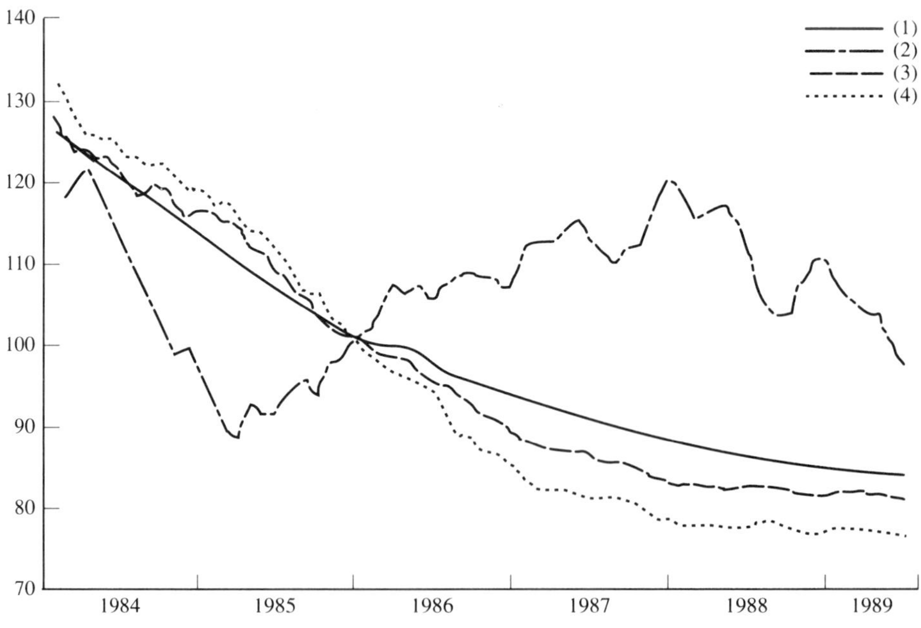

FIG. 10.2 The escudo exchange rate (December 1985 = 100). (1) Effective exchange rate of the Escudo (weighted basket of 13 currencies) (EER); (2) US dollar; (3) ECU; (4) DM

situation originated in 1975, when all credit institutions, with the exception of savings banks, foreign banks operating in Portugal and agricultural credit cooperatives, had been nationalized; the entry of new banks was constitutionally forbidden until 1984. During this period the behaviour of the Portuguese banking industry was highly collusive and to a large extent determined by the monetary and fiscal authorities.

Credit ceilings, still the major instrument of monetary policy, were implemented in 1978 as an instrument to correct balance-of-payments disequilibria. The domestic credit ceiling was obtained as a residual, after taking into account the goals for GDP growth and inflation rates, an intermediate target for the expansion of liquidity held by the non-financial resident sector and assumptions on public sector borrowing requirements (PSBRs). The ceiling for each bank was computed according to its share in the weighted resources of the banking system and its type of portfolio in order to stimulate bank deposits not intermediated into loans.

Explicit reserve requirements have played, comparatively, a rather secondary role in the conduct of monetary policy. Eligible liabilities have consisted of sight and time deposits, certificates of deposits, repurchase agreements and other quasi-monetary liabilities. Until April 1989, reserve ratios varied according to maturity and type of liability (15 per cent on sight deposits, 12 per cent on deposits between 30 and 180 days, 3 per cent on deposits between 180 and 365 days and 1 per cent on deposits over one year and on emigrants' foreign currency deposits). This would translate into an average rate of 9.3 per cent (from 1979 to 1988) – see Fig. 10.3 for international comparison.

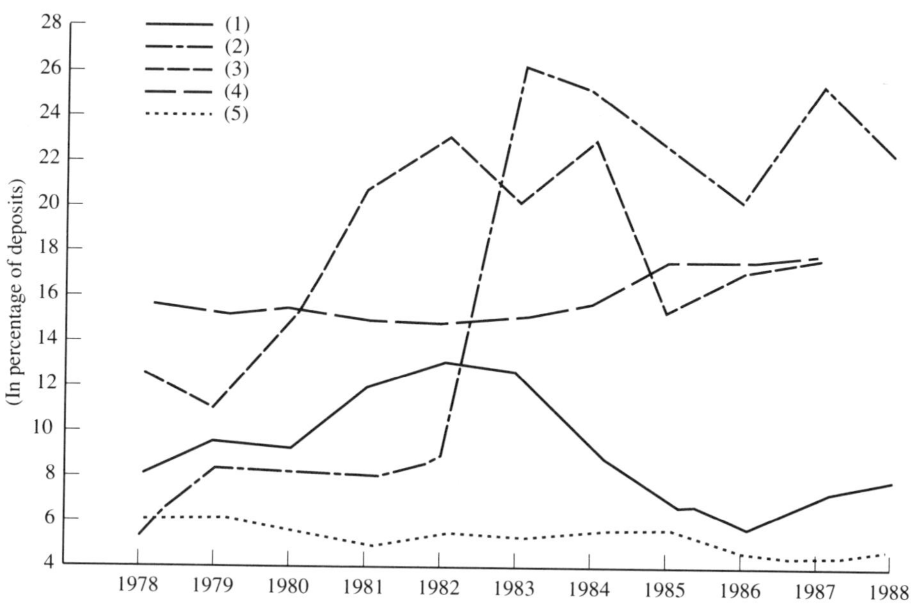

FIG. 10.3 Bank reserves. (1) Portugal; (2) Spain; (3) Greece; (4) Italy; (5) ERM countries (except Italy). *Source*: IMF, *International Financial Statistics*, lines 20, 24 and 25; Bank of Portugal, *Monetary and Financial Statistics*

Against this background, several new instruments have been issued since 1986 allowing for better management of short-term liquidity by the monetary authorities.[7] Controls have accordingly been reduced. Since September 1988 only a minimum rate of deposits with a maturity of more than six months has been administratively set. In April 1989, a uniform reserve requirement of 17 per cent has been set; the Bank of Portugal has, however, compensated part of the costs of the increase of compulsory reserves through interest payments, as it is the case for Greece, Italy and Spain (see note in Fig. 10.1). Since July 1989, new credit to the public sector is given the same treatment as credits to firms and households.

MONETARY POLICY AND IMPLICIT TAXATION

Since the introduction of credit ceilings in 1978, and due to the fact that budget deficits were mainly financed by the central bank (as can be seen in Fig. 10.4), excess liquidity rose steadily within the banking system. In order to provide banks with investment opportunities for these idle balances, an interbank securities market (ISM) was created. In the ISM, the central bank sells public debt bonds of its portfolio, under repurchase agreements of 4–13 weeks, to other monetary institutions; by

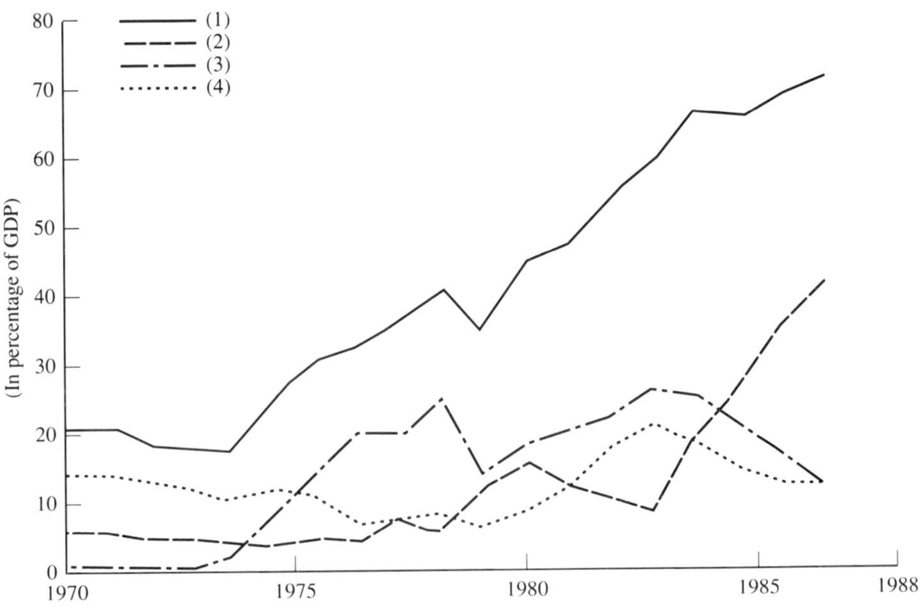

FIG. 10.4 Portuguese public sector debt. (1) Total public sector debt; (2) domestic private; (3) central bank; (4) external. *Source*: Bank of Portugal, *Annual Reports*.

doing so it rewards this frozen excess liquidity. These yields, although having recently followed the deposit rate, have, however, remained far below the would-be lending rates. Throughout the reported period that induced liquidity corresponded to a higher seigniorage revenue than apparently indicated by the reserve ratio, in the sense that it led to a substantial implicit taxation. In fact, despite the positive impact on the correction of unsustainable external imbalances (1976–77 and 1981–83), the efficiency of credit ceilings in periods of economic expansion has been limited to the implicit taxation of the productive sector.

Beleza and Macedo (1988) provide some evidence on this hidden form of taxation. They suggest that Treasury implicit revenues have been collected not only in the form of currency or bank reserves but also through the imposition of the above-mentioned controls (exchange controls, credit ceilings and administratively set interest rates). This policy has induced an increase in demand for public debt on the part of the banking system; the costs involved have been then partly shifted on to private borrowers, to whom credit has been rationed, in the form of excessively high interest rates and hence implicit taxation (this situation is illustrated in Fig. 10A.1 in the Appendix).

These implicit revenues (reported in column (4′) in Table 10.1) correspond in fact to a higher tax base (monetary base). This is because credit ceilings on private

TABLE 10.1 The Portuguese debt accumulation equation

Years	$D(b_t)$	Debt cancelling	$g_t - t_t$	$(r - n)\, b_t$	$D(H_t) / P_t Y_t$		Residual	
	(1)	(1′)	(2)	(3)	(4)	(4′)	(5)	(5′)
1978	12.1		7.3	–6.6	2.8	4.9	14.2	16.3
1979	11.6		5.1	–7.6	5.4	4.6	19.5	18.7
1980	–8.3	(13.7)	–7.6	–6.0	4.0	4.7	9.3	10.0
1981	24.7		5.5	–2.9	6.7	5.4	28.8	27.5
1982	5.0		6.3	–7.1	5.8	9.3	11.6	15.1
1983	12.4		4.0	–5.8	2.8	8.9	17.0	23.1
1984	9.6		6.3	–6.3	0.6	9.0	10.2	18.6
1985	10.1		3.2	– 8.5	1.1	6.6	16.5	22.0
1986	–1.0		–0.8	–6.3	1.4	3.0	7.5	9.1
1987	4.8		–0.3	–3.4	3.0	3.9	11.5	12.4
1988	3.2	(2.3)	–0.2	–3.6	2.1	3.5	9.1	10.5

Sources and definitions: All symbols are defined as in equation [2] in the text. All data are from the Bank of Portugal. (4') Obtained from Beleza and Macedo (1988), annex table 5, and updated to 1988. (1') refers to the cancelling of public debt (as proportion of GDP) by counterpart of revaluation of gold reserves in the Bank of Portugal. The effective interest rate used in (3) is the ratio of interest payments to a two year moving average of total debt. (4) The change in the monetary base. (4') The implicit intermediation tax revenue (assuming interest to be paid up-front and an intermediation rate of 3%) used as an upward estimate of seigniorage derived from a higher tax base. (5) = (1) –(2) –(3) +(4); (5') = (1) –(2) –(3) +(4').

borrowing are a portfolio constraint that leads to the same implicit taxation on the allocation of financial resources as non-interest-bearing reserve requirements or compulsory investments in certain types of securities (see Modigliani *et al.* 1987 for a discussion). This is especially true in a situation where these constraints on banking activities are enhanced by administratively set interest rates and foreign exchange restrictions.

THE PORTUGUESE PUBLIC DEBT DYNAMICS

In the period 1975–85 the ratio of public debt to GDP increased steadily despite a substantial negative contribution of the debt service ratio ($(r - n)b_t$ in equation [2]): high growth and negative real interest rates. In 1980 and 1988, the revaluation of the Treasury stock of gold reserves led to debt write-off operations, diminishing the central bank component of public debt as a percentage of GDP. Throughout that period government primary deficits accounted for the entire debt accumulation; seigniorage revenue had an important countervailing effect. Only by 1985 Treasury bills (short-term public debt sold with discount to other banks by the central bank, which can then be traded with the public or between banks) were issued improving in some way the non-monetary financing of the PSBR. Domestic privately held public debt then increased sharply, allowing for a reduction of both the central bank and the external components of total debt through 1988 (see Fig. 10.4); by the end of 1988, a new public debt instrument very similar to Treasury bills, the CLIP (a long-term revolving credit to the Treasury, auctioned among credit institutions every six months), was issued.

Official budget figures provided by the Bank of Portugal and the Ministry of Finance do not fit our government's budget constraint.[8] Reasons are three-fold, and are given in the following paragraph.

The PSBRs include, besides the official government primary deficits, the so-called Treasury (lending) operations which, in fact, should be taken as mere government transfers (expenditure) within the public sector; they have accounted for 1.8 per cent, 1.5 per cent and 1.1 per cent of GDP in the last three years. The yearly change in the stock of outstanding public debt also reflects other operations such as the take-over of debts and other hidden past deficits of the enlarged public sector (general government and non-financial public enterprises); the ratio of these debt take-overs to GDP represented 5.1 per cent in 1986, 3 per cent in 1987 and 2 per cent in 1988. Finally, exchange rate variations, by affecting the value in escudos of the external component of the debt, may contribute to the discrepancy.

IS THE DEBT SUSTAINABLE?

Despite the recent move towards domestic liberalization, implicit taxation has remained high. It is to be expected, however, that the current reform of the financial sector will substantially reduce these revenues to the level of the standard measure of seigniorage. In Table 10.1 we use two alternative measures of seigniorage: the change in the monetary base (column 4) and an upward-biased measure of it given by the implicit intermediation tax (column 4′). The rationale for the latter is as follows: the controls used by the authorities to induce this implicit tax have an equivalent yield to a higher monetary base. However, part of the 'tax' imposed by these costly controls (especially to private borrowers) is lost in the process.

Besides the conventional deadweight losses, this 'taxation' has led to a sharp decrease in the profitability of public banks, which had to be compensated for by the Treasury and the Bank of Portugal. This effect partly offset the revenue from implicit taxes and eventually showed up as increased Treasury (lending) operations (this is represented by the area ABEF in Fig. 10A.1) requiring, in turn, higher hidden taxation.

In this sense, domestic liberalization has a clear welfare gain although it negatively affects the public debt dynamics in the form of a lower degree of implicit financing and (especially) higher interest rates. Disinflation will further aggravate this effect by reducing seigniorage revenues. Membership of the EMS may come then as a positive contribution to debt stabilization: the reduction of the inflation risk premium (see Fig. 10A.2) and, as a consequence, the reduction in the output costs of the stabilization programme, will translate into a lower interest net of growth factor.

The sustainability of the public debt equation relies, however, on the extent to which the government is capable of generating primary surpluses to stabilize the debt ratio. While the official primary deficit is turning into a surplus, a substantial residual (whose composition was discussed above) remains to be eliminated. For 1989, the forecast primary surplus is sufficient to cover the Treasury (lending) operations, and a new factor will contribute to the reduction of the residual: the revenue from privatizations of public enterprises. The extent to which this factor may in the future compensate for debt take-overs (hidden deficits of the past) and stabilize the ratio of debt to GDP however, remains to be seen.[9]

4. Domestic and external financial liberalization

The liberalization of capital movements in 1992 renders domestic liberalization and stabilization even more urgent. Other liberalization attempts have failed because of the removal of financial protection before domestic liberalization was achieved. Portugal has to remove most capital controls by 1992,[10] and there is still a long way to go before domestic liberalization and stabilization are completed.

However, it should be stressed that the current Portuguese situation is considerably different from the examples provided by some liberalization experiences in Latin America: Portugal is integrated in the EC with, comparatively, a much higher degree of trade liberalization which can only increase. Financial liberalization is not expected to be reversed either – the commitment to the European internal market objective is fully credible. Other liberalization attempts have suffered from a high probability of policy reversals. In this case the private sector may expect the monetary authorities to return to capital controls when facing a speculative run; speculative attacks triggered by self-fulfilling expectations then generate balance-of-payments crises. As put forward by Dellas and Stockman (1988), the potential rapid access (through an international institution) to sufficient foreign exchange reserves eliminates the risk of a speculative run. Various credit facilities of the EMS could supply potentially large amounts of foreign exchange reserves for problems of this kind.

Moreover, as emphasized by Modigliani *et al.* (1987), as less recourse to hidden taxation is made, the level and structure of domestic interest rates become increasingly determined by the market, and more in line with international interest rates. This reduces the need for controls on capital flows for any given exchange rate or balance-of-payments target.

CAPITAL CONTROLS IN PORTUGAL

Data on capital flows and interest rate differentials suggest that capital controls have not been very effective in preventing capital movements. Computing the flows of capital both in absolute terms and as a percentage of GDP for all EC countries it is possible to conclude that trade in capital in both directions is significant. Southern countries, which have relatively severe capital controls, have ratios of trade in capital ((debit + credit)/2 as a percentage of GDP) that are substantially lower than the EC average. This applies in the case of short-term instead of overall capital flows. However, in this case for 1987, Portugal recorded the highest ratio of trade to GDP among the southern countries (1.26 per cent compared to 0.12 per cent; 0.44 per cent and 0.47 per cent for Italy, Greece and Spain respectively) which is even higher than the ratio for the FRG (0.85 per cent).[11] Moreover, in 1987, the extent to which short-term capital moves in both directions, as measured by an index of intra-industry trade (1 – absolute value of [(debit – credit)/(debit + credit)]), is again the highest for Portugal (0.95).

Another way to assess the effectiveness of capital controls is to look at domestic and offshore interest rates. One of the arguments used to defend capital controls is the fact that, in the presence of significant inflation differentials, domestic interest rates would have to rise substantially to prevent massive outflows of capital; this would lead to too high an interest level with the consequent negative effects for the economy.

Effectiveness of capital controls would then be translated into a permanent 'offshore'/'onshore' interest rate differential. In Fig. 10.5 we test covered interest parity which is the difference between the (average) domestic interbank in Lisbon and covered (in Portuguese escudos) Euro deposits. Since mid-1986, there have been no significant differences between the two rates (0.00 for 1988)[12]; this evidence

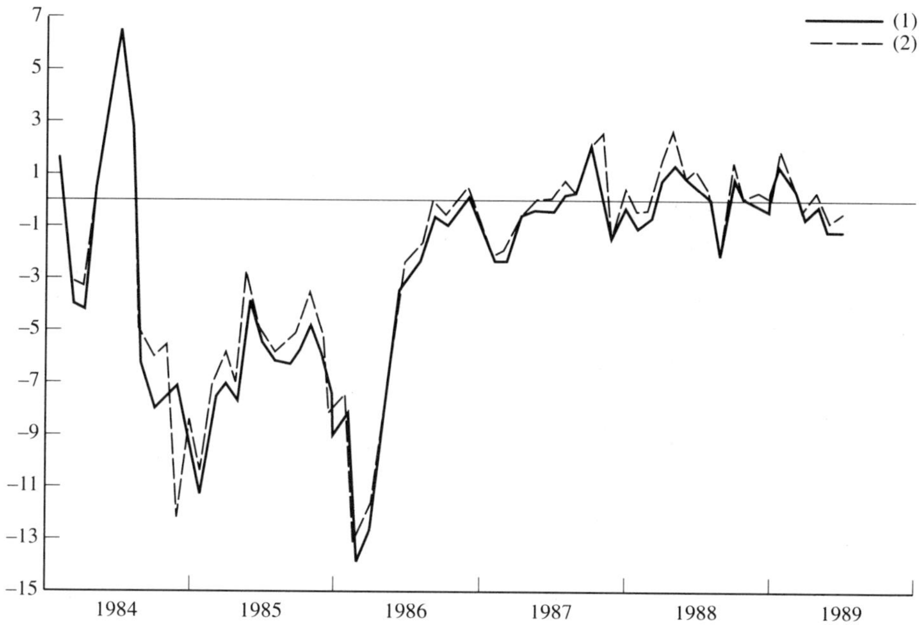

FIG. 10.5 'Onshore'/'offshore' interest rate differential (difference between the (average) interbank rate in Lisbon and covered (in Portuguese escudos) Eurodollar (1) or DM (2)). *Source*: Bank of Portugal

again suggests that in the long term capital controls have not been sufficiently effective to maintain a permanent differential between domestic and 'offshore' rates. The data presented above for short-term capital movements reflect the corresponding arbitrage funds. We can therefore conclude that the present system of capital controls could not be used as a way of neutralizing permanent inflation differentials.

In this light, the impact of the liberalization of capital controls does not need to have disruptive consequences. The immediate effect on government bond yields, and consequently on public debt dynamics, seems to be rather small. The potential short-term increase in interest rate volatility in the wake of expected parity changes (which could be avoided in the very short-term with costly controls) could be eliminated by a smooth adjustment of the escudo within overlapping changing bands. Moreover, this increased interest rate volatility would tend to reinforce (or substitute) the usual competitiveness penalties as a means of enforcing domestically the rules of the system.

5. EMS discipline for Portugal: why and how

The rationale for a country like Portugal to join the EMS was given in section 2 and has been thoroughly discussed in the credibility literature (the best example is Giavazzi and Giovannini 1989). Gros (1990) reinforces the credibility argument for countries with large public debts.[13]

The theoretical reasoning is as follows: as a disciplinary device, the EMS reduces the output costs of a given disinflation process. This is because tight money will face low inflation expectations because of the established disinflationary reputation of the EMS. If the authorities announce a new contractionary stance of monetary policy without this mechanism, they have to gain the necessary reputation by continuously sticking (in a non-optimal way) to contraction. Changing expectations in this way might be too costly and/or take too long, undermining the success of the intended stabilization package.[14] The EMS, representing a clear change of regime, shifts expectations and reduces the output–inflation trade-off. Empirically, the merits of the EMS as a disinflationary mechanism with comparatively low costs in terms of output are less clear. Some authors (see De Grauwe 1989 and Dornbush 1989) provide some evidence against the theoretical arguments developed above: the decline in inflation was stronger in the non-EMS Organization for Economic Co-operation and Development (OECD) countries until 1986 and sacrifice ratios (measured by inflation–unemployment trade-offs) were higher for some EMS countries. However, one can argue that EMS countries went further in eliminating inflation in comparison with other European countries (see De Grauwe 1989). Moreover, other measures of disinflation costs (as deviations of real GDP from its linear trend growth) tend to confirm this theory; Giavazzi and Spaventa (1989) provide evidence drawing on the cases of Italy and the UK.

Giavazzi and Giovannini (1989), looking at the observed shifts in the reduced form equations when there is a change in regime (as predicted by the Lucas critique) confirm broadly the disinflationary role of the EMS. However, this process may only have started some years after the setting up of the EMS: in the beginning economic agents were still learning about its functioning and policy-makers failed to give clear signs of their willingness to enforce domestically the rules of the system.[15] These factors were in turn instrumental in transmitting credibility to the labour market.

Given that the liberalization programme is on course and the need to disinflate, the EMS would be the appropriate device to smooth the adjustment process. In this light, the decision to join the EMS would *a priori* be more beneficial for Portugal than for Spain whose stabilization costs were incurred before full participation in the exchange rate mechanism (ERM). Likewise, it would make much less sense for Portugal to join when the inflation rate had already converged to the EMS average. The usefulness of the EMS as a disciplinary device consists precisely in the help it provides in the process of convergence.

It is worth stressing the present good momentum. The shift in expectations will be clearly faster now than it was at the beginning of the 1980s: the internal market objective, the experience of other countries and the recent increased stability of the system (smaller inflation differentials and fewer realignments) all make it more credible.

The essence of the strategy of joining the EMS is the required change in the pace of nominal depreciation once the escudo enters into the band. The idea is illustrated in Fig. 10.6: line (2) corresponds to a non-overvalued real exchange rate of the escudo (purchasing power parity (PPP) *vis-à-vis* Portugal's 13 main trading partners), and line (2′) to the hypothetical path of the nominal exchange rate inside the EMS that maintains PPP (lower inflation due to a possible shift in inflation expectations); line (1) gives the simulated divergence indicator (adjusted escudo/ECU rate) with the actual crawl of the escudo in effective terms. A 6 per cent fluctuation band allows for a gradual (and sustainable) disinflation process. This is because at the time of realignments the actual rate of the escudo crawls into the new band without any discrete jumps.

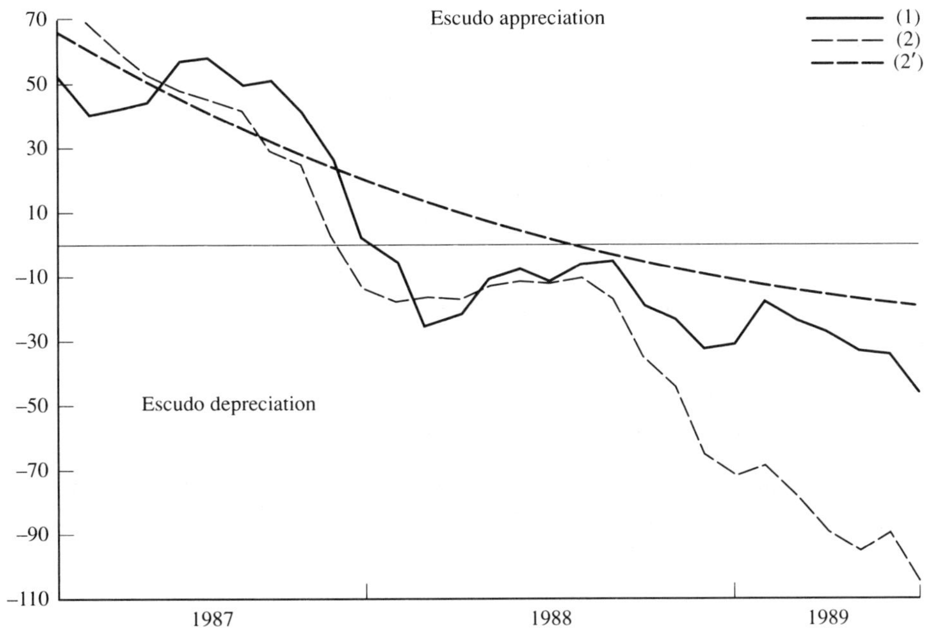

FIG. 10.6 Simulated divergence indicator of the escudo in the ERM (6 per cent fluctuation band). (1) Divergence indicator had the same crawling peg been pursued; (2) divergence indicator had exchange rate policy compensated in each period the inflation differential between Portugal and a weighted average of its 13 main trading partners; (2′) hypothetical effect of EMS discipline and credibility (invariant real exchange rate as in (2)). Central rate: average 1987/88 exchange rate. *Source:* Bank of Portugal

The initial central rate has to be set in such a way as to place the actual rate close to the top of the band. A preset devaluation in order to compensate for past real exchange appreciation (around 3 per cent for the period reported in Fig. 10.6) has to be regarded with caution. While its credibility effect is unclear, its real effects may be close to nil if they are not coupled with adequate policy tools.

6. Conclusion

As discussed above, the reduction of implicit taxation, achieved by financial liberalization, would have a negative direct impact on the dynamics of debt; higher interest rates would also be required to prevent loss of control over credit growth and avoid consequent negative implications for inflation and the balance of payments.[16] The corresponding benefits come only in the medium term: greater clarity concerning the cost of the public sector on the one hand and lower financial intermediation costs on the other. This latter effect, coupled with an EMS-induced reduction in the inflation risk premium (due to a shift in price expectations), may then compensate for the initial rise in interest rates, allowing for a better allocation of resources in the economy. If the disinflationary process is effective in increasing competitiveness, adjustment will not lead to recession. The transmission of credibility to the labour market plays, however, a key role in the success of the strategy, as is suggested by the disinflation experiences of Italy and Ireland (see Giavazzi and Spaventa 1989 and Dornbusch 1989, respectively).

The probability of speculative attacks against the escudo (a 'peso problem') need not be increased during the stabilization process (the present managed exchange rate system has already experienced eroded capital controls). Moreover, a credible commitment to financial liberalization and disinflation can only reduce that probability by excluding recurrence to financial repression and/or monetization. The possibility of a strong upward pressure on the escudo (the 'peseta effect') due to capital inflows is not to be neglected but, in the short run, these inflows can be sterilized through the amortization of the external component of public debt. Any retreat in the necessarily strong commitment to fiscal adjustment during the transition may, however, trigger the failure of the whole programme.

Appendix

Let us consider a very simple diagrammatic representation of the financial market (Fig. 10A.1).

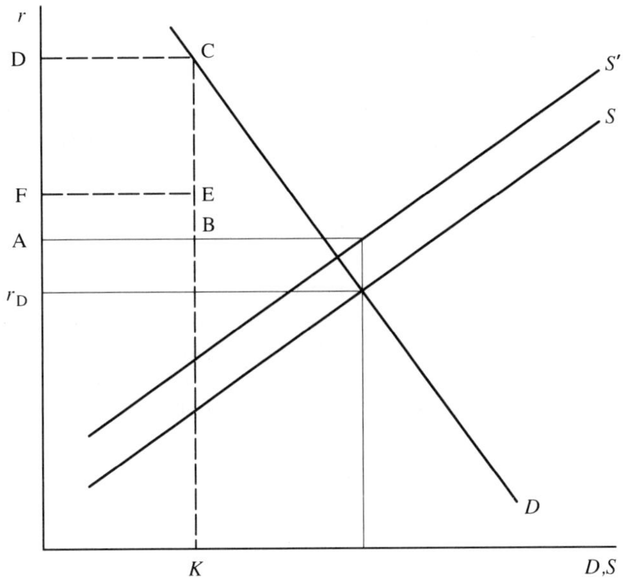

FIG. 10A.1 Credit ceilings and implicit taxation

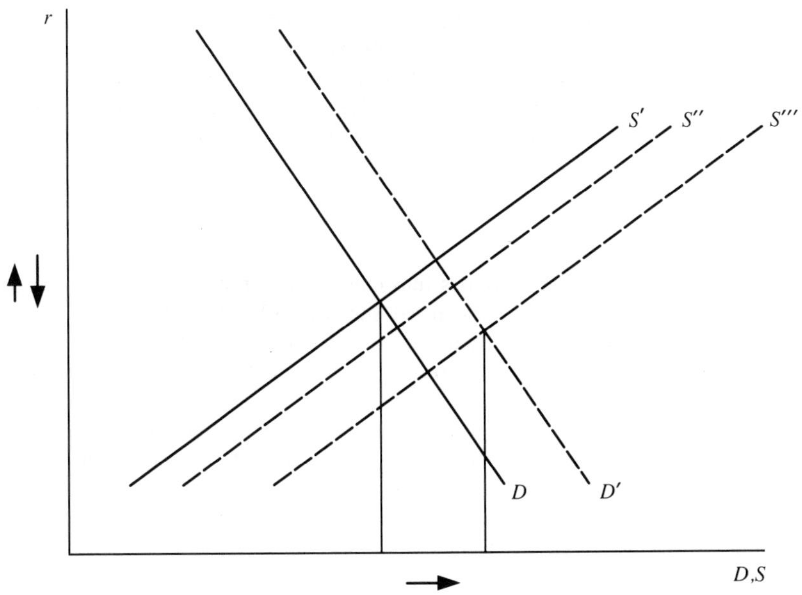

FIG. 10A.2 Liberalization and EMS discipline

The arguments of D (demand for credit) and S (supply of credit) are the expected value and variance of the probability distribution of the real interest rate. Intermediation costs are assumed to be totally shifted on to private borrowers because administratively set deposit rates were designed to stimulate deposits. The intermediation rate is then $A-r_D=c$, K is the credit ceiling and the area *ABCD* the implicit tax revenue (upward-based estimate of seigniorage in Table 10.1). If the deposit rate is set above r_D, government preferential credits ($S'-K$) is increased.

If both borrowers and lenders are risk averse, financial liberalization, enhanced by EMS credibility, shifts S and D to the right (Fig 10A.2). This is due to a reduction on banking intermediation costs (S' shifts to the right, say to S'') and to a decrease of the inflation-risk premium (both curves shift to the right, say to S''' and D'). The resources freed for productive capital formation may then increase substantially as depicted above. The effect on interest rates is unclear. However, as put forward by Modigliani *et al.* (1987), D may be steeper (less elastic with respect to its arguments) than S, especially if the public sector is a large borrower; in this case interest rates decrease.

Notes

1. As stressed by Canzoneri and Rogers (1988), optimal tax rates depend not only upon supply and demand elasticities of the good taxed but also upon the menu of taxes that a government can impose. Separate inflation rates might therefore have tax-smoothing properties. The substitutability between the inflation tax and other revenues depends on the interest rate elasticity of demand and on the money-to-income ratio. Among the extensive literature on optimal tax programmes, see Lucas (1986) and Mankiw (1987) for a discussion of the merits of the inflation tax in a second-best world.
2. This reasoning draws on the well-known unpleasant monetarist arithmetic of Sargent and Wallace (1981); see also Dornbusch (1989) for the recent Irish stabilization experience.
3. The temptation to cheat translates into considering an *ex post* real interest rate in expression [2] incorporating the usual surprise inflation effect: $E_t(P_t) - P_t$. This incentive to inflate and the actual inflation (equal to $E_t(P_t)$ in equilibrium), are increasing with b. See Gros (Chapter 7, above) for the analytical treatment of this issue.
4. Latin American experiences tell us about the danger of liberalizing foreign capital transactions and removing protectionism before domestic liberalization is achieved; the financial sequence of this process is also of the utmost relevance for the success of the liberalization attempt. Beleza and Macedo (1988) stress this aspect for Portugal; see also Edwards (1983) for a survey on the order of liberalization of foreign accounts and its relation to domestic stabilization.
5. See Giavazzi and Spaventa (1989) and Dornbusch (1989) for a thorough discussion of the Italian and Irish cases respectively.

6. A similar policy package had been adopted in 1980; it involved a reduction of the announced rate of the crawl and a discrete revaluation of the escudo of 6 per cent.
7. For a thorough discussion of the Portuguese financial system see Lygum *et al.* (1988).
8. Beleza and Macedo (1988), using a different debt growth equation, already reached this conclusion.
9. Revenues from privatization are expected to amount to 0.7 per cent of GDP for 1989, while debt take-overs will be around 5 per cent. Moreover, in order to privatize, the government might have first to take over the debts of public enterprises; this reduces the revenues from privatizations. There is, however, a clear consensus that, from 1990 onwards, revenues will be more than sufficient to offset past hidden deficits.
10. Direct investment in Portugal is to be liberalized by 1990, outflows of a personal nature, together with purchases of foreign securities by 1991 and direct investment abroad by 1993. Some items such as financial credits, money market securities, some private capital transactions and the opening-up of deposits abroad (for residents) and at home (for the non-resident banks) may be delayed until 1995.
11. Data for 1985–86 point, (although not so clearly) to the same result. In both cases France is well above the four southern countries and the FRG for 1987; in 1985, however, the ratio of short-term capital flows to GDP in France was smaller than in Portugal. All data are from Eurostat, *Balance of Payments*, 2-B, Table II-D.4.
12. While Portugal has enjoyed a 'tranquil period' since mid-1986 in terms of covered interest parity (CIP), Spain has gone through a 'turbulent' period' (capital controls being binding for inflows rather than outflows) because of her shadowing of the EMS. Since the escudo follows a crawling peg, CIP might translate the Portuguese shadowing (see Macedo and Torres 1989).
13. Gros (1990) computes the critical value of b (debt to GDP ratio) that would make it optimal for a country to join a zero-inflation EMS; the resulting condition translates approximately into a ratio of public debt to monetary base >1. We can then say that the higher this ratio the more advantageous it is for a 'fiscally weak' country to join a zero-inflation EMS. This ratio was 2.6 for Italy in 1979 and 3.6, 4.6 and 2.1 for Greece, Portugal and Spain respectively, in 1988.
14. As put forward by Kremers (1989), a stabilization package lacking credibility may undermine the private sector's willingness to moderate wage settlements.
15. The authors refer to the U-turn in the French economic policy stance in 1982–83 and the breakdown of wage indexation rules in Italy in 1984. According to Kremers (1989), in the case of Ireland the credibility process took place in various stages between 1979 and 1982.
16. This is already the case for 1987 if we recall the large inflow of unrecorded short-term capital and the amounts of uncontrolled credit (non-monetary financial institutions and some banking categories of credit exempted from ceilings).

References

Beleza, M. and **Macedo, J. B.** (1988) Implicit taxes and credit ceilings: the Treasury and the banks in Portugal, Universidada Nova de Lisboa, *Working Paper,* No. 106, December.

Canzoneri, M. and **Rogers C. A.** (1988) Is the European Community an optimal currency area? Optimal tax smoothing versus the costs of multiple currencies, mimeo, Georgetown University.

De Grauwe, P. (1989) The cost of disinflation and the European Monetary System, *CEPS Working Document*, 40.

Dellas, H. and **Stockman, A.** (1988) Self-fulfilling expectations, speculative attacks and capital controls, *NBER Working Paper* No. 2625.

Dornbusch, R. (1988) The EMS, the dollar and the yen, in Giavazzi, F., Micossi, S. and Miller, M. (eds) *The European Monetary System*, Cambridge University Press, Cambridge, pp. 23–36.

Dornbusch, R. (1989) Credibility, debt and unemployment: Ireland's failed stabilization, *Economic Policy*, **8**, April, pp 173–209.

Edwards, S. (1983) The order of liberalization of the current and capital accounts of the balance of payments, *NBER Working Paper*, No. 1507.

Giavazzi, F. (1989) The exchange rate question in Europe, *CEPR Discussion Paper*, No. 298.

Giavazzi, F. and **Giovannini, A.** (1987) Exchange rates and prices in Europe, *Weltwirtschaftliches Archiv*, **4**, (December), pp. 592–605.

Giavazzi, F. and **Giovannini, A.** (1989) *Limiting Exchange Rate Flexibility: The European Monetary System,* MIT Press, Cambridge, Mass.

Giavazzi, F. and **Pagano, M.** (1988) The advantage of tying one's hands: EMS discipline and central bank credibility, *European Economic Review*, **32**, pp. 1055–75.

Giavazzi, F. and **Spaventa, L.** (1989) Italy: the real effects of inflation and disinflation, *Economic Policy*, **8**, April, pp 133–71.

Gros, D. (1990) Seigniorage and EMS discipline, Chapter 7 in this volume.

Kremers, J. (1989) Gaining credibility for a disinflation: Ireland's experience in the EMS, *IMF Staff Papers*, forthcoming.

Lucas, R.E. Jr. (1986) Principles of fiscal and monetary policy, *Journal of Monetary Economics*, **17**, pp. 117–34.

Lygum, B., Ottolenghi, D. and **Steinherr, A.** (1988) The Portuguese financial system, *EIB Papers*, **7**, December.

Mankiw, G., (1987) The optimal collection of seigniorage, *Journal of Monetary Economics*, **20**, pp. 327–41.

Macedo, J.B. and **Torres, F.S.** (1989) Real interest differentials and European integration: Portugal and a comparison to Spain, draft, CEPS.

Modigliani, F., Monti, M., Drèze, J., Giersch H. and **Layard, R.** (1987) Reducing unemployment in Europe: the role of capital formation, in Layard, R. and Calmfors, L. (eds), *The Fight Against Unemployment*, MIT Press, Cambridge, Mass., pp. 11–47.

Sargent, T. and **Wallace, N.** (1981) Some unpleasant monetarist arithmetic, *Federal Reserve Bank of Minneapolis Quarterly Review*, **5**, pp. 1–17.

Comment: Gunter Baer

Portugal, when faced with the decision of whether to join an exchange rate arrangement prescribing stable, though adjustable, parities must naturally weigh the advantages of greater exchange rate stability against the disadvantages of restricting the use of the exchange rate as a policy instrument. This assessment will take into consideration the probability of economic imbalances emanating from divergent developments at home and abroad, the possibility of external shocks having asymmetric effects on the countries participating in the arrangement, the availability and effectiveness of alternative adjustment mechanisms, but also, of course, the implications of the exchange rate commitment for domestic economic policies.

In his chapter Francisco Torres focuses on this latter aspect and concentrates especially on the repercussions of participation in the EMS exchange rate mechanism and financial liberalization on Portugal's fiscal policy. While recognizing that the timing and the conditions of Portugal's entry into the EMS will be influenced by the nature of the external constraint at the time a decision is made, he views the emergence of an external constraint as primarily the result of an unsustainable fiscal policy. This emphasis is understandable, given the far-reaching implications that the removal of capital controls and the creation of a unified market for financial services in the Community by 1993 will have on Portugal's budgetary position. On the other hand, he dismisses perhaps too quickly a number of issues which are likely to arise if a country with a relatively low level of productivity and a need to catch up with more developed European neighbours considers relinquishing the freedom to manage its exchange rate. After all, Portugal has fared relatively well in generating growth and employment in recent years, and there remains the question of whether market mechanisms are sufficiently flexible and whether external assistance is needed in order to mitigate the output costs which might arise from adhering to an exchange rate commitment. The answer to these questions will certainly influence the decision on the timing of EMS entry but also, of course, on the degree of flexibility, i.e. the width of the fluctuation band, that Portugal should choose. These considerations are of particular importance, as there can be no doubt that frequent realignments, simulating Portugal's present crawling-peg approach, are not in the spirit of the EMS arrangement. Recourse to exchange rate adjustment to offset the effects of external shocks may therefore not always be a readily available policy option. Much would seem to favour a cautious approach with wider margins, but this may have some consequences for the EMS itself in the sense that the system would display a growing North–South divide between members with wider and narrower bands.

Two interrelated considerations suggest, however, that the fiscal policy implications of entry in the EMS are a matter of particular concern in Portugal. First, financial market liberalization and the need to lower substantially the current rate of inflation will significantly reduce the revenues currently accruing to the government in the form of seigniorage and implicit taxation. Second, a rapid move to a sustainable fiscal policy is an important requirement for underpinning the credibility of the authorities' decision to join the EMS.

The second argument rests, of course, on the assumption that a firm commitment to peg the exchange rate to that of a low-inflation country can have a favourable impact on the wage- and price-setting behaviour of firms and trade unions – provided the adoption of the exchange rate target is credible, which in turn implies that it is supported convincingly by sound monetary and fiscal policies. If this is the case, inflationary expectations could decline fairly quickly and thereby help to reduce the output costs of domestic stabilization policies.

The first argument has gained considerable prominence in recent discussions and has led some economists to counsel against high-inflation countries adopting an exchange rate target. In order to put this argument in perspective, we can by way of illustration use equation [2][1] to calculate the order of magnitude of revenue losses that Portugal might experience after lowering the rate of inflation and deregulating the domestic financial market. If it is assumed that the ratio of government debt to GDP remains constant, equation [2] restates the familiar steady-state budget constraint, with the government's primary deficit being equal to the sum of seigniorage on the monetary base and the implicit tax derived from the issuance of remunerated government debt. If round figures are used for Portugal's real rate of growth, inflation and the real rate of interest as well as for base money and government debt as ratios of GDP, the equation would yield a primary budget deficit consistent with the steady-state budget constraint of 2.2 per cent, about 0.5 of a percentage point less than the actual borrowing requirement net of interest payments in 1988.

By how much would fiscal policy have to be tightened if entry into the EMS were backed up by a reduction in inflation and if deregulation eliminated the preferential terms on which the Portuguese government can borrow at present? If the rate of inflation were brought down to 2 per cent, and if the real rate of interest – in the process of deregulation – rose from the present 2.5 per cent to the level in the FRG (where the long-term bond yield exceeds the GDP deflator by 5 percentage points), the government's gains from seigniorage would drop by 1.2 per cent of GDP and the implicit tax on remunerated debt in Portugal (0.4 per cent of GDP in our example) would disappear and give way to a negative tax of 1.6 per cent of GDP. In conclusion, the example would suggest that a major retrenchment of fiscal policy – shifting the current primary deficit of 2.7 per cent of GDP to a surplus of around 1 per cent of GDP – could be needed.

These calculations are purely illustrative and subject to many qualifications, but they indicate that if sustainable fiscal policies were defined to maintain a constant debt/GDP ratio, Portugal would have to undertake a major fiscal consolidation effort. However, is it realistic to assume that such a retrenchment could be achieved in a relatively short period of time, given the need to modernize and restructure the economy – an objective which can hardly be attained without large budgetary expenditures on infrastructure investment?

Against this background some doubts might arise as to whether Portugal's quest for disinflation and its intention to join the EMS are an optimal course of action. Indeed, if the loss of seigniorage and implicit taxation were to be recouped through higher direct and indirect taxation, this could have adverse supply-side effects and hamper the authorities' efforts to catch up with more prosperous European partners. On the other hand, the continued pursuit of relatively loose monetary and fiscal policies in combination with an array of regulatory measures would hardly provide a meaningful alternative. Such policies could at best have some success in the short term, but their longer-term effects would be detrimental to the objective of higher growth and accelerated development. There are four arguments in support of this view.

First, if Portugal is not to come under pressure to curtail demand in order to prevent a quickening of inflation and the emergence of excessive external constraints, it would have to be able to pursue policies which would ensure a constant rate of relatively high, though tolerable, price increase. So far, at least, it has proved impossible for any country to devise such policies. Moreover, there would still be the risk that the government would be tempted to resort to surprise inflation.

Second, in view of the global trend towards deregulation and liberalization, individual countries will find it increasingly difficult to insulate their economies and to maintain strictly controlled and regulated regimes. However, once liberalization has been started it tends to produce pressure for further deregulation, and administrative measures giving preferential treatment to the public sector would become ineffective.

Third, as the author suggests, the effectiveness of Portugal's capital controls, which are indispensable for maintaining a domestically regulated regime, may have declined in recent years. Incidentally, and more as a footnote, does the test really prove that capital controls have become ineffective? For instance, could it not be argued that the measured equivalence of onshore/offshore interest rates masks the existence of an underlying interest rate differential which would open up once capital controls were lifted? In other words, the 'true' short-term Portuguese interest rate is higher than the current one, possibly reflecting such factors as country risk considerations. Moreover, long-term real rates of interest have been persistently lower in Portugal than abroad. While the differential has narrowed, this may not necessarily indicate a decline in the effectiveness of capital controls, but may rather be the result of deliberate policies in preparation for liberalization by 1993.

Fourth, while the system of domestic regulation has helped the government to collect implicit taxes and provided a source of hidden government financing, there can be little doubt that that regime has bred inefficiencies and contributed to low productivity and lagging standards of living. In part this must be the consequence of inconsistencies in macroeconomic management, which, relying partly on administrative measures, gave the illusion of having two independent instruments – the domestic rate of interest and the exchange rate – for different policy objectives. In part also, the allocation of resources was misguided at the microlevel by the government's crowding-out of the private sector by rationing credit, penalizing savers and inducing banks to take on excessive credit risks in the search for investment opportunities. The elimination of such distortions would, in the longer term, be a more promising supply-side policy than attempts to create relatively high seigniorage gains.

Of course, deregulation and liberalization do not necessarily depend on entry into the EMS. However, acceptance of the exchange rate commitment could send an important signal to markets and, in fact, facilitate rather than aggravate the revision of the authorities' approach to policy-making. This is not to say that the strategy based on liberalization and EMS entry is free of risks, and Portugal may need considerable support from the Community and its individual member countries.

Note

1. Reformulating equation [2] for the steady-state situation yields:

$(g-t) = (n+\pi)\, m + (n-r)b$

where $g-t$ denotes the primary government budget (the borrowing requirement net of interest payments) as a ratio of GDP, m the ratio of base money (currency and unremunerated reserves) and b the ratio of remunerated government debt to GDP. The government sector is consolidated with the central bank. The parameters n, π and r denote the real rate of growth, the rate of inflation and the real rate of interest respectively.

For the illustrative example for Portugal the following values were used: for π, the GDP deflator of 12 per cent; for n, the 10-year average growth rate of 3 per cent; for r the difference between yields on long-term Portuguese government bonds and the GDP deflator, viz. 2.5 per cent; and for m and b 0.12 and 0.8 respectively.

CHAPTER ELEVEN

Greece and the EMS: issues, prospects and a framework for analysis

Lucas Papademos

1. Introduction

The process towards Economic and Monetary Union in the European Community (EC) gained momentum in 1989, following the submission of the Report of the Delors Committee and the Conclusions of the European Council held in Madrid. Although no consensus was reached concerning all stages proposed by the Delors Report leading towards the final objective, the Council decided that the implementation of the first stage would begin on July 1, 1990 and it initiated the process for the organization of an intergovernmental conference to lay down the subsequent stages.

One of the principal steps to be taken in stage one is the inclusion of all Community currencies in the EMS exchange rate mechanism (ERM). There is no explicit timetable. The terminal date of the first stage has not been predetermined, no agreement has yet been reached on proceeding with the subsequent two stages, and the unanimity required for revising the Treaty of Rome could delay the launching of the second stage. Nevertheless, it is implicitly understood and expected by many that the second stage should begin sometime not much beyond 1992, when the internal market programme is to be completed. Indeed, a view which has received considerable support is that the financial integration of the Community requires implementation of the second stage, which would involve institutional changes and more centralized monetary management at the European level.

These developments have increased the pressure on member states whose currencies do not participate fully in the EMS to join the exchange rate mechanism sooner than they might have previously envisaged. The Greek government has supported, in principle, the process towards economic and monetary union. Nevertheless, the issue of Greece's participation in this process has not yet been addressed adequately and explicitly. The simple reason for these seemingly contradictory attitudes towards monetary integration is that the magnitude of the imbalances characterizing the Greek economy has precluded serious consideration of full membership before substantial progress is made towards nominal convergence to the Community norms. The lack of a specific commitment to join the ERM has reflected an understanding that such a step is clearly unfeasible at present and in the immediate future rather than any reservations about the desirability of such action.

The choice of the appropriate exchange rate policy for the present state of the Greek economy – an economy characterized by high inflation, high and rising public debt, and structural inefficiencies – is not obvious. At the theoretical level, arguments can be advanced to support opposing views concerning the effective use of the exchange rate instrument during the transition period leading to low inflation and sustainable economic growth in the new environment of a unified European market. Deciding on the 'correct' view requires an assessment of the relevance of alternative theoretical propositions to the realities of the market structure and political economy in Greece. It is necessary, however, to proceed with the adoption of an economic strategy aiming at internal and external monetary stability, and of a programme of policy measures, both macroeconomic and structural, for attaining these objectives in the not too distant future. The time has come for Greece to express its commitment to European economic and monetary union by specifying a timetable for becoming a full member of the EMS. The choice, however, of the right time to do so is not going to be easy. It will require careful analysis, planning, and consistent implementation of macroeconomic policy to establish conditions which will ensure that full membership is not only feasible but also viable.

The purpose of this chapter is twofold: first, to address a number of fundamental issues relating to the adoption of policies and a timetable for the drachma's participation in the ERM and, second, to provide a framework for a more precise and systematic evaluation of these policies and of anticipated structural changes, both domestic and Community-wide, which will affect the functioning of the Greek economy and its transition to full EMS membership.

This chapter is organized as follows: Section 2 provides an overview of macroeconomic developments in the Greek economy during the last decade and an assessment of the process of, and the prospects for, nominal convergence. Section 3 focuses on certain policy issues, which should be addressed before deciding on the 'right approach' and the 'right time' for joining the ERM. The appendix presents a theoretical framework which can serve as the basis for a further quantitative analysis of these policy issues. This framework emphasises three aspects of the economy which are essential for such an analysis: (1) the financial structure and the determination of monetary equilibrium during a period of deregulation and removal of exchange controls; (2) the dynamics of public debt and the interaction of monetary and fiscal policies; and (3) the inflationary process, with particular reference to the effects of wage indexation, inflationary expectations and exchange rate policy.

2. Economic performance and convergence

The performance of the Greek economy in the 1980s was characterized by high inflation, relatively low GDP growth and high current account and public sector deficits relative to GDP. The macroeconomic performance was not uniformly unsatisfactory over the whole decade. There were periods, notably the 1986-1987 period of the stabilization programme, during which most economic indicators improved substantially. Nevertheless, the average track record was relatively disappointing, compared with both the average performance of the Community as well as the country's own post-war standards.

The purpose of this section is not to provide a comprehensive evaluation of economic performance and policies in Greece over the last ten years, but to offer a broad overview so as to set the stage for an assessment of the prospects for convergence and for an analysis of the anticipated benefits and potential transitory costs from the drachma's entry into the ERM. Consequently, the presentation will focus on certain key features of economic performance and on an appraisal of the effectiveness of economic policies in reducing inflation and current-account and fiscal imbalances.

The macroeconomic performance and policies of the past decade are summarized in Table 11.1, which presents the evolution of twenty-five indicators. Table 11.2 provides a comparison of the evolution of six of these indicators for Greece, all present members of the Community, and the members participating in the exchange rate mechanism of the EMS. In reviewing the performance of the Greek economy, it is instructive to start with 1979, a year which is marked with the creation of the EMS, the second oil-shock and the beginning of a seven-year period of expansionary policies in Greece, policies which culminated in the economic crisis of 1985.

TABLE 11.1 Greece: Economic Indicators (annual average percentage changes unless otherwise indicated)

	1979	1980	1981	1982	1983	1984	1985	1986	1987	1988
Output and employment										
1. Real GDP	3.6	2.1	0.2	0.6	0.4	2.9	3.4	0.8	0.0	4.3
2. Employment	2.7	1.1	1.1	0.1	–1.2	0.4	–1.2	0.1	1.3	1.2
3. Unemployment rate (in percent)	1.9	2.8	4.0	5.8	7.8	8.1	7.8	7.4	7.4	7.7
Prices and wages										
4. GDP deflator	18.2	19.9	21.8	23.5	17.8	19.5	19.0	16.1	12.7	13.4
5. Consumer Price Index	19.0	24.8	24.5	20.9	20.2	18.5	19.3	23.0	16.4	13.5
6. Average hourly wages in manufacturing	20.6	27.2	27.2	33.5	19.4	26.3	19.8	12.7	9.6	18.4
7. Unit labour costs in manufacturing	15.7	21.3	24.6	25.8	16.1	21.8	18.6	13.3	10.5	19.3

Table 11.1 continued

	1979	1980	1981	1982	1983	1984	1985	1986	1987	1988
Balance of Payments (as percent of GDP)										
8. Trade balance	–16.0	–17.0	–18.1	–15.4	–15.4	–15.9	–18.8	–14.4	–14.7	–14.5
9. Invisible balance	–11.	11.4	11.6	10.5	10.0	9.5	9.0	9.9	12.1	12.6
10. Current account balance	–4.9	–5.5	–6.5	–4.9	–5.4	–6.3	–9.8	–4.5	–2.6	–1.8
11. Overall balance	0.4	0.2	–0.4	–0.4	0.2	0.1	1.8	1.5	2.9	1.6
12. External debt (end of period)	13.1	17.4	22.3	25.6	33.9	41.7	50.2	45.8	41.5	40.6
Exchange rates										
13. Effective exchange rate	–6.2	–13.4	–6.0	–8.9	–16.9	–11.5	–17.9	–22.2	–11.0	–7.0
14. Real effective exchange rate (CPI)	3.4	–2.4	5.7	3.9	–7.2	–2.2	–4.2	–6.5	1.5	2.8
15. Real effective exchange rate (ULC)	0.1	0.1	7.1	16.2	–4.4	6.2	–3.0	–14.2	–4.0	9.7
Fiscal policy indicators (as percent of GDP)										
16. Central government expenditures	26.6	26.9	33.7	30.4	34.1	35.1	38.4	38.5	41.9	42.6
17. Central government revenues	22.0	21.0	21.0	23.1	24.1	24.7	24.3	27.0	27.6	26.4
18. Central government net borrowing requirement	6.1	7.3	12.5	10.5	9.7	12.6	14.4	10.4	11.5	14.8
19. Public sector borrowing requirement (cash basis)	5.9	8.8	14.7	12.8	11.4	15.4	17.9	14.0	13.2	16.3
20. Public sector debt (end of period)	28.3	30.4	38.9	44.3	52.4	64.1	76.4	77.6	81.8	90.2
Monetary policy indicators										
21. Money stock (MI) (end of period)	16.0	13.8	25.2	16.2	28.1	8.6	24.4	9.4	14.6	14.9
22. Money stock (M3) (end of period)	18.6	23.6	35.7	27.9	20.9	29.5	27.3	19.1	24.7	22.9
23. Domestic credit (end of period)	24.3	23.8	34.5	32.5	20.6	26.6	26.2	20.3	16.6	20.3
24. Nominal interest rates										
Bank loans (short-term)	17.7	22.3	22.3	21.5	21.5	21.5	21.5	21.5	22.3	22.9
25. Real interest rates (ex post)										
Bank loans (short-term)	–1.1	–2.0	–1.8	0.5	1.1	2.5	1.8	–1.2	5.1	8.3
Treasury bills (3-months)	–6.6	–8.8	–8.6	–5.0	–4.5	–1.0	–1.8	–4.9	0.8	2.5

TABLE 11.2 Indicators of Economic Convergence (annual average percentage changes unless otherwise indicated)

	1980	1981	1982	1983	1984	1985	1986	1987	1988	1989 *(a)*
1. Consumer Prices										
Greece	24.8	24.3	20.9	20.2	18.5	19.3	23.0	16.4	13.5	14.6
EC12	13.7	13.6	12.4	10.3	9.5	7.6	5.4	4.3	4.5	5.1
EMS	11.2	11.7	10.2	7.8	6.3	4.8	2.2	2.1	2.4	3.1
2. Unit Labour Costs										
Greece	21.3	24.6	25.8	16.1	21.8	18.6	13.3	10.5	19.3	15.4
EC12	13.4	12.7	10.5	9.2	6.5	6.3	5.4	5.1	3.8	4.6
EMS	10.9	9.9	8.3	6.3	3.2	3.4	3.4	3.3	1.2	2.2
3. Real GDP										
Greece	2.1	0.2	0.6	0.4	2.9	3.4	0.8	0.0	4.3	3.0
EC12	1.8	0.0	1.1	1.2	2.6	2.7	2.5	2.5	3.4	3.2
EMS	1.9	0.1	0.9	1.1	3.1	2.5	2.2	2.0	3.1	3.1
4. Current Account (% of GDP)										
Greece	–5.5	–6.5	–4.9	–5.4	–6.3	–9.8	–4.5	–2.6	–1,8	–2.1
EC12	–3.5	–3.8	–3.4	–1.9	–1.2	m0.7	0.2	0.2	–0.1	–0.6
EMS	–3.8	–3.3	–2.6	–1.0	–0.7	–0.3	0.3	0.7	1.0	0.7
5. Government Balances *(b)* (% of GDP)										
Greece	–8.8	–14.7	–12.8	–11.4	–15.4	–17.9	–14.0	–13.2	–16.3	–16.5
EC12	–4.7	–7.2	–7.1	–6.4	–6.2	–5.8	–4.9	–4.3	–4.3	–3.9
EMS	–4.6	–7.4	–7.4	–6.4	–5.3	–4.6	–4.1	–3.7	–3.3	–3.1
6. Money Stock *(c)*										
Greece	19.6	31.3	32.3	21.9	25.8	30.0	22.0	22.0	24.7	
EC12	12.9	14.8	15.2	13.4	13.2	13.0	11.5	10.9	10.9	9.3
EMS	8.4	10.4	11.4	11.0	10.1	8.3	7.2	6.5	7.1	6.5

Notes: EC12 refers to all present members of the European Communities
EMS refers to EC members participating in the exchange rate mechanism of the EMS

All averages are unweighted

(a) Forecasts made by the EC Commission (May 1989)
(b) For the EC, the general government deficit, for Greece the PSBR (on a cash basis)
(c) Broad measure of the money stock; National definitions; for Greece M3.

THE SEVEN YEAR NOMINAL EXPANSION: 1979-1985

Over this period, macroeconomic policies were on average very expansionary. Although there was a two-year interval when certain policies were tightened and the policy-mix changed, the overall stance remained inflationary and aggravated the chronic balance-of-payments disequilibrium. Over this period, consumer price inflation fluctuated between 18.5 and 24.5 per cent, the current-account deficit averaged about 6 per cent of GDP, and output growth remained low on average, although it exhibited significant cyclical variations.

These developments reflected, to a large extent, the macroeconomic policies pursued. Following the second oil-shock in 1979, fiscal policy became increasingly expansionary as indicated by the net public sector borrowing requirement (PSBR), which rose from 5.9 per cent of GDP in 1979 to 14.7 per cent in 1981. Monetary policy was accommodating, with broad money growth accelerating to 31 per cent in 1981, while unit labour costs rose by 24.6 per cent in the same year. After the 1981 general election, budgetary policy became restrictive, with the PSBR falling by more than three percentage points of GDP in the two years 1982-83. But incomes policy did not adjust at the same time; on the contrary, unit labour costs rose by another 26 per cent in 1982, after two years of annual increases averaging about 23 per cent. Nominal wage increases moderated only in 1983. Moreover, although monetary and credit expansion slowed down over this period, the deceleration was modest, while inflation-adjusted interest rates remained very low and were often negative, e.g. on government securities. Thus although macroeconomic policy became partly restrictive in 1982-1983, the adjustment effort was insufficient, not well coordinated and, more importantly, short-lived.

During the next two years, both election years, budgetary policy became strongly expansionary again, with the net PSBR rising by 6.5 percentage points to a peak of 17.9 per cent of GDP in 1985. The growth rate of the money stock (M3) accelerated to 30 per cent in the same year and real interest rates, though higher than before, remained relatively low and continued to be negative on short-term treasury bills.

The cumulative effect of macroeconomic policies on the economy over this seven-year period is reflected in the staggering rise of public sector and external debt. Public sector debt increased from 28.3 per cent of GDP at the end of 1979 to 76.4 per cent at the end of 1985. The relative increase in total external debt was even higher; the external debt-to-GDP ratio rose from 13.1 per cent at the end of 1979 to 50 per cent at the end of 1985 (see Figure 11.1).

These expansionary policies were pursued at a time when most Community countries, especially after 1982, were progressively implementing anti-inflationary policies. As a result, significant nominal divergences developed between Greece and the other EC countries, especially those participating in the ERM (Table 11.2). The annual average inflation differential between Greece and the ERM countries reached a peak of 14.5 percentage points in 1985. In the same year, broad money was growing at a rate which exceeded the ERM average by 22 percentage points, and the PSBR reached the record level of 17.9 per cent of GDP, which was al-

FIG. 11.1 Public sector and external debt as % of GDP

most four times the ERM average and three times the Community average. The current account deficit also reached a peak of 9.8 per cent of GDP in 1985, a year when the overall current account of the Community was almost in balance and only three other countries besides Greece had recorded external deficits.

The large nominal divergences between Greece and the Community, especially the ERM members, were not compensated by superior economic growth. On the contrary, real GDP growth remained very close to the Community average throughout that period. Real economic convergence was achieved but at the unsatisfactory low Community level of the period in question. The failure of expansionary macroeconomic policies to stimulate investment and growth reflected to a considerable extent the structural inefficiencies of the productive sector, inefficiencies which became more apparent after Greece's accession to the European Community. Moreover the productivity of investment declined steadily from 25 per cent in 1979 to about 4 per cent in 1983, real labour costs increased in parallel and real productive investment stagnated. The manufacturing sector, which had operated in an environment of protectionism and subsidisation for many years, did not adjust promptly to the new competitive environment following Greece's entry into the EC. In addition, inefficiencies in the labour and financial markets and an inequitable and ineffective tax system compounded the other problems faced by the productive sector. As a result, the supply side of the economy failed to respond adequately to the policy stimulus on nominal aggregate demand.

THE 1986–1987 STABILIZATION PROGRAMME

The sharp deterioration of economic performance experienced in 1985 forced the government to adopt a two-year stabilization programme, launched in October 1985 and aimed at rapid disinflation, a drastic reduction in the current account deficit and stabilization of the country's external debt. The stabilization programme was comprehensive, courageous and ambitious. It implied a radical change in the stance of macroeconomic policies. It involved substantial adjustments in fiscal, monetary and, especially, incomes policy, and an initial devaluation of the drachma by 15 per cent.

The centrepiece of the stabilization programme was the modification of the wage indexation scheme. According to the new scheme, wages would be adjusted on the basis of the official forecast of inflation (instead of past inflation), after deducting the effect of imported inflation. Moreover, the new wage indexation scheme became legally binding on both the public and private sectors until the end of 1987. The stabilization programme included measures aiming at reducing the PSBR by 4 per cent of GDP in 1986 and by a similar percentage in 1987, and it called for a more restrictive monetary policy involving increases in preferential interest rates and measures to curb money and credit growth. The programme also included special measures, such as the six-month advance deposit requirements imposed on the value of certain categories of imports.

The results achieved by the end of the two-year stabilization period were rather impressive. Inflation was reduced by almost 10 percentage points below the record of 25 per cent reached at the end of 1985 and the current account deficit shrank from 9.8 per cent of GDP in 1985 to 2.6 per cent, the lowest percentage since the early 1970s. Moreover, net, nondebt–creating, private capital inflows increased substantially and exceeded the current account deficit. There was a marked improvement in the external position of the country. The external debt fell to 41.5 per cent of GDP at the end of 1987 from 50.2 per cent at the end of 1985 (Figure 11.1).

On the policy front, the achievements were significant, but the overall picture is mixed and not as impressive as the performance of final economic variables. Although the PSBR declined by 4.7 percentage points of GDP over the two-year period, it failed to reach the admittedly ambitious target. Similarly, although domestic credit expansion decelerated sharply (from 26.2 to 16.6 per cent), it overshot the target due to the higher than projected public borrowing, while money growth by the end of 1987 had declined only moderately from its 1985 peak level. Real short-term lending rates to the private sector rose progressively to an average of 5.1 per cent in 1987, but the average real yield on 3-month treasury bills remained just below 1 percentage point. Incomes policy was fully implemented as planned. The new wage indexation scheme, in conjunction with the initial devaluation of the drachma, resulted in a rapid deceleration of nominal wages, and real wages declined by about 13 per cent over the two-year period. After the October 1985 devaluation of the drachma, exchange-rate policy aimed at maintaining competitiveness as measured by relative unit labor costs (Figure 11.2b). The deceleration in the rate of nominal depreciation of the drachma and the new incomes policy adopted played a major role in slowing down inflation since the beginning of 1986.

FIG. 11.2a Nominal and real effective exchange rates, 1979=100

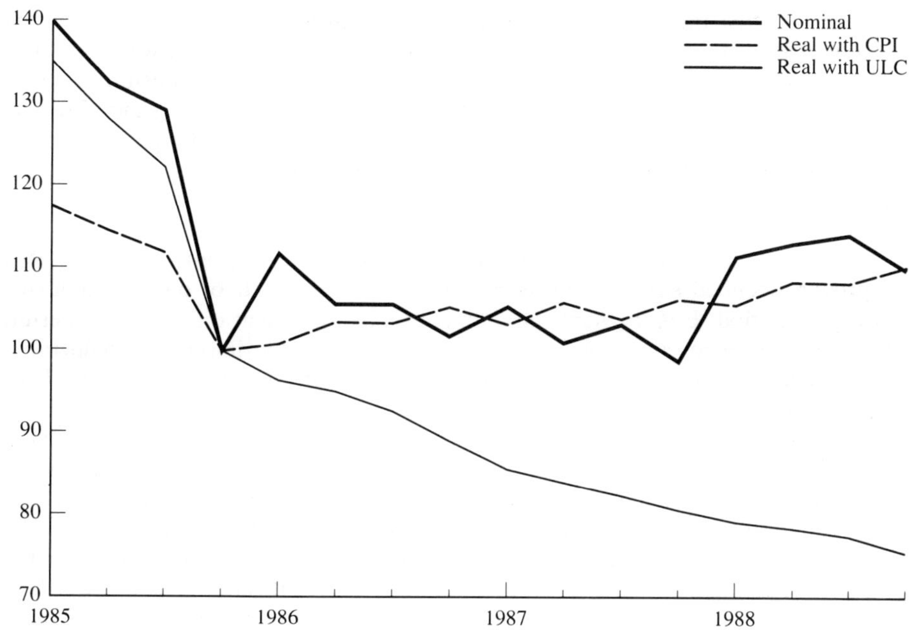

Fig. 11.2b Nominal and real exchange rates, 1986=100

PROSPECTS FOR CONVERGENCE

Experience from the stabilization programme leads to certain observations on the effectiveness of macroeconomic policy in reducing financial and real imbalances and on the nature of the adjustment process. These observations and the more recent economic developments are relevant for assessing the prospects for full EMS membership and for evaluating its implications as regards the economy and the effectiveness of policy.

First, the stabilization period showed that, on the whole, substantial and fairly rapid progress towards *nominal* convergence is feasible. In view of the considerable lags in the effects of policies on the economy, the steady improvement in inflation and in the current account recorded in 1988 – a year when the stance of fiscal and incomes policies changed – should be attributed partly to the delayed influence of stabilization policies. The improvement, however, also reflects the exchange-rate and interest-rate policies pursued in that year.

Second, the effectiveness of the stabilization policies pursued should also be assessed considering that the policy-mix *actually* implemented was neither optimal nor equitable. As already noted, the incomes policy and the exchange rate policy bore the burden of the stabilization effort throughout the period. Interest rate policy was not effectively employed during the first year in the aftermath of the devaluation – a notable policy error. More importantly, the adjustment of fiscal policy was essentially exhausted in the first year and, despite the impressive reduction in the PSBR in that year, the *real* adjustment was rather limited. Much of the decrease in the PSBR was due to the fact that the government took advantage of a sharp fall in oil prices that year to increase taxes without raising final prices. This action, which was prejudiced against the short-term inflation performance, raised revenue by transferring funds from the oil producers to the Greek Treasury rather than by improving the efficiency of the tax system and reducing tax evasion. A more effective and equitable policy-mix could have been employed and would have had a better outcome. The failure to implement a different policy-mix reflects, to a considerable extent, difficulties in tackling fundamental structural problems in the public sector.

Third, the real adjustment, though predictable, was unsatisfactory. Real GDP growth declined sharply and averaged less than one half of one per cent over the two-year period. Employment fell, although unemployment did not rise, presumably owing to changes in labour force participation. Despite improved competitiveness, the decline of the trade-balance, as a proportion of GDP, was negligible if one adjusts for the effect of changes in oil prices.

The period of stabilization ended formally and, to a large extent, effectively in 1987. As can be seen from the policy indicators of Table 11.1, fiscal and incomes policies were relaxed substantially in 1988. The PSBR rose in that year by 3 percentage points of GDP while unit labour costs in manufacturing increased by 19.3 per cent, after two years of average annual increases of about 12 per cent. Monetary and exchange-rate policies had to bear the burden of stabilization since then. Short-term real interest rates rose sharply, and the real lending rate to the private sector averaged 8.3 per cent in 1988. The drachma appreciated in real effective terms by

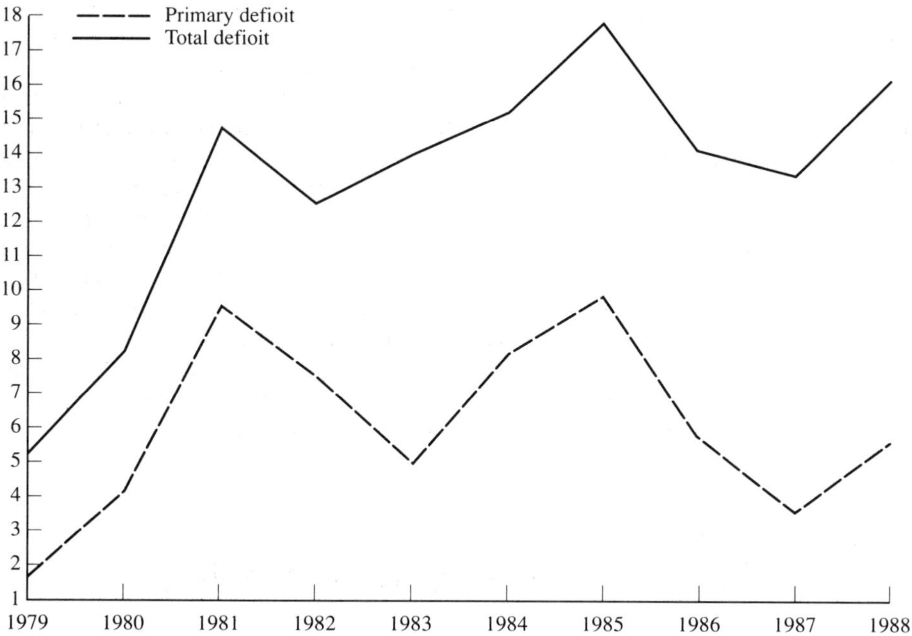

FIG. 11.3 Primary and total public sector deficit as % of GDP

about 9 per cent, based on relative unit labour costs, and by about 3 per cent, on the basis of relative consumer prices. Despite the reversal of macroeconomic policy, inflation and the current account continued to improve, while real output expanded vigorously by 4.3 per cent.

The relaxation of macroeconomic policy which started in 1988 continued in 1989. Earlier forecasts, such as the one by the EC Commission (Table 11.2), suggested a deterioration in economic performance. But these forecasts were based on what have turned out to be optimistic projections concerning the evolution of policy-controlled economic aggregates. More recently available data show substantial divergences from the initial official projections. In particular, it is now expected that the PSBR, as a percentage of GDP, will exceed the record of 18 per cent reached in 1985, while the increase in nominal wages in 1989, combined with that recorded in 1988, is likely to imply an increase in average real wages which will almost fully offset the sharp drop that took place during the two-year stabilization period. Although inflation and the current account have not yet worsened appreciably, the underlying trends are not favourable. Disinflation and external equilibrium cannot be maintained by relying exclusively on exchange rate and interest rate policies.

This overview of recent macroeconomic performance and policies leads to a number of general conclusions. First, the prospects for convergence are not favourable. There is uncertainty about the precise magnitude of the likely divergences in 1990. But there is no uncertainty regarding the order of magnitude of financial imbalances, which will be large, in terms of both flows and stocks. In the fiscal area, the initial conditions from which stabilization policy will have to proceed will be considerably less favourable than in 1985. This is already suggested by the recent trends shown in Figures 11.1 and 11.3, which do not yet include data for 1989. A second general conclusion which emerges is that the political business cycle is very visible in the Greek economy. The large swings in the behaviour of policy-controlled magnitudes and the commensurate swings, with due allowance for time lags, in the behaviour of final economic variables have been apparent throughout the past ten years. Interestingly, only the behaviour of aggregate real output does not seem to fit this pattern consistently. With the exception of the 1986–1987 stabilization period, output growth appears to vary more in line with the average Community growth rather than in response to domestic policy stimuli. The statistical validity of this observation should be further explored. The importance of political business cycles in the Greek economy suggests the need for *systemic* changes which can improve the framework for policy implementation and provide the discipline required for regulating the practices and forces which have destabilized economic performance.

3. The EMS and economic policy

This section addresses certain policy issues which are pertinent to the choice of the 'right time' for the drachma's participation in the ERM.

DISINFLATION, CREDIBILITY AND REAL ADJUSTMENT

It was argued in the previous section that a systemic change which could limit the causes of political business cycles is necessary for achieving internal stability in Greece. It could be argued that accession to full EMS membership would accomplish this by forcing changes in the behaviour of both the public and the policy makers, by influencing expectations and making disinflation policy more credible and thus more effective. The validity of this proposition is supported by the experience of a number of countries (e.g. France, Ireland) that have used participation in the EMS as a catalyst for disinflation (Giavazzi and Pagano 1988).

The general validity of the credibility proposition has to depend on two factors: the magnitude of divergences before full membership and the structure of labour markets and institutional conditions of a country's industrial relations system. In the case of Greece, the size of imbalances is too large and requires substantial policy adjustments especially in the fiscal area. If the necessary radical change in the stance of fiscal policy is not likely to occur promptly, then a premature accession to full membership would undermine credibility and lead to instability. Moreover, it is doubtful that labour union behaviour could be strongly affected by an ERM entry when inflation is substantially higher than the Community average. Trade unions may not respond to the new economic environment implied by the exchange rate regime, especially in a country with a long history of high inflation and if fiscal consolidation appears doubtful. This would result in either an unstable outcome or in substantial and prolonged unemployment, in the event that policy did become restrictive but contrary to expectations.

Thus, given the present state of the Greek economy, the right approach to full membership is to first achieve greater convergence of nominal magnitudes, employing a consistent set of policies, before deciding on participation in the ERM. This does not imply that I take the view that it would be optimal to wait until inflation has stabilized at the average level of the ERM countries. An overdose of EMS discipline may be hazardous to the economy's health before sufficient convergence is achieved. But this does not mean that Greece should not take advantage of the discipline that the EMS can impose on domestic authorities to cure the country's chronic inflation problems. As inflation approaches the highest level experienced by other ERM members, it would be desirable to join the ERM within a 6 per cent band, provided that other policies are consistently implemented. It would be effective to join as soon as feasible within the wider 6 per cent band (for a transitory period) so as to consolidate the progress made and accelerate the process of disinflation, rather than postpone entry aiming at joining within the narrow band. Participation within the wider band would also help to minimise potential employment losses, which can be substantial for an inflation-prone country. The Irish experience has demonstrated that, although a hard currency policy can be ultimately successful, it can entail high unemployment costs over a long period.

The speed with which inflation can be expected to decline in Greece, for a given degree of fiscal and monetary tightening, and the associated employment costs before and after entering the ERM, will depend on certain characteristics of the labour and product markets such as the mechanism and extent of wage indexation, the effects of excess aggregate demand and employment on the speed with which prices and wages adjust, the staggering of labour contracts, the degree of openness of the economy and, more elusive factors such as the nature of expectations, which are likely to be influenced by the change in the exchange rate regime. The model of aggregate price-wage dynamics presented in the next section can serve as a basis for a quantitative assessment of the effects of these factors on the speed and costs of disinflation.

PUBLIC FINANCE AND THE EMS

Another important issue which is relevant for choosing the 'right time' for full membership for a country like Greece relates to the debt accumulation process and the revenue from seigniorage. This issue has been recently emphasized by many, notably Dornbusch (1988) who noted that in Southern Europe 'the quest for disinflation has been pursued without recognition of the long-term budget consequences'. He argued that for a country with a debt problem, which is presumably related to an inefficient tax structure, there is scope for financing a relatively large budget deficit by relatively moderate rates of inflation, provided the velocity of high-powered money is low. The implication of this view is that rapid disinflation, by reducing the revenue from money creation, will accelerate the growth of debt unless it is compensated by fiscal measures. Moreover, aiming at a higher degree of exchange rate fixity may require a higher level of real interest rates, which will further speed up the debt accumulation process both directly, by increasing the interest payments on debt, and indirectly by reducing the demand for high powered money and the growth rate of output. Dornbusch has argued that it is not optimal for a 'low-velocity' country with a debt problem to aim at achieving average ERM inflation – at least not until appropriate fiscal measures can be adopted to reduce the 'optimal' inflation rate.

This view has been challenged by Gros (1990) and Thygesen (1988). Gros has noted that the benefits from seigniorage rest on the assumption that a country is in a position to choose the optimal amount of seigniorage, but that the authorities of a country with a high public debt have an incentive to reduce the real cost of servicing the debt through unanticipated inflation. But an informed public aware of this incentive will expect higher inflation and this will prevent choosing the 'optimal' inflation rate. It can thus be argued that for countries with high public debt, which is usually much larger than the monetary base, the potential revenue from unanticipated inflation is more important than the revenue from seigniorage, and consequently these countries would gain from ERM participation. Thygesen (1988) has also argued that by joining the ERM, a country might be able to lower real interest rates, thus enhancing the sustainability of debt. If a country does not join the ERM and adopts instead a 'crawling peg' exchange-rate policy, the burden of ensuring the stability of inflation will be born by domestic monetary policy.

To assess quantitively the implications of alternative propositions concerning the effects on the debt accumulation process of alternative inflation and exchange-rate policies, the model of the next section specifies the determinants of the dynamic behaviour of public sector debt taking into account the structure of the debt and the existence of implicit forms of taxation via the banking system.

DEREGULATION, LIBERALIZATION AND THE EFFECTIVENESS OF POLICY INSTRUMENTS

A third relevant issue relates to the planned deregulation of the domestic financial markets and their progressive integration into the unified European financial market. Deregulation and financial integration will, of course, affect the functioning of the markets, thus the determinants of monetary equilibrium, and the *modus operandi* of monetary authorities. These effects will be particularly significant in the case of

Greece because the financial system still operates subject to considerable restrictions and extensive foreign exchange controls. It can be expected that financial deregulation and integration will result, other things being equal, in a higher level of real interest rates which will adversely affect debt accumulation and impose additional constraints on monetary management.

The question that must be answered is whether this important institutional and structural change should be completed before the country proceeds to increase the degree of fixity of the exchange rate. Posing this question differently: can the potential adverse effects of this financial shock for the stochastic and dynamic stability of aggregate nominal income be contained more effectively by allowing a certain flexibility in the exchange rate rather than by joining the ERM (on the assumption that the appropriate degree of convergence has been achieved)? The answer to this question partly depends on the initial structure of domestic financial markets and thus on the nature of the structural change, but it also depends on characteristics of market behaviour, the nature of expectations, and the origin and relative size of shocks, including those induced by fiscal policy. Consequently, to answer this question, it will be useful to explore the implications of disturbances which are likely to be dominant and of plausible hypotheses on expectations, on the basis of a model which approximates to the present Greek financial structure and regulations and the process of liberalization.

Appendix

In this appendix we present a theoretical framework which can serve as a basis for a more systematic and quantitative evaluation of issues addressed in Section 3. This model focuses on three aspects of the economy which are essential for the analysis: (1) the structure of domestic financial markets, their integration with international financial markets, and the determinants of monetary equilibrium; (2) the dynamics of public sector debt and the interaction of fiscal and monetary policies; and (3) the dynamics of the inflationary process.

The model is relatively compact concentrating on key characteristics of the financial structure and the determinants of aggregate price-wage dynamics. On the other hand, it cannot be a very simple aggregative model because the analysis requires a description of certain institutional features such as the nature and extent of financial regulation, the degree of possible substitution between domestic and foreign assets, and the mechanism of wage indexation. Under special assumptions concerning market behaviour and the nature of expectations, the model can be simplified and distilled. The remainder of this section describes in some detail the three basic parts of the framework.

FINANCIAL STRUCTURE AND MONETARY EQUILIBRIUM

This section presents an aggregate model of the financial structure of the Greek economy and of the determinants of equilibrium in the financial markets. The model incorporates the banking system and specifies the determinants of demand and supply in both money and credit markets in terms of the behaviour of households (primarily net lenders), firms (primarily net borrowers), and the public sector (net borrower). Domestic residents consider that, in general, domestic and foreign financial instruments are imperfect substitutes. But the model is constructed so as to allow an analysis of the implications of the increased substitutability between domestic and foreign financial instruments which will result from the integration of financial markets in the Community.

The basic financial structure of the economy is summarized in Table 11.3 which shows the financial instruments held by four domestic sectors: the private non-

TABLE 11.3 The Financial Structure of the Greek Economy

Financial Instruments	Sectors			
	Private Nonbank (p)	Banks (b)	Central Bank (c)	Government (g) and other public sector
1. Currency and bank reserves (H)	H_p	H_b	$-H$	H_g
2. Demand and savings deposits (D)	D_p	$-D$		D_g
3. Time and other deposits (T)	T_p	$-T$		T_g
4. Bank Borrowing (B')	B_p'	$-B'$	B_c'	
5. Bonds and bills (B)	B_p	B_b	B_c	$-B_g$
6. Bank loans (L)	$-L_p$	L_b	L_c	$-L_g$
7. Value of equity capital (V)	V_p	$-V_b$		V_g
8. Foreign currency and gold (H^*)	$EH_p{}^*$		$EH_c{}^*$	
9. Foreign deposits (D^*)	$ED_p{}^*$	$-ED_b{}^*$	$ED_c{}^*$	
10. Other foreign financial assets (B^*)	$RB_p{}^*$	$EB_b{}^*$	$EB_c{}^*$	$-EB_g{}^*$
11. Foreign bank loans (L^*)	$-EL_p{}^*$	$-EL_b{}^*$	$-EL_c{}^*$	$-EL_g{}^*$

bank sector (p) which includes households and private firms, the bank sector (b) which includes all bank-type financial institutions (commercial banks and specialized credit institutions), the central bank (c), and the public sector (g), which includes the central government, public enterprises, social insurance funds and other entities of the public sector.

Each row of the Table 11.3 shows the quantities of a financial instrument held as an asset (+) or as a liability (–) by each sector. Each column of the Table shows the quantities of the various financial instruments held by that sector. The zero elements indicate that certain sectors hold at present relatively small amounts of certain instruments. The sum of the elements of each column corresponds to the balance sheet constraint of each sector and defines that sector's net worth. Because at present foreign residents hold very small quantities of domestic currency assets, with the exception of real capital, the first six rows of the Table correspond to market equilibrium conditions, that is the sum of sectoral demands is equal to the total quantity supplied of each financial instrument.

The financial structure of the Greek economy summarized by the Table includes eleven financial instruments, seven of which are denominated in domestic currency units and four in foreign currency units. The larger number of domestic assets included in the Table reflects the finer disaggregation of domestic bank liabilities and assets which is useful for the analysis and the small holdings of foreign corporate equity and real capital by domestic residents. The domestic financial instruments are: currency and bank reserves (H), demand and savings deposits (D), time and other types of bank deposits such as certificates of deposit (T), bank borrowing (B'), which includes both bonds issued by banks and specialized credit institutions and held by the public (B_p') and also banks' borrowing from the central bank (B_c'), other marketable debt instruments issued by nonbanks which at present consist of treasury bills and government bonds (B), bank loans (L), and the value of equity capital (V). This latter quantity is defined to include the equity of firms and the value of the real capital (housing and real estate) owned by households. Domestic residents hold four foreign-currency financial instruments: foreign currency and gold (H^*), foreign bank deposits of all types (D^*), held with financial institutions both at home and abroad, other foreign financial assets (B^*) which are primarily market debt instruments and shares in unit trusts, and foreign-currency bank loans (L^*). The nominal quantities with an asterisk(*) are measured in terms of foreign currency and thus are multiplied by the nominal exchange rate (E), the price of foreign currency in terms of domestic currency. A variable with a subscript ($_{p,b,c,g}$) indicates the quantity of an asset or liability held by the corresponding sector. A variable without a subscript indicates the total quantity of a financial instrument, which is supplied by a single sector.

Financial institutions and markets in Greece have been for many years subjected to extensive and excessive regulations and financial controls. Until only recently, interest rates on all bank assets and liabilities were set administratively by the central bank, and an extensive system of credit rules and regulations constrained the portfolio choices of banks and the borrowing opportunities of the nonbank public. Until 1984 foreign exchange controls prevented domestic residents from legally holding any foreign currency assets, although banks operating in Greece had (rather substantial) foreign currency deposits legally owned by Greeks residing and working abroad. The overregulation of the Greek financial system inhibited the development of money and capital markets which until 1985 accounted for only a negligible fraction of domestic financial assets.

Since 1982 substantial progress has been made towards the deregulation of the banking system, the development of money and capital markets and the relaxation of foreign exchange controls.[1] For example, interest rates on most bank assets and liabilities are now market determined, most specialized credit rules and regulations restricting the financing of specific sectors and activities have been abolished, and the nonbank market for government securities, which was virtually nonexistent before 1984, has developed rapidly and it financed a significant part of the central government's deficit in 1988. Nevertheless, despite the progress made in recent years, the Greek financial system is still functioning subject to important constraints which impinge on the determination of the general level of domestic interest rates and restrict the portfolio choices of banks and the nonbank public. The aggregative model presented here aims at capturing the essential institutional features and constraints of the Greek financial system in a relatively simple specification.

THE DEMAND FOR FINANCIAL ASSETS

The nonbank public's demands for financial assets are assumed to be proportional to the price level P and to also depend upon the nominal rates of return on all assets, measured in terms of domestic currency, anticipated real income Y and initial real wealth W_p/P. Thus the demand for the representative domestic asset A is given by:

$$A_p/P = f_A[i, i*, Y, (W_p/P)_{-1}] \qquad [1]$$

where:

$$P = P_y^{\theta}[EP_y*]^{(1-\theta)} \qquad [2]$$

The price level is measured by an index defined as the geometric average of the price P_y of the domestically produced composite good Y and the price EP_y* of imported final goods, in domestic-currency units. The domestically produced goods and the imported final goods are viewed as imperfect substitutes. The weight in the price index represents the average share of domestic goods in total private expenditures by domestic residents. The vector of nominal rates on the domestic financial assets shown in Table 11.3 has in general seven elements:

$$i + [i_H, i_D, i_T, i_{B'}, i_B, i_L, i_V] \qquad [3]$$

Three of these rates of return are either determined administratively or are not effectively varied, although set by banks. The average nominal rate of return on base money, i_H, has a zero currency component and a rate set by the central bank for the bank reserve component; the interest rate on savings deposits, the largest component of D, has also effectively been fixed by the central bank. Banks have been allowed to set the rates on sight deposits but they change them infrequently. The rate of return

on government securities, i_B, is determined by the government and is not changed very frequently either. The government offers treasury bills regularly, at the beginning of each month, at given interest rates; it also sells medium-term bonds at less regular time intervals. Since the introduction of treasury bills sales directly to the public in 1985, the interest rate on three-month treasury bills has been changed infrequently. The equilibrium quantity in the (nonbank) market for government securities is demand determined at the set interest rates.

Banks can set competitively the interest rates on time deposits and certificates of deposit, i_T, bank bonds $i_{B'}$ and on the bulk of the largest part of their loans to the private sector, i_L. The rate on time deposits can be expressed as a linear function of the loan rate i_L and the rate on treasury bills and bonds i_B:

$$i_T = \kappa_L i_L + \kappa_B i_B - q_T. \qquad [4]$$

The parameters κ_L, κ_B and q_T reflect the effects of reserve requirements, portfolio requirements and operating costs per unit of deposits. The interest rate on bank bonds differs by a fairly constant spread from the interest rate on government paper of the same maturity, that is:

$$i_{B'} = i_B + q_B. \qquad [5]$$

The spread q_B is also affected by interest rate subsidies received by certain specialized credit institutions. Finally, the rate of return on equity capital, i_V, can be expressed in terms of the rate of return on real capital and the risk premium required by households for holding corporate equity. It is assumed for analytical convenience that the risk premium is invariant to the level of interest rates. Thus the vector of nominal rates of return on domestic assets which is relevant for the portfolio choices of the nonbank public has three key elements: (i_D, i_B, i_L). The first two are set 'exogenously' by the authorities while the bank loan i_L rate is market determined, reflecting indirectly the effects of i_D and i_B. We refer to the bank loan rate as the domestic market rate and for notational simplicity we will denote it hereafter by i.

For analytical convenience, it is assumed that the rates of return on foreign deposits, other financial assets and foreign loans, measured in terms of foreign currency, differ by spreads which are invariant to the general level of foreign interest rates and reflect differential transaction costs, risk characteristics and other stochastic factors. The expected nominal rates of return on foreign assets expressed in terms of domestic currency reflect the anticipated rate of depreciation of the drachma, denoted by $\hat{\varepsilon}$. If we denote by i^* the rate of return on foreign bank loans measured in terms of foreign currency, the corresponding rate expressed in terms of domestic currency is:

$$i^* + \hat{\varepsilon} = i^* + \hat{e}_{+1} - e, \qquad [6]$$

where e is the logarithm of the nominal exchange rate. In the empirical analysis we have employed a log-linear specification for the demands for financial assets:

$$\alpha_P - p = k_{AO} + k_A i + k_A^* (i^* + \hat{\varepsilon}) + b_A y + c_A (w_p - p)_{-1} + v_A \qquad [7]$$

where α_p, p, y, w_p are the logarithms of the quantity of asset A_p, the price level, real aggregate income, and wealth of the nonbank private sector, respectively. $i = (i_D, i_B, i)$ is the vector of the levels of the three key domestic rates, and v_A represents the random component of the demand for the asset A_P. The net worth of the private nonbank sector is defined by:

$$W_P = M3_P + B_P' + B_P - L_P + F_P \quad [8]$$

where

$$M3_P = H_P + D_P + T_P \quad [8a]$$
$$F_P = E[H_P^* + D_P^* + B_P^* - L_P^*] \quad [8b]$$

Employing the balance sheet constraints of the other sectors, obtained by summing up the elements of the respective columns of Table 11.3, we find that aggregate real net worth is given by

$$W_P = V + F \quad [8']$$

where

$$V = V_P + V_g, \quad F = F_P + F_b + F_c + F_g.$$

F is the domestic currency value of the net foreign assets of all sectors.

The Bank of Greece has employed as an intermediate target in recent years a broad measure of the money stock, denoted by $M3$, which corresponds to the aggregate $M3_P$ defined above. The demand for this monetary aggregate has been found to have a relatively more stable relation to nominal income than the demand for more narrow measures of the money stock. A specification for the aggregate demand for $M3$, analogous to the one for individual assets, was estimated directly and employed in the simulation analysis. This specification also allowed for the gradual adjustment of the actual demand for real money balances to the desired level $m3^d$. Thus:

$$m3^d - p = k_o + k_3 i + k_{3^*}(i^* + \hat{\varepsilon}) + b_3 y + c_3(w_P - p)_{-1} + v_3$$

$$m3 = \lambda_m m3^d + (1 - \lambda_m)\, m3_{-1}$$

Note that the interest semi-elasticities k_3 and k_{3^*} are by construction weighted averages of the corresponding semi-elasticities of the demand for the component assets. Consequently, the total effect of the rates of return on bank deposits, i_D and i_T' on the demand for $M3$ reflects their offsetting effects on the components of $M3$ and it is thus expected to be small. By contrast, the semi-elasticities of $M3$ with respects to i_B and $(i^* + /)$ will be greater in absolute terms than the corresponding interest elasticities of the component assets.

THE PRIVATE SECTOR'S DEMAND FOR BANK CREDIT

The demand for bank loans by the private sector reflects primarily the demand for credit by firms and to a lesser extent, households' demand for housing loans. (Real estate loans accounted for only a small fraction of the outstanding debt of the private sector at the end of 1988.)

Firms in Greece have financed their investment primarily through bank loans and retained earnings. The financing of capital by issuing shares has been very small while firms' direct borrowing from the market has been negligible until very recently. The size of Greek firms and the relatively undeveloped state of domestic capital markets are not likely to change significantly over the next three to four years and it can thus reasonably be assumed that firms' domestic debt will consist of bank loans. Since the recent abolition of restrictions on foreign borrowing, domestic firms can obtain foreign currency loans from foreign and domestic banks. Domestic and foreign loans are considered imperfect substitutes in part because of the exchange rate risk associated with the different currencies of denomination.

The total demand for bank loans is postulated to be proportional to the total value of firms' tangible assets and to also depend on aggregate nominal income:[2]

$$L_{Tp}{}^{d} = 1_2(\overline{\pi})P_Y K + 1_2(i_A)\, P_Y Y \qquad [9]$$

where the firms' capital is valued at its current replacement cost and i_A is the average cost of firms' borrowing defined below [17a]. The proportionality factor 1_1, the debt-to-capital ratio, is considered to be a function of the average anticipated inflation rate X and not to be very sensitive to transitory fluctuations of the nominal interest rate on bank loans. The average value of 1_1 reflects the effects of institutional factors, the tax structure of the economy and bankruptcy costs which determine the contribution of leverage to the value of the firm. Note that an increase in the level of interest rates reduces the demand for credit indirectly by reducing the demand for investment and thus *K* and *Y* and also by affecting negatively the debt-to-income ratio 1_2. The second term of [9] captures the effects of short-term cyclical factors on the demand for working capital by firms.

The firms' demand for domestic and foreign-currency loans depends on the interest rate differential on such loans, in domestic currency units, and the total demand for credit:

$$L_p d = \varphi[i - (i^* + \hat{\varepsilon})] L_{T_p}$$

$$[EL_p{}^*]^d = [1 - \varphi[i - (i^* + \hat{\varepsilon})]]\, L_{T_p} \qquad [10]$$

where $0 < \varphi(.) < 1$ and $\varphi' < 0$.

THE SUPPLY OF BANK LOANS TO THE PRIVATE SECTOR

As noted above, the portfolio choices of financial institutions are still restricted by constraints other than the conventional reserve requirements imposed for the control of the overall size of bank deposits. These constraints are different for commercial banks and other financial institutions. The presentation here focuses on the relevant constraints and the determinants of the supply of private credit by commercial banks. The balance sheet constraint of banks implied by Table 11.3 is:

$$H_b + L_b + B_b + F_b = D + T + B_p' + B_c' + V_b \qquad [11]$$

where $F_b = E\,(L_b^* - D_b^*)$ denotes the net foreign assets of banks. The asset structure is subject to the following restrictions. Banks are required to hold ordinary reserves equal to a fraction (Z_m) of their total deposit liabilities; they are required to invest a proportion (Z_b) of their deposits in government bills and bonds; in addition, they have to allocate a proportion (Z_g) of their deposits for the financing of public sector enterprises, and a proportion (Z_f) for the financing of small and medium-size firms. If the demand for credit by public enterprises and by small and medium-size firms is smaller than the available supply, commercial banks are required to deposit the excess funds with the Bank of Greece. In what follows, we abstract from the restrictions imposed for the financing of small and medium-sized firms. These restrictions are likely to be abolished in the near future. In addition to the required holdings of H_b and B_b, banks may find it desirable to hold ordinary bank reserves and government securities in excess of the required amounts. Thus in general:

$$H_b = Z_m(D + T + B_p') + H_b^{\,E}, \qquad [12]$$

$$B_b = z_b(D + T + B_p') + B_b^{\,E}. \qquad [13]$$

Banks extend loans to both private and public sector enterprises:
Thus:

$$L_b = L_p + L_{bg} = L_p + z_g(D + T + B_p') + L_{bg}^{\,E} \qquad [14]$$

where $L_{bg}^{\,E}$ denotes bank credit to public sector enterprises in excess of the required amount. Since loans to public sector enterprises are (usually) guaranteed by the government it is reasonable to assume that the quantity $L_{bg}^{\,E}$ is largely demand determined.

Substitution of [12]–[14] into [11], allowing that $D + T + B_p{}' = M4 - H_p$ and on the reasonable assumption that on average banks match their foreign currency assets and liabilities, we obtain

$$H_b^{\,F} + L_p + L_{bg}^{\,E} + B_b^{\,E} = (1 - Z)\,[M4 - H_p] + V_b \qquad [15]$$

where $H_b^{\,F} = (H_b^{\,E} - B_c{}')$ is the quantity of free reserves, excess minus borrowed reserves, held by banks and $z = z_m + z_b + z_g$ which can be interpreted as an effective total required reserve ratio on bank deposits. The demand for free reserves can be expressed as a function of i, i_B and the rate at which banks can borrow reserves from the central bank, denoted i_{CB}.

The supply of bank loans to the private sector can be expressed as a fraction Ψ of banks' unrestricted sources of funds, with the fraction Ψ depending upon the spread between the loan and bond rates:

$$L_p{}^s = \psi(i - i_B)\,[M4 - H_p] + u_L, \quad 0<\psi<1, \quad \psi'>o \qquad [16]$$

where u_L is a stochastic term.

EQUILIBRIUM IN THE CREDIT AND MONEY MARKETS

Equilibrium in the financial markets can be summarized by stating the conditions for equilibrium in the credit and money markets and specifying the balance sheet and budget constraints which restrict the behaviour of the public and the authorities. It follows from [9], [10] and [16] that equilibrium in the market for private bank credit requires that:

$$\varphi\,[\,i - (i* + \hat{\varepsilon})]\,[l_1(\bar{\pi})P_YK + l_2\,(i_A)P_YY] = \psi(i - i_B)[M4 - H_p] + v_L \qquad [17]$$

where

$$i_A = \varphi i + (1 - \varphi)\,(i* + \hat{\varepsilon}) \qquad [17a]$$

$$\varepsilon = \hat{e}_{+1} - e, \quad \pi = p_{+1} - p, \quad p = \theta p_y + (1 - \theta)\,(P_y* + e). \qquad [17b]$$

and v_L is a stochastic term representing the *net* random disturbance in the market for bank loans. This condition depends on the stocks of broad and narrow money which must satisfy the following:

$$Pf_H\,[i_D, i_B, i, i* + \hat{\varepsilon}, Y, (W_p/P) - 1] + v_H = H_p \qquad [18]$$

and

$$Pf_{m_4}\,(i_D, i_B, i, i* + \hat{\varepsilon}, Y, (W_p/P) - 1] + v_{M_4} = M4 \qquad [19]$$

where H and $M4$ are the stocks of currency and broad money supplied by the banking system. The central bank can aim at controlling the monetary base (H) or the nonborrowed base (MO), but the currency component of the base is demand determined, as a function of the variables shown on the left-hand side of [18].

The Bank of Greece has aimed in recent years at controlling the broad measure of the stock money partly by influencing its demand via interest rates and partly by measures which directly affect the supply of bank liabilities. The control of the supply, however, has been subject to the serious constraints imposed by the borrowing needs of the public sector. In previous years, before 1985, the Bank had aimed at controlling directly the supply of bank loans to the private sector relying on credit ceilings imposed on specialized credit institutions and on interest rates to control the liquidity of commercial banks. In the limiting case when the supply of bank loans is the primary financial target of the monetary authorities and on the assumption that it can be controlled effectively, the right-hand side of [17] must be replaced by the policy-determined quantity of bank loans to the private sector, $\bar{L}_p$. However, the effectiveness of such credit controls, especially on the credit extended by commercial banks, was also hampered by the public sector's demand for credit.

The specification of financial markets equilibrium, given by [17]–[19] and the associated definitional relations, involves the following variables which, in general, can be considered as being determined *endogenously*, at least in part: $(i, P_Y, P, Y, E, H_p, M3)$. The nominal exchange rate E and the stock of the broad money $M3$ are variables that are being controlled by the authorities to varying degrees. In addition to the above variables, the system depends upon the policy-determined variables i_D,i_B and MO, the exogenous variables (i^*,Py^*), expectations of the level of E and P_y in the next period and initial conditions, the values of real net worth and the stock of $M3$ in the previous period.

MONETARY EXPANSION AND PUBLIC FINANCE

The relationship between the public sector's debt, borrowing requirements and the stock of broad money can be established from two basic identities: the balance sheet (stock) constraint of the consolidated banking system and the budget (flow) constraint of the public sector. These identities, of course, also relate the stock of domestic money with the economy's net foreign assets and the balance of payments. From Table 11.3 we find that the consolidated balance sheets of banks and the central bank imply that:

$$(B_b + B_c) + (L_b + L_c) + (F_b + F_c) = M3_p + M3_g \qquad [20]$$

where F_j denotes the net foreign assets of sector j ($j = b, c$)in domestic currency and $M3_p = H_p + D_p + T_p + B_p'$, $M3_g = H_g + D_g + T_g$. The sum of the first four terms on the left-hand side of [20] is the total domestic credit (DC) created by the domestic banking system in the form of loans or marketable securities. From the fourth and fifth rows of Table 11.3, it follows that domestic credit can be written as the sum of the public domestic debt held by the banking system and the stock of bank credit to the nonbank private sector:

$$DC = B_b + B_c + L_b + L_c = [B_g + L_g - B_p] + L_p \qquad [21]$$

Let the D^N denote the stock of *net* public sector debt:

$$D^N = (B_g + L_g) + E\,[B_g* + L_g*] - M3_g = (B_g + L_g - F_g) - M3_g \qquad [22]$$

and $P\ (G^T - TX)$ the total nominal deficit of the public sector, where G^T is the real value of total public sector expenditures and TX is the real value of net public sector revenues. A public sector deficit leads to a change in the stock of *net* public sector debt:

$$P(G^T - TX) = D^N - D^N{}_{-1} = \Delta[B_g + L_g - F_f] - \Delta M3_g \qquad [23]$$

Employing [20], [21] and [23] we obtain the following fundamental identity:

$$P(G^T - TX) + \Delta(F_b + F_c + F_g) + \Delta L_p = \Delta M3_p + \Delta B_p \qquad [24]$$

The public sector borrowing requirement (PSBR) = P(G-TX), the credit expansion to the private sector(ΔL_p) and changes in the net foreign assets of the banking system and of the government must be financed by an increase in the stock of broad money and the stock of government securities held by the nonbank public. This identity has played a central role in the formulation of monetary policy in Greece for many years; it is the identity underlying the 'monetary programmes' adopted in previous years, which involved 'targets' and 'projections' for all the major terms of [24]. In the last two years the Bank has announced a target for the rate of growth of M3 = $M3_p$ and consistent projections for ΔL_p and ΔB_p .

We next obtain a different constraint which relates the deficit of the public sector to changes in the *narrow* measure of the stock of money, $M0$, and the interest-bearing public sector debt. This is the conventional budget constraint derived by consolidating the public sector and the central bank. From this the dynamic behaviour of the public sector debt can be described. Equation [22] above defined the net liabilities of the public sector. Noting that the stock of government bills and bonds is held by all three domestic sectors, $B_g = B_p + B_b + B_c$, loans to the public sector are extended by both the central bank and the other banks, $L_g = L_{bg} + L_c$, and rearranging terms we rewrite [22] as:

$$D^N = [B_p + B_b + L_{bg} - M3_g] + [B_c + L_c] + E[B_g* + L_g*]. \qquad [25]$$

But the balance sheet constraint of the central bank is:

$$B_c + L_c + F_c = M0 + H_g \qquad [26]$$

where $M0 = H_p + H_b - B_c'$ is the nonborrowed monetary base, held by the private sector (both bank and nonbank). Substituting [26] into [25] we rewrite [25] as follows:

$$D^N = M0 + B_G + EB_G* - F_c = M0 + B - F_c \qquad [27]$$

where

$$B_G = B_p + B_b + L_{bg} - D_g - T_g \qquad [27a]$$

$$B_G* = B_g* + L_g* \qquad [27b]$$

$$B = B_G + EB_G*. \qquad [27c]$$

The net liabilities of the public sector have been expressed as the sum of the monetary base, $M0$, the total interest-bearing domestic debt (net of public sector deposits) held by the private sector, B_G, the total foreign debt of the public sector, B_G*, and the net foreign assets of the central bank.

The public sector's borrowing requirement can be separated into two components:

$$\text{PSBR} = P(G - TX) + i_{g,-1}B_{-1} \qquad [28]$$

where $P(G\text{-}TX)$ is the nominal value of the primary deficit (net of interest payments), $i_{g-1}\ B_{-1}$ is the value of interest payments on the total outstanding stock of public debt, defined by [27a], and is the *average* cost of public sector borrowing from the domestic private sector and abroad, expressed in domestic currency. The public sector's constraint can now be written in the familiar form:

$$P\ (G - TX) + (i_g B)_{-1} = \Delta B + \Delta M0 - \Delta F_c \qquad [29]$$

The dynamics of public sector debt and their implication for monetary controls can be analyzed from the above equation after expressing all variables as ratios to nominal GDP.

$$\text{Let } d = \text{PSBR}/P_Y Y,\ \bar{d} = P(G - TX)/P_Y Y, \qquad [30]$$

$$b = B/P_Y Y,\ mo = M0/P_Y Y,\ f_c = \text{F}_c/\text{P}_\text{Y}\text{Y}$$

Substituting [30] into [29] and solving for b we get:[3]

$$b - b_{-1} = \bar{d} + (r_g - g)_{-1}\ b_{-1} - (\pi_y + g)\ (mo - f_c)_{-1} - \Delta mo + \Delta f_c, \qquad [31]$$

where π_y is the rate of inflation, g is the growth rate of real GDP and $r_g = i_g - \pi_y$, is the real average interest rate on government debt. The equation, which describes the evolution of the debt-income ratio over time, depends on the 'pure' fiscal variable, d, the primary deficit as a ratio to GDP, the difference between the average cost of public sector debt and real GDP growth, the inflation rate and the evolution of the ratios of narrow money and central bank net foreign assets to GDP. The equation also depends on the exchange rate and its rate of change which affect both the value of b and the average real cost of borrowing. Note also that since mo is the liquidity ratio or the inverse of the income velocity of the monetary base, it is also influenced by inflation and real interest rates. Analyses of the debt accumulation process often assume that the ratios mo and f_c do not vary over time, so that $\Delta mo = \Delta f_c = 0$, and that the real rate is constant. It is important to note, especially for the purposes of the present analysis, that the latter assumption can yield misleading results for two reasons. First, the composition of government debt has been changing over time and the real interest rates on increasing components of the debt have been and will be rising as a consequence of the ongoing process of deregulation and liberalization of financial markets. Second, as the country proceeds with the gradual abolition of exchange controls, it is possible that the overall level of domestic real rates will have to rise. An analysis of the dynamics of public sector debt in Greece should not overlook the implications of the likely increase in the average real cost of government borrowing in the future.

AGGREGATE DEMAND AND PRICE-WAGE DYNAMICS

Aggregate Output

Aggregate output is demand-determined in the short run. Equilibrium in the market for domestic output requires that:

$$P_Y Y = \theta(Q)\, P[C(Y_D) + I(r, r*, K_{-1}) + G] + P_Y X(Q, Y^*) \qquad [32]$$

where $Q = EP_Y*/P_Y$.

The value of aggregate expenditures by domestic residents on domestic goods has been expressed as a fraction θ of the value of total aggregate domestic demand. The fraction is assumed to depend only on the terms of trade, Q.

Total real consumption is taken to depend on anticipated real disposable income. Real disposable income, Y^D is the sum of real income out of current production; $P_Y Y/P$ minus real taxes net of domestic transfers, $P_Y TX/P$, plus real capital gains on the initial stock of capital and investment less depreciation, Y^K, plus the real (asset) income, Y^A, on the net claims of domestic private residents on the government and the rest of the world:

$$Y^D = P_Y(Y - TX)/P + Y^K + Y^A \qquad [33]$$

This definition of real disposable income corresponds to a measure of real saving which equals the change in real household net worth. Anticipated real capital gains on all assets are assumed to equal their long run values. All real income from transitory real capital gains is assumed to be saved. The demand for gross investment by corporate firms depends on domestic and foreign real interest rates and the initial stock of capital, K_{-1}. Exports depend on the terms of trade and foreign output, $Y*$.

Equilibrium in the market for domestic output is expressed in deviations from the full-employment level Y. Approximating aggregate real consumption, net investment, exports and the share of domestic goods in total domestic spending, by linear functions of their arguments around the full-employment equilibrium and also allowing for random disturbances which are proportional to the full-employment equilibrium values (denoted with a -) of the variables they affect, we have:

$$C = \overline{C} + c'(\hat{Y}^D - \overline{Y}^D) + u_c\overline{C} \qquad c'>0$$

$$I = \delta K_{-1} + g_1(r - \overline{r}) + g_i*\,(r - \overline{r}) + u_i\delta\overline{K}, \qquad g_1, g_2*<0$$

$$X = \overline{X} + x'(Q - \overline{Q}) + u_x\overline{X}, \qquad x'>0$$

$$\theta = \overline{\theta} + \theta'(Q - \overline{Q}) + u_\Theta\overline{\theta}, \qquad [34]$$

Substituting [34] and [33] into [32], linearizing the resulting expression around the full-employment equilibrium, and employing the approximation $x - \bar{x} = \log X - \log \bar{X} = X/\bar{X}^{-1}$, yields the following log-linear specification for effective aggregate demand:

$$(41)\ y^{d} = \bar{y} + a_1[r - \bar{r}] + a_1*[r* - \bar{r}*] + a_2[q - \bar{q}] + u_d, \qquad [35]$$

where u_d is the overall random component of aggregate demand, which is equal to a multiple of a weighted average of the stochastic components of consumption, investment and exports, weighted by their respective shares in total output. The variable u_d also captures changes in exports induced by changes in foreign output. Note that y and q are now expressed in logarithms while the interest rates are expressed in percentages.

AGGREGATE PRICE AND WAGE DYNAMICS

The structural specification of the determinants of aggregate price-wage dynamics consists of the following equations:

(i) Wage adjustment The evolution of wages over time reflects the effects of two different processes: the formal indexation of wages to price-level changes and the adjustment of real wages to labour market conditions. Wage indexation has been applied in various forms to the determination of salaries and wages in the public sector since 1979. It has also been employed in the private sector to various degrees. During the period of the stabilization program (1986-1987) the same wage indexation scheme was legally imposed on wages in both the public and private sectors. A general, yet simple, specification of the wage indexation scheme used can be expressed as:

$$(w - w_{-1}) = \lambda(p^{e} - p_{-1}) \qquad [36]$$

where w and p denote respectively the logarithms of the nominal wage rate and the price level, measured by the consumer price index; p^e is the official forecast-expectation of the price level for period t formed (employed) by the authorities in period $t - 1$ when setting the nominal wages to be paid to public employees in period t. This official forecast will, of course, differ in general from the expectations of price level changes formed by the public. The indexation parameter λ reflects the specifics of the indexation mechanism employed, which have varied over time. The effective value of the indexation parameter λ has been estimated as .925 for the average wage (salary) in the public sector and in the nonfarm business sector during the years 1986-1988.

In addition to the effects of indexation, the adjustment of real wages in the short-run can be expected to respond to labour market conditions. Specifically, it is assumed that:

$$(w - w_{-1}) = \psi'(n - \bar{n}) + (\hat{p} - p_{-1}) \quad [37]$$

where n is the logarithm of the actual level of employment, $\bar{n}$ is the long-run 'full-employment' level, and $\hat{p}$ is the (logarithm of) the consumer price level anticipated by the public. The specification [37] is an expectations-adjusted wage Phillips curve expressed in terms of the deviations of employment (rather than unemployment) from its 'natural' full-employment level. It is a relation describing the dynamics of nominal wages, or of anticipated real wages ($w/\hat{p}$) in the short run; at the long run full-employment equilibrium the aggregate real wage is independent of the level of employment.

Nominal wages generally reflect the effects of both processes described by [36] and [37]. It is thus postulated that:

$$w - w_{-1} = s_i\lambda(p^e - p_{-1}) + (1 - s_i)\psi(n - \bar{n}) + (1 - s_i)(\hat{p} - p_{-1}) + u_w' \quad [38]$$

where s_i [4] measures the degree to which aggregate nominal wages are affected by formal wage indexation arrangements and u_w' is a stochastic term. If the expectations of the public and the official forecast differ only by a random element , that is $\hat{p} = p^e + u_e$, then the above equation reduces to:

$$w - w_{-1} = \alpha_1(n - \bar{n}) + \alpha_2(\hat{p} - p_{-1}) + u_w$$

$$\alpha_1 = (1 - s_i)\psi, \quad \alpha_2 = [1 - s_i(1 - \lambda)], \quad u_w = u_w' - s_i\lambda u_e. \quad [39]$$

The above relation can be expressed in terms of the deviations of aggregate real output from its full-employment level by employing the following log-linear Okun-type approximation of the productive technology:

$$y - \bar{y} = \alpha_n(n - \bar{n}) + u_n \quad [40]$$

where u_n is a stochastic term.

(ii) Price level determination and dynamics It is supposed that the target (or equilibrium) aggregate price level is determined as a mark up (μ) over total unit cost (UTC):

$$P_Y{}^T = \mu(\text{UTC}) = \mu[WN + P_R X_R + P_A X_A]/Y, \quad \mu > 1, \quad [41]$$

where P_R and P_A are the prices of imported and agricultural inputs; N, X_R and X_A are the quantities of labour, imported and agricultural inputs respectively required to produce a quantity Y of real output. It is assumed that the target price is formed on a 'standard' unit labour cost based on normal capacity utilization, that is $WN/Y = W/Y_N$, where $Y_N = (Y/N)$ denotes the 'standard' or average labour productivity. On the further assumption that the target price is formed on average ratios of real imported and agricultural inputs, we can deduce from the price equation that:

$$\Delta p_y{}^T = \mu s_L[\Delta w - \Delta y_N] + \mu s_R \Delta p_R + \mu s_A \Delta p_A + u_\mu \quad [42]$$

where

$$s_L = WN/PY, \quad s_R = P_R X_A/PY, \quad s_A = P_A X_A/PY$$

The lower-case variables $p_Y{}^T$, w, y_N, p_R, p_T denote the logarithms of the corresponding upper-case variables and $\Delta x = x - x_{-1}$.

The actual price level adjusts gradually to the target level, which implies to a first approximation that:

$$\Delta p_y = \beta \Delta p_y{}^T + (1 - \beta)\Delta p_{y,-1}, \quad 0<\beta<1 \quad [43]$$

If we express, as before, the domestic price level, P, as a geometric average of the price P_Y of the domestically produced composite good Y and the price of final imported goods in domestic currency units EP_Y* that is:

$$P = P_Y{}^\theta [EP_Y*]^{(1-\theta)},$$

then it follows that:

$$\Delta p = \theta \Delta p_y + (1 - \theta)[\Delta e + \Delta p_y *] \quad [44]$$

Equations [39] – [40], [42] and [43] imply:

$$\Delta p = \alpha_1(y - \bar{y}) + \alpha_2 \Delta \hat{p} + \alpha_3 \Delta \hat{e} + \Delta x + (1 - \beta)\theta \Delta p_{y,-1} + u_p \quad [45]$$

$$\text{where: } \alpha_1 = \kappa s_L(1 - s_i)\psi/\alpha_n, \; \alpha_2 = \kappa s_L[1 - s_i(1 - \lambda)], \; \kappa = \theta\beta\mu \quad [45a]$$

$$\alpha_3 = (1 - \theta) + \kappa(s_R + s_A) \quad [45b]$$

$$\Delta x = -\kappa s_L \Delta y_N + (1 - \theta)p* + \kappa(s_R \Delta p_R* + s_A \Delta p_A*) \quad [45c]$$

$$u_p = u_p(u_w, u_n, u_q, u_\mu). \quad [45d]$$

To complete the model, it is necessary to make hypotheses on the nature of expectations. The analysis should be based on alternative hypotheses of expectations-formulation so as to allow an assessment of their implications for the dynamic behaviour of the economy. Two obvious candidates are: (1) the hypothesis of adaptive expectations; and (2) the assumption that expectations are formed 'rationally', that is they are model-consistent and take into account the actions of the monetary and fiscal authorities. The model is closed by adding the simple dynamic relations, relating real wealth and capital to saving and investment, respectively, and a parametric specification of exchange-rate policy.

REFERENCES

Alogoskoufis, G.S. (1985) Macroeconomic Policy and Aggregate Fluctuations in a Semi-Industrialised Open Economy: Greece 1951-80, *European Economic Review*, 29, pp. 35-61.

Alogoskoufis, G.S. (1989) Macroeconomic Policy and the External Constraint in the Dependent Economy: The case of Greece, Discussion Paper, Birkbeck College, London.

Chalikias, D. (1987) Financial Reform and Problems of Monetary Policy, Papers and Lecture Series No 59, Bank of Greece, Athens.

Committee for the Study of Economic and Monetary Union (Delors Committee) (1989) *Report on Economic and Monetary Union in the European Community (Delors Report)*, Luxembourg.

Dornbusch, R. (1988) The European Monetary System, the dollar and the yen, in Giavazzi F., Micossi S. and Miller M. (eds) *The European Monetary System,* Cambridge University Press, Cambridge pp. 23-41.

Dornbush, R. 1989) Credibility, debt and unemployment: Ireland's failed stabilization, *Economic Policy*, **8**, pp. 173-209.

Fischer, S. (1983) Seigniorage and Fixed Exchange Rates in Aspe, P., Dornbusch R., and Obstfeld M. (eds) *Developing Countries in the World Financial Market,* Chicago University Press, Chicago.

Fischer, S. (1982) Seigniorage and the Case for a National Money, *Journal of Political Economy*, **90**, 2, pp. 295-313.

Friedman, M. (1971) Government Revenue from Inflation, *Journal of Political Economy,* **79**, 4, pp. 846-56.

Giavazzi, F. and **Giovannini. A.** (1989) *Limiting Exchange Rate Flexibility: The European Monetary System,* MIT Press, Cambridge, Mass.

Giavazzi, F., Micossi S. and **Miller M.** (eds) (1988) *The European Monetary System,* Cambridge University Press, Cambridge.

Giavazzi, F. and **Pagano, M.** (1988) The Advantage of Tying One's Hand: EMS Discipline and Central Bank Credibility, *European Economic Review,* **32**, 5, pp. 1055-1082.

Gros, D. (1990) 'Seigniorage and EMS Discipline', chapter 7 in this volume.

Modigliani, F. and **Papademos, L.** (1980) The Structure of Financial Markets and the Monetary Mechanism, in *Controlling Monetary Aggregates III*, Federal Reserve Bank of Boston, pp. 111-155.

Padoa-Schioppa, T. et al. (1987) *Efficiency, Stability and Equity: A Strategy for the Evolution of the Economic System of the European Community,* Oxford University Press.

Papademos, L. and **Modigliani, F.** (1983) Inflation, Financial and Fiscal Structure, and the Monetary Mechanism, *European Economic Review.* **21**, March/April, pp. 203-50.

Papademos, L. and **Rozwadowski, F.** (1983) Monetary and Credit Targets in an Open Economy, in Hodgman, D. (ed) *The Political Economy of Monetary Policy: National and International Aspects*, Federal Reserve Bank of Boston (Boston), pp. 275-306.

Sargent, T.J. and **Wallace, N.** (1981) Some Unpleasant Monetarist Arithmetic, *Federal Reserve Bank of Minneapolis Quarterly Review,* Fall, pp. 1-17.

Spaventa, L. (1987) The Growth of Public Debt: Sustainability, Fiscal Rules and Monetary Rules, *IMF Staff Papers*, **34**, 2, pp. 374-399.

Notes

1 For a more detailed description, see Chalikias (1987) and recent Annual Reports of the Bank of Greece (1986, 1987, 1988).

2 The determinants of the capital structure of corporate firms have been analysed extensively in the financial literature. The nature of the aggregate demand for debt in a macroeconomic context has been examined by Modigliani and Papademos (1980) and Papademos and Modigliani (1983).

3 Ignoring second order terms such as and letting.

4 During 1986–87, $s_i = 1$

Comment: Hans-Jürgen Vosgerau

The chapter by Lucas Papademos, which I have the privilege and the pleasure to discuss, contains an elaborate and very differentiated argument and concludes with a clear message – at least as I read it.

There are two distinct parts of the chapter: the first is a lucid description of the Greek macroeconomic performance during the last 10 years, which serves as a background for the discussion of policy problems posed by the necessity to decide when to enter the exchange rate mechanism of the EMS.

The second part is subdivided into a non-technical discussion, which is still rather vague, and the outline of a model which is designed eventually to give more precision to the necessary answers. I shall take up these two, or – if you prefer – three, parts one after the other and conclude by stating the message as I perceive it.

First, the story of the Greek overall economic performance and its policy foundations, told by a detached economist, is a masterpiece of economo-diplomatic formulation which skilfully conveys the dramatic if not tragic aspects of this part of recent Greek history. Three periods are distinguished. One (the first) from 1979 to 1985: the period of massive nominal expansion, when almost everything was meant to change – αλλαγη is the Greek word, which was used to describe the transformation of a society using among other things misplaced Keynesian instruments originally designed for completely different situations. A first correction was forced upon this development by the stabilization period – the second phase – in 1986 and 1987. Some of the nominal magnitudes were effectively corrected, almost two- thirds of the gain in real wages had to be given up and some real consequences could be reported: GNP growth took off again for a short time.

But the nation as a whole had not yet learned the lesson: politically inspired expansion resumed and resulted in the third and still unfinished period since 1988 in a macroeconomic situation which will probably get worse for some time ahead.

The author calls this a political business cycle – and rightly so, because economic instruments were used for political purposes: the winning of elections. This phenomenon has been extensively described in the public choice literature, and eventually the results must influence our thinking about institutions. In the case of a society in transition from traditional agricultural and oligarchic structures of the Greek variety there is more to it than a business cycle aspect: it is a development problem which is posed.

I reluctantly resist the temptation to comment more on this aspect. For our discussion during this conference it is nevertheless important to learn the lesson which Greece is about to learn the hard way: the lesson that institutionalized strength for those agents to whom responsibility for economic stability is assigned must not be surrendered to populism in the guise of democracy – or else a price has to be paid. The data presented by Papademos showing massive nominal wage increases and excessive public spending with the intended election results (which he mentions only in passing) and their problematic long-run consequences for the performance of the economy (weak real growth) show this clearly.

The question to be posed thus is could an effective resistance by the central bank have stopped this development? The answer to this question has significant implications not only for Greece but also for Europe as a whole, especially the design of a future system of central banks.

I now turn to the second part of the chapter, the discussion of policy problems with respect to EMS.

This discussion concentrates on what is seen to be imminently relevant for Greece today and in the next one or two years. So the problems of membership and of eventual full participation in the monetary union are neither posed nor discussed. There is also no discussion of the optimal currency syndrome, although in the case of Greece with her geographical position at the European margin and her special connections with the Balkans, and the eastern Mediterranean countries this might be an interesting question. The discussion is confined to the problem of finding the right time for full ERM participation.

The right time will have come – so the chapter says – when convergence of nominal magnitudes has sufficiently developed, i.e. when Greek inflation has come down to the maximum of ERM members. This presupposes fiscal and wage discipline, and this in turn cannot be had without what Papademos calls diplomatically success in 'tackling fundamental structural problems in the public sector' on the one hand, and reform of labour market institutions (abolition of wage indexation) on the other.

A final paragraph contains some remarks on deregulation especially in financial markets. This is under way, but far from completed. The author poses the question, whether giving up the exchange rate instrument (i.e. joining the ERM) will positively or negatively affect this development. The answer is postponed until there are results from the model, to which I shall turn in the paragraph following the next one.

Before commenting on the model I want to insert a digression, in order to make a few remarks on the complex of optimal currency areas and international factor mobility – mentioned several times during this conference – and their relation with monetary policy, especially exchange rate policy.

The mobility of Greek factors of production has always been relatively high. This is true for labour mobility as well as for capital mobility. Migration, e.g. to the USA and Australia, has been predominantly long term, while recent migration especially to the FRG has been confined to 5 – 10 years.

Capital mobility is apparently very high, and to a large degree it takes the form of non-debt-creating capital movements, consisting of emigrants' remittances and portfolio shifts of shipowners. Since the accession of Greece to the Common Market, capital movements have increasingly occurred as public international transfers via European structural, agricultural and regional funds mainly in the form of subsidies.

It is true that Greek factor mobility so far has not been confined to EC countries, but nevertheless there seems to be some chance that adjustments to exogenous shocks can be brought about by factor mobility instead of exchange rate adjustments. At any rate the whole complex deserves further attention.

The model is presented as a theoretical framework for analysis of two sets of problems:

1. The macroeconomic performance of the Greek economy;
2. The likely effects of institutional changes mainly in the financial and in the public sector on this performance.

The combination of these two aspects in a single model is an extremely ambitious undertaking. And as the model is more in the stage of a research project than of a working machine it is too early to pass judgement. In addition the time for studying it was really too short, so I have to confine my remarks to a few comments.

1. The model seems to be a combination of economically estimated parts and a general equilibrium model which will rely on informed guesses about magnitudes of parameters and coefficients. The latter part then calls for stimulations and numerical solutions. Problems with both conventional econometric models (structural breaks) and more recent numerical general equilibrium models (definition of equilibrium points in time) are known from the literature. They are possibly accumulating here.
2. The model focuses on the monetary and financial sector. Real parts are outlined only.
3. It is in its real parts short-term and demand oriented and thus neglects supply and (micro)incentive aspects. I think this is a major shortcoming. But this may reflect my personal long-term and real-economic bias.

4. Unless the model has been put to work, solved, estimated at least provisionally and in parts, one cannot say more than that the components seem to be put up reasonably and that the model deserves to be worked out and be tested.

As a referee I would recommend the research programme to be supported.

I conclude by interpreting the chapter as a telegram and stating the chapter's message as I read it. It consists of two phrases.

1. Give the central bank more strength *vis-à-vis* the public sector;
2. Give us more time to work on the research programme and perhaps cooperate with us in this research.

My personal attitude is one of great sympathy on both counters – not only and perhaps not mainly because of the special and unique role of Greece in European history but also because of these reasons.

CHAPTER TWELVE

The United Kingdom and the EMS

Michael Artis

1. Introduction

The long-standing reluctance of the UK to participate fully in the European Monetary System (EMS) is well known. To rationalize the decision to stand off from full participation a changing set of reasons has been offered by successive administrations and today there remains doubt about the substantive extent of the apparent change in approach evoked by the Madrid Summit of July 1989. This might be interpreted as a clear indication that there are deep underlying objective reasons governing the British attitude, were it not for the fact that large bodies of opinion in the UK outside the government (or, more precisely, outside prime ministerial circles) take a favourable attitude to the prospect of full participation. This suggests, rather, that the UK's continued non-participation merely represents a very particular sectional opinion.

However, this chapter does not set out to be an exercise in political speculation. Rather, it takes as its theme the question whether economic analysis can provide some convincing reasons for the British attitude. The chapter starts by reviewing the principal landmarks in the evolution of British opinion on the subject and goes on to examine more closely the particular reasons cited at the time for non-participation. It does appear that the method of conduct of British macro-economic policy at the present time is inimical to joining the EMS; we draw this out in section 3. However, this is not a fatal objection in itself, although as will be seen the problem identified may not be peculiar to the UK. In conclusion we argue that there is no fundamental, uniquely British problem dictating a continuation of previous policy towards the EMS, though there may be a need for a special adaptation of the terms of entry. Whether this makes it likely that the Madrid 'conditions' will be favourably interpreted when the time comes is left to the reader's speculative capacity.

2. The time is never ripe (right)

THE INCEPTION

The preliminary work to establish the EMS was undertaken during the period of office of the last Labour administration in the UK (that of Mr Callaghan) and (up to a point) UK officials participated fully in it, as described in Ludlow (1982). Nevertheless, the Callaghan government declined to participate in the system it had helped to create on the grounds that to do so would be prejudicial to the economy's competitiveness. What the government had in view was that a system inimical to changing the exchange rate would impose a competitive penalty on an economy prone to inflationary shocks: as Mr Callaghan put it in December 1978, membership of the EMS 'would place obligations on us that might result in unnecessary deflation and unemployment'. The history of the Labour governments 1974–79 clearly indicates the inflation-prone nature of the British system as it must have appeared at the time and the balance-of-payments crises of the period had equally given emphasis to the need to maintain competitiveness. However, it would be fair to say that there was also at the time considerable scepticism about the survival chances of the EMS. The UK had, after all, been a member of the Snake arrangement for an exceptionally short period of time and it was easy to read the fate of the Snake as a forecast for the EMS. Opposition to membership of the EMS, at least at the start, was by no means confined to Labour Party opinions; the expert witnesses testifying to the hearings of the House of Commons Expenditure Committee on the subject in November 1978 were, unusually, united in their opposition to it (see House of Commons 1979: 60–76).[1] In sum, dominant opinion in the UK foresaw the need to devalue more often than not and believed that the EMS, if successful, would tend to prevent this and so condemn the UK to an uncompetitive fate;[2] in any case, the EMS might well not succeed at all.

THE THATCHER GOVERNMENT

Upon assuming power in 1979 Mrs Thatcher's first administration had the opportunity to reverse the Labour government's decision but did not do so. The reasons for remaining aloof from the system changed, however. The new government was intent upon beating inflation by following a gradualist monetary strategy; this pre-empted the EMS option as a regime of fixed or quasi-fixed exchange rates is inconsistent with an independent monetary policy. The full statement of the new policy – the medium term financial strategy (MTFS) – when it became available in 1980 was in fact unusually forthright in its explicit unconcern for the exchange rate stating that the exchange rate 'is assumed to be determined by market forces' (see Table 12.1).

TABLE 12.1 Design of the MTFS: extracts from the financial statement and budget report

March 1980

To maintain a progressive reduction in monetary growth . . . it may be necessary to change policies in ways not reflected in the above projections . . . But there would be no question of departing from the money supply policy, which is essential to the success of any anti-inflationary strategy . . . The exchange rate is assumed to be determined by market forces.

March 1982 (i)

External or domestic developments that change the relationship between the domestic money supply and the exchange rate may . . . disturb the link between money and prices. Such changes cannot readily be taken into account in setting monetary targets. But they are a reason why the Government considers it appropriate to look at the exchange rate in monitoring domestic monetary conditions and in taking decisions about policy.

March 1982(ii)

. . . Interpretation of monetary conditions will continue to take account of all the available evidence, including the behaviour of the exchange rate.

and

. . . structural changes in financial markets, saving behaviour and the level and structure of interest rates.

March 1985

. . . Equal weight will be given to the performance of MO and £M3, which will continue to be interpreted in the light of other indicators and of monetary conditions. Significant changes in the exchange rate are also important. It will be necessary to judge the appropriate combination of monetary growth and the exchange rate needed to keep financial policy on track: there is no mechanistic formula.

. . . The Government's overriding aim will be to maintain monetary conditions consistent with a declining growth rate of money GDP and inflation. Short term interest rates will be held at the levels needed to achieve this.

March 1986

Policy will be directed at maintaining monetary conditions that will bring about a gradual reduction in the growth of money GDP over the medium term. . . .

Monetary conditions are assessed in the light of movements in narrow and broad money and the behaviour of other financial indicators, in particular the exchange rate. . . .

There is no mechanical formula for taking the exchange rate into account. . . a balance must be struck between the exchange rate and domestic monetary growth. . .

March 1987

No target for £M3 'which remains difficult to interpret. . . .'

March 1988

A declining path for money GDP growth requires a reduction in monetary growth over the medium term.

> MO has continued to be a reliable indicator of monetary conditions.
>
> While, as last year, there is no explicit target range for broad money, the assessment of monetary conditions continues to take broad money, or liquidity, into account.
>
> Interest rate decisions are based on a comprehensive assessment of monetary conditions so as to maintain downward pressure on inflation. Increases in domestic costs will not be accommodated either by monetary expansion or by exchange rate depreciation. Exchange rates play a central role in both domestic monetary decisions and international policy co-ordination.
>
> The PSBR is now assumed to be zero over the medium term: a balanced budget. This is a prudent and cautious level and can be maintained over the medium term. It also provides a clear and simple rule with a good historical pedigree.

THE EXPERIMENT IN ACTION

The experience of the Thatcher government experiment in independent monetary policy produced widespread disillusionment and a swing of both opinion and policy in favour of exchange rate targets. The paper by Artis and Currie (1981) yielded an analytical landmark, providing as it did a comparison of the merits of monetary and exchange rate targets as intermediate means of the control of inflation. This was fertile ground for a further shift of opinion in favour of full participation in the EMS.

The Thatcher experiment turned out unexpectedly in a number of respects. First, far from adhering to its 'gradualist' credentials the experiment involved, by mistake, a precipitate exchange rate appreciation and a sharp and deep economic recession. Secondly, the experiment succeeded in reducing inflation – ahead of what was being achieved in Europe – despite continuing large increases in the money supply, as measured in the MTFS by a broad money concept, £M3.

The principal causes of the surprise seem to be threefold: first, there was an autonomous shift (increase) in the demand for (broad) money; second, there was the impact of the second Organization of Petroleum Exporting Countries (OPEC) oil shock on the exchange rate as the UK became self-sufficient in oil at this time; third, there was a lack of understanding of the effects ('overshooting') on the current exchange rate of perceptions that policy was and would remain 'tough'.

The instability in the demand for money was particularly critical because an important ingredient in the new policy was its self-declared precommitment to a path of monetary deceleration. Because of this, to have executed a U-turn immediately after announcing the strategy would have been received as a first order defeat for the programme. Thus the degree of flexibility that might have been expected of the policy was not present.

Nevertheless, the pressures were so strong that the stringency of policy was relaxed[3] and the policy itself reformulated so as to give greater room to the exchange rate in diagnosing the need for monetary correction; this was practised before it was announced but it was made very clear in the restatement of the MTFS in 1982. Tables 12.1 and 12.2 illustrate this change, together with the accompanying de-emphasis of

TABLE 12.2: Content of the MTFS

	Four-year forward ranges quoted (1)
March 1980	£M3:PSBR
March 1981	£M3: PSBR
March 1982	£M3: M1: PSL2:PSBR (2)
March 1983	£M3: M1: PSL2: PSBR
March 1984	£M3: MO: PSBR
March 1985	£M3: MO: money GDP: PSBR
March 1986	MO: money GDP: PSBR: £M3
March 1987	MO: money GDP: PSBR (3)
March 1988	MO: money GDP; PSBR (zero) (4)

Notes: (1) Target ranges except as noted below, PSBR as % GDP; (2) broad medium term objective; (3) illustrative ranges for 1987/88 on; (4) illustrative ranges for 1988/89 on.

targets for the broad monetary aggregate £M3, the subsequent de-emphasis of monetary targets altogether and their replacement by targets for nominal gross domestic product (GDP) with narrow money as an indicator variable. Several observers (e.g. Pliatzky, 1989) have complained that the MTFS offends the Trade Descriptions Act by describing as the same thing policies of quite different types; this point aside, however, it also seems clear that the most recent formal expression of the MTFS has entirely failed to capture the attention of informed observers. Rather, the dominant perception of current monetary policy is that policy actions focus on the control of interest rates with inflation as a direct target and the exchange rate as an intermediate one (we return to this formulation later). In 1987, following the Louvre Accord, the Chancellor of the Exchequer hardened the concern for the exchange rate into a policy of shadowing the Deutschmark with a ceiling of 3 DM to the £. Figure 12.1 illustrates the force of this policy.

This phase came to an end, amid recriminations, in February 1988 when the exchange rate was allowed to rise strongly and there was a return to a more pragmatic policy stance, one in which the exchange rate was certainly still important but not so privileged as it had been in the Louvre episode. The immediate cause of the recriminations is now recognized as the 'excess credibility' problem. During the period in which the policy of shadowing the DM was pursued there were signs of a gathering inflationary pressure (itself due to earlier stimulatory policies). But to prevent the exchange rate from rising beyond the unofficial ceiling of 3 DM required interest rates to be held down at a time when, for counter-inflationary reasons, a rise (and/or a rise in the exchange rate) seemed to be the required policy response.

There has therefore been a substantial evolution of policy in the UK. Starting from the pursuit of monetary targets without regard for the exchange rate through a 180 degree U- turn the opposite pole was reached during the 1987/88 phase of DM

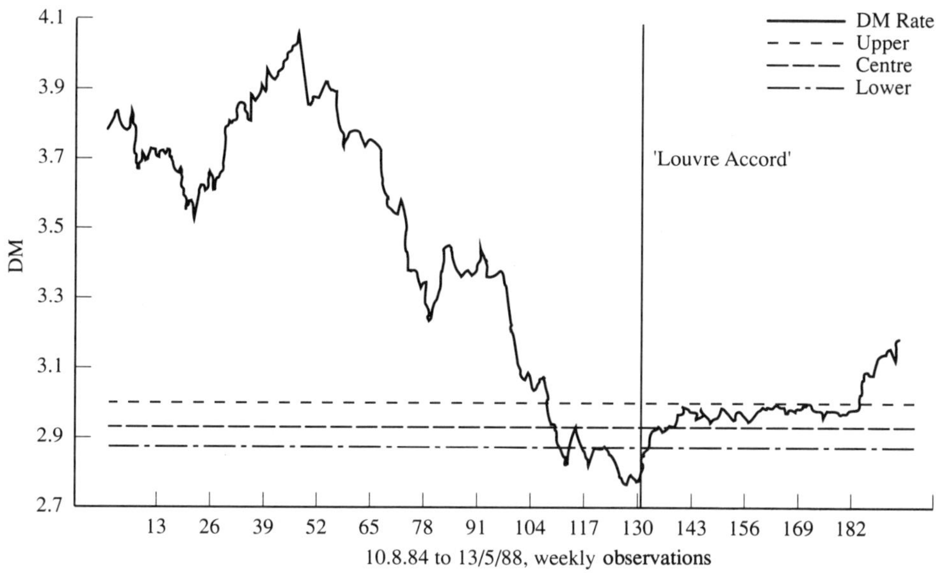

FIG . 12.1 Sterling/DM rate

'shadowing'. That phase might have led on, in other circumstances, to full participation in the EMS. In fact it was an experience which led to a restatement of monetary policy in which the interest rate is used to realize, directly, an objective for inflation, responding to the exchange rate in the light of this target.

ATTITUDES TO THE EMS

The policy evolution described above could not help but lead to a reappraisal of British attitudes to the EMS given the parallel and successful evolution of the EMS itself.

THE HOUSE OF LORDS REPORT

A report prepared by a committee of the House of Lords in 1983 was an important early marker of this process of reappraisal. That report concluded that the UK should seek 'early, though not necessarily immediate' entry into the full EMS (House of Lords 1983: xxiv). Important evidence provided to the committee included that of Neils Thygesen. Thygesen emphasized that the experience of the EMS to date provided evidence of considerable flexibility, in contrast to the rigidity which had been apprehended by its critics in the UK, while at the same time the system produced greater stability in exchange rates than might otherwise have come about. Thygesen also anticipated a future 'hardening' of the system, much as has in fact eventuated. This achievement (and the prognosis) appealed to the committee which, however, noted reservations about full UK membership of the system in two respects: first, the problem of oil; second, the prospect of speculation in what would be a 'bipolar' (London–Frankfurt) system. At this time it was only just becoming possible to show that the EMS had exerted a stabilizing effect on exchange rates (Ungerer *et al.* 1983)– Sam Brittain in a famous phrase had been led by the system's flexibility in its early phase of operations to characterize it dismissively as 'a mere crawling peg' (Financial Times, 24 March 1983). Nevertheless, by contrast with recent *British* experience, there was an attractive degree of exchange rate stability. Moreover, the system had survived, albeit at the cost of incurring Sam Brittain's withering description; and it became clearer with the passage of time that this first phase of accommodating flexibility was the price of a survival which enabled the system thereafter to become a harder counter-inflationary discipline.

The House of Lords (1983) report presaged a considerable development of interest in the EMS within the UK. Two further parliamentary reports were to come, one each from the House of Commons (1985) and the House of Lords (1988) which were addressed directly to the issue, while a number of other investigations by the influential House of Commons Treasury and Civil Service Committee (e.g. the First Report 1981–82 and the Fifth Report 1983–84 and 1984–85) devoted a substantial amount of time to the EMS question. The policy evolution towards an exchange rate target provided a natural trigger: it was easy to see that such a target would be more credible as part of an EMS commitment than as a go-it-alone option. The reduction of inflation in Europe at large brought attention to the possible benefits of using the EMS as a beneficial framework for counter-inflationary policies, reducing the costs of controlling inflation. The argument has been set in terms of the value of the added credibility given by a commitment to the EMS (which is in effect a commitment to a peg against a low inflation currency, the DM)[4] and has been given added strength by reason of the continued instability in the principal monetary aggregates. Thus, Currie and Dicks (1989) have argued that renewing the MTFS is an unconvincing option in view of its past history of changing content in the light of the unstable behaviour of the monetary aggregates (see Tables 12.1 and 12.2 again), leaving membership of the EMS as the only way of asserting a credible precommitment to a tough monetary policy. Implicitly, they rate the current policy of using interest rates to target inflation directly as lacking in precommitment value.

At the same time, the benefits of the EMS for exchange rate stability became ever better established. Many studies are now available to show that intra-EMS exchange rates have been stabilized by the EMS;[5] there is some dispute in respect of the effect of the EMS on member countries' overall effective exchange rates. It is perfectly possible that a country could find that in stabilizing its EMS (mainly DM) rate it destabilizes its dollar rate with ambiguous effect for its overall effective rate.[6] This is particularly important for the UK, the composition of its effective rate being more heavily weighted towards the dollar and less heavily weighted towards the DM than that of any other EMS country.[7] However, trade patterns have changed markedly

TABLE 12.3: Effective index weights (%)

	Old index				New index			
	$	DM	ERM	£	$	DM	ERM	£
UK	24.6	14.1	41.6	–	20.4	20.1	51.1	–
Belgium	16.2	23.2	62.0	2.1	9.2	27.6	65.8	10.1
Denmark	24.0	11.2	35.3	7.1	9.1	24.7	44.7	11.8
France	22.7	20.1	46.0	4.1	12.1	27.4	57.2	10.1
FRG	21.6	–	41.7	4.8	13.4	–	46.7	10.9
Italy	20.7	27.8	48.5	5.1	11.6	27.6	57.6	9.3
Netherlands	19.3	20.2	54.6	3.2	10.2	31.0	62.4	10.9

Note: The figures show the weight in the index, for any country, of the currencies listed. ERM is the sum of the weights of the ERM currencies (excluding Spain). The basis of the new and old indices is explained in the source references. In the new index, introduced in November 1988, Australia was dropped from the list of countries involved.

Source: Quarterly Bulletin of the Bank of England, March 1981 and November 1988.

for the UK, as Table 12.3 shows. The data in Table 12.3 show the proportionate weights in the effective rate indices of the dollar, DM, the ERM currencies as a whole and sterling, for the UK and for the exchange rate mechanism (ERM) countries individually (excluding Spain). As can be seen, the proportionate weight of the dollar in the UK index has fallen between the old and the new indices[8] and that of the DM and the ERM currencies has risen sharply. Correspondingly, the weight of sterling for the ERM countries has risen along with the weight of the ERM currencies; that of the dollar has fallen sharply. As a result, the dollar has become relatively more important for the UK than for ERM members than it was, though the weight of ERM currencies in the UK index now exceeds 50 per cent. According to results obtained by Fratianni (1988) the operation of the system has in fact produced a net destabilizing effect on overall effective rates for most countries, though Artis and Taylor (1989), using different techniques, contradict this – albeit they find evidence of a less strong stabilizing effect on overall effective than on intra-EMS exchange rates.[9]

For these reasons, opinion at large in the UK has been increasingly receptive to the prospect of full participation in the system. Nevertheless, the dominant view in the British government has remained opposed. The change of formal approach at the Madrid Summit in July from the previous unspecific 'when the time is ripe' conditional agreement to one in which explicit conditions have been laid down appears highly significant at some levels.[10] But while there is a clear sense that a concession was made, there has been no sense of a genuine shift in opinion; still less any sign of even qualified enthusiasm. It might be pointed out that there is little available by way of reasoned reservation either. However, the book by Alan Walters, *Britain's Economic Renaissance* (Walters 1986), does contain some reasoned reservations and as his advice is influential with the Prime Minister it seems fair to assume that it may be consulted as an authoritative source to explain British government attitudes.

3. Reservations

The principal points of reservation mentioned either in official reports (including reports of parliamentary committees) or in Professor Walters's book are the following:

1. The vulnerability of sterling to oil price movements.
2. The prospect of speculation in a bi-polar system.
3. The loss of monetary independence of the EMS.
4. The exchange control 'logic' of the EMS;
5. The insufficiency of instruments to control competitiveness inside the EMS.
6. The insufficiency of instruments to control inflation inside the EMS.

This is not an exhaustive list of reservations, but includes the principal serious and non-ephemeral ones; an associated issue – not so much a reservation as a comment on the terms of entry – concerns the rate at which to join and the width of the band. This we deal with in an ensuing section of the chapter.

OIL

The problem posed by the 'petrocurrency' status of sterling was twofold: normative and positive. First, 'permanent' changes in oil prices ought to be allowed to affect the sterling exchange rate in the light of the UK's self-sufficient position. (HM Treasury calculations suggested, as of 1985, an elasticity of the equilibrium sterling effective exchange rate to the oil price of about 0.3, see House of Commons 1985, HMT Evidence: 41.) There was a perception that this adjustment might not be conceded inside the EMS. The positive problem perceived was that oil-price shocks would, willy-nilly, blow the system apart if sterling was not able to be revalued within it. In retrospect it may seem that both these concerns were overdone. Indeed, outside the EMS, sterling was vulnerable to an 'excess' oil-price response, which membership of the EMS might have removed (this point was made in House of Lords 1983).

SPECULATION

The problem of speculation was addressed more generally, e.g. in House of Lords (1983). The perception was that as sterling still retained some status as a vehicle currency, the potential for destabilizing speculative shifts of funds between sterling and the DM was bigger than the potential for such shifts between, say, the French franc or the lira and the DM; in any case these currencies were protected by exchange controls. Continental observers exhibited some doubts about the capacity of sterling to adhere to the system without the benefit of such controls (see e.g. the evidence given by Melitz to the House of Commons 1985 inquiry).

The perception that sterling membership of the system might pose special problems of the management of speculation may have been reduced in the light of the system's increased capacity (since the Basle-Nyborg Agreement) to counter speculation and the discovery by the UK Chancellor of the Exchequer of the 'paradigm' EMS realignment – the changing of the central rate and bands without affecting the market rate.[11] Nevertheless, it remains a prominent consideration, recently cited by the Bank of England in its evidence to the 1988 House of Lords enquiry and again in the governor's speech reprinted in Bank of England (1989). The problem of speculation could be largely solved by sufficient cooperation but this raises the third objection, the key reservation of principle of the Thatcher government.

LOSS OF SOVEREIGNTY

Adherence to a fixed, or quasi-fixed exchange rate system makes a country's money supply and interest rate endogenous to that goal. Monetary policy cannot therefore be used to pursue any other policy goal. Although this is true, it seems fair to say that hitherto the proponents of EMS membership for the UK have so far had the better of the argument. In the kind of 'natural rate' model taken as standard in much policy discussion these days, the only virtue of an independent monetary policy (and hence, a floating exchange rate regime) is the ability to 'choose' a different inflation rate. But this choice seems a negligible advantage when the inflation rate apparently offered by EMS membership is so low and steady. Thus, broadly speaking, the point of the reservation has been accepted in logic but turned on its head in practice.

THE EXCHANGE CONTROL 'LOGIC' OF THE EMS

It is notable, however, that until the recent trend towards the removal of exchange controls the existing member countries of the EMS did not feel too strongly the constraint upon their monetary independence. Rightly so, for exchange controls provide an added 'degree of freedom' enabling a country to recover a degree of monetary autonomy.[12] Not accidentally, it is with the removal of these controls that the movement towards economic and monetary union (EMU) has been instigated, a movement which promises the recovery of a degree of sovereignty by sharing in collective decision-making.

Short of the EMU solution, however, it is not difficult to appreciate why the EMS can be thought of (Walters 1986) as predisposed towards exchange controls.[13] These yield monetary independence as well as serving a counter-speculative function. Since British policy abolished exchange controls in 1979 there was no inclination to be forced to adopt them again. (None of the proponents of EMS entry for the UK has argued for this, it might be noted.)

COMPETITIVENESS: AN INSUFFICIENCY OF INSTRUMENTS

This reservation is a repetition, essentially, of the Callaghan government's viewpoint, and also can be found, sharply expressed, in the House of Commons 1985. The argument is that nominal exchange rate variation is essential to control competitiveness and that this control would be jeopardized by membership of the EMS. The counter-inflationary objectives of EMS lend support to this view: for, with these objectives in mind, EMS policy has been to ensure that exchange rate realignments 'under-index' the exchange rate as a means of exerting a discipline on inflation. Over the long term such a policy, in the face of persistent country-specific inflation shocks simply forces the real rates of exchange cumulatively away from equilibrium. There is some evidence that this is in fact what has happened: Artis and Taylor (1989) tested the intra-EMS bilateral-DM real exchange rates for evidence of 'mean reversion'. In other words, they looked to see whether or not real exchange rates appeared to be self-stabilizing. Their finding was negative: so far, real exchange rates seem to be drifting away from equilibrium. The competitiveness reservation has not so far re-established itself as a central objection, however, for two reasons. First, the real sterling exchange rate has fluctuated enormously during the late 1970s and 1980s outside the EMS. It seems inconceivable that it could have become as sharply misaligned had sterling been in the exchange rate mechanism of the EMS. Second, the efficacy of nominal exchange rate adjustment for lasting real rate adjustment is now widely questioned: the effects appear to be short term, though not unimportant.

INFLATION CONTROL: AN INSUFFICIENCY OF INSTRUMENTS

Perhaps more surprising at first sight is the objection that membership of the EMS would not yield the best available framework for beating inflation. But this reservation appears in Walters (1986) and is in fact now more than ever of significance in the UK.

In Walters (1986) the argument is put as follows: in a fixed exchange rate system, nominal rates of interest must be the same in every participating country. Then, a country experiencing a positive inflationary shock will find that its real rate of interest falls while a country experiencing a negative shock will experience a rise in its real rate. But these movements are contrary to the direction of adjustment required for a stabilizing reaction. The argument belies the EMS in that it ignores the

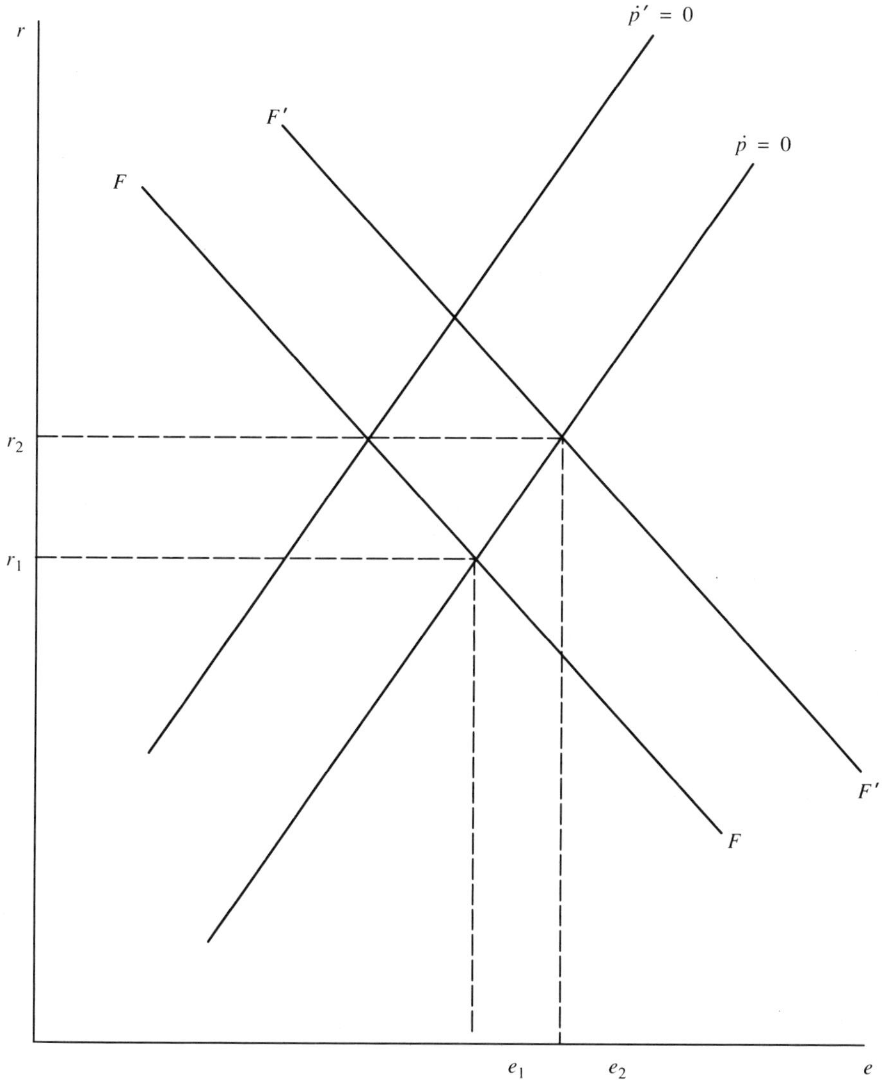

FIG 12.1 Diagram 1 (depreciation ⟶)

possibility that a currency could be expected to fall (or rise) within the bands, but it is apposite for the case where the market invests the current exchange rate with credibility whether this be at the band limits or at an intermediate position.

In current policy conditions in the UK the argument can be restated as follows. There are two types of policy available in principle, fiscal and monetary; however, government spending is determined by medium term planning considerations having nothing to do with inflation while tax rates can only be changed once a year in one (downward) direction. This is a political constraint, but a constraint just the same. Monetary policy consists in changing the rate of interest with a view to hitting demand and the exchange rate, impacting on inflation. Fig. 12.1 (due to Walter Eltis) illustrates the argument. Here $\dot{p} = 0$ is the locus of zero inflation combinations of the rate of interest and the exchange rate, and *FF* is a foreign exchange market line relating the rate of interest and the exchange rate. If *FF* should shift, say to *F′F′*, then the rate of interest should be increased from r_1 to r_2 to offset the inflationary effect of the depreciation as the exchange rate depreciates from e_1 to e_2. Suppose now that $p = 0$ shifts, say to $p' = 0$. Then, for a given exchange rate, the rate of interest must be increased to keep inflation down. This cannot happen if the rate of interest is constrained to stay the same. The argument relies on less than perfect goods market integration (for in that case an exchange rate peg would be sufficient inflation control and $p' = 0$ would be vertical) and on the absence of an alternative stabilization tool. The former is a reasonable assumption but the latter is an imposed political constraint which could be removed: fiscal policy could be used if necessary to supply the counter-inflationary pressure required.

The argument is, however, important not just for the UK but for any other EMS country which may now experience an insufficiency of policy instruments to control inflation: once again, countries deploying measures of exchange control were in effect giving themselves an additional policy instrument which, under the provisions of 1992, they are constrained to give up.[14]

4. The rate upon entry

Evidently some of the reservations mentioned are less important now than they were at the time they were first voiced. In other cases, perception of the scope for policy has changed so that former reservations are no longer so important. A problem that is recurrent, however, is that of the 'appropriate rate upon entry'. This problem is particularly important in current circumstances. There is a general perception that sterling is overvalued at the moment. For example, sterling was some 16 per cent above its 'fundamental equilibrium level' in mid-1988, as calculated by Barrell and Wren-Lewis (1989). Since part of the point of joining would be to ensure a favourable climate for counter-inflationary policy the option of 'arranging' a prior devaluation does not seem very sensible. It might be possible to anticipate an early realignment, but the objection to this is that it would be undesirable from the viewpoint of credibility even if it was allowed. A solution is to join at the top of the band, i.e. with the central rate some way below the market rate.[15] This option might be extended to include a wider band, not only to accommodate a larger adjustment but also because this can be advocated as a suitable counter-speculative modification. With a wider band, speculative movements could be absorbed more frequently in a rate adjustment and would less often require an interest rate adjustment which might not be desirable on domestic grounds.[16]

5. Conclusions

The UK has remained aloof from full participation in the EMS so far, for a mix of reasons. One of these, the 'petro-currency' reservation, has clearly waned in significance. Of the remainder, the speculative vulnerability of sterling in an EMS framework, if less strongly apprehended than was the case before Nyborg, nevertheless remains a plausible apprehension. Wider bands might be a suitable modification. The objection from loss of control over competitiveness suffers from comparing EMS membership with a hypothetical regime itself sharply different from what the UK has actually experienced. The other reservations hang together. Adherence to the EMS would undermine monetary sovereignty and failing solution by EMU or by exchange control, would compromise UK counter-inflationary policy as at present practised. However, there is a solution to this, so the reservation is not ultimately fundamental.

Notes

1. This unusual display of unity among economists provoked comment from the committee's chairman at the time, as Ludlow (1982) notes. However, the reasoning offered for the common opinion was far from uniform.
2. There was a recrudescence of this view much later in House of Commons (1985), by which time, however, it had become unrepresentative of mainstream opinion.
3. Walters (1986) notes how evidence from Niehans was critical in this regard. Niehans's evidence consisted in showing that measures of narrow money indicated that policy had been very harsh – contrary to the impression generated by the over-target expansion of broad money. (For those who prefer to regard narrow money as an endogenous variable, Niehans's figures were simply another way of showing that the UK had entered a severe recession.)
4. In a variant of this argument de Grauwe (1989) has argued that while the 'shdort sharp shock' may provide credibility more quickly, because of the excess appreciation of the exchange rate, membership of the EMS may make it harder to lose credibility, once it has been earned. It must be admitted that the facts do not appear to strongly support the value of the system as a counter-inflationary device – see Artis and Nachane (1989), De Grauwe (1989), Giavazzi and Pagano (1988).
5. Representative of the predominant approach is Ungerer *et al.* (1986).
6. This is, after all, simply the reverse side of the interest of the Federal Republic of Germany (FRG) in promoting an EMS in order to dilute the vulnerability of the DM to swings of opinion about the dollar.
7. These statements refer to the composition of the IMF's MERM- weighted effective rate indices.
8. The old index, based on 1977 total trade flows was replaced by the new one, based on 1980 manufacturing trade flows, in November 1988. The change in trade flow

definition is responsible for part of the difference shown between the old and new indices.

9. Some opponents of EMS membership also stress the possibility of another 'volatility transfer', from exchange rates to interest rates; however, Artis and Taylor (1987) find that EMS experience (which, however, may be dependent on the presence of capital exchange controls) does not confirm any such transfer.

10. These conditions are that, before entry: (a) there should be a lower inflation rate in the UK; (b) exchange controls within the EMS should have been removed; (c) sufficient progress should have been made towards the single EC market; (d) financial services should be liberalized; (d) there should be agreement on competition policy.

11. Peter Kenen (1988) has computed that some 70 per cent of EMS currency realignments have been of this type. The UK Chancellor advertised the paradigm to wider circles in his address to the International Monetary Fund in September 1987.

12. The exchange controls in force in Italy and France have been outward-looking, yielding an opportunity to maintain lower interest rates than otherwise would have been required.

13. See also, again, Melitz's observations on the question in House of Commons (1985).

14. Currie and Dicks (1989) treat this difficulty as one only of transition. It is certainly true that the problem illustrated is most acute for a high-inflation country like the UK contemplating a transition to low inflation inside the EMS. But the argument is just as true for inflationary shocks arising in an intially low- inflation context.

15. Note that the solution of joining at the top of the band is feasible only if the 'excess credibility' problem has already been solved: otherwise, the expected downward drift will not materialize and counter-inflationary policy will be weakened as interest rates are reduced to prevent the rate rising through the top of the band.

16. Against this, if exchange rate expectations are extrapolative it may never be useful to exploit a wider band.

References

Artis, M. J. and **Currie, D. A., (1981)** Monetary and exchange rate targets**,** *Oxford Economic Papers*, July, **33**, pp. 176–200.

Artis, M. J. and **Nachane, D.** (1990) Wages and prices in Europe: a test of the German leadership thesis, *Weltwirtschaftliches Archiv*, March, **126**, pp. 59–77.

Artis, M. J. and **Taylor, M. P.** (1989) The achievements of the European Monetary System, *Economic and Social Review*, **20**, January, pp. 121–45.

Bank of England (1989) The future of monetary arrangements in Europe, *Quarterly Bulletin of the Bank of England*, August, pp. 368–77.

Barrell, R. and **Wren-Lewis, S.** (1989) Fundamental equilibrium exchange rates for the G7, *CEPR Discussion Papers*, No. 323.

Currie, D. and **Dicks, G.** (1989) The MTFS or the EMS: which way for credible monetary policy, *LBS Economic Outlook*, June, pp. 12–24.

De Grauwe, P. (1989) The cost of disinflation and the European Monetary System, *CEPR Discussion Paper*, No. 326.

Fratianni, M. (1988) The European Monetary System: how well has it worked?, paper presented to a Cato Institute Conference, February, Washington D.C.

Giavazzi, F. and **Pagano, M.** (1989) The advantage of tying one's hands: EMS discipline and central bank credibility, *European Economic Review*, **32**, pp. 1055–82.

House of Commons (1979) *The European Monetary System, Report of the Expenditure Committee, Session 1978–79.*

House of Commons (1985) *The European Monetary System*, 13th Report from the Treasury and Civil Service Committee and Evidence.

House of Lords (1983) European Monetary System, *Report of the Select Committee on the European Communities*, 5th Report 1983–84.

House of Lords (1988) European financial area, *Report of the Select Committee on the European Communities*, 21st Report, 1987–88.

Kenen, P. B. (1988) *Managing Exchange Rates*, Routledge/Royal Institute of International Affairs, London.

Ludlow, P. (1982) *The Making of the European Monetary System*, Butterworths, London.

Pliatsky, L. (1989) *The Treasury Under Mrs Thatcher*, Blackwell, Oxford.

Ungerer, H., Evans, O. and **Nyberg, P.** (1983) The European Monetary System: the experience, 1979–82, *IMF Occasional Papers*, **19**, May.

Ungerer, H., Evans, O., Mayer, T. and **Young P.** (1986) The European Monetary System: recent developments', *IMF Occasional Papers*, **48**, December.

Walters, A. A. (1986) *Britain's Economic Renaissance*, Oxford University Press, Oxford.

Comment: Jean-Jacques Rey

Having read Professor Artis's chapter, I could not resist the temptation to imagine a resurrected Madame de Sévigné writing to Madame de Grignan something like this:

> My dear daughter, you know how most people feel in London today, yet the King still feels otherwise. You must be dying to hear how it is fashionable to argue the case in the Court these days. As you know, the wisdom changes while the ruling remains. The arguments are more than ripe, it is just the time that isn't. . . .

The point is that, like Madame de Sévigné's letters, Professor Artis's chapter is an in-depth analysis, delivered in a most condensed format. And the more the author seems to step back behind the story he tells, the more he succeeds in conveying his message.

In commenting on Professor Artis's contribution, I would like to make four points. None of them is intended to challenge the author's findings. I would like to take a slightly different approach to the subject-matter, first by presenting an outsider's view – I mean as an outsider to the UK – and second, by keeping at some distance of pure economic analysis though, like Professor Artis, I do not want to embark on an exercise in political speculation.

First, let me observe that the debate on the UK and the ERM has been carried along in terms of both economic analysis and political science. This is quite normal and would apply for any country where a major change in exchange rate management were subjected to public discussion before it occurs. However, in this particular case, I see a danger that, as time goes by, the weight of arguments might shift from sound economic judgement to the plain tactics of the political arena. I would like to express the hope that when sterling eventually joins the ERM, this does reflect a healthy balance of economic conviction and broadly based political consensus, rather than the outcome of a major showdown between political forces, with economists left to watch the game.

There is an international dimension to this preoccupation since the discussion goes on not only in the UK but also throughout the Community. This leads me to my second comment: I sometimes wonder if it is well advised to put a lot of pressure from outside on our British friends to cross the bridge.

As more countries join the ERM, it is important that the act of joining be perceived by the newcomers as a genuine systemic progress undertaken in their own lasting interest. The Spanish move was unambiguous in this respect and I welcome this. Surely, we want sterling in, but we want the British on the side of the defenders of the system for its merits as an engine for stability, both internal and external, and not merely as a party having made a concession to the majority or to the *acquis communautaire*. I think it will be important to keep this in mind now that adherence to the ERM has been made a major ingredient of the first stage towards EMU. The ERM itself would not gain from adding a half-hearted country to its participants.

Does this mean that we should be satisfied with the present state of affairs and that outsiders should abstain from expressing any views as to sterling exchange rate management? That is going too far, and here is my third point.

The Artis chapter provides illuminating evidence of the changes in the content of the MTFS as well as in the British authorities' views on the exchange rate over the last 10 years. Although they have always stopped short of pegging the rate for sterling, clearly these changes have been of interest and of some consequence for other countries. These changes now escape the requirement for mutual agreement in the Community since they do not involve a formal alignment or realignment of central rates. They are subject to IMF surveillance under Article IV of the Articles of Agreement, but little has been done by the IMF to give substance to that surveillance.

While I am not advocating strong pressure on the UK for the entry of sterling in the ERM, the present framework according to which sterling is neither pegged, nor freely floating, nor subjected to any specific Community consensus-building procedure should also be regarded as less than satisfactory.

If it is argued that sterling should not take part in the ERM because (a) sovereignty over monetary policy must be retained, (b) monetary policy is the only available weapon against inflation and (c) the exchange rate must be allowed to appreciate in response to interest rate differentials, one may be led to interpret this as saying that sovereignty would allow the UK to export its own inflation to neighbouring countries. This is not an issue for the time being, but the problem remains in principle.

The conclusion that may be drawn is that while we should avoid building up alternatives to the ERM, there might be a case for setting up a transitory framework, based perhaps on some form of target zones, which would ensure that mutual agreement on exchange rate patterns and policies is a component of EMS even for countries whose currencies still remain outside the ERM. Such an arrangement could perhaps pioneer an international monetary system, where a greater degree of consensus on exchange rate formation would help stem the tide towards creeping protectionism.

My last comment will be to fully endorse the point made by Artis about the need for available instruments given the objectives to be pursued. If one advocates freedom for the movement of goods, services and capital, a high priority for internal stability and an internationally cooperative climate, then it is not enough, indeed, to allocate monetary policy as the sole instrument to combine all aims. Monetary policy should not be overburdened. Rather, there is a strong case for moving all the way to a one-currency area and drop 'local' sovereignty rather than individual freedom, price stability or peace between nations. But that is another hurdle, I assume, for another conference.

CHAPTER THIRTEEN

Panel discussion: from the EMS to the EMU

Contribution by Niels Thygesen: Benefits and costs of an economic and monetary union relative to EMS

This chapter addresses the likely benefits and costs of a full economic and monetary union (EMU) relative to the European Monetary System (EMS) as it presently functions. The *Delors Report* was conspicuously silent on such an assessment of benefits and costs. The committee simply took the objective of EMU as given because of its mandate, so what I have to say on this subject lies strictly outside the agreed framework of the *Delors Report*.

An undertaking of this kind is necessary, but hazardous. There is no fundamental dissatisfaction with the present working of the EMS. Indeed, one may see the debate on EMU as a tribute to the past success of the stepping-stone of the EMS and ask why it is necessary to take explicit steps towards fixing exchange rates permanently and replacing national currencies by a single currency. The alternative of moving *de facto* towards ever more stable exchange rates might seem preferable.

Chapter 1 in this volume (Thygesen 1990), discusses various arguments as to why it is necessary to move beyond voluntary coordination to a more mandatory form of coordination in the second and third stages of the Delors process and, particularly, how it might be done. Here I shall not resume my discussion of why an institutional approach appears superior to purely voluntary coordination. It is only necessary to recall the two main danger elements in continued reliance on the present mechanisms. First, the present workings of the EMS may be inadequate in the more symmetrical world which is emerging. Financial competitiveness among national currencies within the system, enhanced by the credibility effects of a long period of fully stable exchange rates, has reshuffled the roles of countries within the system. It is now more necessary to make joint assessments of policy and possibly to take joint actions. Secondly, the entry of new members may require a firmer structure if the present stability features are to be preserved. These two danger elements raise doubt whether the option of persisting in the present framework is available. There is no need to dramatize this point, though obviously to those who believe the present system will become unstable that is a decisive argument in favour of moving explicitly towards EMU. I not only wish to underline the risks of status quo, but subsequently to base my argument mainly on a comparison of the present EMS and full EMU, assuming both to be sufficiently stable to be feasible.

There is an unfortunate tendency for discussions of benefits and costs of EMU to be monopolized by those who employ largely political arguments. There are indeed significant political arguments to be made: a single currency is an important political step like the removal of physical frontiers between the participating countries; monetary identity and influence in the global system may require that the EMS participants opt for full EMU and a single currency; and there is a linkage to the 1992 programme and a need to consolidate that by a further bold initiative. These arguments are advanced primarily by European politicians who are in favour of EMU, though also increasingly by European industry. I take note here of the conclusion in Chapter 3 of this volume (Krugman 1990), namely that the ultimate argument in favour of EMU may be political. Nevertheless, there are several more technical points on which economists ought to concentrate in order to clarify the choice. EMU and a single currency deserve to be assessed on their own merits rather than for their political symbolism.

1. Costs of giving up exchange rates as a policy instrument

Open-economy macroeconomics suggests a general answer why governments find it useful to retain separate currencies and a possibility of changing their relative prices: realignments become desirable if the economies for which governments are held to be responsible to their electorate experience differentiated shocks. These shocks may be external or domestic in origin; a major energy price hike or a domestic cost explosion are examples that come readily to mind. A government that has experienced such a shock to its economy would come to regret a precommitment to keep the exchange rate fixed, since accommodation of a shock through a realignment may entail lower costs of adjustment than the alternative of prolonged adjustment of relative national price levels. If European governments anticipated that important differentiated shocks were likely to occur in the future regardless of the exchange rate regime, they would indeed be taking a serious risk by committing themselves to maintaining completely fixed exchange rates. The emerging acceptance of EMU as an objective is, above all, an implicit recognition by most European Community (EC) governments that the likelihood of large and nationally differentiated shocks is fading.

Even if this recognition is widely shared, governments are correct in perceiving that their ability to conduct activist stabilization policies is constrained by irrevocably fixing exchange rates. Moreover, modern macroeconomic theory points out that since monetary expansion and devaluation are at their most effective when they are the least expected, the short-term rewards for breaking the fixed exchange rate commitment could be seen as rising for a time after the declaration of an intention to keep the exchange rate irrevocably fixed.

These arguments suggest that governments may have, or discover, incentives to opt out, if they can, in order to pursue more efficiently their macroeconomic objectives. For one major category of shocks to a participating economy – changes in domestic economic policy that make the fixed exchange rate unsustainable – there is no independence of the exchange rate regime. In an EMU policy shocks would have to be constrained to those that do not threaten to upset fixed rates. Governments that see *a priori* the remaining scope of action as too narrow will perceive a likely cost of joining EMU. Could that cost be upset by benefits?

A government which explicitly wants to retain freedom to realign its exchange rate pays a price. Agents in the national markets for goods, labour and financial assets will assume that this freedom of manoeuvre will occasionally be used. They will tend, therefore, to set a more rapid rate of increase of prices and costs and to add a risk premium to the required return on assets denominated in that currency. Higher inflationary expectations would raise actual inflation and nominal interest rates. If the exchange rate in fact remains fixed, there will be temporarily higher inflation and lower output than in the situation where the commitment to fixity is seen as truly irrevocable. If the currency is in fact devalued, the critical perceptions of private economic agents will have been borne out and a non-inflationary reputation will be that much harder to build up in the future. The EMS experience has shown that markets have a very long memory. The pace with which convergence in inflationary expectations and interest rates takes place will depend critically on the extent to which firms, households, labour unions and other economic agents are convinced that the decision to freeze exchange rates cannot be reversed. There is no substitute for the final state of EMU with its irrevocable freezing of exchange rates in achieving such convergence.

In macroeconomic terms the cost–benefit assessment of taking the step has to evaluate the cost of giving up the possibility of accommodating differentiated major and non-transitory shocks, occasionally directly induced by national policy-makers, against the benefit of more definitively strengthening confidence in the long-term predictability and stability of the price level. Obviously the level at which exchange rates are set initially would also have to be regarded as broadly acceptable. The verdict on how the balance comes out for any particular participant must necessarily be subjective, since it depends on the likelihood of future shocks and the degree of credibility of the agreements. All that can be said with confidence is that the balance between costs and benefits has shifted in favour of the latter as the likelihood of differentiated shocks within the EC is reduced, while the benefits of full convergence of interest rates and of inflationary expectations at a low level have become more clearly perceived.

With the general background of the previous discussion it may be useful to examine two more specific arguments often advanced for retaining the exchange rate as a policy instrument within Europe. They serve to place the debate on EMU more squarely in the environment facing the European economies in the 1990s than the general and somewhat ahistorical context of the *Delors Report* and general macroeconomic arguments. According to these arguments realignments of central rates may continue to be seen as necessary either because they can modify the real exchange rate as part of a current account adjustment, or because they enable some participants to continue to make use of an inflation tax.

Even if one adopts the optimistic view that national inflation rates may converge fully in EMU, some trend-wise changes in real exchange rates might be required to sustain simultaneous external and internal balance in each participating country. Differences in growth rates of capacity output and/or in income elasticities in the foreign trade of participants are potential sources of external or internal imbalances in the medium term. If, say, France and Italy need to grow faster than the Federal Republic of Germany) (FRG), for demographic or other reasons, to preserve internal balance, or if the income elasticity in the world demand for German-produced goods is more permanently above those for French- and Italian-produced goods for an extended period, some trend-wise real appreciation of the Deutschmark (DM) against the other two currencies might be warranted. Most international macroeconomic models of interaction do report evidence of systematic differences in income elasticities in foreign trade within the EC, suggesting, for example, that France would face trend-wise deterioration of her trade balance at growth rates of demand parallel to those of the FRG. Furthermore, differences in labour force growth between on the one hand France, Italy and Spain, which all presently have relatively high unemployment, and on the other hand the FRG, suggest that the former three might need to grow faster than the FRG.

Are large trade imbalances sustainable in an EMU where intra-union exchange rates are fixed? And could participants collectively reduce their external surplus *vis-à-vis* the USA without some intra-European exchange rate modifications, given their different starting positions? There are two reasons for saying that neither the trend-wise arguments on imbalances, nor the more transitory need for adjustment to a reduced US deficit, justifies continued reliance on nominal exchange rate changes within Europe as an instrument of policy.

The first, and most important, argument is that the price elasticities in the foreign trade of European countries appear to be too low to be relied upon to bring about a major part of an adjustment. Realignments might have to be so large that they would more permanently upset the results of inflationary convergence and monetary cohesion achieved in the EMS since 1983. Most of the adjustment will have to come from other policy instruments. Furthermore, in an EMU, large external imbalances will be more readily financeable than in a system relying on regular, though modest, realignments.

The second argument is that changes in price competitiveness are not blocked by fixing exchange rates. The experience of some EMS countries suggests that real effective exchange rates do change to some extent independently of the policy of pegging to other EMS currencies (see De Grauwe and Vanhaverbecke 1989). For example, Belgium has improved her competitive position (measured by relative unit labour costs) by approximately 10 per cent in the 1983–89 period while the Belgian franc was broadly stable in the EMS. Domestic cost and price performance is more important than exchange rate policy in influencing competitiveness over the medium term and the major effort has to be directed at that performance.

In summary, the cost of not being able to facilitate changes in competitiveness through realignments cannot be dismissed as insignificant, though it is smaller than the traditional literature assumes. More important, much of it has already been incurred in the current EMS with its diminishing recourse to realignments since 1983. Broadly, this implies that the present distribution of economic activity has been accepted in the EC; otherwise it would have been reckless to adopt the 1992 programme and for the participants in the EMS to have managed the system as tightly as they have recently done. Small and infrequent realignments will continue to be possible in stages one and two envisaged in the *Delors Report*; they will not in themselves bring about major adjustment, but at best moderately facilitate it. The more such realignments are resorted to, the more necessary it becomes to make it clear that participants do aim to create a single currency area in the future. Otherwise realignments may lose even their limited capacity to affect real exchange rates.

The second argument in favour of retaining the exchange rate as a policy instrument lies in the area of public finance. Within an EMU, governments in Italy, Spain, Portugal and Greece would find it hard to compensate (through increases in other taxes or by cutting expenditures) for the seigniorage gains they have made in the past decade and a half of relatively high inflation and automatic deficit financing through money creation. A rapid increase in the demand for non-interest-bearing currency, rising broadly in line with nominal incomes, and for required reserves held by the banking system, typically remunerated at interest rates well below the market level, has provided automatic financing of an important part of deficits. Becoming part of an EMU committed to low inflation would remove most of this inflation tax, which is not easily replaceable by other forms of taxation or expenditure cuts.

On closer examination much of this alleged cost of exchange rate fixity turns out to be of secondary importance. The seigniorage gains were exceptionally large in the decade of 1975–85; they have already been very significantly reduced; they are currently of the order of 0.5 per cent of gross national product for Italy and Spain and about twice that for Portugal and Greece (see Gros 1990). Regardless of whether or not EMU is established, the scope for extracting seigniorage would narrow, as financial integration forces countries with relatively high reserve requirements and low interest paid on such reserves to reduce this tax on their banking systems. Part of the loss of revenue would be offset by the seigniorage gains made by a European system of central banks (ESCB), once the latter begins to issue a common currency and to remit part of the proceeds thereof in some form to participants. The actual loss before that occurred would be far smaller than the figures mentioned, because even in a zero-inflation economy there are some seigniorage gains. On the whole, this issue does not provide an important justification for high and differentiated inflation rates.

In summary, the two more specific arguments for retaining the use of realignments as a policy instrument do not appear to be decisive; most of the costs of not using the exchange rate as a policy instrument have already occurred in the present EMS and time is working to reduce these further. The macroeconomic benefits have been stated more briefly. They accrue primarily in the form of greater predictability and stability of the future price level for most participants and protection against nationally engineered policy shocks.

These benefits are still some way from being realized. Nor is it obvious that they could be realized fully without the additional step of introducing a common currency to underline the definitive nature of EMU and eliminate the inconveniences that would remain in managing an economically and financially integrated area with 12 (or more) national currencies. The balance between macroeconomic costs and benefits of moving to EMU may already in themselves be sufficiently promising to justify EMU as a superior outcome to the present EMS. But the move to a common currency would more definitively shift the balance of costs and benefits in favour of the latter. Hence I turn to a consideration of those additional benefits.

2. Macroeconomic benefits for firms and consumers

The most readily quantifiable benefit of the common currency, but also arguably the least important, is to remove completely all transaction costs in moving from one participating currency to another. But bid-ask spreads and other charges of foreign exchange traders are only large for cash–2–5 per cent. However, tourism and other activities which require the use of cash are of limited economic importance. Intra-EMU trade could amount to 15–20 per cent of gross national product (GNP), but here the transaction costs are of a much lower order of magnitude. Large multinational enterprises typically pay 0.1 per cent or even less, but for smaller firms which play an important role in the trade of some countries charges may be up to 0.5 per cent. The total savings of transaction costs for firms and consumers may on this basis be assessed to between 0.25 and 0.5 per cent of the EC's GNP or 80–160 million ECUs.

Much more important, but difficult to quantify, are the savings to firms in using the single currency which removes the need for up-to-date information about trends in different national currencies and the obligation to cover risks associated with changes in their exchange rates. In this broader category of information costs one may also include the savings for multinational firms in being able to keep their accounts in a common unit, to make internal calculations and settlements and to organize sales efforts on the basis of a price policy expressed in a single unit. It is a major purpose of the internal market that price discrimination between national markets should gradually disappear and be replaced by clear and uniform prices – apart from indirect taxes which will continue to be different from country to country. Only then would the internal market approximate the situation known in the USA where strategies of producers are based on a national price (exclusive of state sales taxes). A common price policy of this type in European firms would greatly sharpen competition and imply substantial gains for consumers.

The so-called Cecchini Report of 1988 tried, through a number of sectoral studies, to assess the benefits of realizing the internal market and arrived at surprisingly high figures: a total removal of all remaining restrictions on intra-EC trade might imply a rise in the total GNP of the EC of 4.5–6.5 per cent over a five-year period – assuming appropriate macroeconomic policies. It is possible that these estimates are too high, at least if national currency areas continue to exist as a brake on complete specialization of firms and economies of scale. Many large European firms have estimated that they might save 0.5–1 per cent of their total turnover by moving to a single currency. Firms that foresee higher costs from a single currency are very few. Survey studies of this kind strengthen the expectation that a single currency could give a significant boost to real income in the EC, probably not less than 2 per cent or 80 million ECUs some years later.

The Cecchini Report stressed the importance of increased competition within the financial sector. The report observed large price differences for apparently identical financial products and assumed, as a rule of thumb, that prices might level off towards the average level in the four 'cheapest' EC member states. Such assumed effects of competition may be excessive; yet it is clear that, not least, financial integration could bring large gains for the users of financial services and that these gains are very sensitive to whether the full passage to a common currency is made. Only on that basis will savers and borrowers have an opportunity for directly comparing pensions, other insurance schemes, financial instruments and borrowing facilities which the financial systems in different EC countries are providing.

Both the Cecchini Report and other elements of the assessment of welfare gains to which I have referred see the benefits as a once-and-for-all rise in real incomes which leaves the rate of growth of individual countries unchanged when the effects have shown up fully. This may well be too pessimistic. In particular, it could be expected that the improved intermediation from saving to investment through the financial system which would be a consequence of greater clarity and certainty inside the common currency area would also lead to a more permanent increase in the rate of growth.

Some of the benefits to firms and consumers will be achieved at the expense of the financial sector. This is most obvious in saving of transaction costs in dealing in European currencies, in the provision of financial products to protect firms against currency risk and for the effect of intensified competition in the European financial area. Some other benefits are net: in particular the reduction of information costs in firms. But it is not surprising if European banks and financial institutions have a more critical view of the prospect of a common currency than their customers. Important sources of revenue will be reduced. However, from welfare–economic perspectives these redistributions of benefits do not affect the main conclusion: a common currency would imply significant net gains. Higher incomes would make it possible to more than compensate the producers of financial and other products for a temporary reduction of earnings from certain activities.

The benefits discussed so far would accrue to those taking part in intra-European economic transactions. But there would also be benefits to firms and consumers who do not take part in such transactions. However, the latter category of benefits would depend crucially on the qualities of the new common currency. To the extent that the intentions of the *Delors Report* are met, that currency would be managed to give a maximum degree of predictability and stability in its purchasing power. This is also a precondition for the participation of the low-inflation countries in the present EMS; they could not be expected to agree to EMU, unless the common currency would have approximately the same quality as their own might continue to have in a more decentralized EMS.

Assuming that the common currency will be approximately as stable as the present low-inflation currencies in the EMS, the replacement of other national currencies through participation in EMU would imply a lower and more stable level of interest rates than most EC countries could otherwise expect. Expected depreciation and a risk premium would be squeezed out of interest rates in those other currencies. At the same time the predictability of future prices, goods and services would improve. This is of increasing importance regarding the length of the contract that agents are engaged in. Long-term contracts can be made with greater certainty of the economic outcome, and fewer costs in negotiating revisions in case the general level of prices develops differently from that expected. Residual uncertainty will relate to possible changes in relative prices and no longer in any significant way to fluctuations in the general purchasing power of the currency.

It is important in this perspective to keep in mind the benefits beyond the purely macroeconomic area. When the latter are taken into account and the perspective is broadened beyond that of the policy-maker, the benefits appear to outweigh the costs. In any case, the previous conclusion that benefits are likely to have risen relative to costs in recent years is strengthened. While there can never be any complete assessment of costs and benefits, the crude evaluation made here suggests to me that there would indeed be benefits of moving from the present EMS to EMU.

References

De Grauwe, P. and **Vanhaverbecke, W.** (1989) Exchange rate experiences of small EMS countries: the cases of Belgium, Denmark and the Netherlands, paper for conference, Exchange rate policy in Selected Industrial Countries, at the Centre for European Policy Studies, co-sponsored by the International Monetary Fund, Macquarie University and Katholieke Universiteit, Louvain, forthcoming in volume of International Monetary Fund and *CEPS Working Document*, No, 42.

Gros, D. (1990) Seigniorage and EMS discipline, this volume, Chapter 7.

Krugman, P. (1990) Policy problems of a monetary union, this volume, Chapter 3.

Thygesen, N. (1990) Institutional developments in the evolution from EMS towards EMU, this volume, Chapter 1.

Contribution by Gunter Baer

No other single suggestion in the approach of the *Delors Report* towards economic and monetary union has received more criticism than the proposal to develop binding rules and procedures for budgetary policies. As spelled out in paragraph 33, these rules should involve effective upper limits on budget deficits in individual member countries and the definition of the overall stance of fiscal policy over the medium term on the basis of the aggregate budgetary balance comprising both the national and the Community positions (Delors Committee, 1989).

The criticism is not so much directed at the type of rules; rather, the whole idea of discretionary fiscal constraints imposed at the Community level is rejected out of hand. Let me quote one source which can hardly be suspected of favouring fiscal laxity. In its study on a monetary order for the single European market, the FRG's Board of Academic Advisers to the Federal Ministry of Economics states that 'in itself, a European monetary union does not require any formal restriction on national autonomy in fiscal policy beyond the ban on central bank financing of state expenditure' and goes on to say that in a monetary union the possibility of suddenly lowering the real value of a government debt will no longer exist. 'The fact that one must pay interest and debts with money one cannot create oneself is the prime mover of discipline; it creates informal pressures towards a convergence in the form of sound fiscal conduct' (Watrin 1989). This view has been echoed by a large number of academics, but has also been expressed in some official reactions to the *Delors Report*.

Leaving aside for a moment the tricky problems involved in drafting practical rules (in fact, the problems may turn out to be so extensive that even those who, as a matter of principle, are strongly in favour of formal rules might ultimately settle for a less formal system), the discussion about rules hinges on two basic questions. First, can markets be expected to produce sufficiently strong signals to prompt national governments to pursue sound fiscal policies and therefore eliminate the risks of excessive government borrowing, with adverse effects on the Community's interest rate level and its exchange rate *vis-à-vis* the rest of the world? Second, is there a need for a deliberate fiscal policy for the Community as a whole, both for the purpose of domestic macroeconomic management in the Community and in support of its exchange rate policy *vis-à-vis* third currencies?

As my answer to the first question would tend to be 'no', and to the second question 'yes', I feel that economic and monetary union in Europe would be better served by a system of explicit fiscal constraints than by one that relied solely on an informal and potentially disruptive approach, with conflicting or even incompatible government policies brought into line by market forces.

The view that market signals will discipline national governments in their budgetary policies through market-induced interest rate spreads, reflecting growing risk premiums for profligate borrowers, is said to follow from two assumptions. First, as noted by the Board of Advisers quoted above, public sector authorities would be denied access to monetary financing and would therefore not be able to depreciate the real value of their debt through inflation. Second, a troubled borrower could not count on being bailed out by the Community; in other words, there would be no explicit or implicit guarantee that the Community would underwrite the borrowing of an individual government.

These two conditions, it is argued, would put governments on the same footing as private borrowers, who cannot resort to central bank credit or, owing to competition, pass on increasing borrowing costs in higher prices or expect to be bailed out by others. Faced with the threat of bankruptcy, governments, like private borrowers, would therefore revert to more prudent budgetary policies.

For this to be the case, however, we would have to have sufficient confidence that markets price risks adequately and that the borrowers react responsibly to such signals. In fact there are a number of examples of markets having failed to impose the necessary discipline even on private sector borrowers, especially where large corporations have been involved. Furthermore, there are clearly limits to how great an analogy can be made between private and public sector borrowers. Even with recourse to monetary financing being ruled out, national governments in the union will retain their power to raise additional revenues through taxation, although the scope for increasing national taxes may be limited in a union. Governments are therefore more likely to be judged 'safe' borrowers in comparison with private sector borrowers. In fact, this assessment receives 'official' support from the proposed risk-weighted solvency ratios (ancillary to the Community's Second Banking Directive), which prescribe a zero weight for bank holdings of EC government paper. Moreover, there is certainly a different perception of sovereign risks compared with private sector risks, not least because practical experience suggests that in a union built on solidarity it will be extremely difficult, if not politically impossible, to let a national government default. Even an explicit no-bail-out provision is not likely to be credible, leaving aside the political pressure that investors in other Community countries would try to exert if their claims on a troubled national EC government were put in jeopardy.

For these reasons it would seem probable that in a situation of fixed exchange rates (or after a common currency has been introduced) debt issued by different governments would be perfectly substitutable in the eyes of market participants and earn the same interest rate. Any substantial increase in the deficit of one member country would therefore result in an increase in interest rates on all EC government debt rather than a mark-up of the risk premium on the debt of the deficit country.

There are also serious doubts about the responsiveness of governments to interest rate spreads, should such spreads develop at all. Under the present EMS arrangement the large differences between interest rates on the debts of individual EC governments obviously reflect the perception of exchange risks much more than credit risks, and the fear of provoking exchange rate tensions has frequently been cited as a deterrent to greater fiscal laxity. With the move to irrevocably final exchange rates, currency risks would vanish and high interest rates converge towards a lower average. Is it wholly realistic to assume that under these conditions small spreads would discipline some of the EC governments with a history of loose fiscal policy? And, more generally, is it realistic to assume that governments would respond to small differences in relative borrowing costs if the overall level of interest rates fluctuated widely under international influences? And finally, given that the consequences of recourse to capital markets, e.g. higher taxation in the future, are usually borne by successor governments, would interest rate increases really induce the authorities to refrain from additional borrowing, especially if they considered it to be only a temporary measure? There is every reason to be sceptical.

Those who are less sceptical frequently combine their reasoning with the view that there is no need for a centralized, coordinated fiscal policy for demand management purposes either because fiscal policy is denied a role as a demand-management instrument altogether, or because the use of a Community fiscal policy should be reserved for situations of serious disequilibrium, in which case it could be administered in an *ad hoc* fashion and without a system of formal constraints. A review of the pros and cons of an active fiscal policy would indeed suggest using this instrument cautiously. But as long as individual countries are advised in international policy debates to pursue more restrictive or more expansionary fiscal policies, it would seem unrealistic to assume that the Community as a whole could abandon the idea of managing its aggregate budgetary position.

Clearly, if it is believed that market forces will impose prudent fiscal policies in all Community countries and that any form of aggregate fiscal policy management is undesirable, there is logically no room for formal fiscal constraints in an economic and monetary union. However, for anyone not sharing either of these views, there would be a case for a system of rules and procedures: in the first place, if market forces did not succeed in disciplining budgetary policies, such rules would be required to keep the aggregate budgetary position in balance even though fiscal policy was not to be used actively as a macroeconomic policy tool; second, rules would be needed in order to manage actively a centralized fiscal policy, even if market forces resulted in sound fiscal policies in all member countries of the Community.

The opponents of formal budgetary constraints usually support their reasoning by pointing out that existing federal states, with the exception of Australia, do not impose limitations on the budgetary policies of regional and local authorities and that no major problems have been encountered in these states. As has been mentioned recently by the Governor of the Bank of England, the available empirical evidence does not suggest that there is a painless route to federal fiscal soundness. For example, in the mid-nineteenth century some American states ran up large debts and defaulted, and it was against this background that it was found expedient to amend states' constitutions, restricting their powers to borrow (Leigh-Pemberton 1989). Indeed, when forming an economic and monetary union among different nations, the current experience of federal states appears to be of limited significance. First, there is the important structural difference between major federal states, which have sizeable central budgets, and the Community, which on the basis of present forecasts will have only a very small central budget. Second, the prudence in budgetary policies generally exhibited by regional authorities may have much to do with the fact that the regions do not engage in any kind of demand-management policy and, in most cases, limit their borrowing to capital spending.

For these reasons the case put forward by the opponents of formal constraints is rather weak, and it seems advisable that at this delicate stage of building and consolidating ECU in Europe caution should be exercised. Explicit fiscal policy coordination would indeed appear to be a vital component of such a union (Lamfalussy 1989).

Obviously, formal and binding constraints on fiscal policy as proposed in the *Delors Report* affect national sovereignty, and that is why some politicians strongly object to this part of the Delors approach. However, as the *Delors Report* states at the outset, ECU involves a transfer of decision-making power from member states to the Community in many areas of economic policy-making. This does not imply that centralized decisions cannot take account of the situation of individual member states, nor does the *Delors Report* suggest that under a system of formal budgetary rules each country would need to have the same fiscal policy. But the aggregate outcome will have to be consistent with macroeconomic stability, without which the resolve of the participating countries would be severely tested. And there can be no doubt that many problems will have to be overcome.

In concluding, I mention a problem which arises from the legacy of past fiscal divergence. At present there are enormous differences in the levels of general government debt between Community countries, ranging, as a percentage of their current budgetary receipts, from 26 per cent in Luxembourg and 76 per cent in France to far above 200 per cent in Italy, Belgium and Ireland. In an economic and monetary union the interest service on this outstanding debt will be made at roughly identical interest rates, and, if it is assumed that the burden of taxation imposed on each country's residents cannot diverge widely, this implies that government spending net of interest payments will differ considerably. This in turn means that the level of government services provided within national borders will vary significantly a development which in the longer term could give rise to major structural imbalances within the Community.

References

Committee for the Study of Economic and Monetary Union (the Delors Committee) (1989) *Report on Economic and Monetary Union in the European Community* (The *Delors Report*) (with Collection of Papers), Office for Official Publication of the European Communities, Luxemburg.

Lamfalussy, A. (1989) Macro-co-ordination of fiscal policies in an economic and monetary union in Europe, in Collection of Papers submitted to the Committee for the Study of Economic and Monetary Union attached to the *Delors Report*, Luxembourg.

Leigh-Pemberton, R. (1989) The future of monetary arrangements in Europe, *Bank of England/Quarterly Bulletin*, London, August.

Watrin, C. (1989) *A Monetary Order for the Single European Market* (English translation), Bonn.

Contribution by Antonio Maria Costa

On the subject of the benefits or otherwise of EMU I will address four questions:

1. Why is EMU now on the Community's agenda?
2. What do we have to gain from the EMU in terms of welfare: namely, is it worth it?
3. How shall we get there? In particular, what does the *Delors Report* (Delors Committee 1989) say about the process?
4. What is the appropriate budgetary regime, its institutional centralization and political accountability?

THE ECONOMIC, INSTITUTIONAL AND POLITICAL ROOTS OF THE EMU PROCESS

History provides important elements for a proper understanding of the reasons behind the present drive towards economic integration in the Community. I see at least three sets of closely interrelated factors: economic, institutional and political.

First, I see the events at the turn of the 1990s as a deliberate response to the 'Eurosclerosis' and 'Europessimism' of the 1970s and early 1980s. These were terms used to describe the systemic under-performance of the European economy during that period with respect to Europe's own past performance as well as to that of its main trading partners.

The European under-performance during that period concerned economic, financial and monetary issues. Between 1974 and 1985, the European economy substantially under-performed those of its international competitors, with EC economic growth at an average of 1.9 per cent p.a. compared with 2.4 per cent in the USA and 3.8 per cent in Japan. This slow growth was combined with high inflation (11 per cent on average for the Community), compared with the USA (7.0 per cent) and Japan (6.3 per cent).

The integration of world financial markets has been under way since the late 1970s. Most Europeans have realized that without full liberalization of capital movements and of financial markets within the Community, it would be very difficult for Europe to play an active and influential part in this world-wide process.

The exchange rate swings that took place between 1980 and 1987 (a period during which the dollar appreciated by 100 per cent, only to return to its starting point) has led to the realization that, while a policy aiming at currency stabilization world-wide is needed, it should involve a European monetary cohesion and a homogeneous participation in international fora.

But much more appears in the background to the monetary union process than just the economic, monetary and financial troubles of the past two decades.

Indeed, and *second*, within the EC there have been significant institutional developments during the 1980s. To a large extent, the deliberate political decision to go ahead with EMU (lately reiterated at the European Council in Madrid) and the continuing drive towards it (as shown by the efforts to put stage one in place) build upon the major institutional accomplishments during this decade now ending.

Outstanding among Community successes are as follows:

1. The EMS, which recently celebrated its tenth birthday. The EMS has contributed to disinflation in participating countries as well as to greater stability of exchange rates throughout most of the Community.
2. The European Single Act which was approved in 1985. It democratized decision-making by introducing majority voting for much Community legislation, by strengthening the roles of the elected bodies (e.g. the European Parliament) and by implementing microeconomic subsidiarity.
3. The drive towards the internal market and the goal of 1992. With 60 per cent of the legislative acts envisaged for the completion of the single market already approved, the process is on target compared with the goals set by the Commission's White Paper of 1985.

Third, and finally, the new momentum towards the European construction is in my view a deliberate political reaction to the major geopolitical changes that have taken place in the course of the 1980s and are likely to continue:

1. The waning of Pax Americana;
2. The emergence of Japan as a commercial and financial power;
3. The political and economic democratization in Eastern Europe.

This complex background to EMU involves economic, institutional as well as political issues at the same time. However, a fourth component should also be considered: the present Commission's commitment to implement fully the Treaty of Rome, especially its call for EMU first and European union later.

ON THE COSTS AND BENEFITS OF EMU

I now turn to my second topic.

An economic and monetary union has to be judged on its ability to improve the economic welfare of its citizens. What are then the costs and the benefits one could expect from such a union? Addressing the same question, some members of the economic profession have arrived at a puzzling conclusion. Since the analysis of the welfare implications of an EMU are quite complex and not fully amenable to quantification and to firm evaluation, some (including Paul Krugman, in Ch. 3 of this book) have argued that economic science is unlikely to give an unambiguous answer. As a consequence, the major benefit to be gained from the process now under way is a fact of a political nature: EMU is seen as an important prolegomenon to the European union reaffirned in the Single Act.

I have two comments to make on this. First, I do not disagree on the political dimensions of EMU – not at all, in fact, given what I said above about evolving world geopolitics. Yet this political debate is not on the agenda (at least not on my own professional agenda). Second, as an economist, I find it disturbing that my profession is incapable of providing a clear answer as to the costs and benefits of EMU. This cannot be right and the Commission staff are now working hard on this problem. In the meantime, I shall attempt to treat the question in a stylized form, to a large extent building upon the experience in this sort of analysis the Commission has accumulated in the context of the 'Cost of Non-Europe' Project.

If we envisage EMU as an optimum currency area (OCA) with irrevocably fixed exchange rates, then the decision-making (public and private) in the Community will undergo enormous changes, all loaded with consequences.

First (but not foremost) are the direct, static benefits deriving from the reduction of transaction costs and exchange rate uncertainty. These advantages – operational in nature and amenable to quantitative estimate – will accrue to the private sector: producers and traders. Their importance will increase with the volume of cross-border commercial and financial transactions relative to the total transactions that take place within the Community. These benefits will be one-off, in the sense that they will add to economic growth as, and after, EMU takes place. Namely, once EMU has been established, producers and traders will be permanently better off by operating under a much improved regime.

Second, and more difficult albeit more promising, is the evaluation of the indirect consequences of EMU, in other words, the dynamic gains. What needs to be proved in this regard is that all types of economic behaviour, public and private, at the national as well as at the Community level, will be affected – and positively so.

To begin with, EMU will improve the incentives and expectations of the private sector by abolishing what (in 1993) will be the last major economic barrier separating member countries: exchange rate changes. Exchange rate risks discourage cross-border investment. The longer term a business project, the more its planning is affected by exchange rate risk. Yet it is precisely this type of long-term major investment decision that needs to be made on a Community-wide basis if we are to benefit from the better allocation of resources and increased efficiency resulting fron the internal market (namely 1992). If you are not convinced that it is here, at the micro level, that the main dynamic benefits of a single currency will come, just approach the argument with a reverse reasoning – since benefits are the mirror image of costs (the lower the latter, the higher the former), just think about the costs US business would face if the New Jersey dollar were worth more (or less) than the Texas dollar. Now multiply that by 50 (the number of US states) and see what you get for the USA. There are 12 countries in the EC, 11 currencies and 10 intra-EC exchange rates!

At the same time, public sectors, both governments and central banks, will compete with each other in aiming to provide the best service at the lowest cost. This should induce a better overall policy-making environment within the Community than would otherwise be the case. For example, given that the European monetary policy will be as stability orientated as that of the German Bundesbank, there will be a credibility gain for countries with poor reputations on the monetary side.

There will be costs as well. They will consist in giving up nominal exchange rate policy instruments in response to real shocks. But, these costs will decrease over time. This is because the completion of the internal market in 1992 will result in an increase in the share of intra-Community transactions (compared with trade with the rest of the world); in an increase of factor mobility (both capital and labour) and in an improvement in the efficiency of markets. In this context, the argument that the economic and monetary construction of the Community should take advantage of the 1992 goal (by becoming its natural development) is very persuasive. (Queen Beatrix's intimation is well rooted in economics.) In fact, the argument could be strengthened by advocating the bimodal nature of the EMU – 1992 relationship. Namely, the EMU (a) will contribute value added to the internal market, increasing the benefits one expects from it in the process, (b) it will add to stability, by abolishing the exchange rate barrier, in addition to the removal (by 1992) of the technical, physical and fiscal frontiers.

It is interesting to note that the gains from EMU – in terms of greater decision-making options–will be felt mostly at the microeconomic level (the firm and the individual), whereas at the macroeconomic level EMU will mostly turn into a constraint upon national decision-making.

This ought not to be a problem to the extent that national policy autonomy losses will be turned into Community policy sovereignty gains. This means that as all member states will increasingly submit to the self-discipline required to take into account mutual interests, everybody will be better off.

Before closing this discussion on the costs and benefits of EMU, let me turn to structural and regional questions. These are important, and not only to the less advanced countries. Will the loss of the freedom to devalue be a disadvantage especially for the less developed member states? I believe that the balance of advantages will be strongly positive on account of the different and offsetting shocks that may result for those countries from the process of economic integration. The *Delors Report* has a well-balanced approach to EMU.

The revenue from seigniorage, namely, printing money to finance government deficits and thereby causing additional inflation, will no longer be available. Good riddance! Though studies show that revenue from seigniorage has been declining in recent years, this hidden tax is still quite significant in many member states. Similarly, the tendency of governments to tax their banking systems, through reserve requirements held interest-free or at below market rates with the central bank, will have to end at the risk of disadvantaging the domestic banking sector.

The above will have to be seen in the light of the enormous benefits countries will derive from better policy, improved expectations and generally the switch towards a different Community regime – one characterized by stability and sustainable growth.

Of course, the overall costs and benefits will depend on the shape, type and form of EMU. Let me now give an outline of the proposals of the Delors Committee (1989) for a better understanding of the issues debated today.

PROPOSALS AND COUNTER-PROPOSALS

The *Delors Report* on EMU is based on three main principles:

1. *Parallelism*: namely, integration of the monetary and of the economic aspects of the union (see below).
2. *Subsidiarity*; this is the systemic, macroeconomic counterpart of the principle of mutual recognition of norms and standards (see above). The attribution of competences to the Community in the context of the EMU should be confined to those situations in which collective decision-making is necessary to guarantee better results.
3. *Plurality*: the Community is made up of member states, each with different economic, social, cultural and political characteristics. The preservation of this plurality requires that member states keep control of their own developments to the greatest extent possible. President Delors is fond of saying that 'l'Union européenne se fera dans la pluralité, ou elle ne se fera pas.' In the context of today's debate, this expression means that the specificity of each national situation has to be considered an asset upon which to build the EMU, not an obstacle making the process harder.

The *Delors Report* defines three irrevocable conditions as necessary for a monetary union:

1. irrevocable convertibility of currencies;
2. irrevocable capital liberalization and financial integration;
3. the irrevocable fixing of exchange rate parities.

If these three conditions are accepted, for economic as well as psychological and political reasons, the adoption of a single currency would be a natural and desirable consequence. I honestly find it difficult to tell a businessman that 'at a point in time *t* dealing in currency *X* or currency *Y* of the EC will carry exactly the same foreign exchange risk', without adding that 'at that time the exchange rate between currencies *X* and *Y* will be abolished'. Former Chancellor Schmidt went, jokingly, even further when he added that 'at that point in time, unless the EC currencies are replaced by a single EC currency, markets in the Community will still be more chaotic than in Marrakesh, where only one money is used'.

Once we accept this consequence (i.e. fixed exchange rates leading to a single currency), the question of the appropriate single monetary institution within the Community, for issuing the single currency and running a single monetary policy is solved: a single currency must mean a single European central bank.

Economic Union, a less obvious concept, is described in terms of the internal market (namely 1992) with its four freedoms of movement for persons, goods, services and capital. But organized markets need rules of behaviour. Hence emphasis is placed on:

(a) competition policy and other measures aimed at strengthening market mechanisms;

(b) common structural and regional policies;
(c) macroeconomic policy coordination, including budget policies. This means developing a system of 'safety nets' for constraining sharply divergent policies of economic management in other countries.

The monetary union process proposed above focuses on a single EC monetary policy, a single currency and a single central bank. In contrast, economic union does not require a new economic policy institution. In order to respect the principles of subsidiarity and plurality, it is proposed to leave economic policies largely in the hands of national governments. And this is, of course, loaded with implications.

Before turning to these implications, let me address the question of implementation. The Delors Committee (1989) proposes a single process consisting of three stages.

Stage one, which was accepted by the European Council in Madrid in June 1989 and will start on July 1 1990, comprises on the economic side the completion of an internal market programme (by 1992) together with the legislation necessary to provide a framework for greater coordination of economic policy, especially budgetary policy. On the monetary side, it includes the creation of a single financial area (through capital movement liberalization), the inclusion of all currencies in the EMS, removal of all impediments to the private use of the ECU, and a legal text to strengthen the role of the Committee of Central Bank Governors of the European Community. Stage one would also include the preparation and ratification of a change in the Treaty of Rome.

The second and third stages proposed by the Delors Committee (1989) would see the gradual reinforcement of coordination procedures on the economic side and the creation of a new institution, the system of European central banks, on the monetary side.

When should all this happen? The Delors Committee(1989) proposes no specific timetable for the transition to stages two and three. And for good reason. It is possible to legislate for the elimination of physical, technical and fiscal barriers (as was done in the White Paper of 1985, which set the target of the achievement of a single market by 1992), but it is not possible to legislate for an appropriate degree of economic convergence – namely, to dictate the timing for having the basic EMU conditions in place and for turning to stages two and three.

The *Delors Report* represents the only fully articulated and consistent blueprint of EMU and the way to get there. It met the tough test of unanimity on this fact by all EC central bank governors, who were members of the Delors group (in their personal capacities). Other views (but no alternative blueprint) on the EMU process have emerged. Let us look at their contents and implications.

Two other concepts of monetary union have surfaced in informal debates thus far. Both are characterized by a greater degree of exchange rate flexibility than is envisaged in the *Delors Report*.

First, a currency competition concept, as proposed by such illustrious writers as von Hayek and Vaubel and recently endorsed by the UK Treasury. According to this definition, an optimal currency area need not be characterized by fixed exchange rates. All exchange controls should be lifted (namely, in our jargon, 1992 should be in place) and transactions could be conducted in any of the currencies of the member states at the choice of the transactors. According to this approach, market efficiency – defined by the degree of competition taking place in it – is more important than price stability and exchange rate fixity. Governments and central banks would be forced to compete to provide stability, as the most stable currency would soon become the one most heavily in demand.

The incentive for authorities to engage in currency competition would be twofold:

1. A push element, whereby the seigniorage accrued to a central bank issuing an internationally demanded currency would be increased if that currency were increasingly utilized outside the issuing country;
2. A pull element due to the loss of monetary control in countries with softer currencies from the domestic use of foreign currency.

Considerable surrendering of sovereignty would take place – but not to monetary or other institutions. The transfer of sovereignty would be to markets and to citizens, the ultimate judges of the quality of a currency and of the adequacy of policy.

I shall return to this notion of currency competition. Before then, let me compare this competitive model with another view of the EMU process. I am referring to an asymmetric peg system, which views the EMU as an optimal currency area (OCA) analogous to a strengthened EMS with progressively greater fixity of exchange rates. Free capital movements and currency convertibility are other aspects of this asymmetric peg.

The system is called 'asymmetric' because one currency would emerge as leader, identifiable by its responsibility for sterilizing reserve flows so as to control the money supply. Other currencies would borrow credibility from the leader, but would not (not fully at least) sterilize these flows.

This system is characterized by a powerful centripetal force. Why? Because the incentive to peg on to a leading reserve currency is obviously greater for smaller economies and less widely used currencies. Therefore, if a number of such smaller currencies were to peg to an already strong currency, even the currencies of other major countries would become smaller with respect to the currency zone of the leader. Such an asymmetric peg would therefore tend to privilege, and increasingly so through time, one national currency and its underlying economy, making the rest of the OCA subservient to the interest of the leader. (It is interesting to note that UK commentators have been unanimous in concluding that both the currency competition and the asymmetric peg models would result in the crowning of a national currency and its underlying economy to become the standards of the EC systems. I agree with this conclusion to which I just want to add that the *Delors Report* is by far the more balanced and symmetrical in its implications, and as a consequence, more acceptable and realistic.)

I find the debate about different EMU options fascinating: the final outcome will definitely be richer because of it. In this light the following questions are addressed.

First: Are the various ideas floated reflecting monetary union, alternative to, and mutually exclusive with respect to, the full blueprint proposed by the Delors Committee (1989)?

I believe they are most certainly mutually exclusive if each is seen as an alternative terminal point in the Community monetary construction. For example, if currency competition or the asymmetric peg is seen as the only and ultimate form of monetary union, then clearly there can be no agreement between these views and those expressed by the Delors Committee (1989).

However, and this is vital, these views may not be radically incompatible with those of the Delors Committee (1989) if they are seen as contributing to different phases of a monotonic process of convergence towards full monetary union as defined in the *Delors Report*. Namely, there cannot be outright incompatibility if there is a political commitment on the part of member states (even those who may be infatuated with alternative options) to accept a key aspect of the *Delors Report*, which sees continuity of the monetary construction process towards the ultimate goal as defined in the report itself.

In other words, we ought to separate:

(a) the EMU, seen as a final outcome leading to a constitutional change (a treaty revision) which is the product of a political decision and a commitment to accept the report of the Delors Committee (1989) in its broad formulation; from
(b) the actual transition to such monetary union, which is a process. Such a transition needs to be gradual and may incorporate features from alternative definitions of an optimal currency area.

Second: How much can these alternative definitions learn from each other? A great deal. Indeed, between now and the moment EMU will prevail, there will be much currency competition as the other EC monies try to emulate the best (DM), as well as much EMS hardening through pegging of currencies to the leading (DM) money.

In the process towards monetary union, much currency competition will take place. In fact, a great deal of it is going to occur between now and 1992, as economic agents, economic systems and even governments (and perhaps central banks) compete to achieve more appropriate and more efficient management of their own affairs.

Also, during the early phases of the process, the EMS will consolidate further (either by law or by market appreciation of what is taking place). The leading role of one (or more) of the major currencies within the system will be maintained. In fact, there is evidence of growing substitutability between the DM and other strong currencies in the system, among them the French franc. The conclusion of this, currency competition and a more stable EMS will no doubt support the convergence of the monetary arrangements in Europe towards the only monetary blueprint available so far: that defined by the Delors Committee (1989).

THE BUDGETARY REGIME

Now I turn to the final set of interesting issues, beginning with budgetary coordination.

Macroeconomic policy coordination implies a limitation of a sort on the conduct of national policy – budgetary policy in particular. What kind of limitation is politically realistic and economically effective?

All agree that governments should not have access to direct central bank credit or to other forms of monetary financing. This condition, though necessary, is not sufficient for the efficiency of EMU: budget deficits could still have an externality impact, throughout the Community. (Namely, taxpayers in other countries may be taxed by inadequate policies in any given member state.)

All agree at the same time that the best way to finance public deficits is by means of financial market intermediation.

But could this be limited and if so how? There is no single answer to this question. Our answer depends on whether we believe that markets or governments are more likely to fail, since we all agree that failures are a reality both in spontaneous markets (those exposed to competition) and in organized markets (e.g. governments). So it is a question of the degree to which one or other type of arrangement is better situated.

History is littered with evidence of government failures. The 1970s in particular have provided ample evidence of budgetary mismanagement, excessive national debts, inefficient resource allocation by political criteria and costly interference with the allocative mechanism of markets. In most countries it has taken over 10 years (the 1980s) to remedy excesses of the previous decade.

Monetary union will only be viable, therefore, if some sort of surveillance of government behaviour is put into operation to minimize the chances, and the consequences, of government failure.

But surveillance by what means? By means of the market, and the financial market in particular. Certainly. But exclusively? I do not think that this would be wise since market failures are also likely and for several reasons. Economic literature has extensively dealt with market failures in the presence of non-convex economies (e.g. in cases of discontinuities in decision-making in zero–one solutions, etc.); in the presence of externalities; or in the presence of collective goods. This is all very relevant to monetary union.

But over and above what is stated in academic circles, the Delors Committee (1989) claims, correctly in my view, that market forces alone, tremendously powerful and important although they are, are also 'too slow and weak or too sudden and disruptive' to provide an appropriate deterrent to the misbehaviour of governments, and therefore to serve as a remedy for their failures. The examples of the collapse of New York City's finances or the stampeding into lending to least developed countries by private banks in the 1980s, are all evidence of market failures – or at least of the inefficient self-policing of markets.

All this is, of course, related to the issue of institutional centralization and democratic accountability. The final objective of EMU is irrevocably fixed exchange rates, a single currency, a unique monetary policy and a sole centralized monetary institution (a Community central bank). What kind of institutional set-up do we need on the budgetary side as a counterpart to this?

At least three budgetary regimes have emerged in the EMU debate:

1. A decentralized market-based regime, supported by the exclusion of monetary financing and of no mutual bailing out in the Community;
2. Multilateral surveillance of national budgetary policy, at the Community level, which would combine coordination procedures with a safety net concerning limits on the size of deficits and debts, as well as on the techniques of their financing;
3. Binding annual guidelines on the size and structures of budget deficits and of government debts and on their financing. These would be decided at Community level, but not necessarily in a new institution.

Differences between the three schools are of course a product of political, even ideological preferences, but also the result of alternative approaches to economic science and to the working of our economic systems.

For example, the decentralized market-based regime, opposes limits on a country's freedom to run deficits (or to build up debts), because:

(a) fiscal policy is ill suited to short-term demand management; and
(b) with fixed exchange rates, fiscal policy is needed to maintain internal balance (it being sanctioned only by markets).

The multilateral surveillance approach supported by a safety net comes from:

(a) fears that the market discipline is indeed inadequate or disruptive in the way it polices poor policies; and
(b) questions the firmness of political commitment that in a monetary union, especially if seen as a first step to a political union, there will be no bailing out. Indeed, governments, facing electorates reluctant to service debt obligations, may extort solidarity from fellow member states by threatening to default or to renege on their EMU commitment or even to opt out of the process towards monetary union entirely.

Those that support binding budgetary guidelines see them as a necessary counterpart to: (a) a single central banking institution in Europe, and (b) a single currency. Otherwise, there may be a risk of instability and economic sub-optimality resulting from the maintenance of a small Community budget, national budgetary decision-making, and centralized monetary policy.

It seems worthwhile to ask what the average economist thinks of these alternative options. For example, what do the average Keynesian economist or the typical neo-classical economist or typical Ricardian have to say about the above? Of course, there is no such thing as a typical adherent to any of the above-mentioned schools, nor is there a single answer to any of the issues raised above. It would depend on:

(a) the degree of openness, the size and the exchange regime of an economy;
(b) the causes of a budget deficit, whether brought about by low tax receipts or high expenditure;
(c) the nature of the deficit itself (whether transitory or permanent; expected or not and so forth).

Nevertheless, and with these qualifications in mind, it would appear reasonable to characterize the thinking of the various economic schools as follows:

1. A Keynesian economist would probably stress the likelihood of deflationary bias in EMU if national policies were run independently. Why? Because of the growing import leakages (even more likely in the post-1992 environment and in the EMU regime), countries may refrain from expansionary budgetary policy due to fears of deficits (little increase in real revenue would take place for any added volume of public demand). Therefore, the Keynesian economist is likely to argue that budgetary policy is a useful instrument to promote domestic demand and to derive output gains if it is accompanied by joint (i.e. at a Community level) determination of budgetary stances.
2. For a neo-classicist, since permanent public deficits crowd out private capital information and trade higher present consumption for lower future growth, the EC budgetary regime ought to be designed so as to foster convergence towards low public deficits. Why? Because the negative externality caused by shared monetary conditions throughout the EMU area is to be fought by setting limits on public deficits. Indeed, the neo-classicist is likely to argue that EMU will bring about an increased risk of uncontrolled budgetary regimes, i.e. for a bias towards fiscal laxity in EMU (as opposed to the bias towards fiscal rigour expected by the Keynesian).

   The risk of fiscal laxity will occur because, in an EMU regime, increases in the public deficits of member countries would increase interest rates in the whole union and cause a deterioration in the balance of payments of the union. In other words, others will share the negative externality of public finance mismanagement. That could become a temptation for member countries to engage in beggar-thy-neighbour budgetary policies.
3. According to the Ricardian approach, the rationality of the private sector is believed to be able to discount the future (taxed) impact of current budget deficits. In other words, the real effects of deficit spending, or variations of it, are nil. Therefore, the Ricardian would presumably be indifferent to the design of the budgetary regime to accompany EMU.

The empirical evidence on the three different views on the working of budgetary policy is abundant and quite familiar. One must distinguish between moderate and large deficits.

1. Moderate deficits do not seem to validate the Ricardian school. They do validate the Keynesian approach, since an increase in deficits has a

short-term and positive impact on real growth. But they also validate the neo-classical paradigm, in the longer term, as the increasing public deficit will have a negative impact on savings and investment.

2. For larger deficits (i.e. for the unsustainable situation, such as that of one major country, Italy, and many minor countries, Greece, Belgium, etc.), aggregate demand is relatively unaffected by changes in the budget. This seems to lend support to an extent to the Ricardian theory of Neutrality.

What lessons do we derive from the above in the design of the budgetary side of monetary union? The following six conclusions are offered as food for thought.

1. All schools agree that a serious uncertainty exists on how to calculate the most advisable budgetary policy.
2. The principle of subsidiarity should also systematically apply to macroeconomics, to overcome inconsistencies in national budgetary policy and between budgetary and monetary policy with each country.
3. Spill-over effects of small changes in budgetary policy may be insignificant. Only if national budgetary policy poses a serious threat to the internal and external balance of the Community at large, should they be contested at the Community level and perhaps preceded by Community measures.
4. For Keynesians and neo-classicists alike, the decentralized market-based regime fails to respond to the threat of monetary instability due to excessive budgetary deficits. In these circumstances, the EC needs to have in its arsenal the means to act against the villain. In contrast, the Ricardian school could live with such a regime.
5. Strict binding guidelines for budgets could not be in line with the subsidiarity principle. It would be supported by the Keynesian but not by the classicist (and also opposed by the Ricardian).
6. Mutual multilateral surveillance, accompanied by a budgetary safety net, would not seem to pose major problems to either a reasonable Keynesian or to a moderate neo-classicist.

As a personal conclusion, I find it difficult to disagree with the Delors Committee's (1989) suggestion that budgetary policy coordination in the Community within the context of monetary union should respect the principle of subsidiarity. Therefore, it should be accomplished by

(a) non-monetary financing of budget deficits;
(b) the use of financial market instruments;
(c) limitation on external borrowing in non-EC currencies;
(d) upper limits on budget deficits in individual member countries.

I close on this issue with the hope that the economics profession will assist both member countries and the Commission in their efforts to understand the various options, to be better aware of the implications and, eventually, to provide viable support to intergovernmental deliberations.

Contribution by Andrew Crockett

INTRODUCTION

In these concluding remarks, I will try and focus on the concerns that the UK has about the proposals made by some of the more enthusiastic advocates of rapid progress towards monetary union.

First, however, I want to deal with an important issue that is part of stage one, namely, sterling's membership of the ERM. The British government's policy in this respect has been set out: sterling will join the ERM when certain conditions, which were made somewhat clearer at the Madrid Summit, have been met. My personal view is that membership is a good thing and will eventually bring significant benefits. However, it would be a mistake to think that simply by joining the ERM, the UK will be able magically to reduce the costs of bringing down inflation, as some commentators appear to believe.

Part of the misunderstanding arises from a failure to appreciate how the anti-inflationary credibility of ERM membership comes about. Credibility cannot be acquired by simply joining the ERM. It has to be earned, and it has to be earned by sustained policies. Provided, however, that the UK can demonstrate by its actions that it will do what is necessary to bring its inflation rate into line with that of the FRG, the *de facto* leader of the system, a commitment to join the ERM can, I believe, lend both discipline and credibility to the government's medium-term anti-inflationary strategy.

Another problem is that the constraints of ERM membership do not always produce the right result from a domestic perspective. In 1987/88, for example, shadowing the DM required the UK authorities to lower interest rates in a way that added to domestic liquidity and increased inflationary pressures. This episode underlines the importance, first, of choosing the right rate at which to join, and second, of joining the mechanism at a time when its constraints are consistent with the requirements of domestic macroeconomic policy. Also, shadowing in some sense gives the worst of both worlds: it provides less benefit in terms of credibility, since the currency is not in the mechanism but only shadowing it; and it increases the adjustment costs because the intervention or policy adjustment needed to stay within the shadowing range falls only on the shadowing country, rather than being shared more symmetrically with other countries.

The conclusion is that full membership can be of assistance in deriving the full benefit of an anti-inflationary policy, but it cannot by any means take the place of such a policy. More importantly, however, the benefits of ERM participation should not be seen only in terms of the effects on inflation. The other advantages of membership are in terms of what it can contribute to exchange rate stability, and the contribution that exchange rate stability in turn makes to objectives such as the promotion of trade and investment within the community and the creation of a more symmetrical mechanism for policy decisions. Middle-sized open economies such as that of the UK are increasingly constrained in their monetary policy – their freedom of action is circumscribed by the environment in which they find themselves. So any move towards a situation in which there was a sharing of responsibility for policy-making would be advantageous.

BEYOND STAGE ONE

With this introduction let me pass on to the situation as it will be once the conditions of stage one have been fulfilled – that is to say, once we have free capital mobility, once the Single European Act is complete, once all large members of the Community are members of the ERM. There are two major headings under which the key policy issues can be grouped. First, what is the nature of eventual economic and monetary union to which we will move? Second, how fast should we move towards such a union? Under both headings there are clear differences of view, particularly (but not only) between the UK government and the views of a number of other Community members.

I will start with the second question, because the reasons for a cautious approach are, I believe, independent of the precise nature of the ultimate union. That this is still in dispute is itself a good reason for caution. We have heard a variety of views during this conference concerning the speed with which we should expect to achieve stage three, and eventually the complete monetary union in which there would be a single currency. A number of speakers have envisaged full monetary union within a very few years. Such rapid progress would clearly be desirable if all were agreed on some ultimate objective of political union and wished to use the symbolism of monetary union to move towards it. Whatever one thinks of the objective of political union, there is clearly no consensus on that subject at this time so that to use monetary union as a stalking-horse to achieve it would be both inappropriate and counter-productive.

If one considers EMU on its own merits, that is in terms of the balance of economic benefits and costs, there are also reasons for proceeding slowly. The basic economic rationale for monetary union, in whatever country or group of countries, is that the region for which a common currency is proposed constitutes an optimal currency area. Europe is not yet an optimal currency area in the sense that the USA is. Of course, Europe is becoming more integrated in ways that will eventually bring it much closer to being an optimal currency area than it is now. As Paul Krugman points out in Chapter 3, however, it is very difficult to be categoric about when the stage is reached at which a group of countries can be said to constitute an optimal currency area. Let me simply note, without elaborating, some of the criteria for an optimal currency area. First, the *degree of trade integration*: as Krugman points out, this is more limited in Europe than it is, say, between Canada and the USA. Of course, the degree of trade integration in Europe is increasing over time. But for the big four economies in the Community it is still relatively modest (roughly 10 per cent of the GDP of the four major economies is exported to the rest of the Community).

Second, *factor mobility*: this is limited at present and, for obvious cultural reasons, labour mobility will continue to be more limited than in culturally and linguistically more homogeneous areas such as the USA. Third, the *mechanisms of adjustment* to economic disturbances: there is no transfer mechanism comparable to that in existing nation-states to cushion the effects of disturbances that have differential effects on different regions. In particular, the automatic stabilizing properties of tax and social security provisions do not operate to transfer income from regions where economic activity is rising at above-average rates.

None of the factors I have mentioned should preclude progress towards closer monetary links; neither, however, should they be ignored, for in combination they make a powerful case for not allowing monetary arrangements to get too far ahead of real economic integration. The Single European Act will be a very forceful element for change and for greater integration. It would be a mistake, however, to assume that by 1 January 1993 effects of an integrated European market will have been felt. That is simply not true. The *legal elements* of the Single European Act will have been overcome. But it will take time for what the Single European Act allows and encourages actually to happen.

I turn now to the nature of the EMU to which we are moving. A key question here is whether the Delors model is the only model that can be envisaged. And are all the individual elements of the Delors model equally necessary for the overall plan? In this connection, one can single out the proposals included in the *Delors Report* on fiscal policy coordination and the strengthening of regional policies. In my opinion, both of those proposals are flawed, at least in the way they have been interpreted. In dealing with fiscal policy, it is clear that mechanisms should exist that facilitate the coordination of national budgetary policies; it is much less clear that this could be achieved efficiently by centralized and mandatory procedures. We should rely instead on multilateral surveillance and peer pressure. As far as regional policies are concerned, the *Delors Report* nowhere suggested that massive new regional transfers would be needed to make EMU work. If others believe that such transfers are necessary or desirable, I think they are mistaken.

Still, it can be argued, there remain regional income disparities in the Community that should not be ignored. There are problems in moving to a monetary union with a single monetary policy and we need to be sure we have answers to these problems before committing ourselves to such a union. With a single monetary policy there is no monetary means of taking account of regional differences in macroeconomic policy needs. (At the time that the Federal Reserve System was created this problem was recognized and an attempt was made to devise a system in which monetary policies could be differentiated in different regions. It did not succeed, and I do not suppose we could have any greater success with such an objective in Europe. Nevertheless, we do need to have mechanisms that take adequate account of the possibility of different cyclical positions or different cyclical needs across regions.)

This touches on the question of the appropriate anchor for monetary policy. It has been said that principal reliance should be placed on the independence of a central bank committed to the objective of price stability. I submit that while central bank independence and the objective of price stability are important, they are not themselves a complete basis for the kind of institutional adaptation we are seeking.

Consider the goal of democratic accountability for example. Thought has to be given to how the governing council of an independent monetary policy-making institution should be constituted, how it should be elected, the term of office of the governing board, their terms of reference and so on. In addition, there are more technical considerations to be addressed such as the balance of responsibilities between the central institution and the national central banks; the operating instruments that should be employed; the ownership of assets held in common.

My conclusion from all of this is that we need a fairly lengthy period to make stage one work properly. All member states of the Community will have to join the narrow band of the ERM. Beyond that, it would be highly desirable to ensure that the ERM survives a complete business cycle. We need to absorb the effects of the single European Act, so that we know that the system can live with that. That is not just a question of waiting until the Single European Act is on the statute books. It is a question of seeing that the system survives the variety of stresses to which it will become subject. During that period I think that detailed consideration should be given to the nature of whatever central monetary policy-making institution might be established, in the light of the experience gained during the operation of stage one. Only after that would it be appropriate to consider the specific nature of the final goal and the particular legal context in which it should be approached. It would be a serious mistake to set lawyers to work on treaty changes when so many questions remain to be resolved. This is not put forward in a spirit of obstructionism. Ten years, say, would not be a long time given the scope of what we are undertaking. The delay is a very small price to pay for making sure that we do the job right.

Contribution by Xenophon Zolotas

The issue of European EMU has an important political dimension, since it is indisputable that for its successful implementation the member states will have to cede a substantial part of their economic and monetary sovereignty to the governing bodies of the union. For this reason the Delors Committee (1989) rightly set as a fundamental condition from the outset a binding political undertaking from the member states for a gradual movement towards the ultimate goal of EMU.

This condition will influence in a decisive way the decision-making in the private sector which has a prime role to play alongside the institutional and the public sector arrangements towards the achievement of EMU. It is interesting to note that immediately after the announcement of the Single European Act and with the prospect of a unified market by 1992, mergers of companies and the setting up of intra-European entrepreneurial bodies, as well as joint ventures on a greater scale in the member countries have started taking place. From the moment the proposals of the Delors Committee are adopted, this movement will be accelerated and intensified. These developments in the private sector will enhance progressively the pace towards EMU, creating a kind of *fait accompli*, which at the same time will facilitate the work of the economic and monetary authorities in the member countries, forestalling any regression. One could perhaps mention that nearly all the member countries (with the exception of the two smallest), including the UK, have committed themselves to join the exchange rate mechanism during the first stage envisaged by the *Delors Report*.

As we all know, the *Delors Report* recommends the acceptance right from the beginning of the final goal of EMU, to be accomplished in an evolutionary step-by-step approach in three stages, without setting time limits to the sequence. The first stage only is specified to commence on 1 July 1990. It is not my purpose here to deal with the measures which are recommended for a gradual advancement towards the target of EMU. I limit myself to making a few remarks on the proposals concerning the first stage.

The goal in this stage is the achievement of greater convergence in economic performance through the strengthening of economic and monetary policy coordination, and the completion of the single market. In particular, in the monetary field the focus would be on removing all obstacles to financial integration and on intensifying cooperation and coordination of monetary policies.

For the implementation of these goals, an enlargement and strengthening of the responsibilities of the existing Committee of Central Bank Governors is recommended as well as the establishment of three subcommittees with special duties. It is not necessary here to review details of the work of these bodies. I would like, however, to state that the relevant proposals are inadequate to secure the pursued aims. Closer cooperation on a permanent basis should have been sought among central banks, with the transformation of the Committee of Central Bank Governors into a standing institution, with a special management board and its own permanent research staff, which could come from the central banks of the member states. In this manner closer cooperation would be facilitated. And so would constant consultations and the follow-up of the prompt implementation of necessary measures. The main advantage, however, would be to help develop among the central banks a spirit of closer cooperation, confidence and solidarity for the success of the common cause: to safeguard monetary stability. If this scheme were to be accepted there would be no need for a second stage, since all the steps foreseen for this stage would be taken in the first one in an evolutionary way. During the last three years I have recommended this scheme in various publications and on certain occasions, as the most appropriate and efficacious for the interim period.

Two fundamental prerequisites of the monetary union are: first, the irrevocable freezing of exchange rates of the currencies of the member states. Second, the establishment of a European central bank. This bank will formulate the common monetary policy, safeguarding price stability in conjunction with economic growth and employment. For the success of this undertaking, common determination of money supply for the entire European area will be necessary, and in parallel sound fiscal and budgetary policies must be implemented to maintain monetary stability. The *Delors Report* provides for this with particular emphasis on fiscal policies.

I would now like briefly to comment on some of the problems expected to emerge with the elimination of adjustable currencies which are the norm today in the EMS, safeguarding the relative autonomy of the monetary policy of central banks and the corrective capacity they have to face external imbalances with corresponding devaluations and revaluations of their currencies.

In a system of permanently fixed parities the economic imbalances and disparities among member countries will necessarily be effected mainly through the market mechanism. This means that in the case where one country delays introducing technological innovations or organizational improvements in relation to the other and loses its competitiveness, it will have to reduce its production costs in the main through cuts in wages, or through improvements in productivity following new and technologically advanced investments. This requires flexibility in the labour markets, which in many countries, however, is rather limited. This problem deserves particular attention and further research in implementing suitable measures to forestall social tensions and contain other disturbances.

Now, I would like to add a few comments pertaining to the less advanced countries of the EC. These countries are the so-called peripheral ones.

The introduction of a European EMU if special measures are not undertaken by the Community, may bring recession rather than higher growth, with capital and labour flowing towards the stonger economies, due to the substantially higher remuneration of labour, the economies of scale and the advantageous returns to capital in the advanced economies.

With reference to the performance of European union after it is completed following the third stage envisaged in the *Delors Report*, I make reference here to a relevant statement by the President of the Deutsche Bundesbank, Mr Karl Otto Pohl:

> In a monetary union with irreversibly fixed exchange rates the weak would become ever weaker and the strong ever stronger. We would thus experience great tensions in the real economy in Europe. For this reason

alone, monetary union without simultaneous integration in fields like fiscal policy as well as regional and social policy is utterly inconceivable. In this context it is certainly valid to speak of asymmetry in Europe.

To avoid such developments, the *Delors Report* recommends special provisions to reactivate the economies of the countries with lagging development within the Community. These provisions in view of EMU have already started being implemented beginning with the doubling of the capital of the structural funds of the Community. For the success of the goal of a faster development of the weakest countries, to help them close the gap with the developed ones, the formulation of a special plan of regional development in which the creation of infrastructures in industrial zones, technical education, research, communication and, in certain cases, industrial plants, will be necessary.

In conclusion, I would like to add some final remarks:

1. We should keep in mind that a perfect economic union is not feasible without a parallel monetary union, with a European central bank and ultimately a common currency.
2. For EMU to operate smoothly, it is imperative that it should seek to eliminate to a substantial degree the existing disparities and asymmetries in the economies of the weaker countries in relation to the advanced ones.
3. To ensure permanence and security for EMU, a European political union will one day have to come into being.

Select bibliography

Artis, M.J. and **Miller, M.** On joining the EMS, *Midland Bank Review*, Winter 1986, **3**, pp. 176–200.

Artis, M.J. and **Taylor, M.P.** Exchange rates, interest rates, capital controls and the European Monetary System: assessing the track record, Giavazzi, F., Micossi, S. and Miller, M. (eds), *The European Monetary System*, Cambridge University Press, Cambridge, 1988, pp. 185–206.

Artis, M.J. and **Taylor, M.P.** The achievement of the European Monetary System, *Economic and Social Review*, **20** (January, 1989) pp. 121–45.

Artis, M.J. and **Nachane, D.** Wages and prices in Europe: a test of the German leadership thesis, *Weltwirtschaftliches Archiv* **126**, (March 1990) pp. 51–77.

Artus, P. The European Monetary System, exchange rate expectations and the reputation of the authorities, paper presented at the Conference on International Economic Policy Coordination, Aix-en-Provence, 24–25 June 1988.

Begg, D. and **Wyplosz, C.** Why the EMS? Dynamic games and the equilibrium policy regime, in Bryant, R. and Portes, R. (eds), *Global Macroeconomics: Policy Conflict and Cooperation* St Martin's Press, New York, 1987.

Bekx, P. and **Tullio, G.** The European Monetary System and the determination of the DM–US dollar exchange rate, mimeo, Commission of the EEC, 1987.

Bini Smaghi, L. Fiscal prerequisitites for further monetary convergence in the EMS, *Banca Nazionale del Lavoro Quarterly Review*, No. 169, 1989.

Bini Smaghi, L. Progressing towards European Monetary Union: selected issues and a few proposals, mimeo, Banca d'Italia, 1989.

Bini Smaghi, L. and **Masera, R.S.** L'évoluzione degli Accordi di Cambio dello SME, in *L'unificazione monetario e lo SME*, Il Mulino, Bologna, 1987.

Bini Smaghi, L. and **Vona, S.** La Coesione dello SME e il Ruolo dei Fattori Esterni: Un'Analist in Termini di Commercio Estero, *Banca d'Italia, Temi di Discussione*, No 103, 1988.

Bofinger, P. Das Europäische Währungssystem, und die geldpolitische Kooperation in Europa, *Kredit und Kapital* **21** 1989, pp. 317–45.

Canzoneri, M. and **Rogers, C.A.** Is the European Community an optimal currency area? Optimal tax smoothing versus the costs of multiple currencies, Georgetown University, 1988.

Cohen, D. and **Wyplosz, C.** The European Monetary Union: an agnostic evaluation, typescript, 1989

Collins, S. Inflation and the European Monetary System, in Giavazzi, F., Micossi, S. and Miller, M. (eds 1988). *The European Monetary System,* Cambridge, Cambridge University Press, pp. 112–36.

Comité pour l'Union Monetaire de l'Europe *Un Programme pour l'Action*, Crédit National, Paris, 1988.

Committee of Governors of the EEC *Report on the Strengthening of the EMS*, BIS, September 1987.

Committee on the Study of Economic and Monetary Union (the Delors Committee), *Report on Economic and Monetary Union in the European Community (Delors*

Reports) (With Collection of Papers). Office for Official Publications of the European Communities, Luxemburg, 1989.

Currie, D. and **Dicks, G.** The MTFS or the EMS: which way for credible monetary policy, *LBS Economic Outlook*, June 1989, pp. 17–24.

De Cecco, M. and **Giovannini, A.** (eds). A European Central Bank? *Perspectives on Monetary Unification after ten years of the EMS*, Cambridge University Press, Cambridge, 1988.

De Grauwe, P. Fiscal policies in the EMS: a strategic analysis, *International Economics Research Papers* No. 53, Catholic University of Louvain, 1986.

De Grauwe, P. International trade and economic growth in the European Monetary System, *European Economic Review* **31**, (1987), pp. 389–98.

De Grauwe, P. The cost of disinflation and the European Monetary System, *CEPR Discussion Paper*, No. 326, 1988.

De Grauwe, P. Is the European Monetary System a DM-zone? *CEPR Discussion Paper* No. 297, 1988.

De Grauwe, P. and **Verfaille, G** Exchange rate variability misalignment, and the European Monetary System, in Marston, R. (ed) *Misalignment of Exchange Rates: Effects on Trade and Industry,* University of Chicago Press, Chicago, 1988, pp. 77–103.

De Larosière, J. First stages towards the creation of a European Reserve Bank – the creation of a European Reserve Fund, in Collection of Papers of *Delors Report,* 1989, pp. 177–84.

Dini, L. A new phase in the European Monetary System: introductory statement, in Giavazzi, F., Micossi, S. and Miller M., (eds), *The European Monetary System*, Cambridge University Press, Cambridge, 1988 pp. 385–88.

Dornbusch, R. The European Monetary System, the dollar and the yen, Giavazzi, F., Micossi, S., and Miller, M., (eds), *The European Monetary System,* Cambridge University Press, Cambridge, 1988, pp. 23–36.

Dornbusch, R. Credibility, debt and unemployment: Ireland's failed stabilization, *Economic Policy,* **8** (April 1989), pp. 174–204.

Driffill, J. The stability and sustainability of the European Monetary System with perfect capital markets, in Giavazzi, F., Micossi, S., and Miller, M, (eds), *The European Monetary System,* Cambridge University Press, Cambridge, 1988, pp 211–28.

Dudler, H. Monetary policy and exchange market management in Germany, in *Exchange Market Intervention and Monetary Policy,* BIS, March 1988. Basle.

Eizenga, W. The independence of the Deutsche Bundesbank and the Nederlandsche Bank with regard to monetary policy: a comparative study, *SUERF Papers on Monetary Policy and Financial System,* No. 12, SUERF, Tilburg, 1987.

Fratianni, M. The European Monetary System: how well has it worked? return to an adjustable-peg arrangement, *Cato Journal* **8** pp. 477–501. (1988)

Fratianni, M. and **Von Hagen, J.** German dominance in the EMS: the empirical evidence, *Open Economies Review,* (eds) January 1990, pp. 86–87.

Fratianni, M. and **Von Hagen, J.** The European Monetary System ten years after, in Allan H. Meltzer and Charles Plosser (eds), Carnegie-Rochester Conference Series on Public Policy, vol. 32, 1990.

Giavazzi, F. and **Pagano, M.** Capital controls and the European Monetary System, in *Capital Controls and Foreign Exchange Legislation,* Euromobiliare, Occasional Paper 1, June 1985.

Giavazzi, F. and **Giovannini, A.** Models of the EMS: is Europe a greater Deutschmark area? in Bryant, R.C. and Portes, R. (eds), *Global Macroeconomics,* New York, St Martin's Press, 1987, pp. 237–76.

Giavazzi, F. and **Giovannini, A.** Exchange rates and prices in Europe, *Weltwirtschaftliches Archiv,* **4** (December 1987), pp. 592–605.

Giavazzi, F. and **Giovannini, A.** The role of the exchange-rate regime in a disinflation: empirical evidence on the European Monetary system, in Giavazzi, F., Micossi, S. and Miller, M. (eds), *The European Monetary System,* Cambridge, Cambridge University Press, 1988, pp. 85–107.

Giavazzi, F. and **Pagano, M.** The advantage of tying one's hands: EMS discipline and central bank credibility, *European Economic Review* **32** (1988) pp. 1055–82.

Giavazzi, F. The EMS experience, paper presented at the conference 'The EMS: Ten Years Later' Bergamo, 5th May 1989.

Giavazzi, F. and **Giovannini, A.** *Limiting Exchange Rate Flexibility: The European Monetary System,* Cambridge, MIT Press, 1989.

Giavazzi, F. and **Giovannini, A.** Can the EMS be exported? Lessons from ten years of monetary policy coordination in Europe, *CEPR Discussion Paper,* No. 285, January 1989.

Gil, G. Aspectos monetarios y finacieros de la integración española en la Comunidad Económica Europea, Banco de España, Servicio de Estudios, *Estudios Económicos,* No. 37, 1985.

Goodhart, C. The *Delors Report:* was Lawson's reaction justifiable? Financial Markets Group, London School of Economics, London, 1989 (unpublished).

Grilli, V. Seigniorage in Europe, in De Cecco, M. and Giovannini, G. (eds), *A European Central Bank,* Cambridge University Press, Cambridge, 1989.

Gross, D. Capital controls in the EMS: a model with incomplete separation, *CEPS Working Document,* No. 32, August 1987.

Gros, D. Seigniorage versus EMS discipline: some welfare consideration, *CEPS Working Document,* No. 38, Centre for European Policy Studies, Brussels, September, 1988.

Gros, D. *Seigniorage in the EC: The Implications of the EMS and Financial Market Integration,* Washington, International Monetary Fund, IMF WP/89/7. 1989.

Gros, D. and **Thygesen, N.** The EMS: achievements, current issues and directions for the future, *CEPS Paper,* No. 35, Centre for European Policy Studies, Brussels, 1988.

Gros, D. and **Thygesen, N.** Le SME: performances and perspectives, *Observations et Dianostics Economiques 24,* Banque de France, 1988, pp. 55–80.

House of Commons *The European Monetary System,* First Report of the Expenditure Committee, Session 1978–79, 1979.

House of Commons *The European Monetary System,* 13th Report from the Treasury and Civil Service Committee, 1985.

House of Lords European Monetary System, *Report of the Select Committee on the European Communities,* 5th Report 1983–84, 1983.

House of Lords European financial area, *Report of the Select Committee on the European Communities,* 21st Report, 1987–88, 1988.

Información Commercial Española *España y el Sistema Monetario Europeo,* No. 657, May 1988.

Jaans, P. The basic difference between the frameworks for policy-decision making provided by the EMS and EMU, in Collection of Papers of *Delors Report,* 1989, pp. 221–3.

Katseli, L. Macroeconomics policy coordination and the domestic base of national economic policies in major European countries, paper presented at the Conference on the Political Economy of International Macroeconomic Policy Coordination, Andover, Mass., 5–7 November 1987.

Kenen, P. Reflections on EMS Experience, in Giavazzi, F., Micossi, S. and Miller, M. (eds), *The European Monetary System*, Cambridge University Press, Cambridge, 1988.

Kessel Saiz, G. La peseta en el Sistema Monetario Europeo: algunas reconsideraciones, *Informacón Commercial Española,* February 1987.

Kloten, N Der Delors-Bericht, *Europa Archiv* **44** (9), (1989) pp. 251–60.

Kremers, J Gaining credibility for a disinflation: Ireland's experience in the EMS, *IMF Staff Papers,* forthcoming, 1989.

Lamfalussy, A. A proposal for stage two under which monetary policy operations would be centralized in a jointly-owned subsidiary, in Collection of Papers of Delors Report, 1989, pp. 213–19.

Leigh-Pemberton, R. The future of monetary arrangements in Europe, *Quarterly Bulletin of the Bank of England,* London, August 1989, pp. 368–79.

Louis, JV., ***et al***. *Rapport du Groupe Système Européen de Banques Centrales,* CEPREM et Comité Spinelli, Brussels, 1989.

Ludlow, P. *The Making of the European Monetary System,* Butterworths, 1982.

Macedo, J.B. and **Torres, F.S.** Real interest differentials and European integration: Portugal and a comparison to Spain, Draft, CEPS, 1989.

Masera, R.S. European currency: an Italian view, in Giavazzi, F., Micossi, S. and Miller, M., (eds), *The European Monetary System*, Cambridge University Press, Cambridge, 1988 pp. 393–404.

Mastropasqua, C., Micossi, S. and **Rinaldi, R.** Interventions, sterilization and monetary policy in the EMS countries (1979–1987), in Giavazzi, F., Micossi, S. and Miller, M., (eds), *The European Monetary System,* Cambridge University Press, Cambridge, 1988 pp. 252–87.

Melitz, J. The welfare cost of the European Monetary System, *Journal of International Money and Finance,* **4** (1985), pp. 485–506.

Melitz, J. Monetary discipline, Germany and the European Monetary System: a synthesis, in Giavazzi, F., Micossi, S. and Miller, M., (eds), *The European Monetary System,* Cambridge University Press, Cambridge, 1988 pp. 51–79.

Micossi, S. The intervention and financial mechanisms of the EMS and the role of the ECU, *Banca Nazionale des Lavoro Quarterly Review,* December 1985, pp. 327–45.

Micossi, S. and **Padoa-Schioppa, T.** Short-term interest rate linkages between the United States and Europe, *Rivista di Politica economica, Selected Papers,* No. 18, December 1984.

Modigliani, F., Monti, M., Dreze, J., Giersche, H. and **Layard, R.** Reducing unemployment in Europe: The role of capital formation, *CEPS Papers No. 28*, Centre for European Policy Studies, Brussels, 1986.

Padoa-Schioppa Report, *Efficiency, Stability and Equity,* Oxford University Press, Oxford, 1987.

Portes, R. Macroeconomic policy coordination and the European Monetary System, *CEPR Discussion Paper*, No. 342, September 1989.

Radaelli, G. Stabilita dello SME, controlli sui movimenti di capitale e interventi sui mercatidi cambi, *CEEP Economia,* No. 1 (1989), pp. 1–36.

Rogoff, K. Can exchange rate predictability be achieved without monetary convergence? Evidence from the EMS, *European Economic Review,* June–July 1985, **28**, pp. 93–115.

Roubini, N. Sterilization policies, offsetting capital movements and exchange rate intervention policies in the EMS, Chapter 4, Ph.D. dissertation, Harvard University, Cambridge, Mass., 1988.

Russo, M. and **Tullio, G.** Monetary policy coordination within the European monetary system: is there a rule? in Giavazzi, F., Micossi, S. and Miller, M. (eds), *The European Monetary System,* Cambridge University Press, Cambridge, 1988, pp 292–356.

Sarcinelli, M. The EMS and the international monetary system: towards greater stability, *Banca Nazionale del Lavoro Quarterly Review* March 1986, pp. 57–83.

Spaventa, L. The New EMS Symmetry without Coordination, paper presented at the Conference on Managing the EMS in an Integrated Europe, Madrid, 11–12 May 1989.

Thygesen, N. Decentralization and accountability within the central bank: any lessons from the US experience for the potential organization of a European central banking institution? (with comment by Jean-Jacques Rey), in De Grauwe, P. and Peeters, T., (eds), *The ECU and European Monetary Integration,* Macmillan, Basingstoke and London, 1988, pp. 91–118.

Thygesen, N. A European central banking system – some analytical and operational considerations, in Collection of Papers of *Delors Report*, 1989, pp. 157–75.

Tsoukalis, L. The political economy of the European Monetary System, in Guerrieri, P. and Padoan, P.C. (eds), *The Political Economy of European Integration,* Hemel Hempstead, Harvester Wheatsheaf, 1989.

Ungerer, H., Evans, O. and **Nyberg, P.** The European Monetary System: the experience 1979–1982. *Occasional Paper*, No. 19, International Monetary Fund, May 1983.

Ungerer, H., Evans, O. and **Nyberg, P**. The European Monetary System: recent developments, *Occasional Paper,* No. 48, International Monetary Fund, December 1986.

Vaubel, R. The return to the new EMS, in Karl Brunner, K. and Meltzer, A.H. (eds), *Monetary Institutions and the Policy Process,* Carnegie-Rochester Conference, Series vol. 13, Amsterdam, North-Holland, 1980, pp. 173–221.

Vaubel, R. Image and reality of the European Monetary System – a review. *Weltwirtschaftliches Archiv,* **125** (2) (1989), pp. 397–405.

Viñals, J La incorporación de España al Sistema Monetario Europeo y sus consecuencias para la politica monetaria, in *La politica monetaria en España,* FEDEA, 1987

Viñals, J. El SME y Mercado Unico de 1992: perspectivas de futor, *Boletin económico,* Banco de España, June 1988.

Viñals, J. Spain and the 'EEC cum 1992' shock, forthcoming in Bliss, C. and Braga de Macedo, J., (eds), *Unity with Diversity in the European Economy,* Cambridge University Press, Cambridge, 1989.

Viñals, J. and **Domingo, L.** La peseta y el SME: un modelo del tipo de cambio peseta-marco, *Revista Española de Economia*, **4,** (1) (1987).

Vona, S. and **Bini Smaghi, L.** Economic growth and exchange rates in the European Monetary System: their trade effects in a changing external environment, in Giavazzi, F., Micossi, S. and Miller, M., (eds), *The European Monetary System,* Cambridge University Press, Cambridge 1988, pp. 140–78.

Von Hagen, J. and **Fratianni, M.** German dominance in the EMS: evidence from interest rates, Working Paper, Federal Reserve Bank of St Louis and Italian International Economic Center, 1989.

Watrin, C. (Chairman of the Board of Academic Advisers to the Federal Ministry of Economics), A monetary order for the single European market (English translation), Bonn, 1989.

Wyplosz, C. Capital flows, liberalization and the EMS: a French perspective, in *European Economy,* No. 36, 1988 pp. 85–103.

Wyplosz, C. Asymmetry in the EMS: intentional or systemic, *European Economic Review,* March 1989, **33**, pp. 310–20.

List of Contributors

Professor Michael Artis has held a Chair in Economics at Manchester University since 1976. He has previously held posts at Oxford, and Adelaide and Flinders Universities in Australia and at the National Institute of Economic and Social Research in London, with his first Chair at Swansea University College. He has supplied evidence to and acted as technical adviser to committees of both Houses of Parliament.

Gunter Baer is Assistant Manager of the Monetary and Economic Department of the BIS. He has been Secretary of the G–10 Working Party on exchange market intervention (Jurgensen Report) and of the Committee for the study of economic and monetary union in Europe (Delors Report).

Antonio Costa was Director General of the Directorate General of Monetary and Economic Affairs of the EC Commission. He has also held a position at the OECD.

Andrew Crockett is Executive Director of the Bank of England, in charge of Overseas Affairs. He was seconded to the International Monetary Fund in 1972 as Personal Assistant to the Managing Director. He became Chief of the Fund's Special Studies Division in 1974, then Assistant Director of the Middle Eastern Department in 1977.

Henning Dalgaard is Assistant Governor of the Danmarks National Bank. He has been Chairman of the group of foreign exchange experts of the Committee of Governors of the EC Central Banks since 1982.

Michele Fratianni is Professor of Business Economics and Public Policy at the Graduate School of Business at Indiana University and Visiting Professor of Economics at the Catholic University of Louvain. He has been Economic Adviser to the European Economic Commission in Brussels (1976–1979), Senior Staff Economist with the US President's Council of Economic Advisers (1981–1982). He is the co-editor of *Open Economies Review*.

Francesco Giavazzi is Professor of Economics at the University of Bologna. He is also co-director of the International Macroeconomics Programme at the Centre for Economic Policy Research in London, and a Research Associate of the National Bureau of Economic Research in Cambridge, Mass.

Paul De Grauwe is Professor of Economics at the University of Leuven, research fellow at the Centre for European Policy Studies and fellow of the Centre for Economic Policy Research.

Daniel Gros is Senior Research Fellow at the Centre for European Policy Studies. He has been teaching at the University of Leuven as well as being an academic adviser to the European Commission.

Jürgen von Hagen is Assistant Professor of Business Economics and Public Policy at Indiana University and has taught Economics at the University of Bonn. He has been a visiting economist at the Federal Reserve Bank of St. Louis (1987 and 1989) and the Board of Governors of the Federal Reserve System (April 1990), and has worked for the German Federal Bureau for International Trade Information.

Otmar Issing is professor of Economics at the University of Wurzburg, West Germany. He has been appointed a member of the German Council of Economic Experts for the period March 1988 to February 1993. He is also a member of the *Kronberger Kreis*, a group of professors well known for their critical analyses of German economic policy.

Louka Katseli is Professor of Economics at the University of Athens and a Research Fellow of the Centre for Economic Policy Research. She has been the Director of the Centre for Planning and Economic Research in Athens. She has also taught at Yale University.

Paul Krugman is Professor of Economics at the Massachusetts Institute of Technology and a research associate of the National Bureau of Economic Research. He previously taught at Yale University.

Jacques Melitz is an Economist in the Research Division of INSEE, Paris and Professor at the *Institut des Etudes Politiques et Hautes Etudes Commerciales*. He has been managing editor of the *Annales de L'INSEE*.

Stefano Micossi is Head of the Research Department at *Confindustria* (Italian Federation of Industry) and is Professor of Monetary Theory and Policy at the Luiss University of Rome. He has been head of the International Research Division of the Bank of Italy. He has taught at the University of Rome.

Lucas Papademos is the Economic Advisor of the Bank of Greece. He has been teaching at MIT and was a member of the group preparing the Padoa-Scioppa report.

Jean-Jacques Rey is Director at the National Bank of Belgium and Professor at the Free University of Brussels.

Wolfgang Rieke is Head of the International Department at the Deutsche Bundesbank. He has been associated with the OECD and the IMF (European Department).

André Sapir is Professor at the Free University of Brussels and Director of Research at the Institute of European Studies. He was Assistant Professor of Economics at the University of Wisconsin-Madison from 1977 to 1982. He is also a Fellow of the Centre for Economic Policy Research (CEPR). He has been a visiting professor in several universities in Europe and a consultant for numerous international organizations.

Luigi Spaventa is Professor of Economics at the University of Rome, 'La Sapienza'. He was Visiting Fellow at All Souls College, Oxford, 1968–1969 and Visiting Scholar at the IMF, 1984. He was Luigi Einaudi Professor at Cornell University, 1989. From 1976–1983 he was a Member of the Italian Parliament. He was Chairman of the Italian Treasury Committee on debt management, 1988–1989. Currently he is a Member of a Treasury Committee on financial intermediation.

Dr André Szasz is a Member of the Executive Board of the Netherlands Bank. He is also a Member of the Monetary Committee of the EC, and of Working Party 3 of the OECD. He is the Deputy for the Dutch Central Bank Governor in the Group of Ten, and in the Committee of Central Bank Governors of the EC.

Niels Thygesen is Professor of Economics at the University of Copenhagen and Associate Senior Research Fellow at the Centre for European Policy Studies (CEPS). He has served on various expert committees on European integration, including the Marjolin Group 1974–1975 and the Delors Committee 1988–1989.

Francisco Torres is a Research Fellow at the Centre for European Policy Studies. He has been an Economist at the *Banco de Portugal* and Lecturer at the Universidade Catolica Portuguesa.

Loukas Tsoukalis is University Lecturer and Fellow at St Antony's College, Oxford. He is also Director of Economic Studies at the College of Europe, Bruges.

José Viñals is Deputy-Chief at the Research department of the *Banco de España*, in charge of international economics. He has been an Assistant Professor of Economics at Stanford University from 1981 to 1986 and currently teaches international economics at the Graduate Center for Monetary and Financial Studies in Madrid. He has been a consultant for the International Monetary Fund and the World Bank.

Hans-Jürgen Vosgerau is Professor of Economics at the University of Konstanz. He has been a visiting scholar at MIT and King's College, Cambridge and Dean of the Department of Economics at the University of Tübingen.

Xenophon Zolotas has been the Governor of the Bank of Greece for many years. He was also Parliamentary Prime Minister of Greece during 1989–90. He was Governor of the IMF for Greece, Minister of Economic Coordination, Member of the Greek Delegation to the UN General Assembly and Greek Representative at the Economic Commission for Europe. He was Professor of Economics at the University of Thessaloniki and the University of Athens. He is a member of the Academy of Athens and Honorary Governor of the Bank of Greece.

Index